How to Move Your Expensive Office to the Free Cloud

Authored By

Dave Armstrong

Edited By

Marian Armstrong

Another Smarty Pants Books Selection

Smarty Pants Books creates a series of How-to-do book that help you to understand and use emerging technologies that help make your business better.

How to Move Your Expensive Office to the Free Cloud
Published by
Armstrong Publishing and Smarty Pants Books
504 N Main St
Livingston, MT 59047

Copyright © 2013 by David Armstrong
Published by Armstrong Publishing and Smarty Pants Books, Livingston Montana 59047
Print   ISBN: 978-0-9911845-2-1

Manufactured in the United States of America

No part of this publication may be reproduced, stored in a retrieval system or transmitted in any form or by any means, electronic, mechanical, photocopying, recording, scanning or otherwise, except as permitted under Sections 107 or 108 of the 1976 United States Copyright Act, without either the prior written permission of the Publisher. Requests to the Publisher for permission should be addressed to the Permissions Department, Armstrong Publishing, 504 N Main St, Livingston MT 59047, (406) 223-0090

Limit of Liability/Disclaimer of Warranty: The publisher and the author make no representations or warranties with respect to the accuracy or completeness of the contents of this work and specifically disclaim all warranties, including without limitation warranties of fitness for a particular purpose. No warranty may be created or extended by sales or promotional materials. The advice and strategies contained herein may not be suitable for every situation. This work is sold with the understanding that the publisher is not engaged in rendering legal, accounting, or other professional services. If professional assistance is required, the services of a competent professional person should be sought. Neither the publisher nor the author shall be liable for damages arising here from.

The fact that an organization or Web site is referred to in this work as a citation and/or a potential source of further information does not mean that the author or the publisher endorses the information the organization or Web site may provide or recommendations it may make. Further, readers should be aware that Internet Web sites listed in this work may have changed or disappeared between when this work was written and when it is read.

For general information on our other products and services please contact our Customer Care Department (406) 223-0090

Introduction

The Internet has increased the growth of technology to a dizzying pace. I know this technology explosion is scary to some. A well-established business can disappear overnight as some new technology disrupts the established order.

Ever hear of Kodak? Kodak was founded in 1888 in Rochester, New York. George Eastman and his successors built a multibillion business of making cameras, film and printing paper. While the rest of the photography world worked to make digital cameras better, Kodak could not imagine a world without film. They will never be the company they once were.

If you run or manage an information or service type business such as insurance, investing or a web business, you need to see what is coming. There are new technologies now available that could dramatically improve your business. This disruptive, to some, technology will offer a great advantage to those that embrace it and ruin to those that do not see it coming.

You can now run a business with employees working from remote offices and they can be from anywhere in the world. You can dump the overhead expense of an office, save all of the commute time for you and your employees and still have better communication between staff. You can work anywhere you can find Wi-Fi or through your carrier's data plan.

This book is a plan on how to get from here to there. It is a manual on the services available, mostly free, and how they compare. This tsunami is coming. The question is: "*Are you going to be the disruptor or the disruptee?*"

My name is Dave Armstrong and I have been a technical trainer since 1983. I am also a business man since the 1970s. My purpose in writing this book is to help you understand and use the opportunities that these technological changes present.

Dedication

To my editor, proofer, cheer leader, sweetheart and wife, Marian Armstrong. Thank God, one of us knows where commas go.

Table of Contents

Introduction iii

Dedication iii

Chapter 1: What Are We Going to Learn? 1

How to Evaluate Your Business as a Candidate for Virtualization and the Cloud 2
Here is What We Will Do in the Book 2

Chapter 2: What is a Virtual Office? 3

How to Find and Motivate Great Virtual Staff 3
How to Work in the Cloud 4
Work Anywhere with a Tablet or Phone 4
How Microsoft, Zoho and Google's Documents Work 4
The Best Ways to Use Phones and Other Interoffice Communication 5

Chapter 3: The Pros and Cons of a Virtual Office? 7

Good Things with a Virtual Office 7
Cost Savings 7
Quality Employees from Anywhere in the World 8
Think Globally, Think Experts 9
Staff sizing flexibility 10
Temporary Independent Contractors 10
Workspace vs. Workplace 10
Less distraction 10
Up to 30 Percent Increase in Productivity 11
Reduced Employee Turnover and Absenteeism 11
Possible Problems with a Virtual Office 11
Need Self-Reliant and Self-Motivated Staff 11
It is a Matter of Trust 12
Trust but Verify 12
Time Tracking 12
Preventing Computer Misuse 13
Perceived Business Image 13
Virtual Assistant and Receptionist 13

Employee Disconnect and Isolation.. 13
Loss of Employee Recognition 14
Loss of Nonverbal Nuance 14
Renting Physical Space.. 14
Meetings and Interoffice Communication 14

Chapter 4: Your Office in the Clouds 15

What is the Cloud?... 15
    Always Connected Anywhere 15

What does it Cost?... 16
    Ongoing vs. Onetime 16
    Software Always Up to Date 16

Google Drive 17
    Free Google Productivity Apps 17

Microsoft's SkyDrive 17
    You Get a Lot for the Per-User Fee 18
    Personal or Business 18

Zoho CRM and Zoho Docs.. 18

Dropbox 18

Google, Microsoft or Zoho.. 19

Preparing for Mobile Access 19

Chapter 5: Using Microsoft Office in the Cloud 21

Basic Office for Free... 21

Organizing with Folders 25

Uploading Files... 28

Accessing Your Desktop from SkyDrive 31

Using the Word App 32

Using the Excel App 40

Using the PowerPoint App 43

Using the OneNote App 50

Using the Excel Survey 54

Using Office with SkyDrive Pro 59

Office 365 Home Premium 59
    Office 365 Home Premium 60
    Office 365 University 60
Office 365 Small Business 60
Office 365 Small Business Premium 61
Office 365 Midsize Business 61
Office on Demand 62
Lync and Skype 62

Chapter 6: The Outlook Web App 65

Creating New Email 73
Using Outlook People (Contacts) 79
    Uploading Your Existing Contacts 79
Skype Calling 87
Using Outlook Calendar 88
    Main Screen and Month View 88
    Adding a New Appointment 94

Chapter 7: Using Google Docs and Drive 99

Understanding Google Docs and Google Drive 100
Google Desktop Drive 101
Google Docs 103
    What applications are missing? 103
Understanding the Google Drive Dashboard 103
    Google Templates and Add-Ons 106
Using Document 107
    Creating a New Document 108
    The Document Toolbar 109
    The Document Menus 109
Using Presentation 113
    Creating a new Presentation 113
    The Presentation Toolbar 115
    The Presentation Menus 116
Using Spreadsheet 120
    Creating a New Spreadsheet 120

  The Spreadsheet Toolbar 121
  The Spreadsheet Menus 121

 Collaborating using Google Docs 125
  Sharing the Google Doc 125

 Page Setup and Printing Files 128

 Using Form 129
  Picking a From Template 130
  The Form Toolbar 131
  The Form Menus 132
  Creating Your First Survey Form 134
  Sending or Embedding Your Form 139
  Viewing the Response Analytics 143

Chapter 8: Using Gmail and Google Docs Automation 145

 Copying a Prepared Spreadsheet for Names and Email Addresses 145
  Acquiring the Sample Spreadsheet 146

 Creating Your Email Template 147
  Understanding the Merge Fields 147

 Merging Your Email List 147
  Giving Permission for the Script to Run 148
  Running the Mail Merge 150

 Checking Your Results 150

 Getting Back to Your Email Template and Spreadsheet 150

 Warning, Gmail is Watching! 152

 How Google Docs Scripting Works 152
  Analyzing a Google Doc's Script 154

Chapter 9: Using Gmail and Hangouts 157

 Gmail Main Screen 157

 Using Gmail Setting to Collect All of your Email 162

 Letting Your Assistant Access Your Gmail 163

 Managing Your Gmail Folders 165
  Checking Your Spam Folder for False Positives 166
  Composing a New Email 167

 Using Contacts in Gmail 169

Adding Contacts 170
Using Google Tasks in Gmail 171
Using Hangouts to Make Text Messaging, Phone and Video Calls 173
Video calling 174

Chapter 10: Using Google Calendar 177

The Main Screen 177
Month, Week, Day and Agenda Calendar Views 178
Annual Calendar View 180

Adding a New Event 181

Google Docs in the Enterprise 183

Chapter 11: Google Cloud Print 185

Hooking Up a Classic Printer 186
Getting to Your Registered Printer 188
Sharing Your Printers 191

Hooking up a Cloud Reader Printer 192

Chapter 12: Using Zoho CRM 195

What is Zoho 195

What Does CRM Cost? 198

Zoho CRM 199
Working with Leads 202
Adding a New Lead 202
Emailing a Lead 204
Calling a Lead 204
Adding a Task to a Lead 206
Adding an Event to a Lead 207
Editing an Lead's Event 207
Viewing a Lead's History 208
Converting Leads into Contacts 209
The Accounts List 210
The Contacts List 212
The Potential List 213
The Campaigns List 214
Accessing Reports 215
Reading Your Dashboard 217

Cases	218
Activities	219
Solutions	220
Setup Features on the Home Screen	224

Chapter 13: Using Zoho Productivity Apps 227

What are Zoho Productivity Apps?	227
Moving Between Zoho Apps	229
Zoho's Writer App	229
Zoho's Sheet App	230
Let's Explore the Sheet Menu Tabs	231
The Sheet Home Tab	232
The Sheet Format Tab	232
The Sheet Insert Tab	233
The Sheet Formulas Tab	236
The Sheet Data Tab	238
The Sheet View Tab	241
The Sheet Review Tab	241
The Sheet Macros Tab	243
The Share Tab	246
Zoho's Show App	249
Let's Explore Show's Menu Tabs	250
The Show Home Tab	250
The Show Insert Tab	250
The Show Design Tab	251
The Show Transition Tab	251
The Show Animation Tab	251
The Show Slide Show Tab	251
The Show View Tab	252
The Show Review Tab	252
The Show Share Tab	252
The Show Format Tab	252
Creating Folders	253
Zoho Docs for Desktop	254
Integration with Google and Microsoft	256

Chapter 14: Using Skype 257

Skype	258
Downloading Skype	258

    Skype's Main Screen 260
    Searching for, Adding and importing Contacts... 261
    Sending Instant Messages... 262
    Sending SMS Messages to Mobile Phones 264
    Sending Files 266
    To Send a File Using Skype 267
    Quick Trouble Shooting Your Speakers, Microphone and Webcam 268
    Making Skype Calls.. 269
    Sharing Screens 271
    Group Video Conferencing 273
    Calling Landlines and Mobiles 276
    Skype Menus 276

Skype Pricing 280

Chapter 15: Conferencing and Screen Sharing 283

GoToMeeting 284
    My Take on GoToMeeting 285

WebEx 286
    My Take on WebEx 287

My TrueCloud... 288
    My take on My TrueCloud 289

TeamViewer.. 290
    TeamViewer Full Version 291
    TeamViewer QuickSupport 299
    TeamViewer Host... 300
    TeamViewer QuickJoin for Conferencing 301

Chapter 16: Managing Incoming and Interoffice Calls 303

Skype 304

Grasshopper... 304
    Grasshopper Cost 304
    Signing UP for Grasshopper 305
    Configuring Grasshopper 307
    Call Forwarding Setup 308
    Recording Your Voice Greeting.. 311
    How to Use Grasshopper 314
    Going Mobile with Grasshopper 318

RingCentral... 323

    Virtual Phone System Wrap-up 330

Chapter 17: Collaborating With Google Sites 331

    Using Google Sites to Collaborate 331
        Adding a New Project Management Site 332

    Exploring the New Project Management Site 335
        Editing the Project Management Site's Pages 337
        Managing the Project Management Site's Structure 340

    Using Google Sites as an Intranet 343
        Intranet Documents Links 343
        Intranet Calendar Link 344
        Intranet Directory Link 345
        Intranet Discussion Link 345
        Intranet Announcements Link 345
        Intranet Resources Link 346

Chapter 18: Wrapping it All Up 347

    Microsoft, Google or Zoho 347
        Choose Microsoft 347
        Choose Google 347
        Choose Zoho 347

    Compare Your Cost 348

    Employee Training 349

    Transitioning to Virtual 349

Index 351

Chapter 1: What Are We Going to Learn?

The technology explosion has given us a new way of doing business. This means you have a choice of a traditional office place, where you pull a group together, or a virtual office or something in-between. This new technology gives you the freedom to work anywhere, any time, on any computer, tablet or smartphone.

Freedom to work anywhere may be an incentive, but the savings of not having a physical office can turn an average business into a very profitable one. An office, utilities and insurance can represent 35% or more of profits in many information based businesses. Add in the commuting time and cost for you and your employees, and you have a good reason to see if you could turn a cost into additional profit. That is what this book is about and what we are going to explore. When you finish, you will understand the pros and cons of virtual offices and how to set them up.

Even if you are not ready to allow everyone to work at home, there is valuable information in this book on how to connect everyone by chat, audio and video. Have all your meetings at your desk and record for those out today. Better yet, create a wiki for ongoing meetings anyone can join, contribute and leave at any time.

This is very much a how-to-do type of book, but the first few chapters discuss the decisions you will need to make if you go virtual and move much of your work to the cloud. These chapters present the pros and cons in a fair and balanced manner so you can make a good decision. The later chapters give you insight into cloud based tools that make virtual teams possible, namely Microsoft's SkyDrive recently renamed to OneDrive, Google Drive, Zoho CRM and Docs. These are all web based, office type applications.

Even if you are happy with your office, there is much to gain from going virtual or moving to the cloud. You get free cloud based software, cheap phones calls to and from your customers, less staff.

Just keeping staff at their desk can add a 20 to 30% boost in productivity. Be the first to embrace this new technology and lead your competitors.

Chapter 1: What Are We Going to Learn?

How to Evaluate Your Business as a Candidate for Virtualization and the Cloud

Many businesses are not good candidates as their sales depend on a face to face exchange. Brick and mortar retail stores, manufacturing or auto repair are examples. However, if you mostly communicate with your customers over the phone, fill out forms and paperwork and work mostly with computers; you have an information type business in which a virtual office offers many advantages. Examples of this might be insurance, financial and online businesses. This book is a blueprint for taking advantage of these emerging technologies.

Here is What We Will Do in the Book

- We are going to evaluate and compare three free web based office suites that can successfully replace a desktop version of Office. These are:
    - Microsoft's SkyDrive
    - Google's Drive
    - Zoho's CRM and integrated Docs
- We will look at Skype for instant communication and cheap phone calls all over the world. This gives all your staff instant chat, voice and/or video communication, desk to desk, anytime, anywhere.
- We will evaluate virtual web based incoming call management that answers and routes calls.
- We will discover how to print over the Internet so any printer, in any location is yours to use. We will also look at remotely controlling and troubleshooting your staff's computers.
- We will learn about collaboration with virtual video meetings and using wikis to provide what is in effect a 24/7, ongoing meeting that collects and organizes the group's thoughts and input.

Chapter 2: What is a Virtual Office?

Yes, you can save a lot of expense and do business in your house robe, but there are issues you will have to master. We will cover this in detail later, but, in a nutshell, here are both sides:

Pros

- You eliminate much of the office expense.
- You eliminate the time and cost of commuting.
- You extend your reach for great employees to anywhere in the world.
- You get better employees as you offer virtual work.
- Without the usual office distractions, productivity increases by as much as 30%.

Cons

- You need self-motivated staff you can trust.
- Alternately, you need time and activity tools that keep employees doing effective work.
- You might worry about your business image without a physical office.
- You might have web surfers rather than effective workers.
- Employees disconnect and isolation might be an issue.
- The barrier between work and leisure time is vague and can lead to burnout.

This book helps eliminate most of the cons and helps you achieve the many pros.

How to Find and Motivate Great Virtual Staff

Again, we will have more detail later, but many of the best potential candidates already work virtually and want to work that way. They get virtual work because they are first

Chapter 2: What is a Virtual Office?

class employees. Additionally, since they do not have to come to the office, they can work from anywhere.

For example, I live in Montana. It is a great place to live, but wages are much lower than say, New York City. My hourly rate is less than a New York based programmer or consultant and yet I am very happy making what I charge. My big city customers get a bargain and I get to live in paradise.

This also means you can ramp staff up, and then when not needed, ramp staff down by using independent contractors for projects. This means no need to pay FICA or benefits for staff that are not needed on a daily basis.

How to Work in the Cloud

If you have a traditional office, you probably have multiple computers, each with its own hard drive. Each computer has its own files and if you want to work on a file not on your computer, you have to copy that file over to your computer using your network.

Worse, you are at home at your computer and you need that file back in your office. If you anticipated this, you could email them to yourself or carry them home on a thumb drive. Copy back to the thumb drive and carry back to the office and hope you do not get the old and new version confused.

When you work in the cloud, there is only one copy and it is stored on an industrial strength, secure server run by someone like Google or Microsoft. If you need the file from any computer, you access through the web. You work with the file through any web browser much like you do now with a local application like Microsoft Office.

Work Anywhere with a Tablet or Phone

In many cases, you do not even need a traditional PC as you can read and often edit files on tablets and smart phones. The tremendous cost savings and work anywhere methods give you a competitive edge, for now. Early adopters of virtual workspaces will crush traditional office based businesses. They can respond faster, 24/7, and with much less cost. Will you lead this inevitable trend or later play catch-up?

How Microsoft, Zoho and Google's Documents Work

We will explore these three free services in greater depth in the three chapters devoted to each of their services.

We will also take a very high view of Microsoft's Paid Service, Office 365. An in depth tutorial on Office 365 would be a sizeable book in itself. We will give you enough information to decide if you want the more extensive paid service.

Chapter 2: What is a Virtual Office?

- All of the services offer free and paid services.
- All give you free storage where you can upload files: Google 15GB, Microsoft 7GB and Zoho 5GBof space.
- All give you a free, but slightly limited, office suite. For many businesses, it provides all that is needed.
- If you already use Microsoft office, upgrading to Office 365 gives you a much richer experience and you can use your existing office skills. They give you an upgrade to Office 2013 desktop software with a monthly or annual subscription. The small business plan is about $12 a month per person. You can try it free for 30 days.
- Google docs, combined with Gmail and Google Calendar, gives you some of the same functionality for free.
- Zoho provides a similar office suite with email and a calendar. Additionally, this is all integrated into a CRM (client relationship management) app which may make Zoho the best of all virtual apps.
- For all, any major, up to date browser works as well as tablets and smartphones, Apple and Android.
- To access, you need to sign up and get a Gmail address, Windows ID or Zoho user ID and password. Again, for small businesses, they are all free. If you use an Android based phone, you probably already have a Gmail address.

In the how-to, step-by-step chapters, we discus each service in greater detail. You will not need all three, so at some point you will need to commit to one or the other. The purpose of these evaluations is to help you decide which is best for you.

The Best Ways to Use Phones and Other Interoffice Communication

Chapter 2: What is a Virtual Office?

There are two issues: routing incoming phone calls and communication between staff. We will look at several phone services, including Grasshopper, that can answer phones and route calls.

On the interoffice topic, we will explore Lync® from Office 365® and Skype®. Both of these inexpensive solutions offer instant messaging, voice and video connections. You can use them to arrange video online meetings and presentations. Even traditional offices are using these to connect staff and avoid a disruptive walk and visit.

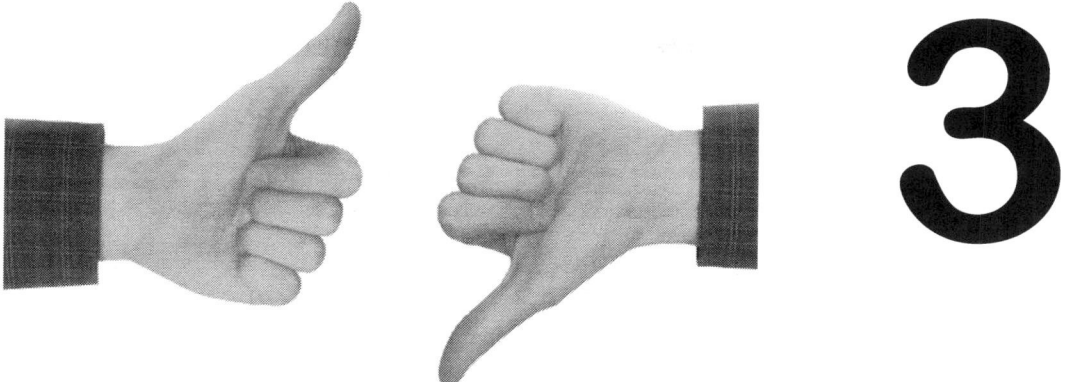

Chapter 3: The Pros and Cons of a Virtual Office?

First, let's cover the motivation for changing to a virtual office. While you might be looking at saving overhead cost, there are many less tangible reasons as we will learn. Later in this chapter, to be fair and balanced, we will look at some detriments and how to overcome them.

Good Things with a Virtual Office

What is the first thing you think of as motivation to explore a virtual office? Most say cost savings. They can be substantial and can double your net profit. However, there are many advantages in improving communication and productivity.

Cost Savings
Office Space

According to an article in Entrepreneur Magazine [1], the national average cost for office space is $23.23 a square foot. If you have a 1,500 square foot office, you will pay $2,903.75 a month. This includes a 2.1% increase over last year, 2012. It can be much higher. For example:

- **San Francisco** - Up 7.2% - $35.99 per square foot (PSF)
- **San Jose** - Up 4.6% - $25.05 PSF
- **New York City** - Up 4.4% - $49.98 PSF

Having a 1,500 square foot office in New York would cost you $6,247.50 a month. Moving to a virtual office would save about 95% of that rental cost.

---

[1] The Best and Worse U.S. Cities for Renting Office Space - Entrepreneur Magazine
http://goo.gl/2CyjNg

Computers

If each of your staff now has a computer, the number of computers will not change. However, you will not need a powerful computer with lots of storage space. You will be accessing your office files over the web and an entry level computer will work as fast as an expensive, high end one. The Internet does not get any faster with a more powerful computer. If you go Google, you might even opt for a Chrome laptop. Think of a simple operating system and a super browser combined. New ones are selling for as little as $200.

Software

If you have purchased several upgrades to Microsoft Office, you know how expensive that can be over time. In cloud computing, you do not necessarily need local software installed with the exception of a browser such as Chrome, Firefox or Internet Explorer. If all you need is Word, Excel and PowerPoint, or Google's equivalents, you may not need to purchase any office type suite.

If you opt for a paid service, such as Office 365, you are, in effect, renting the online service and they are giving you the desktop software in addition. Stop paying and the desktop copies also stop. If you use some of the software applications such as Access, InfoPath (document flow and forms) or Publisher, this might be a good deal.

Commute

What does it cost to travel from your home to your office? Not just money, but time spent traveling. For some of you in the larger cities, this may be hundreds of hours a year; hours you could be working or if you prefer, recreating. What would happen to your gasoline expenditures if your office was in your home?

While you might enjoy ditching the daily travel, your staff will love it. Offering virtual work is a tremendous enticement for top notch employees.

Insurance

Depending on how you feel about insurance, you may be able to stop carrying some of the policies for which you now pay. For one thing, you do not have all your eggs in one basket, your office. Yes, one of your home offices might have a flood, theft or fire, but it is only one computer to replace. Since everything is in the cloud and safe, you only need a quick trip to SAMS or Costco for a replacement.

Quality Employees from Anywhere in the World

If you have a traditional physical office, you hire locally. After all, the employee can't drive across the country just to come to work. Distance becomes somewhat irrelevant with a virtual office.

Chapter 3: The Pros and Cons of a Virtual Office

Think Globally, Think Experts

Your perfect employee may not live anywhere near you. They may not even be in your country. I have trained programmers and other workers from all over the world: India, Eastern Europe and China. Many have world class talents and their wage/hours/benefits and expectations are very reasonable. oDesk[2] is one of the best places to find staff. There you can view portfolios, resumes and ratings on applicants. Other places to look for virtual workers are:

- Freelancer[3]
- Guru[4]
- Elance[5]

You can assume that they have their own computers and Internet access. However, be aware of the time shift if they live far away. Unless they are night owls with insomnia, an out of the country employee might not be available during your working hours. This is not always a bad thing. I once helped on a project that was "rush, all possible". We had a programmer in the US, the Ukraine and Korea. They passed off their code to the next programmer coming on line and the work continued 24/7.

---

[2] oDesk - Top Virtual Employee Pros
http://goo.gl/p27LSP
[3] Freelancer.com
http://goo.gl/8zfcKF
[4] Guru.com
http://www.guru.com/
[5] Elance.com
https://www.elance.com/

Staff sizing flexibility

Many small companies are reluctant to hire new staff during a busy time. What do you do when you are not so busy a short time later? It is painful to hire good people and then to have to lay them off when you no longer have work. Many virtual workers work as independent contractors. They move from one business to another as those companies' work ebbs and flows. You can quickly ramp up and then ramp down staff as needed in a virtual office.

Temporary Independent Contractors

Many of these candidates work as freelancers. This means no FICA, payroll taxes or paid benefits. You simply send them a 1099 at the end of the year if they make more than $500. Make sure that they are properly qualified as independent contractors to satisfy the IRS guidelines. While they can work full time for a short period, they need to have other clients and be willing to work for them. If you find a real treasure, you might talk them out of the independent life.

If you hire foreign workers, you may need to learn the rules on tax reporting on both your side and theirs. Each country is different, but a Google search will get you started.

Workspace vs. Workplace

It is just semantics, but what you call something is important. A workplace is the traditional, physical office. A workspace is anywhere you have Internet access and the ability to connect to your cloud services.

Just as you have the right to require an employee to be at a physical workplace, you can and should require that an employee is at their workspace a certain amount of time. We will talk about how to trust but verify an employee's working effort shortly. This is a major concern for many employers moving to a virtual office.

Less distraction

Offices with many people working in close proximity can make meaningful work difficult and at times chaotic. It is common for one person to leave their desk to visit. While there may be legitimate business reasons, too often the visit digresses into a disruption or distraction.

Up to 30 Percent Increase in Productivity

According to the Wikipedia article Telecommuting:[6], some companies have seen up to a 30% increase in productivity by going virtual. This is partially due to fewer distractions, but having a quiet environment with well-defined expectations and monitoring promotes good productive work habits.

Reduced Employee Turnover and Absenteeism

According to this article in Forbes by Kevin Kruse, he tells new employees, "You can do your job wherever and whenever you want…you can even sit in a beach chair with a cocktail in hand for all I care…as long as you get our desired results."[7] This motivates employees and makes them task oriented.

Possible Problems with a Virtual Office

There are issues and pitfalls you will have to address. You will need to learn some of the tools and train yourself and your employees. All are doable and the payoffs for you and your staff are substantial. Your business will make more money and have better and happier employees. I promised to be fair and balanced, so let's look at some potential issues.

Need Self-Reliant and Self-Motivated Staff

How do you hire or train employees to be good virtual workers? Not everyone does well without someone looking over their shoulder. I once allowed one of my best sales person to work from his home. His sales plummeted and he was back at work in a few weeks. To get you started, here is an excellent article titled "How to Manage Home-Based Workers the Apple Way from Intuit"[8]. You will want to read the full article, but here is a summary of the key points:

1. Make them part of the team.
2. Set expectations during training.
3. Conduct real-time checks.

---

[6] Wikipeida.org article on Telecommuting
http://en.wikipedia.org/wiki/Telecommuting

[7] Top 10 Benefits of Working from Home Survey Results - Forbes
http://goo.gl/Bp2gJQ

[8] How to Manage Home-Based Workers the Apple Way from Intuit
http://goo.gl/Yg0FiZ

Chapter 3: The Pros and Cons of a Virtual Office

Bottom line, you want self-directed staff.

It is a Matter of Trust

If you hire good people, you can let them know that you trust that they will make your companies interest paramount. Read the above article on how Apple trains their At-Home Advisors. When your staff feels they are part of a productive and task driven team, they are reluctant to let the other team members down by slacking or misusing company assets, including their time.

The worse situation is when an employee feels adversarial towards you, their employer. It is beyond the scope of this book to talk about management but trusting employees you do not see often can be a challenge for some types of managers.

Trust but Verify

Not sure you can trust a new hire? You can help them set goals for tasks they must accomplish each day. Do they make calls? How many? Can you track the number and duration? There are several software packages that can monitor their computer activities. They all have a hidden agent or piece of software that can monitor all activity. Here are some of the most popular:

- ActivTrak[9] - This is a cloud based productivity monitoring service. You can see, in real time, what the employee is doing on the web and with any software application. You can even set alarms for nonproductive activity. No trips to Facebook or eBay without you knowing it. Block any website or application from the cloud. **This is Free for up to three employees**.
- SpyAgent[10] - SpyAgent can log anything ranging from what the user typed and the files they downloaded, to who they talked to and emailed, website searches they performed, programs they ran, and much more - all time stamped by date for easy viewing! **Three Licenses for $79.95**.
- TopTenReviews[11] - If you want to evaluate even more packages, this site ranks and reviews them. Note, that SpyAgent above ranks number 1, thanks to its remote monitoring, remote shutdown, ability to block sites and screen replay. When you are discussing a problem with an employee, you might want to show proof.

Time Tracking

---

[9] Free Employee Monitoring Software - ActivTrack.com
http://activtrak.com/
[10] SpyAgent v8 - Herman St
http://store.hermanstreet.com/pc-software/spyagent-v8-download/
[11] TopTenReviews of Monitoring Software
http://monitoring-software-review.toptenreviews.com/

Chapter 3: The Pros and Cons of a Virtual Office

If you have hourly paid employees, you might want to install time card software. Here is a review of the top 10. Many have free trials.[12]

Preventing Computer Misuse

When you provide them with the computer, you might lock it down so they cannot add or delete any software. It is relatively easy and straight forward. When you set the computer up, you make yourself an admin. This allows you complete control. You then create an account for the employee that has reduced privileges. You can prevent them from installing, deleting or changing anything on the computer.

Perceived Business Image

Unfortunately, many people think of offices in a home as a "home business" and that they are small and somehow not a real business. That's not true, but perception always trumps reality.

If you feel that is an issue, you can rent a prestigious address. Regus[13] has several packages that provide a business address. They and other similar services, also, offer a part time space for meetings, a receptionist, phone answering, etc.

Virtual Assistant and Receptionist

Want a live 24/7 real person answering your phones? There are many services that provide that, plus call routing, voice mail and other features.

Here are a few candidates for a real person virtual receptionist:

- Ruby[14] - Starts at $239 a month. This gives you 100 receptionist minutes, voice mail with email notification, unlimited talk time and voicemail time.
- Go Answer[15] - Ask for a pricing quote. They offer bilingual answering if you need it. Again, call routing.

While many people say they do not like them, automated, menu driven answering systems do work well as long as you do not overburden the menus. During working hours, always have a zero option that leads to a real person or a message system after hours.

Employee Disconnect and Isolation

---

[12] Time card software reviews - toptenreviews
http://time-card-software-review.toptenreviews.com/
[13] Virtual office packages and business addresses - Regus.com
http://goo.gl/3rRuoF
[14] Ruby Receptionist
http://www.callruby.com/why-ruby.html
[15] Live answering service - Go Answer
http://www.888goanswer.com/page/24x7_Live_Answering

Chapter 3: The Pros and Cons of a Virtual Office

This can be a real problem and we discuss some remedies below. For many workers, one of the advantages of a physical workspace is the emotional contact with others. We are social animals and need that human contact.

Instant video communication between staff can help. However, physical meetings can help your staff emotionally connect as members of a team.

Loss of Employee Recognition

Good workers are often motivated by the recognition of their fellow workers and managers for doing a good job. This happens often in a physical work environment. In a virtual environment, it may not be as easy to note exceptional performance.

As a manager of a virtual staff, you are going to have to make a point of praising and acknowledging good work. Start virtual meetings with acknowledgements of those that have done exemplary work.

Loss of Nonverbal Nuance

As social animals, we are intuitively tuned into the nonverbal signals we receive from others. A phone call, text message or even face to face video cannot provide all of the nuances we receive in a face to face contact.

This means you and your staff will have to work harder to understand each other in interoffice communication.

Renting Physical Space

The odds are that your customers are not virtual if you do business locally. You may yet need a part time place to meet them. We discussed Regus[13] on the last page. They specialize in physical spaces for virtual businesses.

If you live in a small town, you may have to negotiate your own. Many local Chamber of Commerce organizations provide meeting rooms for their members. You will usually have to schedule time, of course.

Meetings and Interoffice Communication

This is easy to solve with technology. Skype, GoToMeeting, WebEx and several other packages can let staff meet from their own desk. With video, much of the face-to-face experience is preserved.

However, to build a team, you may want to hold real world meetings so staff get to know each other.

Chapter 4: Your Office in the Clouds

In this chapter, we will learn what the cloud is and what it offers our new virtual office. All of the electronic files on all of your office computers can now be safely stored on a secure server managed by the experts at Google, Microsoft or one of several other vendors. For many smaller businesses, it is free.

What is the Cloud?

Since the beginning, many have called the Internet "The Cloud". It is a cloud of interconnected computers and networks. You transverse that cloud at nearly the speed of light minus the connection time of hundreds of connection points. Regardless, it is fast and, most of the time, reliable.

When we talk about storing something in the cloud, we mean we are storing our data on one of the millions of servers out there.

These servers are:

- Industrial strength with numerous fail over systems to keep them from going down. Many boast a 99.999% uptime.
- Redundant in that the data is probably on several servers, each acting as a backup to the others. Even if a server totally failed, you could still reach your data.
- Secure at the highest level. Google, Microsoft and the others have top line security experts and most have never been successfully hacked (as far as we know).

Always Connected Anywhere

Once the data is stored in the cloud, you access it through a web browser. Any recent web browser will work, although, there is some slight advantage in using the vendor's web browser if they have created one. For example, Chrome has a few minor advantages using Google web applications and, of course, Internet Explorer with Microsoft's web applications.

This means you can reach your data from any computer, even those you do not control such as an Internet Café or a library computer. When finished, you sign out and leave no trace of your data behind.

Since web based applications (web pages) cannot provide as much functionality as desktop applications, Microsoft's 365 Office will download a small version of their desktop software, if you need it. This is called Office on Demand and it is then erased when you finish. This is a nice feature if you need the richer, desktop version of their software on a computer that does not have desktop Office. For most of you, most of the time, the web version is just fine.

What does it Cost?

Is anything really free? You can argue that my monthly ISP bill means nothing as the Internet is free. However, Google, Microsoft and Zoho give away an entire suite of office applications including replacements for Microsoft's desktop version of Word, Excel and SharePoint. Yes, it is free unless you are a large business and need more features.

In addition to the Office applications, they all give you storage space: 15GB for Google, 7GB for Microsoft and 5GB for Zoho. For many smaller businesses, this is all you may need. If you do need more space, you can purchase extra for a very reasonable rate. We get a detailed review of these packages in their respective chapters.

Ongoing vs. Onetime

Traditionally, if you wanted Microsoft Office, you bought or upgraded it and then installed it on your computer. Have another computer, you buy and install another copy. Some software vendors sell a license for three computers, but usually a software license is good for only one. It is like a book in that there can only be one copy running at a time. Buy a new computer and you could install it, but you are required to remove it from the old computer.

For those that charge for their online services such as Office 365, you pay a subscription fee monthly or annually. You do not own the software, you rent it. The upside is a low, up front outlay and your software is always up-to-date.

Software Always Up to Date

If you work on Windows, do you get monthly updates? I hope so as these help secure your computer. If you have Microsoft Office, you are also getting updates and fixes. Some of the fixes are for bugs found and security issues discovered. They rarely change how the software actually works. However, unless the bug is a serious risk, you may not get a fix from Microsoft for a month or so.

We do not have these update issues in web based software. There may be bugs to fix, but the software vendor can repair the page as soon as the problem is discovered and the very next visitor to the web page gets the corrected copy. Google, Microsoft and other vendors continually work to improve their products. They change all the time, hopefully, for the better. We have a lot of screen captures in the later, how-to-do chapters that may be somewhat obsolete by the time you read this. Usually, the changes are not so extreme as to cause any confusion.

Let's get a closer, high level view of the competing vendors.

Google Drive

You will need a Google email address and password. To use Google Drive, http://www.google.com/drive.

I admire Google. Who would think a company could grow to be worth $250,000,000,000, (250 Billion), dollars by giving very useful things away free? They are the engine behind my Android Smart Phone, my GPS, my email and calendar.

They do sell things, of course. Go to Google Play and you can purchase movies, books, songs and applications for your Android tablet and smart phone. Much is free and, of course, they give you a free book reader, movie and music player.

Free Google Productivity Apps

For most users, they are free. Any document can be shared and even allows co-authoring where two or more people work on the same document in real time. They look and act like their Microsoft Office counterparts and so, there is no need for extensive retraining.

You get these free applications:

- **Document** - Similar to Microsoft Word.
- **Presentation** - Similar to PowerPoint.
- **Spreadsheet** - Similar to Excel.
- **Form** - Data collection forms. Can be used for surveys.
- **Drawing** - Sort of like a simpler Publisher.
- **Gmail** - Email, contact list and calendar.
- **Hangouts** - Chat, phone and video application.

If you want more, you might consider their enterprise version for $5 a month for each employee. The enterprise version gives you admin tools and improves collaboration.

Microsoft's SkyDrive

To compete against Google, Microsoft offers SkyDrive, http://SkyDrive.com.

You get the most basic office suite applications free:

- **Word** - Classic Office word processing.
- **Excel** - Spreadsheet.
- **PowerPoint** - Presentations.
- **OneNote** - Like a note book for organizing, planning and keeping notes.
- **Excel Survey** - Forms that feed into Excel - Like Google's app Form.
- **Text document** - Web based notepad.
- **Outlook Web App** - An email and calendaring app.

Already know Microsoft Office? Then this might be your best tool.

You Get a Lot for the Per-User Fee

If you opt for Microsoft's Small Business Premium paid services, you also get desktop versions of their complete Office Suite. Additionally, you also get business class email, online conferencing and a free public website.

Personal or Business

While Office 365 Home Premium is only $99.99 a year and can be used on 5 desktops and 5 mobile devices, they warn that it is not for businesses. They also give you desktop applications. I am not sure why it would not work for businesses or even if they could really tell. You decide.

Zoho CRM and Zoho Docs

Zoho, https://www.zoho.com/, is famous for their CRM system for tracking leads and contacts. They are used to manage the pipeline of suspects becoming prospects and prospects becoming customers. They even track the problems (cases) of customers after the sale.

They have a free suite of office type products.

You get these free applications:

- **Writer** - A word processing app.
- **Sheet** - A spreadsheet app.
- **Show** - A presentation app.
- **MailMagnet** - An email app.

What separates Zoho from the others, is the excellent CRM application. All email, letters sent, phone calls made, issue cases are tied to an individual lead or contact. These integrations make Zoho a superb contender for your cloud if CRM is important to you.

Dropbox

Dropbox offers no office applications, just 2 GB of free storage. You can upload any type of file, music, documents, images, etc. You will want to download the desktop app which creates a special folder in your Favorites group in Windows Explorer. Drag or copy any file to the special folder and it syncs/uploads to your cloud Dropbox.

There is a folder called Public and if you place a file in it, you can then right click on the file and a web link to that file is placed in your cut and paste buffer. Paste that into the body of an email and you give someone a link to download the file. Email limits the size of an attachment to around 10 MB depending on the email client.

Dropbox makes their money on paid services they offer to those that need more space.

Google, Microsoft or Zoho

The chapters on these office type apps give you much deeper details on these competing services. If you know and are comfortable with Microsoft office and use OneNote, Access, Outlook or Publisher, you may want to go with the Office 365 Small Business Premium Plan for $12.50 per employee, per month. You get a free 30 day trial to try it out.

If you currently only use the core Office applications, Word, Excel and PowerPoint, you can choose any of the free services: Google Drive, SkyDrive or Zoho. If tracking prospects and customers is important, Zoho competes very well with their integrated CRM.

All are free for small businesses. All give you an email client: Outlook.com vs. Gmail vs. MailMagnet. All give you calendars integrated with email. As mentioned, you get 15GB storage with Google, 7GB with Microsoft and 5GB with Zoho. That is a lot of storage. Google's storage would store 3,000,000 (3 Million) 5 MB files. All offer additional storage for a modest amount.

You may want to read all of the chapters in a cursory manner and then decide which service you like best and want to pursue. If you are still unsure, you might want to try both to get a better feel for what you do and do not like. Obviously, they are parallel services that overlap so you only need one or the other. The good news is all of them, if you want to upgrade to the paid services, offer 30 day evaluations.

Preparing for Mobile Access

If you do not want to be in front of a desktop PC during most of the working day, you need to learn how to use a tablet or smartphone. Tablets can do about 80% of what a PC does for most people.

Conversely, if you are a power user that does a lot of video editing or high end graphics, you may need the PC and big screen. For most business related computing, tablets may be the answer to how to break the tether to your PC.

You might find the smaller screen of a smartphone a bit small for browsing websites, but many of the vendors we discuss have Android and Apple apps that make better use of the small screen. Look at tablets if you want to do serious work. I am an Android fan and I

Chapter 4: Your Office in the Clouds

carry a Nexus 7, 2013 version. When I need it, I have a Bluetooth keyboard and mouse along with a small stand that makes the tablet as easy to use as a laptop.

Internet access using a PC vs. a mobile device is about 50% vs.50% as of January, 2014. Mobile is growing much faster than PC use (*Figure 1*).

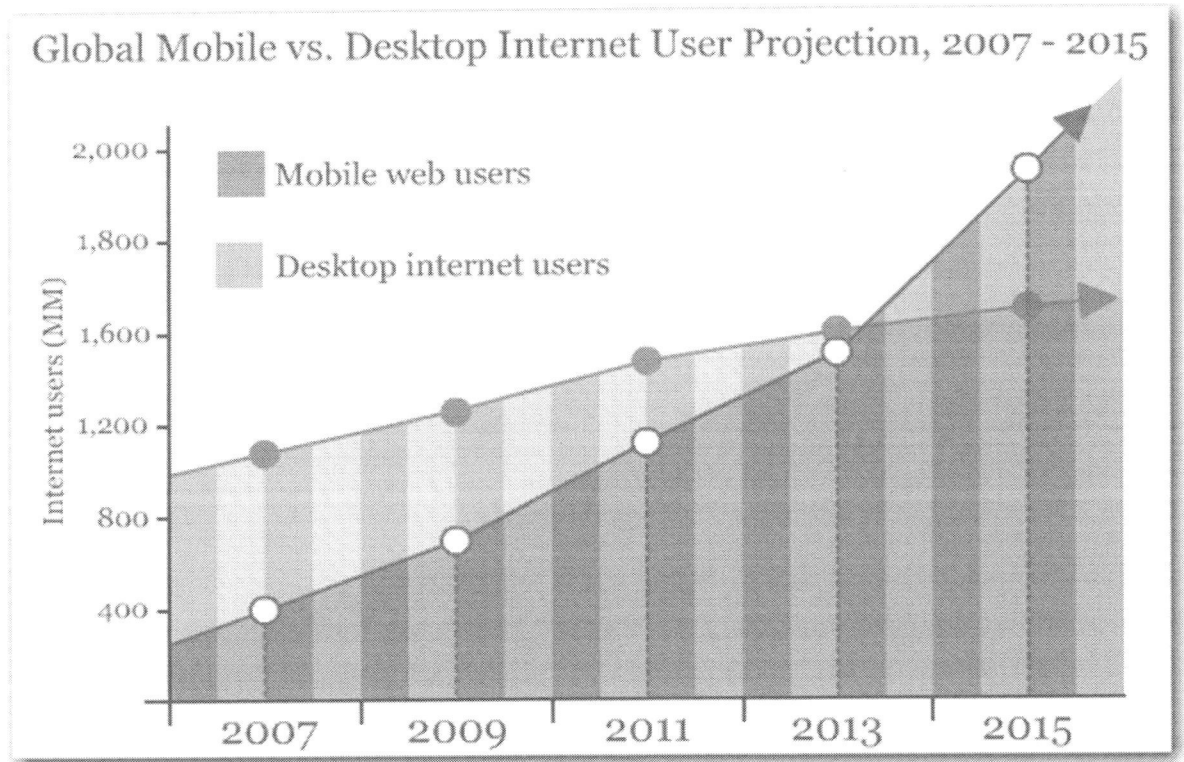

Figure 1: the world is going mobile

Chapter 5: Using Microsoft Office in the Cloud
Basic Office for Free

Microsoft gives away a web based version of their core 2013 Office suite. They throw in 7GB of space, which translates to a lot of documents. It's all free and available anywhere you have a browser, 24/7. Unless you are a serous Microsoft Office user, it may be all you ever need. It is not even necessary that you have purchased their desktop Office suite of products, although, it does help when you reach the limits of what the web apps can do.

Get started by going to http://www.skydrive.com where you can sign in or sign up as seen in (*Figure 2*).

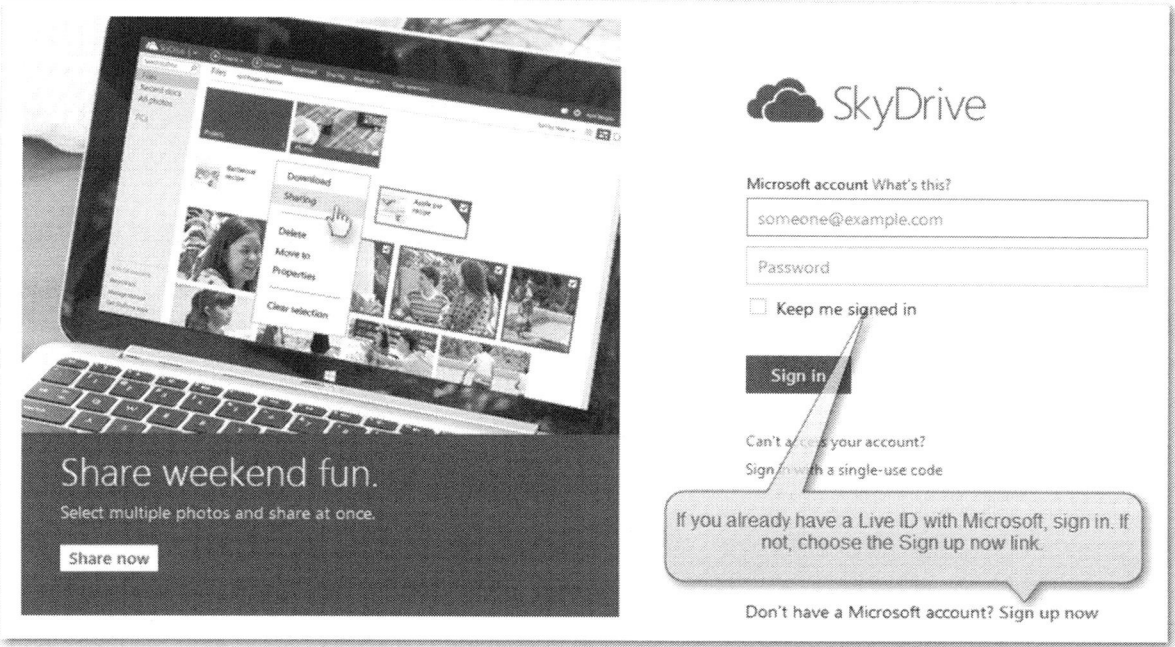

Figure 2: Sign in or sign up to SkyDrive

Chapter 5: Using Microsoft Office in the Cloud

If you are a new sign up, you may need to confirm the address from an email they send to you. Once properly signed up or signed in, you will see the web pages in (*Figure 3*).

Let's explore the main controls:

1. The **Files** tab will show you all the files you have uploaded or created that are not saved into subfolders.
2. This **Recent docs** tab shows documents you recently created. **All photos** shows all the images you uploaded to the Pictures folder.
3. Documents can be **Shared** with others.
4. If you download the SkyDrive app for your PC, you can use a desktop folder to view, up and download files to SkyDrive.
5. Use the link **Get SkyDrive apps** to download apps to your **PC**, Apple or Android devices.
6. There are three systems or built in folders. You can add your own. This shows the Windows 8 type tiles.
7. If you are not on a touch screen, you can change the thumbnails view to a details view.

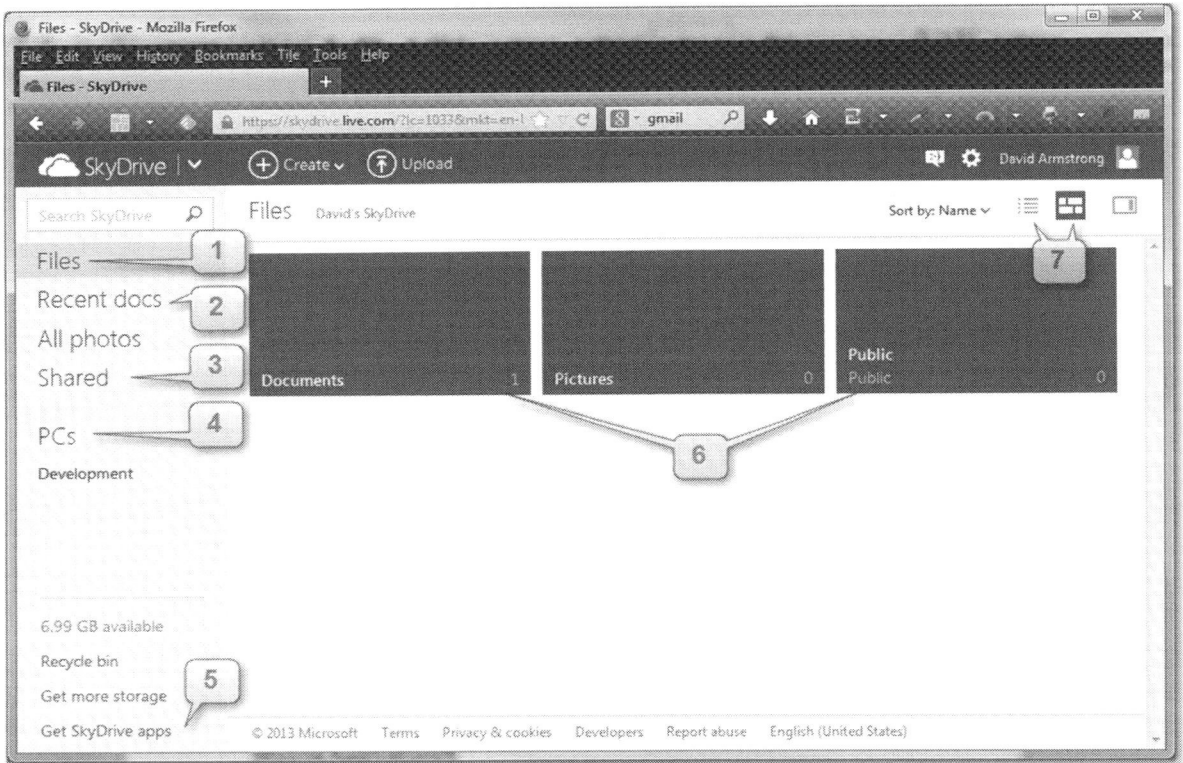

Figure 3: Main SkyDrive screen

If you are on a tablet, phone or PC with a touch screen, you may like the big blocky thumbnails Microsoft embraces in Windows 8. However, the thumbnails make poor use of the limited screen real estate most of us have. You can switch from the blocky thumbnail view to the detail view (*Figure 4*).

This view means less scrolling and is similar to the one you get in Windows Explorer. Additionally, you can see how much space each folder or file uses and whether you are sharing and how.

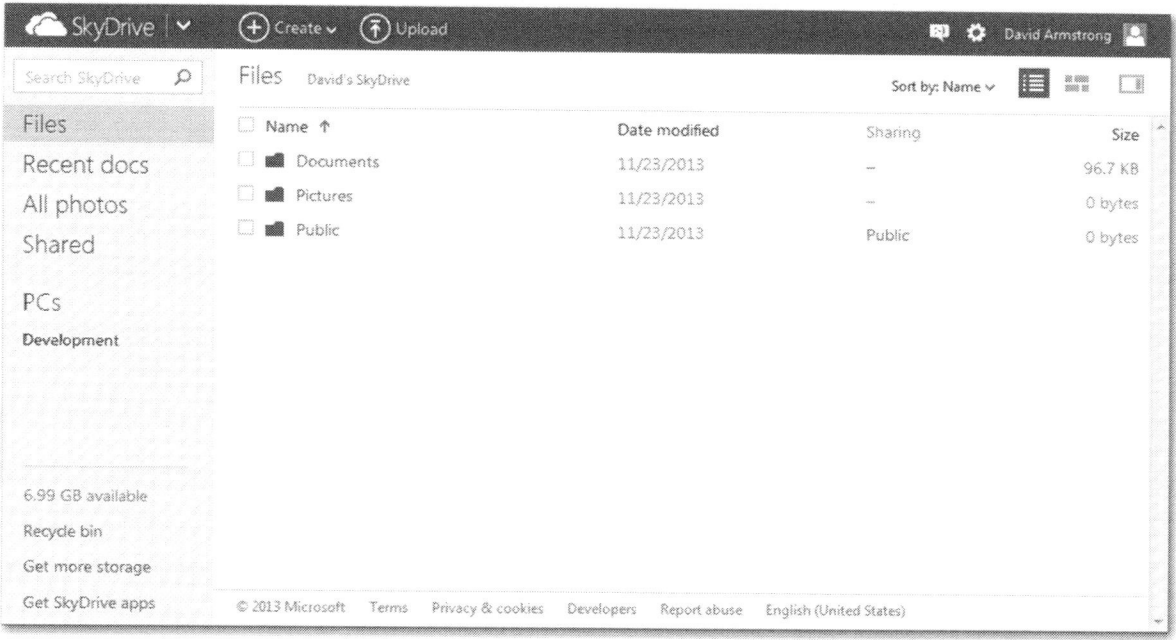

Figure 4: The main screen in list view

You really want the SkyDrive app on your desktop. While it looks and acts like most folders, it gives you a fast and easy way to see and access the documents and folders you created in SkyDrive. To download, click the **Get SkyDrive apps** link at the bottom of the screen (*Figure 4*). When the page loads, you want to click the **Download the desktop app** button (*Figure 5*).

Once downloaded, you want to install by double-clicking the downloaded file and following the installation prompts.

Chapter 5: Using Microsoft Office in the Cloud

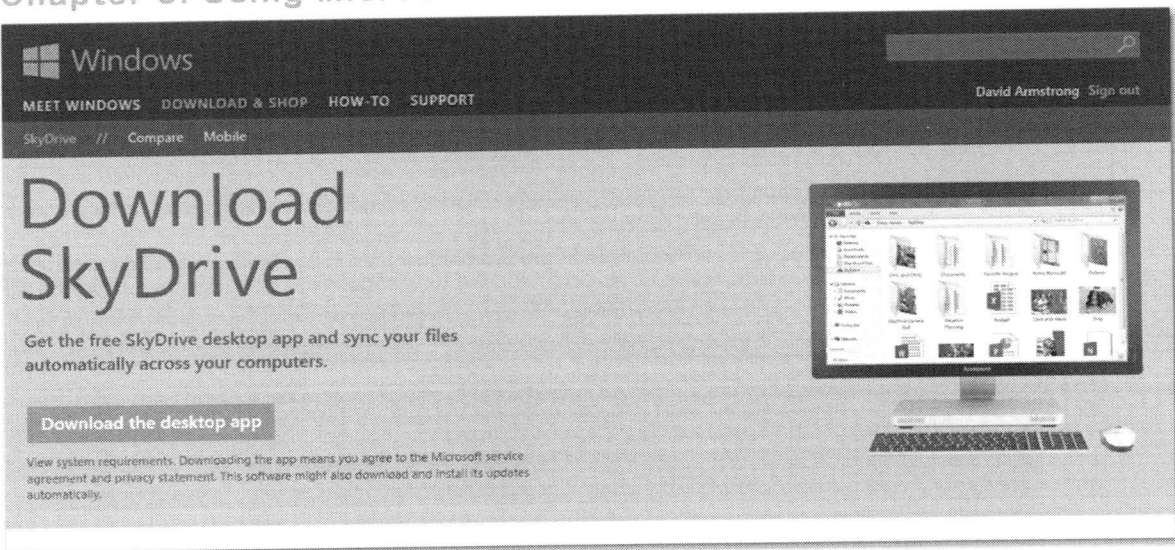

Figure 5: Download the desktop SkyDrive

Once installed, you will have a new folder under your **Favorites** called **SkyDrive** (*Figure 6*).

If this is a new SkyDrive account, you will see three folders that are shared by their counterparts on your web SkyDrive. Having this syncing folder on your desktop, is very convenient for accessing your SkyDrive online storage.

For Example:

- You can drag any file into the SkyDrive folder, and it will automatically upload to SkyDrive.
- If you click on a SkyDrive document from this folder, it will open with the desktop version of Office, if you have it installed.
- Delete a file from the folder, and it is deleted in SkyDrive. You can always reclaim it from the SkyDrive recycle bin, if needed.

Microsoft also provides mobile SkyDrive apps for Apple and Android devices.

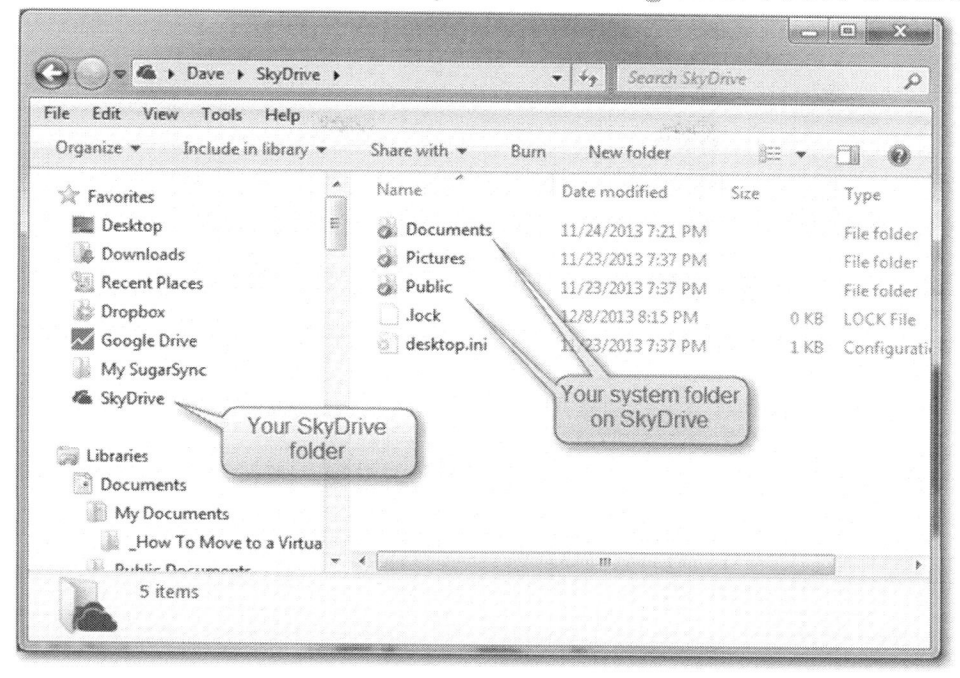

Figure 6: Your desktop SkyDrive folder

Organizing with Folders

Just like in Windows Explorer on your desktop, you can create and nest folders to organize your documents and uploaded files in SkyDrive. Before you add anything, make sure you are in the folder in which you want to add.

In my example, I am adding my folder at the top level. While that might be appropriate, you might also want to add your folders underneath an existing one.

Once you are in the proper place, click the **Create** button on the top of the screen as seen in (*Figure 7*). Then choose the **Folder** menu item.

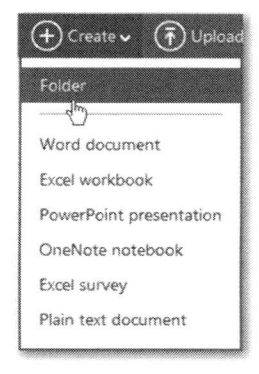

Figure 7: The Create dropdown

A small screen opens allowing you to type the folder's name (*Figure 8*).

Chapter 5: Using Microsoft Office in the Cloud

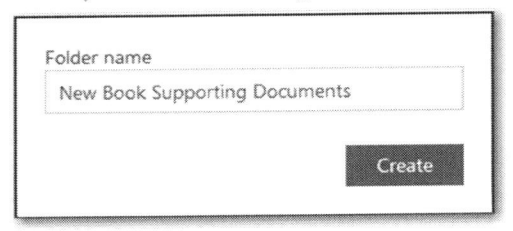

Figure 8: Adding the folder's name screen

In (*Figure 9*), you see the new folder, **New Book Supporting Documents**. The folders are sorted by their name in ascending order, although, you can change the sort method.

Name ↑	Date modified	Sharing	Size
Documents	11/23/2013	--	106 KB
New Book Supporting Documents	12:11 PM	--	0 bytes
Pictures	11/23/2013	--	0 bytes
Public	12:38 PM	Public	54.6 MB

Figure 9: List of folders and documents

You can see the different sorts available. I find the Date created in Descending order to be the most useful (*Figure 10*).

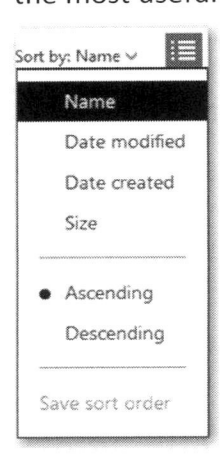

Figure 10: Changing the sort order

When I click on the new folder's link, it opens. SkyDrive gives me instructions on how to create a document (*Figure 11*).

We will add more folders and then documents later, but notice the links at the top that say **David's SkyDrive > New Book Supporting Documents.** If you are new to these, they are usually called breadcrumb links. These links show you where you are in a hierarchy of items. Click on the **David's SkyDrive** link and you move to the top of your SkyDrive as seen in (*Figure 9*).

Once you have a lot of deeply nested folders, this will be very useful for navigation.

Figure 11: An empty folder

Below, I have added three new folders. As we progress, I will upload and create documents within these folders (*Figure 12*).

Figure 12: New folders under New Book Supporting Documents folder

Notice, the small selection check box to the left of a folder or document in the details view. If you check the box and click the Details pane icon in the upper right, you open a side panel that gives you the properties of that folder or file.

The folder contains images as well as documents (*Figure 13*).

Chapter 5: Using Microsoft Office in the Cloud

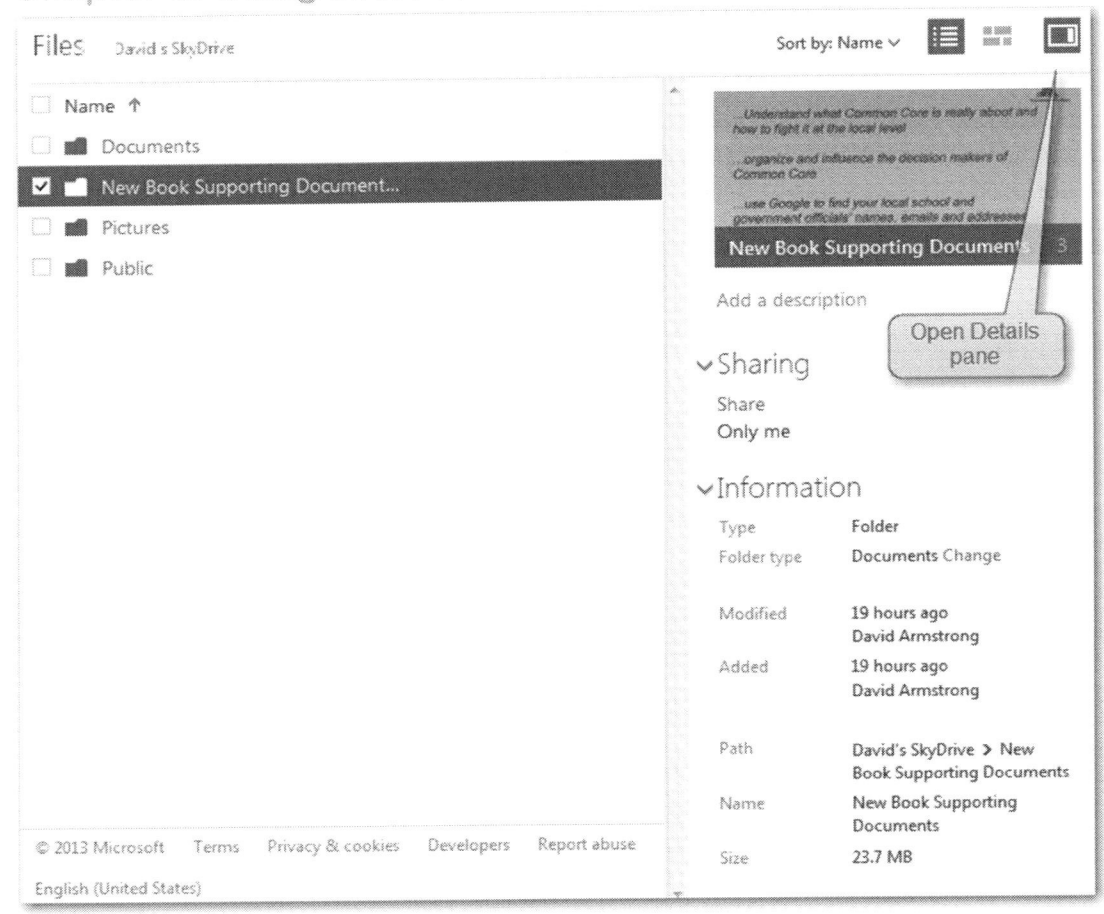

Figure 13: Folder or file Detail's pane

Uploading Files

I have several images I would like to upload into the Images folder seen in (*Figure 13*). To do so, I need to click the Upload button at the top (*Figure 14*).

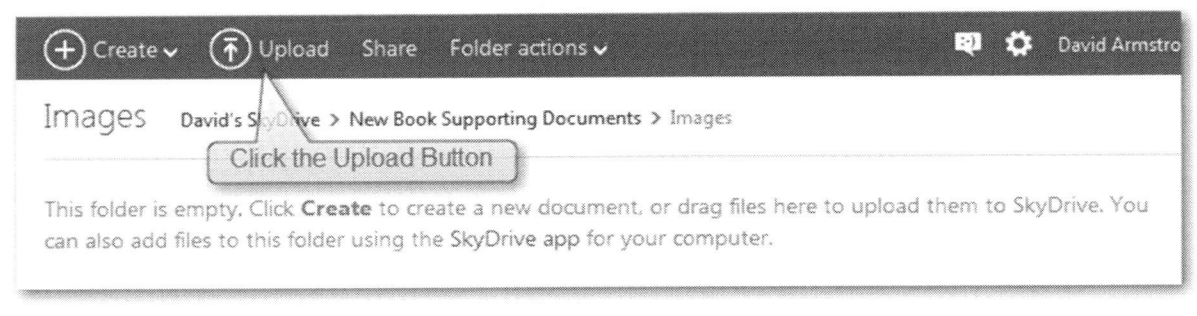

Figure 14: Click the Upload button to start the upload

This will open the Windows standard **File Upload** dialog. Navigate to the location of the images and select one or more images you wish to. Click **Open** to start the upload (*Figure 15*).

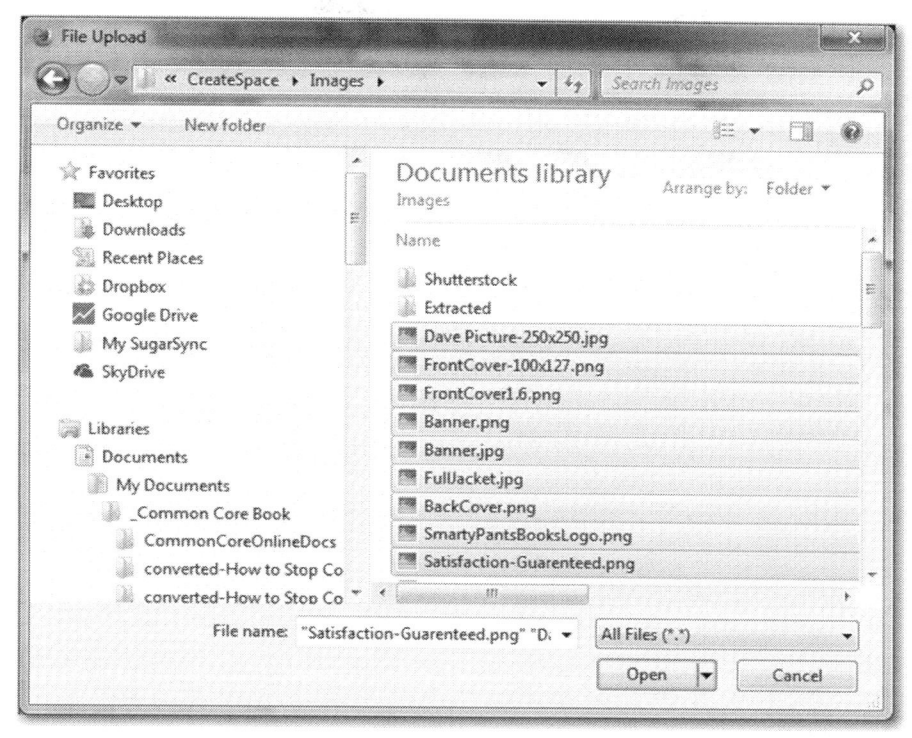

Figure 15: Picking images to upload

A small popup window shows the files uploading with a progress bar (*Figure 16*).

Chapter 5: Using Microsoft Office in the Cloud

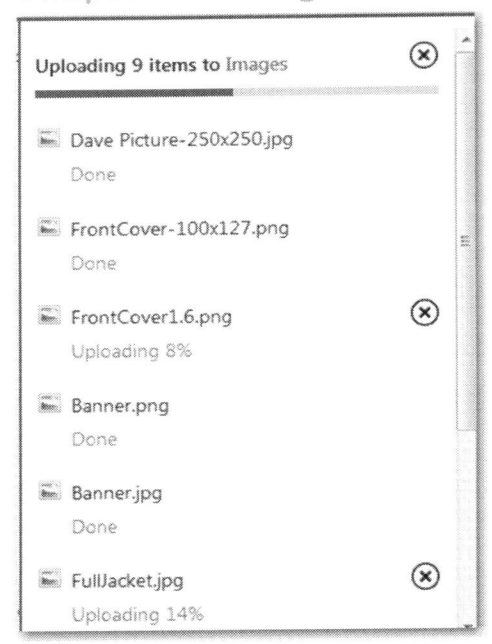

Figure 16: Uploading progress window

See the uploaded images in (*Figure 17*). Again, you can change over to the details view for a more compact listing.

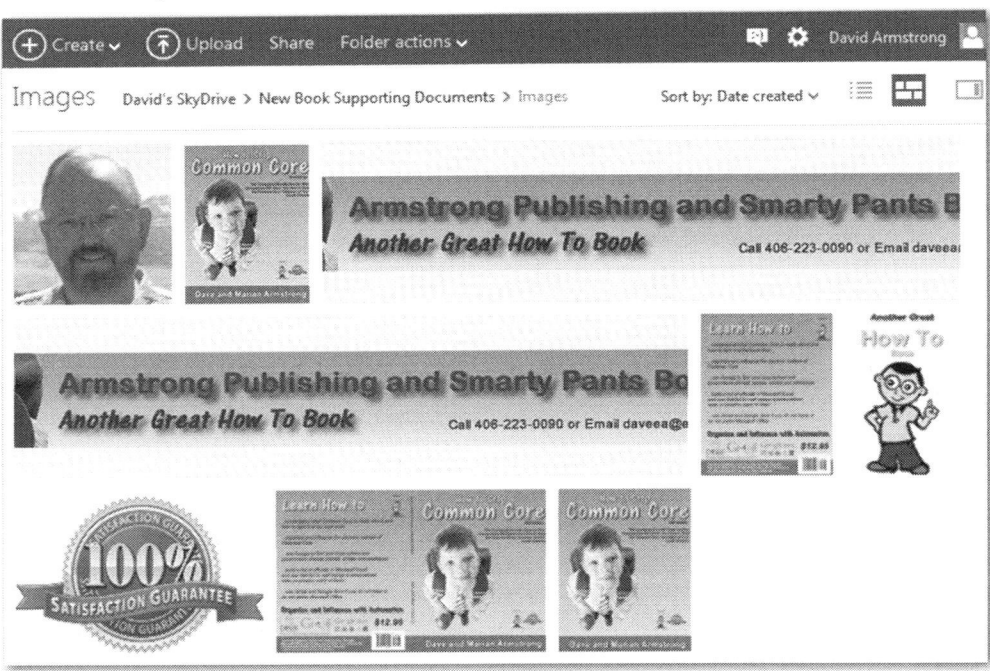

Figure 17: Uploaded images in thumbnail view

I can see the uploaded files in the folder (*Figure 18*).

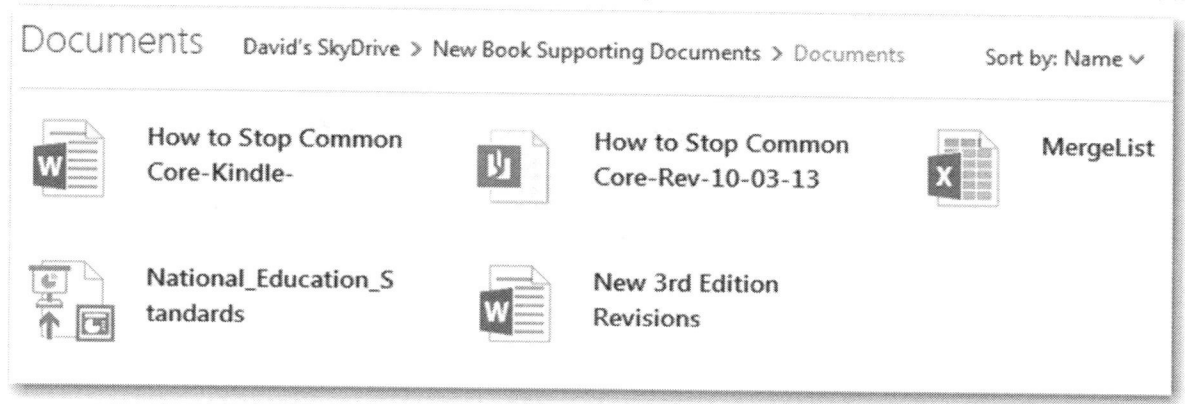

Figure 18: Uploaded documents

Accessing Your Desktop from SkyDrive

If you give SkyDrive permission, you can access files on your PC from anywhere through a browser. After you have downloaded and installed the SkyDrive, within a short time, the name of your computer will show up under the PCs area on the left column of your main SkyDrive screen (*Figure 19*). Be aware that there are many security issues that may not allow this, especially in a corporate office with their higher levels of security.

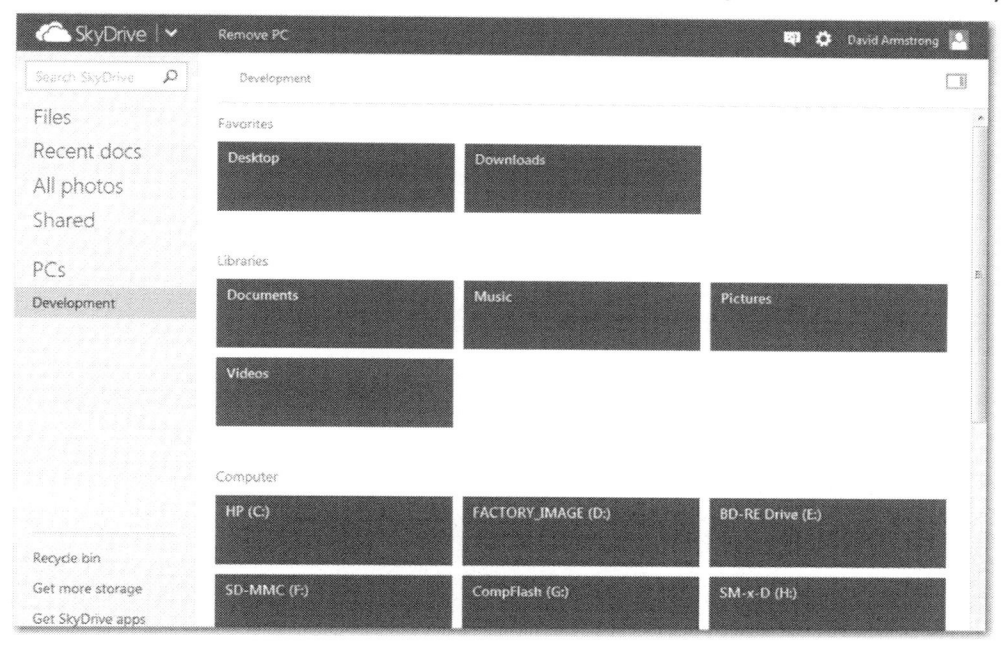

Figure 19: Accessing your computer remotely using SkyDrive

If you are successful, you can drill down into the many folders of your remote PC (*Figure 20*). However, be aware that only a few files can be opened: those that match up with the SkyDrive applications, images and PDF files.

Chapter 5: Using Microsoft Office in the Cloud

If you try to open other files, you will get the option to download. Be careful that you do not accidently download and then leave a file on a public computer. You will need to erase any downloads.

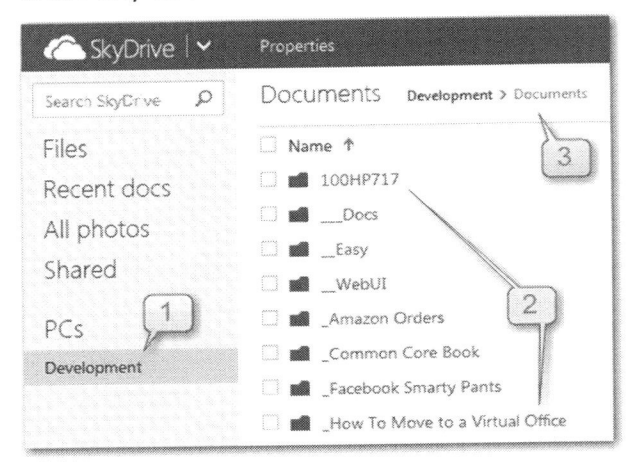

Figure 20: Finding your remote files in SkyDrive

Using the Word App

I am going to have to assume that you have used one of the newer versions of Word. If you are totally new to Microsoft Office apps, you may want to supplement this chapter with a basic book on Office. The Office 2013 for Dummies book is excellent. If I were to make this into an in depth tutorial on all of the features of SkyDrive, it might take several hundred pages just teaching Microsoft Office. My purpose is to give you a high level view so you can make good decisions about which cloud service you want to use.

Your first task is to give the document a meaningful name. Click in the area that contains the default name of Document1 and type a new name (*Figure 21*).

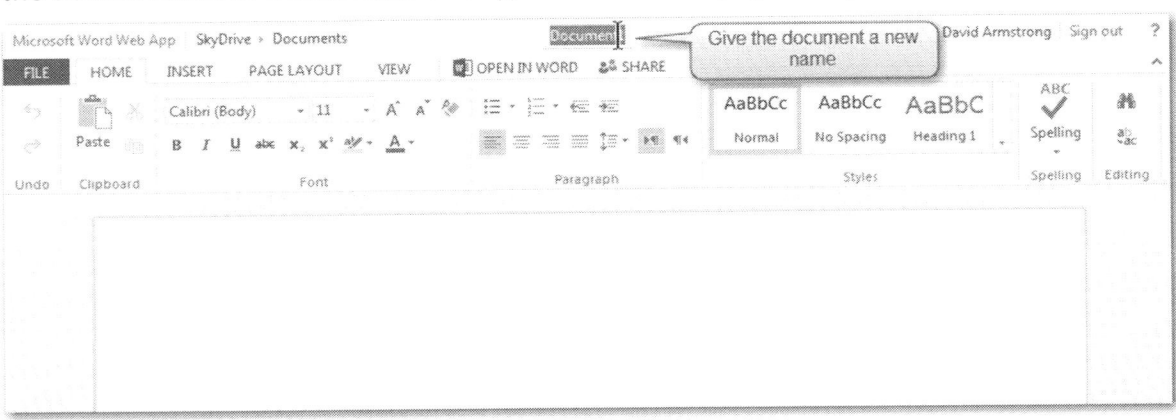

Figure 21: Naming the new word document

Chapter 5: Using Microsoft Office in the Cloud

If you have used any desktop version of Word from 2007 on, you should feel right at home. Office uses a graphical toolbar they call the Ribbon. It has tabs across the top and groups of related controls within each tab. For example, if I wanted to start a numbered list, I would click the **HOME** tab and then the numbered list icon in the **Paragraph** group.

As you can see, The **HOME** tab holds all the formatting options (*Figure 22*).

The groups are:

- **Undo** - Access to the **Undo** and redo actions.
- **Clipboard** - Use this to cut and **Paste.**
- **Font** - Use to pick, size and format a text.
- **Paragraph** - This group allows you to create list, align text and indent.
- **Styles** - Gives access to the many **Styles** included in web Word.
- **Spelling** - Check spelling and allows you to change language dictionaries.
- **Editing** - Search and replace tools.

When you are composing your document, you will mostly be in the **HOME** tab.

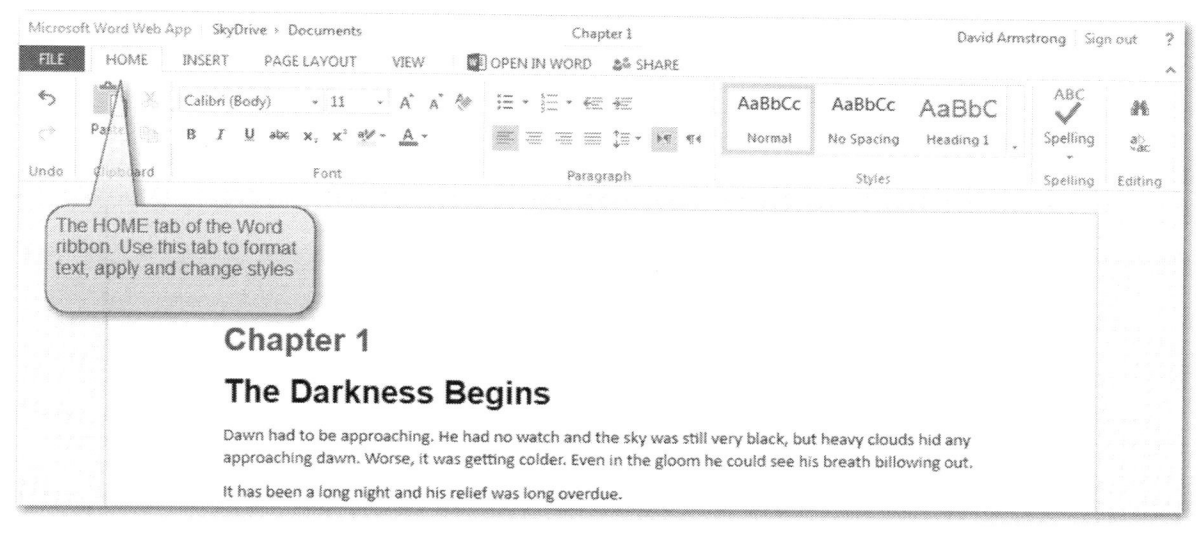

Figure 22: The Word HOME tab

We use the **INSERT** tab to **INSERT** items into our document (*Figure 23*).

The groups are:

- **Page Break** - Use to force the text below the break to move to the next page.
- **Tables** - Insert a Table at the cursor's location.
- **Picture** - Upload and insert a **Picture** from your PC's hard drive.
- **Clip Art** - As you can see in (*Figure 24*), there is an extensive collection of Clip Art and pictures on almost any topic.
- **Link** - Opens a small screen where you can type the visible text and URL.

Chapter 5: Using Microsoft Office in the Cloud

- **Headers & Footers** - This allows you to add repeating text and/or page numbers at the top and/or bottom of the page.
- **Page Numbers** - This will help you quickly format the page numbers.

Figure 23: The Word INSERT tab

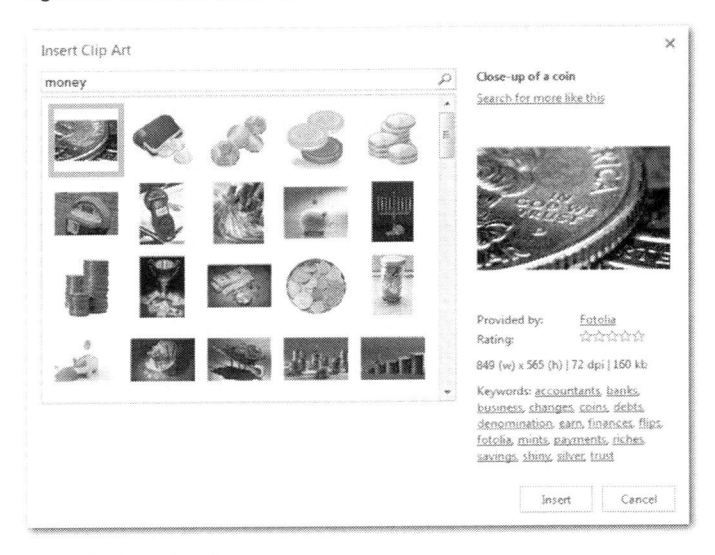

Figure 24: Inserting clip art

The **PAGE LAYOUT** tab allows you to format the page layout. This allows you to set the defaults for **Paragraph Spacing** and **Indenting**.

The groups are:

Page Setup - Set **Margins**, **Orientation** and paper **Size** before starting a document.

Paragraph - Use to set the default indents and spacing before and after paragraphs.

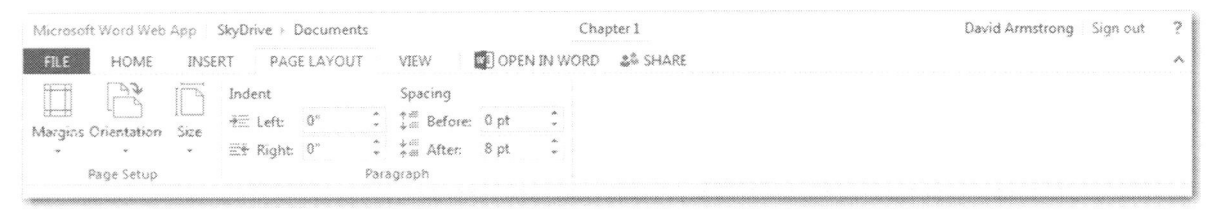

Figure 25: The Word PAGE LAYOUT tab

The **VIEW** tab allows us to change from an editing mode to a view and read mode. In (*Figure 26*), you can see options for how the headers and footers work. For Example, a new chapter's first page generally does not have headers or footers. Setting **Different First Page** removes these.

The Groups are:

- **Document Views** - Use this to switch between **Editing View** and **Reading Viewing.** Editing cannot be done in the reading view.
- **Header & Footer** - While you create the headers and footers in the **INSERT** tab, here you have options for how the headers and footers appear.

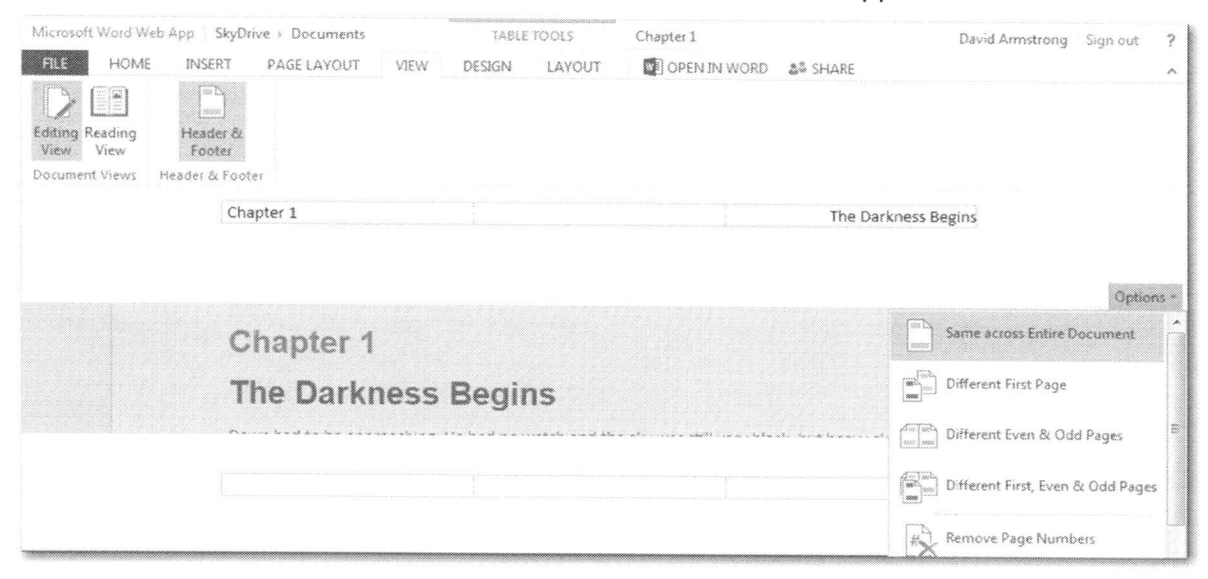

Figure 26: The Word VIEW tab

If you know the desktop version of Word, you realize that there are many advance features missing. If you need to have Word automatically create a table of contents, it is missing in the web versions.

However, by using **OPEN IN WORD**, SkyDrive downloads a copy of this web document and loads it in your desktop version of Word, assuming you have Word desktop installed. Downloading and launching a file is considered a security no-no as this would be a great way to spread viruses. This is not the case, but you will be warned (*Figure 27*). Click the **OK** button and **IF** you have Microsoft Office installed, and **IF** you have the right privileges on your computer, the document will launch in Microsoft Word.

Chapter 5: Using Microsoft Office in the Cloud

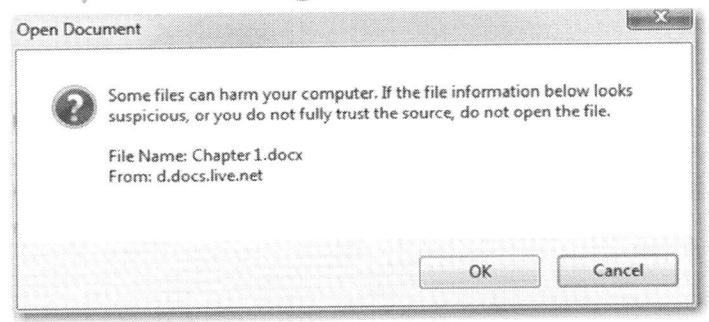

Figure 27: OPEN IN WORD tab and warning

If you get an error or nothing happens, don't despair. Remember your SkyDrive folder we saw in (*Figure 6*)? Close the web file by clicking the SkyDrive link at the top of the page. Open your desktop folder and double-click the file.

If successful, you will open the file locally in the desktop version of Word (*Figure 28*).

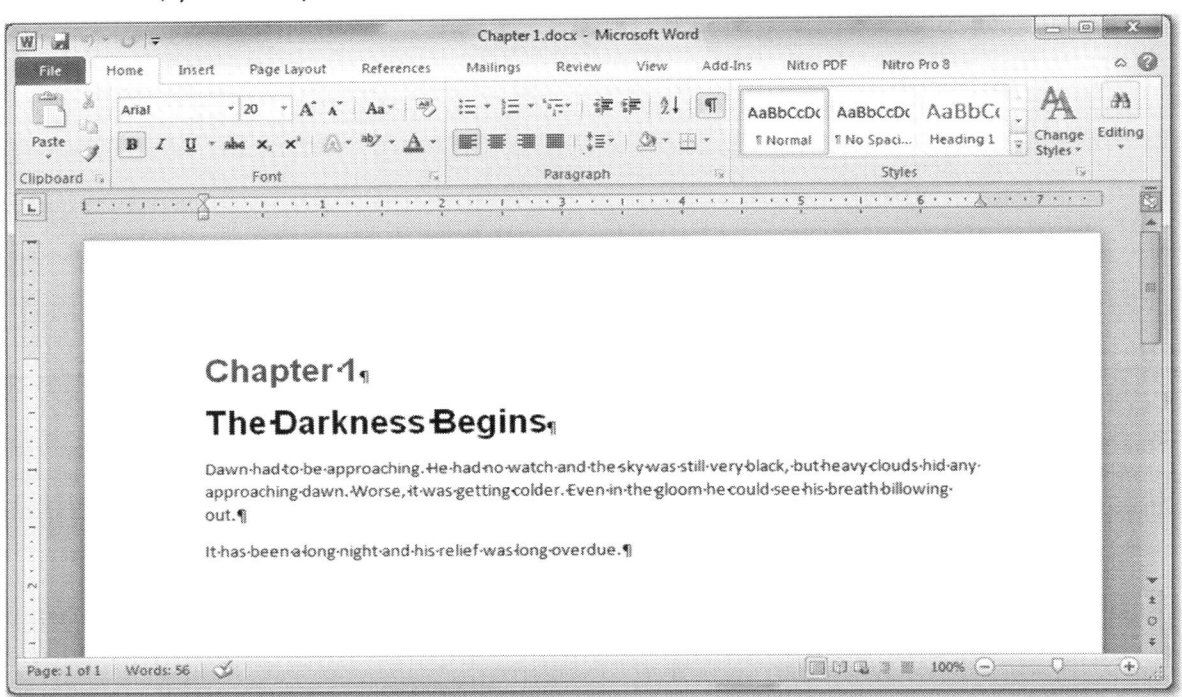

Figure 28: The document opened in desktop Word

The last group on the right is the **SHARE** tab. This does not show a group below as in the other tabs, but instead opens the window you see in (*Figure 29*). The purpose of this menu is to allow other people to have access to the file. You may just want to show it off, or you might want to allow editing by others or collaborators.

Let's explore the dialog. I have partially filled it out so the default screen is a little simpler.

Chapter 5: Using Microsoft Office in the Cloud

1. Do you want to **Invite people**? This means they can join you in viewing and optionally editing the document.
2. If you just want to send a link to the file, click the **Get a link** choice. This will produce a link for anyone, but they will only be able to view.
3. To send an invitation, type one or more email addresses. They each get an email with the link in the email body.
4. You can add a short note to the email telling what this link is about.
5. Do you want them to be able to edit or just view?
6. While you would like others to have a SkyDrive account, so you do not have to coach them in the editing, it is not actually necessary.

Using instant messaging, Skype or another messaging tool such as Google's Hangouts, you can both edit and see each other's edits in real time with just a tiny delay.

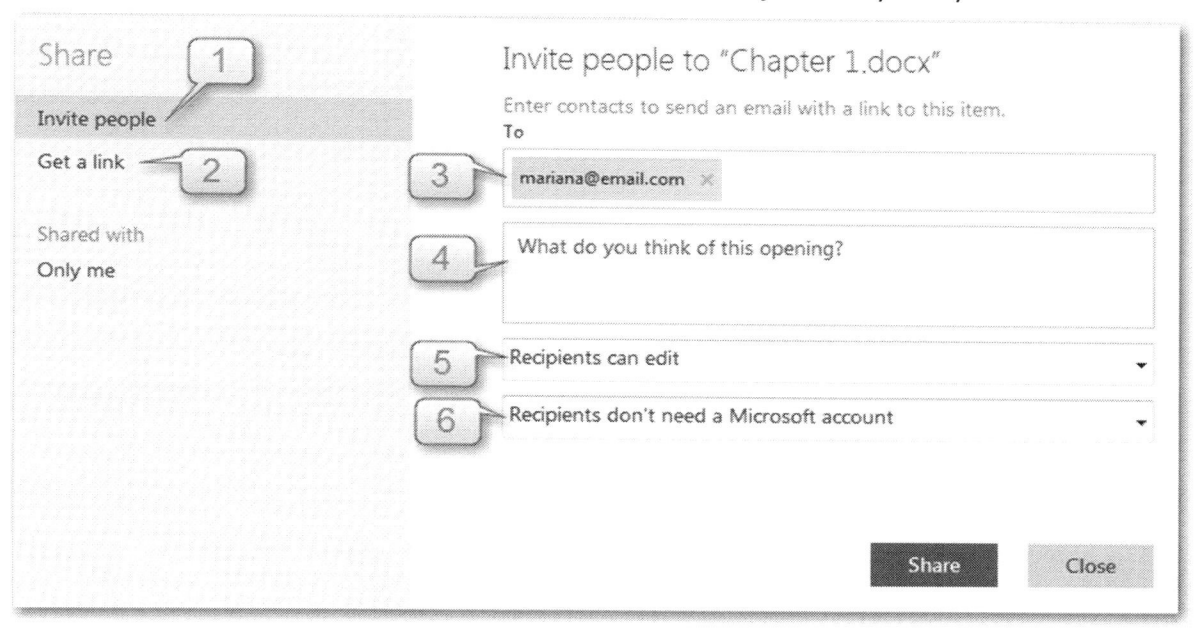

Figure 29: SHARE options

I saved the **FILE** menu to the last because it is unlike the other tab choices.

Let's explore the **FILE** menus (*Figure 30* through *Figure 36*).

Chapter 5: Using Microsoft Office in the Cloud

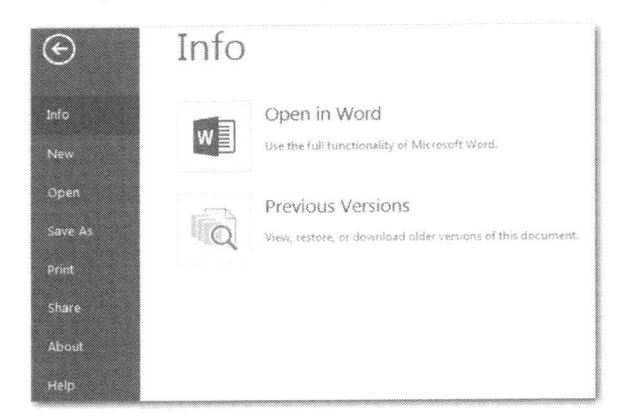

Figure 30: FILE->Info

This menu choice gives you another way to open the file in desktop Word. You can also step back in time should you need an earlier version of the document.

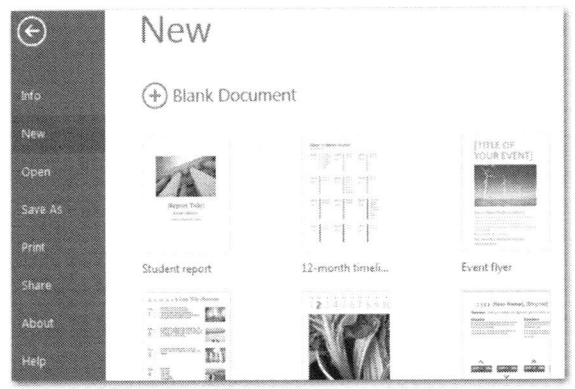

Figure 31: FILE->New

This allows you to create a new web Word document. Notice, that there are many templates that you might want to use as a starting point. This is a quick way to dress up a document for us that are design disabled.

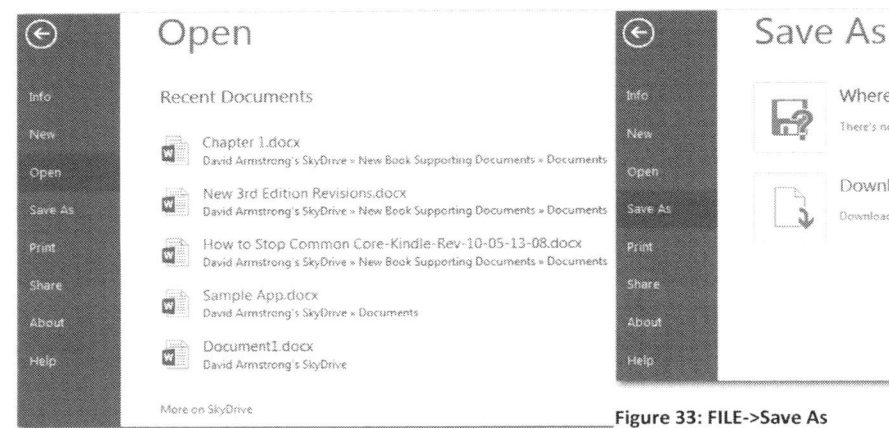

Figure 32: FILE->Open

Like the desktop version of Word, this remembers the most-recent documents you have opened. Great when you want to find yesterday's documents in a hurry.

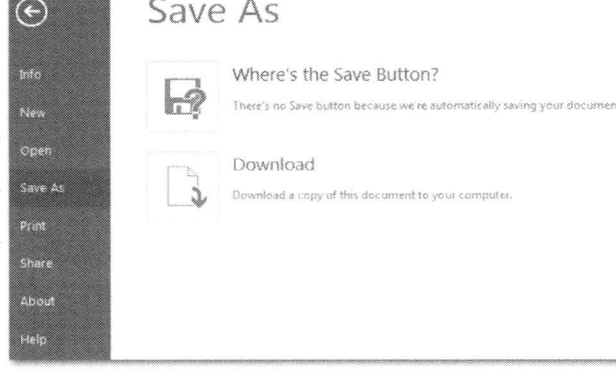

Figure 33: FILE->Save As

As you revise documents, you may want to save a copy with a date embedded in the filename, leaving the original file intact.

Note, that you can also download.

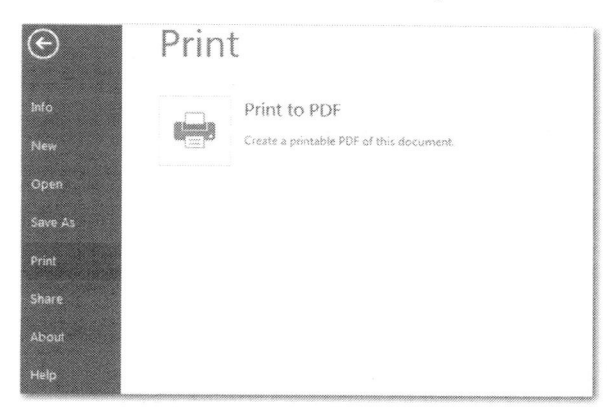

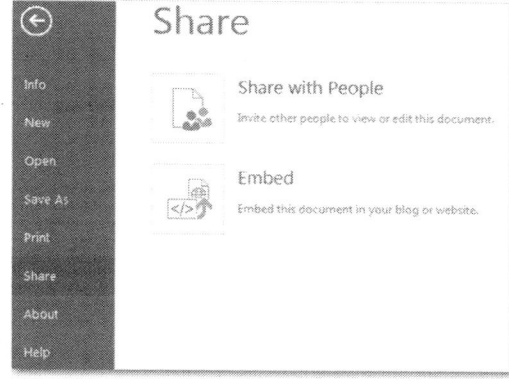

Figure 31: FILE->Print

Since printing web pages is tricky at best and the browser adds links, splits text in arbitrary places, web Word first converts the document into a formatted PDF which you can then print as usual.

Figure 34: FILE->Share

You can share from here as well as the **SHARE** tab (*Figure 29*). You can also get the HTML code which you can use to **Embed** the document into one of your web pages, if you have a website.

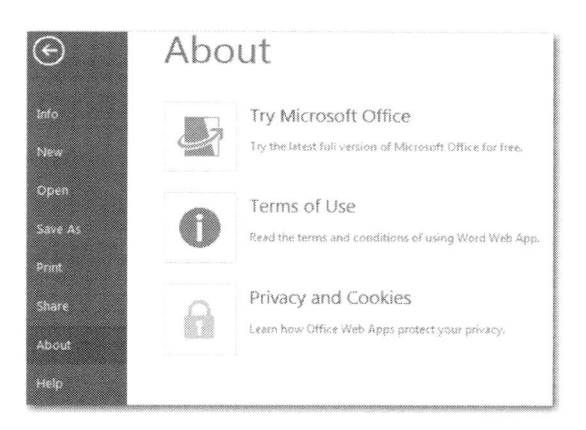

Figure 35: FILE->About

Not much here, just how you can use a promotion to try a paid version of Office.

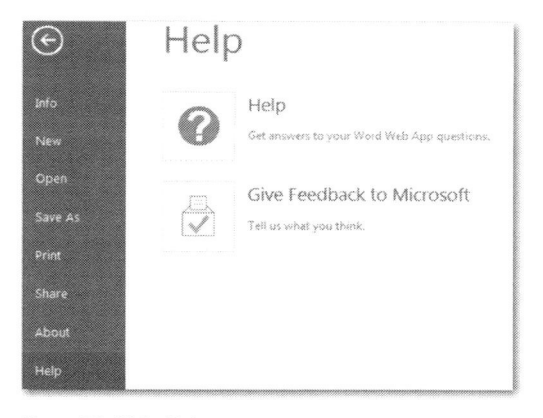

Figure 36: FILE->Help

This choice gives you **Help** on the web Word app. You can, also, complain about the Help as feedback to Microsoft.

If you got this far, you should have a good idea how to get around in Word and most of its features. Practice makes perfect and you should now be able to create routine word processing documents.

Chapter 5: Using Microsoft Office in the Cloud

Using the Excel App

I am assuming that you are reading this chapter from the beginning and have covered Word. You will find that many of the menus in Excel are similar. For example, the FILE tab menus are identical and serve the same purpose.

We will not cover those identical menus and functions. When possible, I will refer you back to the figures that show those features.

I have had a long-term relationship with spreadsheets. In 1980, I bought my first computer, mainly so I could run VisiCalc, the granddaddy of spreadsheets. I graduated to Lotus 123, then to Master Plan (early Microsoft) and then to Excel. I am the oldest computer nerd I know, and I have been there from the start. All businesses must crunch numbers to find the analytics of their business, and they are wonderful tools.

That is not me, of course, but you get the idea. We have the same hair.

As in Word, the first thing we do is name the Excel document by clicking the generic name at the top center on the screen. Type a meaningful name. You can always rename later.

For those of you that have never used spreadsheets, they combine static data, which you enter, and formulas that act on that data to produce calculated results.

In the simple example in (*Figure 37*), I am adding the values I typed into the cells B2 and C2. The equal sign in cell D2 tells Excel I am entering a formula or number. **Sum**, is a built in function and it requires the cell addresses separated by commas.

There are some features in the web app that I miss from the desktop version. In desktop Excel, I can type part of the formula and then drag over B2 and C2. In web Excel, I have to type the actual cell locations. That is your one-minute explanation of spreadsheets. There are many entry level books on Excel 2013. Any of the Dummy series books are good if you are an absolute beginner.

Figure 37: Creating a formula in a calculated cell

The same ribbon type control is on all the web apps as it is in desktop versions. You have a series of tabs. Each tab has one or more groups, and a group holds a number of icons, some of which are dropdowns with further controls.

In the **HOME** tab, we can format our text and cells (*Figure 38*).

Here are the groups:

- **Undo** - Use to Undo your last change or redo if you change your mind. You can **Undo** multiple times.
- **Clipboard** - Use to cut and **Paste**.
- **Font** - For text formatting, colorizing and putting borders around cells.
- **Alignment** - For aligning, inserting text and merging cells.
- **Number** - For formatting numbers.
- **Tables** - For creating and formatting tables. You can, also, start a **Survey,** as we will see later.
- **Cells** - Allow you to insert or delete **Cells**, columns and rows.
- **Editing** - Helps you sort data, use some built-in math formulas, clear data and find and/or replace data.

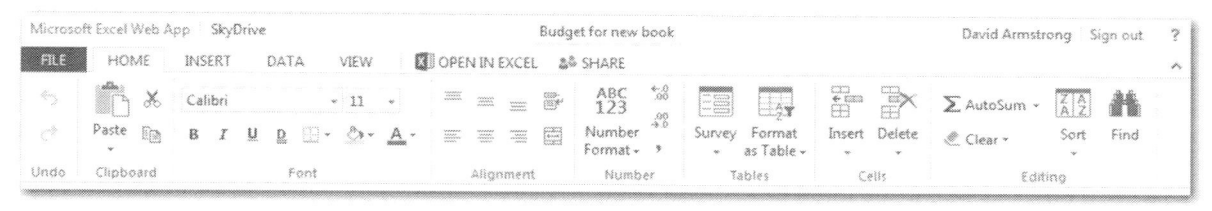

Figure 38: The Excel HOME tab

In the **INSERT** tab, we can insert items into the sheet (*Figure 39*).

Here are the groups:

- **Function** - When you are typing in a calculated cell, you can insert a function as seen in the (*Figure 40*).
- **Tables** - Use to insert a table.
- **Charts** - Use this to insert and map a chart to visually represent data.
- **Links** - Add hyperlinks to web sites or emails.

The **INSERT** tab helps you dress up your sheet's charts. Charts are linked to their underlying data and change as you enter new static numbers.

Chapter 5: Using Microsoft Office in the Cloud

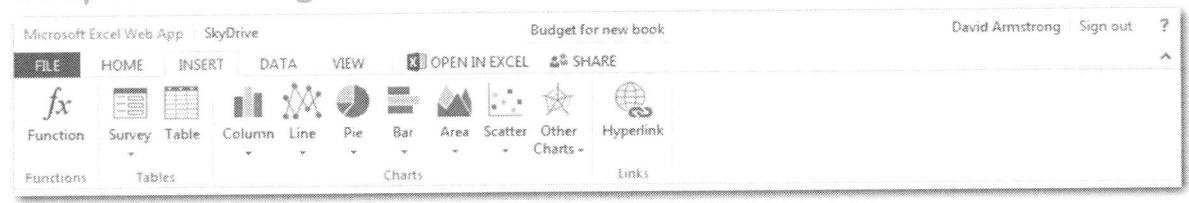

Figure 39: The Excel INSERT tab

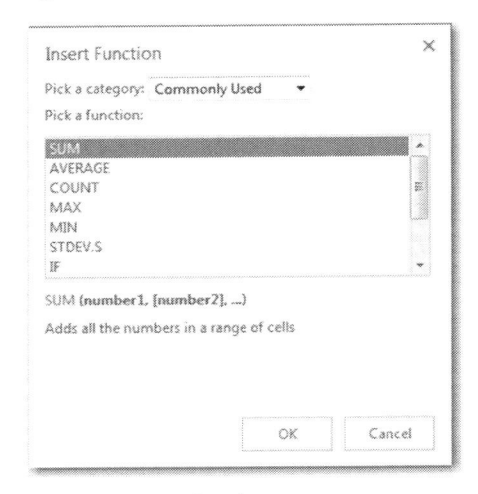

Figure 40: Insert a function screen

Underneath it all, spreadsheets can act as databases. They have size limitations, but like a database, they have a row that holds the information for one record such as a person's data. Each column on the sheet is a field that holds a single piece of that data. You might have columns named First Name, Last Name, Address, etc.

The **DATA** tab holds groups that allow us to work on that data (*Figure 41*).

Here are the groups:

- **Connections** - It is possible to connect a spreadsheet to an external data source. In effect, the spreadsheet becomes a very smart report that pulls data in from the external sources and then calculates sums and/or sorts that data. These icons become active when connected, and they can refresh the latest data.
- **Calculation** - You can force the spreadsheet to recalculate all values. You may need to recalculate after pulling new data in **Connections**.
- **Sort** - Highlight that column of data you wish to sort and then choose ascending or descending. Do not include name headers in the sort.

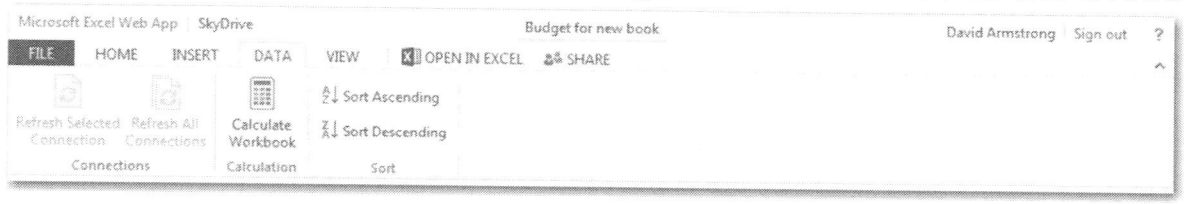

Figure 41: The Excel DATA tab

Like most other web Office apps, the **VIEW** tab can change the **Editing View** to a **Reading View** which represents what the document will look like printed (*Figure 42*).

Figure 42: The Excel VIEW tab

We will not cover the **FILE** tab as it is the same in the entire suite of Office web apps. If you want to review what **FILE** does, check out (*Figure 30*) and subsequent figures.

Using the PowerPoint App

In the business world, teaching and presenting lives on slide shows. If you are a presenter, they keep you on tract and assure you do not skip an important point. In sales, we use presentations to visually sell our product or service.

Microsoft's web PowerPoint is a lite version of desktop PowerPoint. There are missing features such as recording or inserting sound files. However, all the essentials are there and you have the advantage of being able to access and show the slides on any computer, anywhere, that has an Internet connection.

Start by moving to the folder where you want to save the document. Click the **Create** button on the top and then **PowerPoint presentation** from the dropdown menu.

First, give the presentation a meaningful name. Before we explore the tabs, let's tour this opening screen (*Figure 43*).

1. On the left is a visual list of slide thumbnails. Use this to navigate and rearrange slides.
2. In the opening slide, there are two text boxes. Click into the large text box to change the title of the presentation.
3. Most slides have detail text below the title area. Click the lower text box to edit or add text.
4. You can optionally add speaker notes at the bottom of the screen. If you are creating courseware, this might be notes to your instructors.

Chapter 5: Using Microsoft Office in the Cloud

5. This is a very plain slide. We can dress it up by clicking the design menu tab and picking one of the many templates.

Figure 43: A new PowerPoint document

I have dressed the presentation up and have added a new interior type slide. There are several different slide layouts such as the opening and interior slides you see here (*Figure 44*).

The templates help you get started with an attractive layout and color scheme. However, you can modify any layout with additional text boxes, different fonts, etc.

Chapter 5: Using Microsoft Office in the Cloud

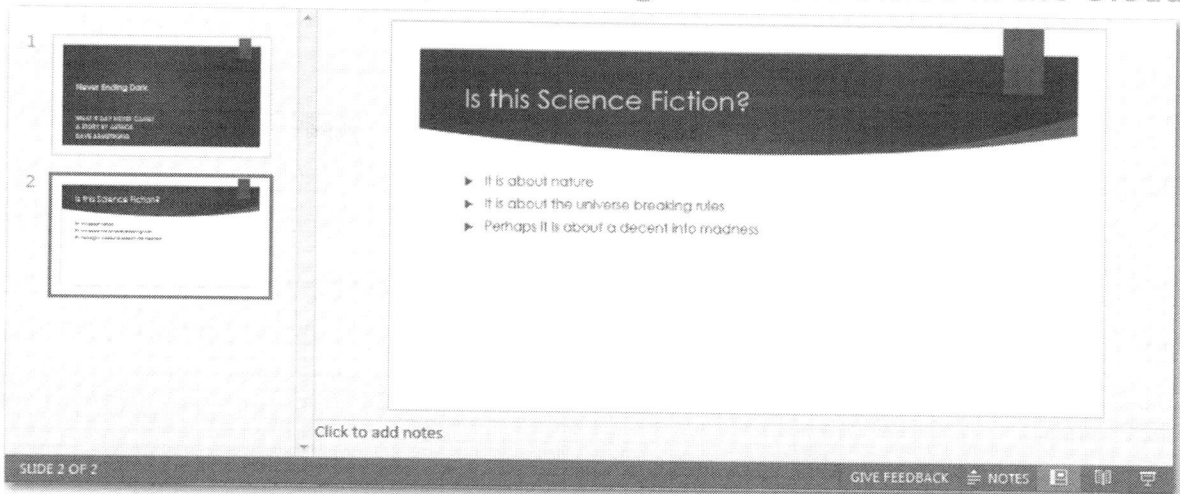

Figure 44: Applied template and interior slide

The ribbon tabs are similar in the different SkyDrive web apps and they serve the same purpose. Each tab holds one or more groups of icons you click to get to the different features and controls.

In the **HOME** tab, we have text, image and shape formatting (*Figure 45*).

These are groups of controls:

- **Undo** - Gives quick access to undoing or redoing a change.
- **Clipboard** - **Copy**, cut and **Paste**.
- **Delete** - Select a slide and click to delete it.
- **Slides** - allow you to insert a new slide, duplicate an existing one, change its layout and hide the slide.
- **Font** - Gives you control over the font's type, size and color.
- **Paragraph** - Helps you with alignment and lists.
- **Drawing** - Allows you to add and format shapes.

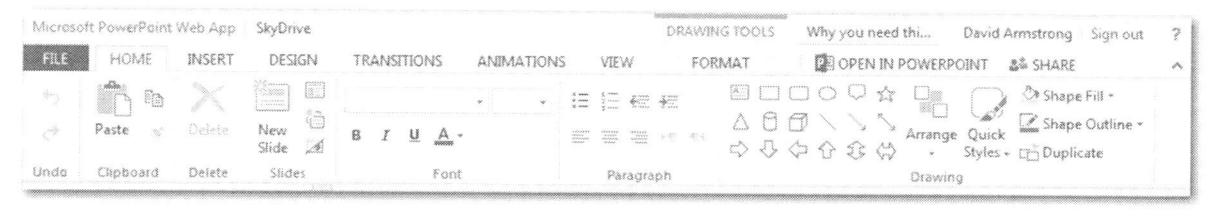

Figure 45: The PowerPoint HOME tab

The **INSERT** tab allows you to insert pictures, shapes, text boxes, etc. (*Figure 46*).

Here are the groups:

Chapter 5: Using Microsoft Office in the Cloud

- **Slides** - This duplicates some of the Slides on the HOME tab. Click to insert a new slide.
- **Images** - Insert a picture from your local drive or from the extensive collection of free clipart.
- **Illustrations** - Insert shapes and SmartArt, a collection of common schemes such as an organizational chart.
- **Links** - Add hyperlinks and accompanying visible text.
- **Text** - This is one of several ways to add a text box.

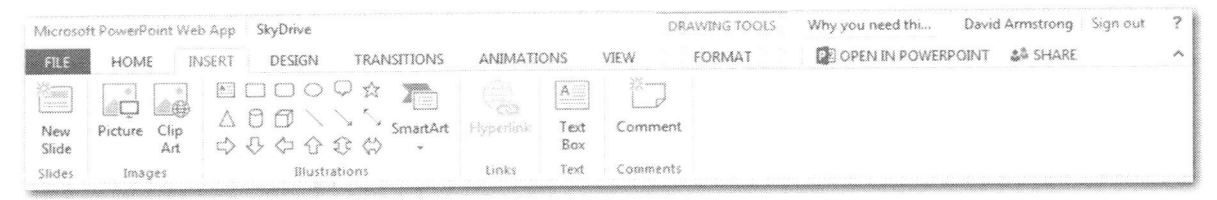

Figure 46: The PowerPoint INSERT tab

The **DESIGN** tab contains a number of themes (*Figure 47*).

Here are the groups:

- **Themes** - There is a generous collection of themes. Use the down arrow to the right of the themes to see more themes *(Figure 48)*.
- **Variants** - After picking a color combination and layout, you can change the colors by picking a variant of that template.

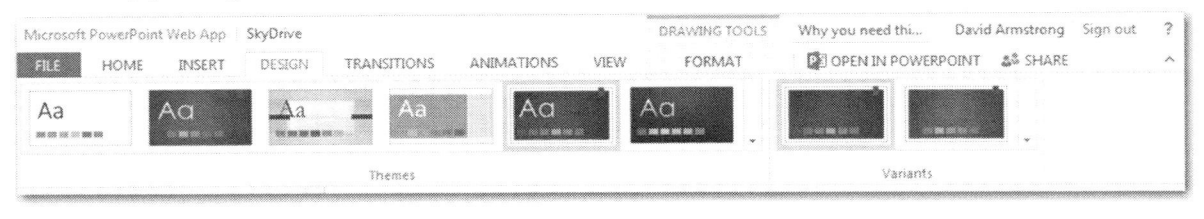

Figure 47: The PowerPoint DESIGN tab

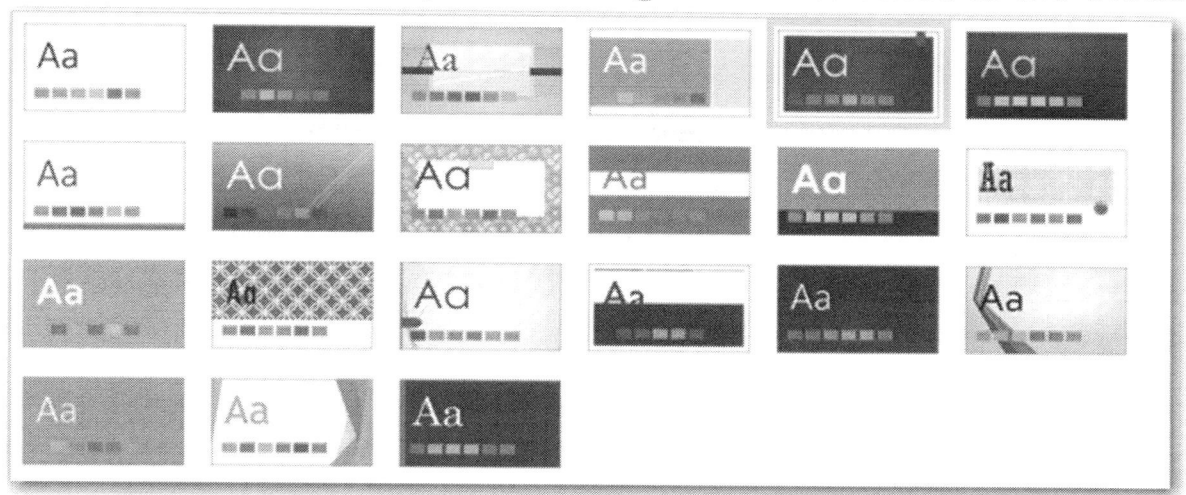

Figure 48: More PowerPoint themes

You can experiment with a new theme at any time as changing themes will not effect your text, images or shapes you have added.

As in desktop PowerPoint, you have a few options in how your slides appear on the screen. You might want your slides to fade in or move up from the bottom. You can do all of that as we see in the **TRANSITIONS** tab (*Figure 49*). Here are the groups:

- **Transitions to This Slide** - Pick one of the choices. If you pick **Fade** or **Push**, you get options on how the slide moves in (*Figure 50*).
- **Transitions** - Allows you to apply a transition to all the slides.

Figure 49: The PowerPoint TRANSITIONS tab

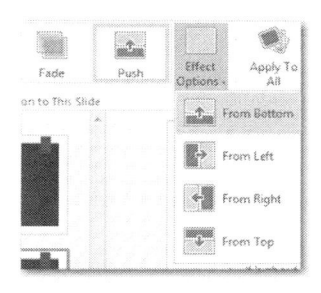

Figure 50: Slide TRANSITIONS options

Chapter 5: Using Microsoft Office in the Cloud

The **ANIMATIONS** tab allows you to add action to slides which, if not overdone, can make a slide more interesting. To start, you need to select an object in a slide you wish to animate. Once you have an item selected, and the tab **ANIMATIONS** open, you will see these groups (*Figure 51*).

Here are the groups:

- **Animation** - Add or remove an animation effect. Depending on the effect you may have options as you see (*Figure 52*).
- **Timing** - Use **Timing** to arrange the order of the animations. For example, you might want a series of arrows to move in as you reveal text boxes.

Don't overdue animations, as they can be distracting. Always ask, "Do the animations help present my point?"

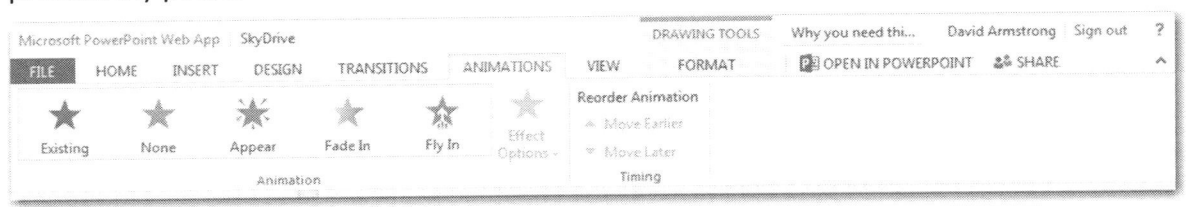

Figure 51: The PowerPoint ANAMATIONS tab

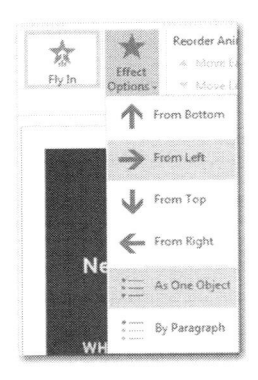

Figure 52: Adding an animation effect option

The **VIEW** tab allows you to run the slide show, see it as it would be printed and if you added hidden comments, you can see them in a list (*Figure 53*).

Here are the groups:

- **Presentations Views** - If you are editing the presentation, you are in the **Editing View**. **Reading View** allows you to paginate through the slides as they would be printed and **Slide Show** opens a new browser window with no menus or toolbars, full screen (*Figure 54*). In the lower left, navigation controls fade in and out as you mouse over them.

- **Show** - This group allows you to open up the **Notes** section at the bottom of the slides, and if you have added comments, you can show them in a pop up area to the right using **Show Comments**.

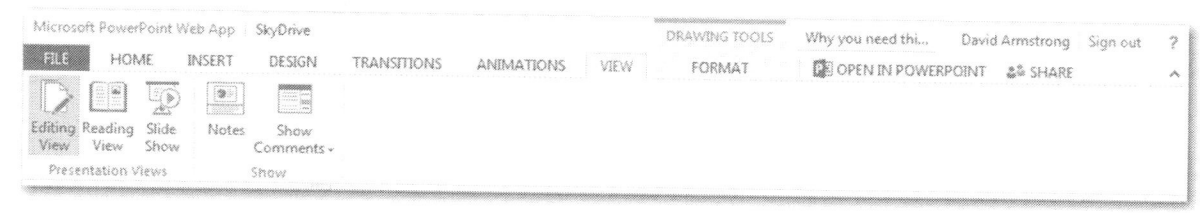

Figure 53: The PowerPoint VIEW tab

Figure 54: Slide in full-screen presentation mode

If you have an object on the slide selected, you will see a **FORMAT** group. As you place objects, such as text boxes, shapes and images, they will often overlap. However, you may need to rearrange the order when an image covers text, for example. You can send an object backward or bring forward.

You may want to add some prepared formatting to the objects and rotate them. All of these can be done with the **FORMAT** tab (*Figure 55*).

The groups are:

- **Insert Shapes** - This group shows up on several tabs. Drag a shape to your slide.
- **Shape Styles** - Use these, ready to use, styles to quickly format a shape. You can expand to see more styles (*Figure 56*).

Chapter 5: Using Microsoft Office in the Cloud

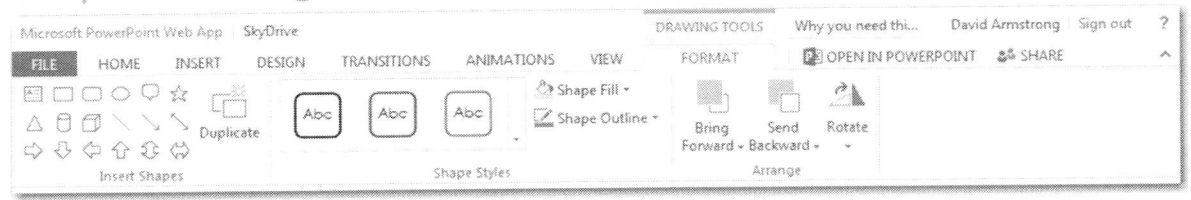

Figure 55: The PowerPoint FORMAT tab

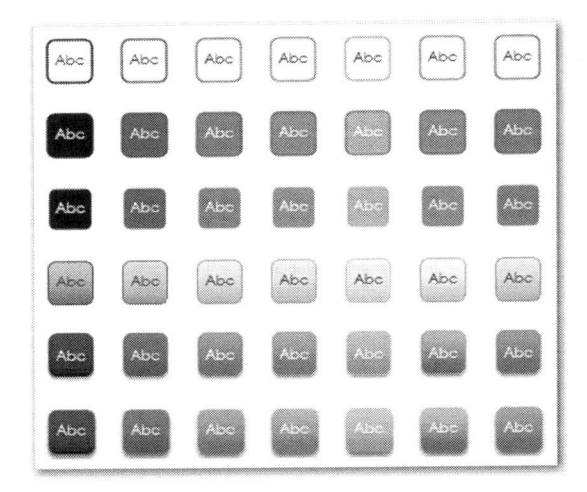

Figure 56: Built-in formatting templates

The PowerPoint web app is more than adequate for most presentations, and you never worry about losing them while they are safely stored on SkyDrive.

Using the OneNote App

Most of us have used paper notebooks in the past. I had one for each class and used bright-colored markers and small stick-it type notes to color code lecture notes, assignments, etc.

With Microsoft's OneNote app, they have taken this form of organizing and moved it into an application. This wonderful tool is also one of the web Office apps. A notebook consists of various sections and each section can have any number of pages.

As usual, start with the **Create** button and choose **OneNote notebook**. The opening screen of the OneNote web app has little content to start. First thing, give the notebook a name as in the other apps.

Let's explore the opening screen (*Figure 57*).

1. Think about how you want to segment or group the different topics you will store. Right-click the link **Untitled Section** and rename. We will see how to add new sections later.

Chapter 5: Using Microsoft Office in the Cloud

2. Your section already has a single page. It shows as **Untitled Page** in the navigation column. Type the page name above the date and its text will transfer to the left.
3. You can add new pages by clicking the + in a circle.
4. All the Office apps allow you to toggle showing the ribbon menus on or off. I have a large monitor and like them on. I pin them so they always stay open. If not pinned, they appear only if you move your cursor to the top.

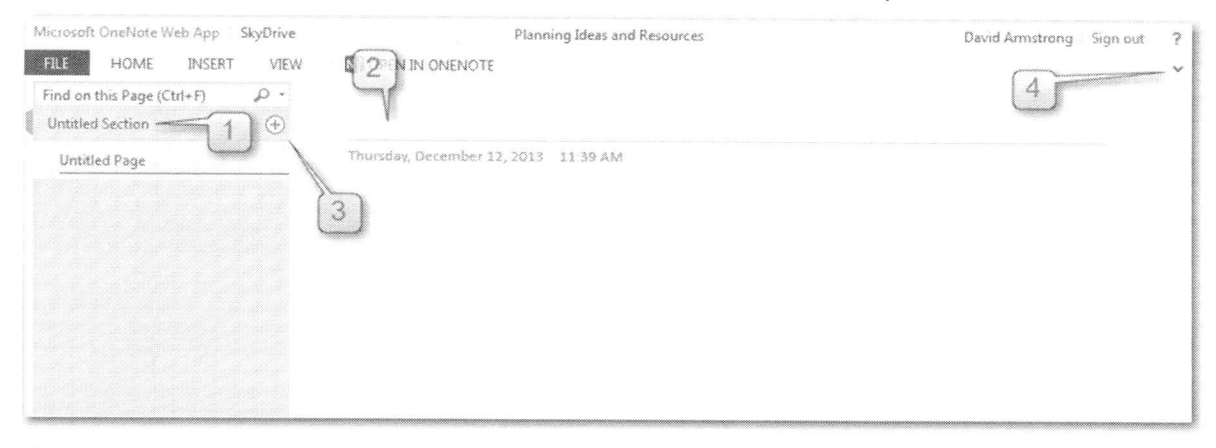

Figure 57: OneNote opening screen

In *(Figure 58)*, you see the beginnings of a notebook. I have renamed the section and named two pages. I copied and pasted an image I am considering for the cover jacket of a possible book. There is new text added to the right of the image.

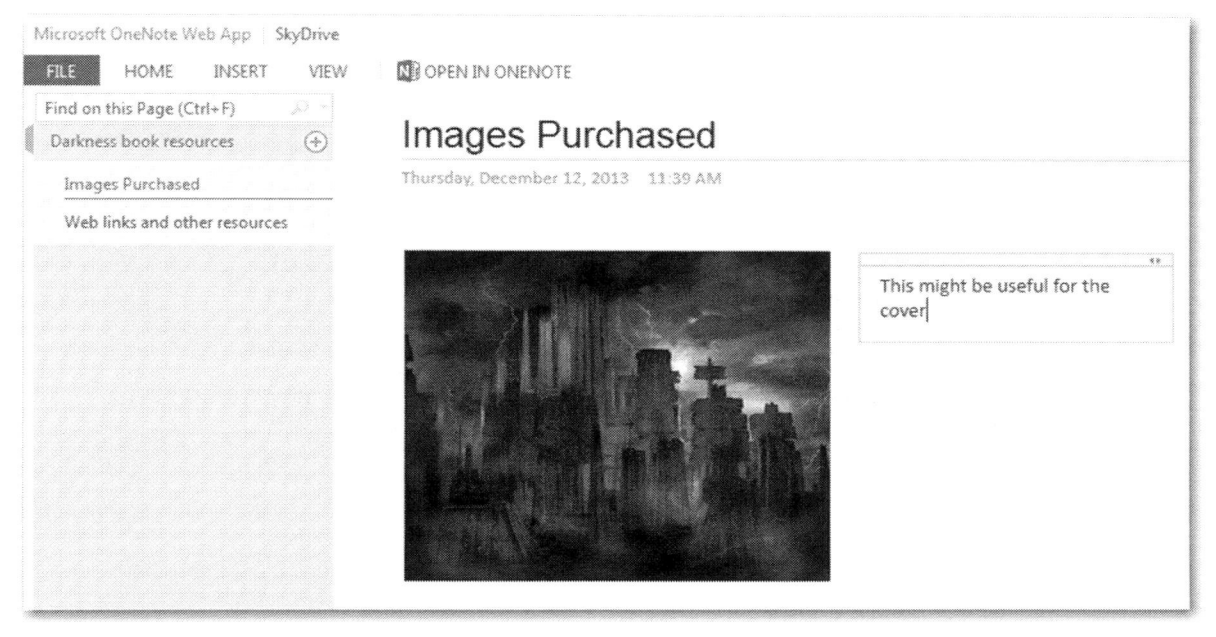

Figure 58: Information added

Chapter 5: Using Microsoft Office in the Cloud

Let's explore the menu tabs. Like most Office web apps, we have a **HOME** menu that contains most of the formatting options (*Figure 59*).

The groups are:

Undo - Use to undo and redo edits.

Paste - Use to copy, cut and **Paste** text and objects.

Basic Text - Use to pick font, size, color alignment and list such as this bulleted list.

- **Styles** - Like the Word web app, you have many styles from which to choose (*Figure 60*).
- **Tags** - There are many tags you can add for follow-up or just to segment even further (*Figure 61*).
- **Spelling** - Check your spelling or change to another language dictionary.

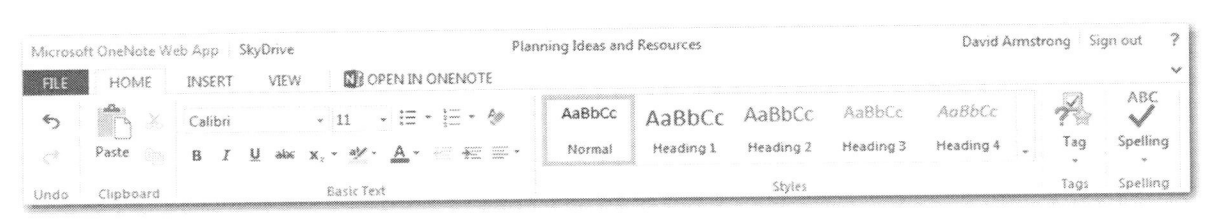

Figure 59: The OneNote HOME tab

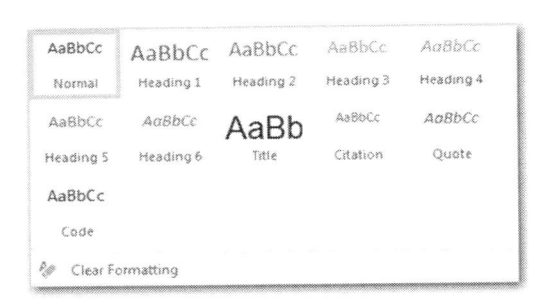

Figure 60: Built-in styles

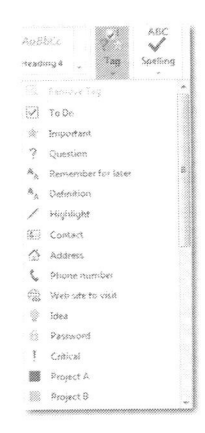

Figure 61: Tagging items

Similar to other **INSERT** tabs, we can add several items (*Figure 62*).

Here are the groups.

- **Notebook** - Here you can insert new segments and pages.
- **Tables** - Insert tables at the location of the cursor.
- **Pictures** - Pictures off of your hard drive or built-in clip art.

Chapter 5: Using Microsoft Office in the Cloud

- **Links** - Add URL or email links to a page.

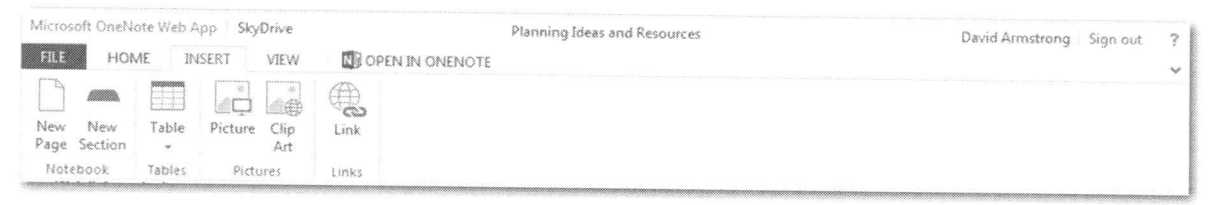

Figure 62: The OneNote INSERT tab

The **VIEW** tab allows you to switch to a read-only view of your notebook and to view previous versions and various authors if you have more than one person working on it (*Figure 63*).

The groups are:

- **Notebook Views** - You can switch to a **Reading View** to prevent accidentally modifying. To return to the **Editing View** from reading, click on the **EDIT NOTEBOOK** link and choose **Edit in OneNote web App** (*Figure 64*).
- **Authors** - See who worked on what if you collaborated on the notebook.
- **Versions** - Previous edits are preserved by date. If you accidentally delete something, you can go back in time to retrieve from an earlier version.

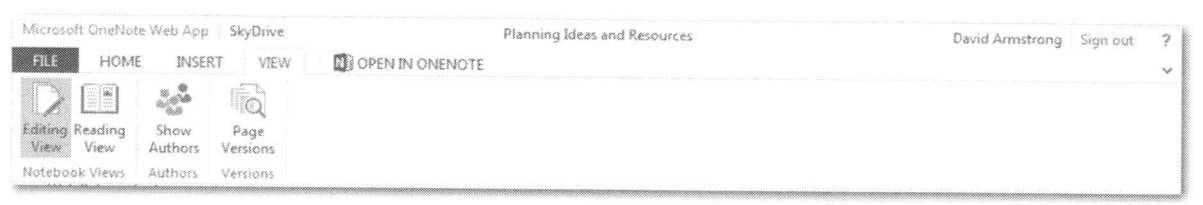

Figure 63: The OneNote VIEW tab

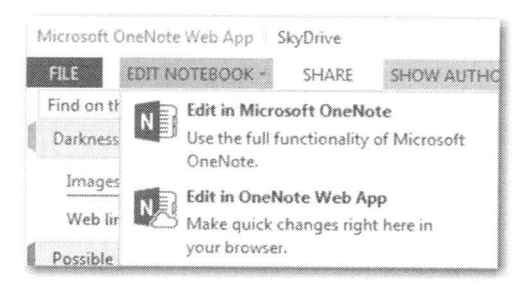

Figure 64: Moving back to the edit mode

You may get additional menu tabs depending on what you are doing with a page. Clicking on the image, added a **PICTURE TOOLS FORMAT** (*Figure 65*).

The groups are:

- **Image Text** - This allows you to add text associated with this picture. This **Alt-Text** is required on web pages provided to sight impaired individuals.

Chapter 5: Using Microsoft Office in the Cloud

- **Image Size** - Adjust the image size.

Figure 65: Image FORMAT tab

OneNote is a great tool for collecting and recording related data. Use it for planning and research.

Using the Excel Survey

What do your customers honestly want? Do you actually know?

Surveys help you plan and shape your products or services to your customer's needs. There are some great paid services that help you create surveys, such as Constant Contact and Survey Monkey. They give you graphs and charts of responses, etc. However, for basic surveys, you can do this in SkyDrive.

To start, click the **Create** button and choose **Excel survey**. A spreadsheet opens and then the survey creation screen opens on top. You will do all of your design here, and the responses to the survey will be inserted as rows in the underlying spreadsheet. We will see the results in the spreadsheet later.

Starting a new survey is very simple and requires just a few short steps (*Figure 66*).

1. Enter a title for the survey. The survey taker will see this at the top of the survey. Keep it short.
2. Enter a short explanation of what the survey is about.
3. When you click on the first question, a form opens to the right (Figure 67) that ask you what type of questions you want.

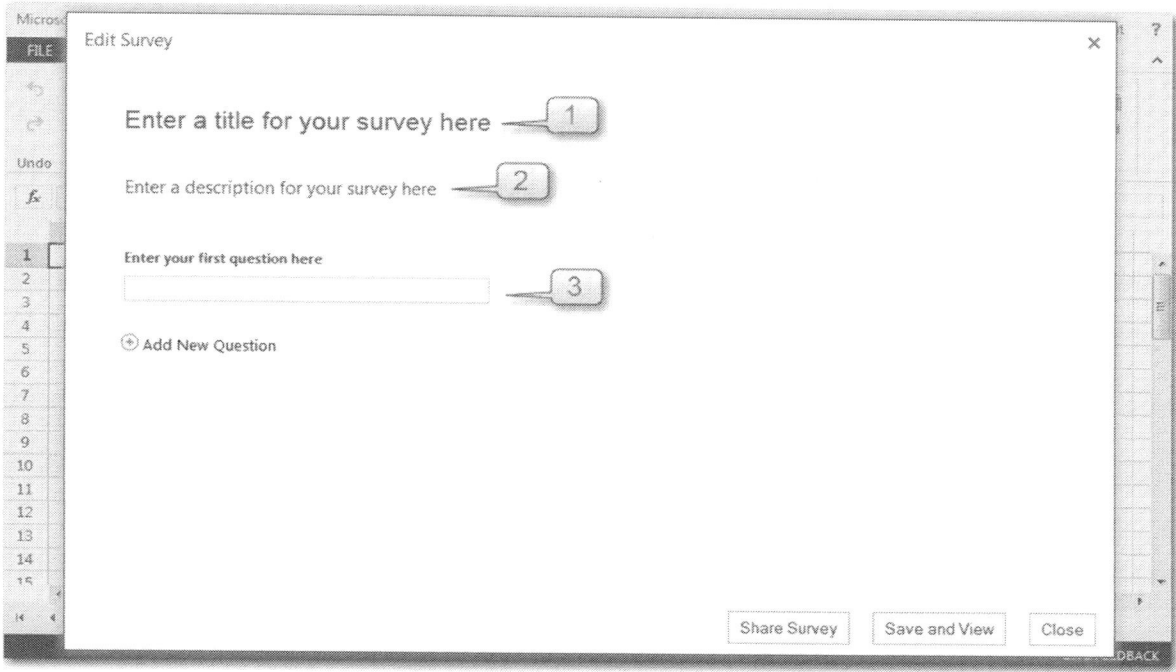

Figure 66: Excel Survey opening screen

As you add each question, an **EDIT QUESTION** box opens to the right that allows you to create a question and a subtitle. As you choose the type of question, the form (*Figure 68*) changes to give you a chance to refine the choices or set the options as you see below.

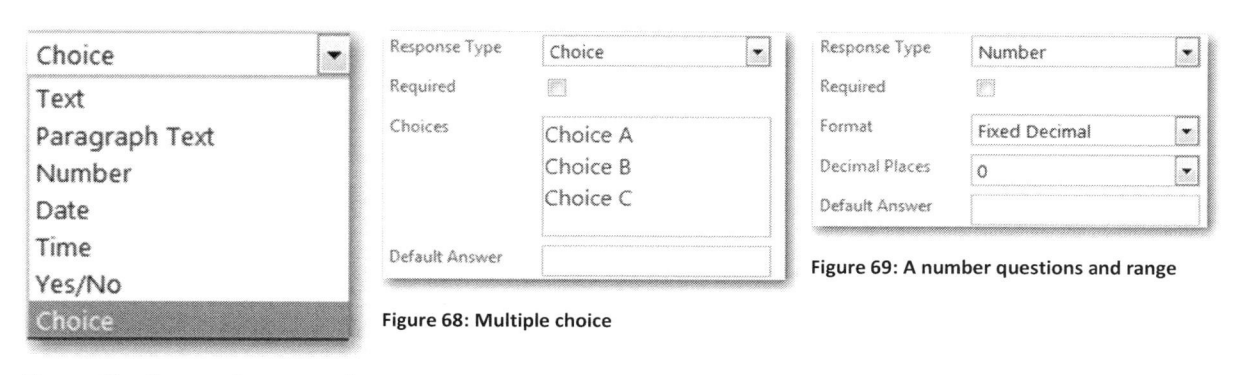

Figure 68: Multiple choice

Figure 69: A number questions and range

Figure 67: Choose the type of question

We can refine numbers to a type and number of decimal places (*Figure 69*). (*Figure 70*) shows adding a yes/no type question.

Chapter 5: Using Microsoft Office in the Cloud

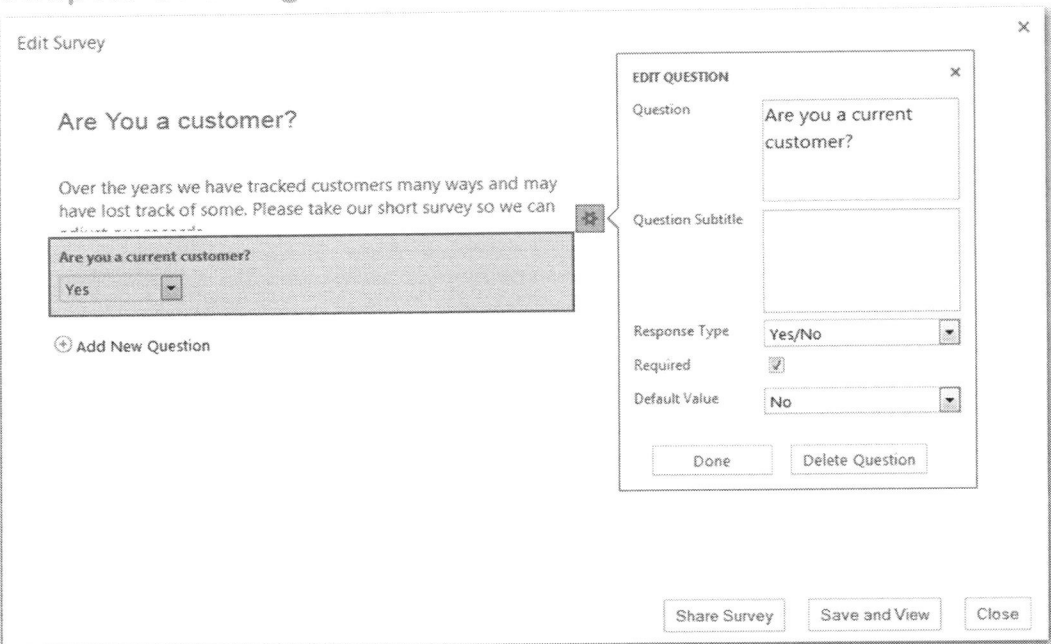

Figure 70: Adding a survey title and question

We added a second question that collects a text response. I could have used a date type question for more precision (*Figure 71*).

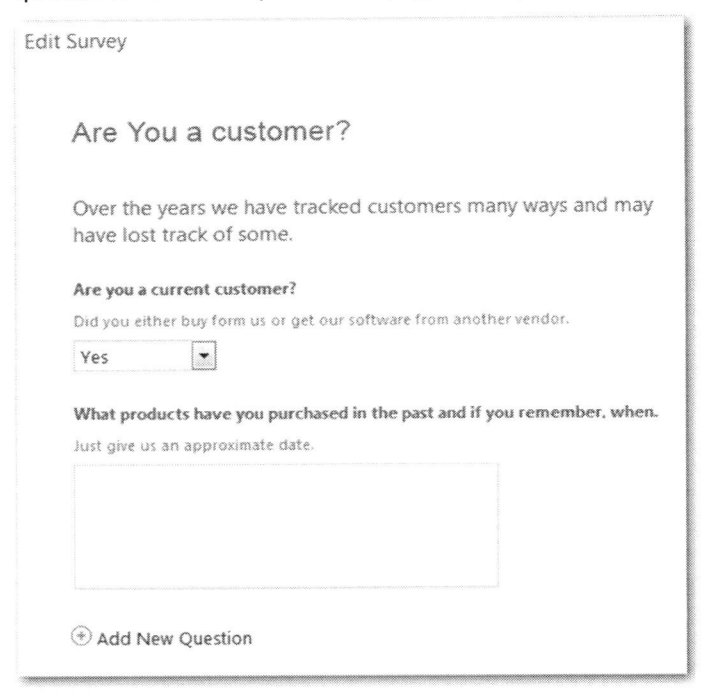

Figure 71: Adding a text answered question

Chapter 5: Using Microsoft Office in the Cloud

As you work, you can view the survey as seen by those taking it. You can add content and click the **Submit** button to test, if you wish (*Figure 72*).

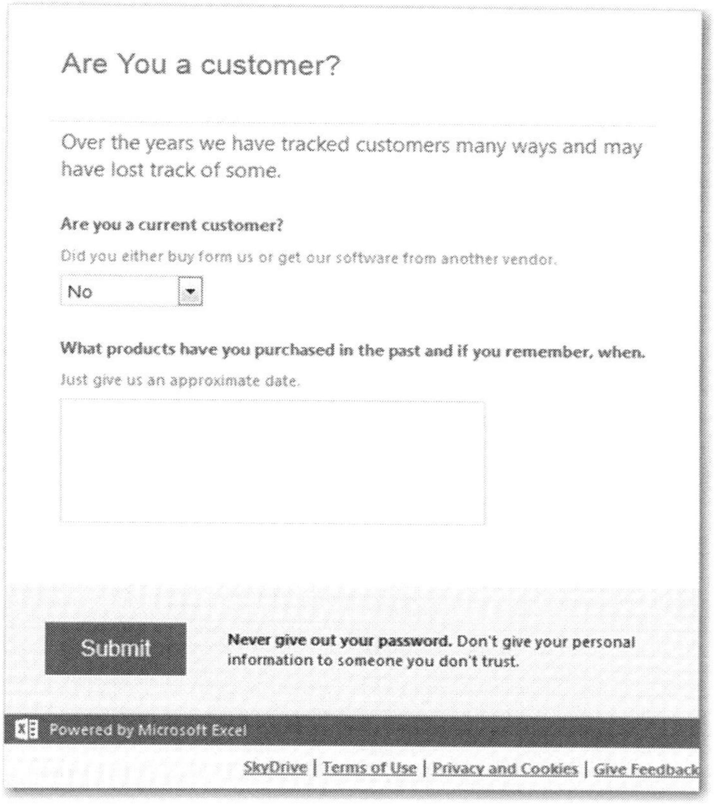

Figure 72: What the survey taker sees

After testing, getting back to the survey form is a little different than just double-clicking the survey link, as that will just open the Excel sheet.

Instead, right click the link and choose **Edit survey** to return to editing the survey form (*Figure 73*).

Chapter 5: Using Microsoft Office in the Cloud

After you have completed the survey, you want to send the survey to those chosen to take it. From the survey link, right click and choose **Share survey**. This opens the **Get a Link to your survey** window (*Figure 74*).

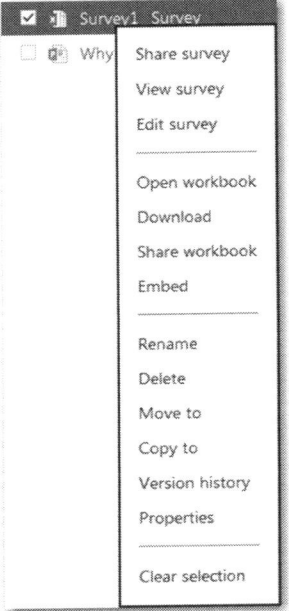

Figure 73: Getting back to the survey

Figure 74: Sharing a survey with a link

Click the **Create Link** button and you get a URL that will take any browser to the survey's web page (*Figure 75*). You can copy this long link, **Ctrl+C**, or you can shorten the link if you use it in any printed documentation. This makes it much easier to type.

Figure 75: Your link with an option to shorten it

Lastly, you can open the spreadsheet after running some test surveys to see the answers (*Figure 76*).

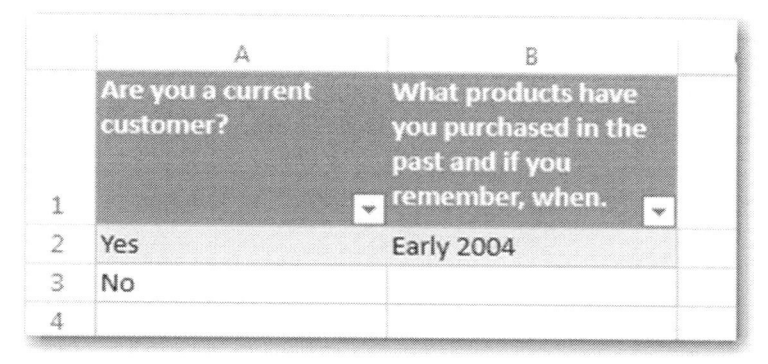

Figure 76: The results collected in Excel

Using Office with SkyDrive Pro

SkyDrive Pro is Microsoft's paid service. The prices we quote are correct as of January, 2013. They change often, and competition with Google is pushing prices down for both parties. Good news for us, but you may see some obsolete information in the book as time goes by. Go to Office 365, http://office.microsoft.com, to see the latest news/cost/features.

They have several offerings: individual/education, and business. The individual and education plans have the same products, but differ in how many licenses they offer. The business plans vary to cover small businesses up to enterprise plans with thousands of users.

We will look at each in the next few sections; however, this book is not really about Office 365 as our tittle says "free or almost free". Much of what you learned earlier in this chapter is similar, but Office 365 offers desktop versions of the software and additional features such as Exchange, Lync and SharePoint services, depending on your subscription.

This section is a very high level look at the paid offerings from Microsoft. You should, however, learn enough to know if you need to look deeper into Office 365.

Office 365 Home Premium

With Office 365, you are renting software, not purchasing a perpetual license as you would have bought in the past. If you stop paying and do not renew, your software stops working. The software is licensed on a per-device basis. You can install on 5 computers; PCs or Macs. The plan specifically prohibits using the software for commercial use.

Office 365 Home Premium

Office 365 Home Premium version is $9.99 USD a month or $99.99 a year.

With the consumer versions, you get these 2013 desktop versions of the Office apps as well as SkyDrive Pro:

- Word
- Excel
- PowerPoint
- OneNote
- Outlook
- Publisher
- Access
- You get the right to install the software on up to five computers.
- They give you an additional 20GB of storage on SkyDrive for a total of 27GB.
- You download and always have the up-to-date desktop versions from your SkyDrive account. There is no need for product keys.
- They give you 60 Skype world minutes a month.

Office 365 University

Office 365 University cost a one-time fee of $79.99.

This offering is the same as the Office 365 Home Premium with these exceptions:

1. The single fee provides four years of coverage.
2. Office may only be installed on two computers.
3. You must be enrolled as a full or part-time student or faculty/staff of an eligible educational institution.

Office 365 Small Business

The business plans are licensed on a per-user basis, not per-device. All business plans are guaranteed to have 99.9% uptime and IT phone support 24/7 for critical issues. They, also, claim premium anti-malware protection and anti-spam filtering.

The Office 365 Small Business is $6.00 a month or billed annually at $60.00 per user. You can add up to 25 users.

Here is what you get:

- Business class email - With 50GB of storage, shared calendars and your domain name addresses.
- Online conferencing.

- A public website that can connect to your own domain name.
- File sharing.
- Office Web Apps.
- Easy to use administrative control.

You get no desktop apps, much like the free SkyDrive. However, you can have your own domain in email addresses and the free website.

Office 365 Small Business Premium

Again, all business plans are licensed on a per-user basis, not per-device. This has the same features as the small business, but provides the full desktop Office suite.

The Office 365 Small Business Premium is $12.50 a month and must be purchased for $150.00 annually per user. You can add up to 25 users.

Here is what you get:

- Word
- Excel
- PowerPoint
- OneNote
- Outlook
- Access
- Publisher
- Lync
- Access on tablets and other mobile devices.
- Business class email - With 50GB of storage, shared calendars and your domain name addresses.
- Online conferencing.
- A public website that can connect to your own domain name.
- File sharing.
- Office Web Apps.
- Easy to use administrative control.
- 25GB of storage per each user.

Office 365 Midsize Business

Again, all business plans are licensed on a per-user basis, not per-device. This has the same features as the small business, but provides the full desktop Office suite.

The Office 365 Midsize Business is $15.00 a month with an annual commitment per user. You can add up to 300 users.

The features and desktop software is the same as the small business premium plus:

- Optional Active Directory integration.
- SharePoint to collaborate and store documents.

Office on Demand

All of the desktop applications are more powerful than their web app counterparts. If you are setting on your computer and have the desktop apps installed, you only need to open the document in the local desktop app.

What if you are at a customer's location using one their computers and you need the desktop version of Office and they do not have Office installed?

All the business plans give you Office on Demand. When you ask to open in Office, a streaming version of the desktop app downloads on their computer allowing you to have the full desktop app available. There is some delay you may have to contend with and when you have finished modifying the document, the downloaded Office app is removed leaving no trace behind.

Lync and Skype

Microsoft bought the popular application Skype in May, 2011. Microsoft has its own communication software, Lync. They share a lot of the same functionality, and both make excellent candidates for interoffice communication.

Unlike Skype, Lync is not free and is usually sold as a server product that would be hosted on a company's server. You do get Lync on the larger Office 365 business plans and Microsoft will host it for you.

In the title of this book, we mention free or almost free. Lync does not fit into that premise so we will give just a quick, high level look at it. It is mentioned here, as it is a Microsoft product and can work in the cloud as a service.

From this screen, you can call, chat and start a video meeting or presentation.

Figure 77: The Lync client

I got this image off the web, and I hope Bill Gates will not mind. It shows a video call going on between the caller and Bill (*Figure 78*).

Chapter 5: Using Microsoft Office in the Cloud

Figure 78: Video calling on Lync

Lync makes individual and group meetings easy, with or without video (*Figure 79*). Since they are made computer to computer, there is no phone or additional fees.

In my opinion, Skype, which offers free computer to computer IM, audio and video, is a better value. Add cheap phone calls and Skype is hard to beat, regardless, of which office suite you decide to use.

Figure 79: Lync meeting

Chapter 6: The Outlook Web App

Microsoft offers a free, web-based version of their Office suite product Outlook. If you have used desktop Outlook, you will feel quite comfortable as the layout is similar. However, the navigation is quite different from the other SkyDrive apps, as you are missing the ribbon bar across the top.

The Outlook Web Application is often called OWA. I am going to use OWA in this text as it saves typing and makes it clear we are not talking about the desktop app. Also, you will notice I have blurred out some of the contact information as the screen captures contains names of real people, and I do not want to reveal their actual names and email addresses.

The top bar in SkyDrive can get you to OWA by clicking the down pointing arrow (*Figure 80*).

Figure 80: Change app menu

That pops up a menu showing SkyDrive and the three apps contained in OWA (*Figure 81*).

OWA contains these three applications:

1. **Outlook.com** - The Outlook email application.
2. **People** - To manage your contacts.
3. **Calendar** - To manage your time, task and events.

Chapter 6: The Outlook Web App

Figure 81: Application choices

The opening screen of OWA looks much like its desktop version (*Figure 82*).

Let's take a quick, high level tour:

1. You organize your email into folders. These are built-in, and you can add your own folders and nest folders within those.
2. You can quickly filter the emails by several different categories, including custom ones you create.
3. The center panel shows all of your emails within that folder, Inbox in this case.
4. You can open and use a chat messaging box from any application in OWA.
5. You can easily connect to your Facebook friends and Google contacts as the Microsoft chat application connects to these other messaging services.
6. As we will see later, you can also connect with audio or video, if you have the free Skype app installed.

Chapter 6: The Outlook Web App

Figure 82: The main screen of OWA

When you open an email, you get a new series of menus that work with the email (*Figure 83*).

Figure 83: The email tool bar/menu

The menu choices are:

1. **New** - You can create a new email by clicking this link.
2. **Reply** - Use to **Reply**, **Reply all** or **Forward.**

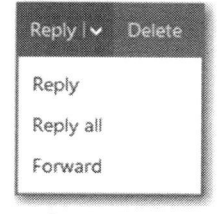

3. **Delete** - Moves the email to the deleted folder.
4. **Archive** - Moves the email to the archive folder.

67

5. **Junk** - Moves the email to the junk folder and teaches OWA that future emails from this source is probably junk. Check the junk folder often for false positives.

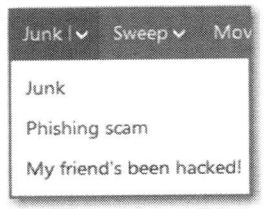

6. **Sweep** - Use this to move one or more emails and for cleanup of folders. You can edit the rules of how automatic **Sweep** works.

7. **Move to** - Sort your email into folders as you read.

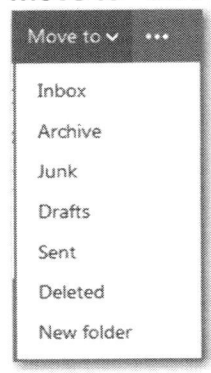

8. **...** - This utility menu (three dots) allows you to categorize, mark email as read or unread, flag or un-flag and print. If you have a message thread, you can collapse the previous messages and view the underlying HTML source.
9. **Messaging** - This opens and closes the messaging panel.
10. **Email** - This shows from whom the email comes.
11. **Add to contacts** - This adds the email sender to your contacts.

Chapter 6: The Outlook Web App

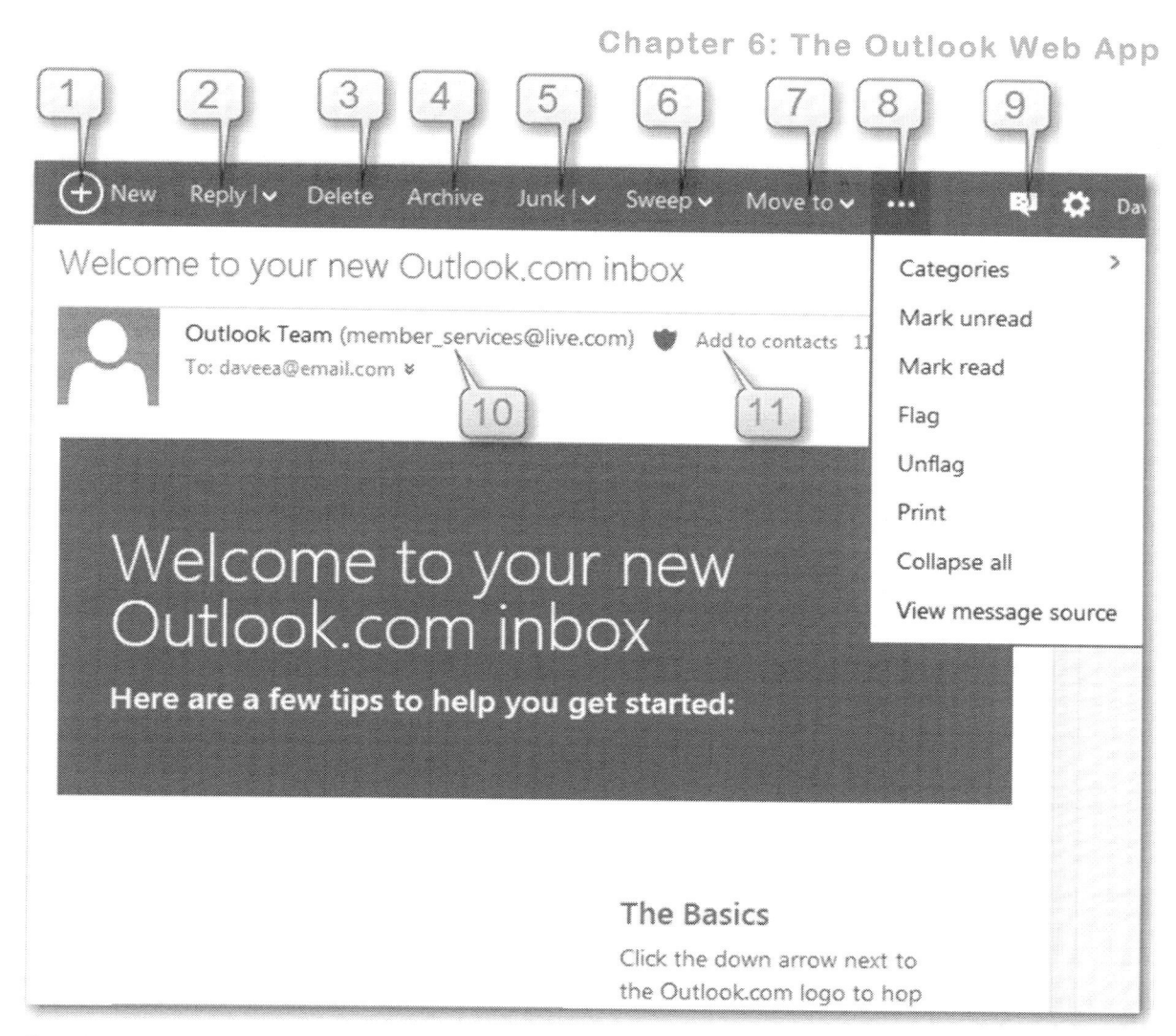

Figure 84: An open email message

The gear icon opens a menu that allows you to open a reading pane, change the color scheme of OWA and access other email settings (***Error! Reference source not found.***).

Chapter 6: The Outlook Web App

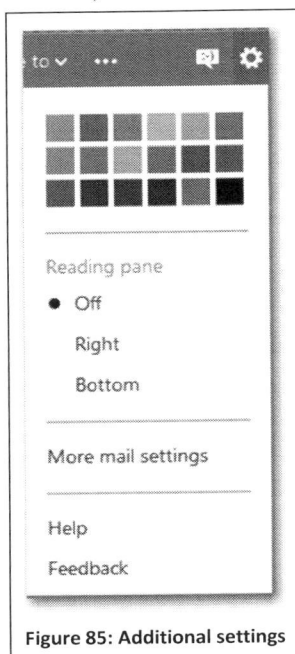

Choosing **More mail settings** off of the menu, opens a screen where you can edit the many settings that control how your email is handled (*Figure 86*).

Figure 85: Additional settings

One of the major flaws in OWA, is that email is "sent has this on behalf of" issue. Many consider this very unprofessional and Microsoft claims they will fix it shortly.

hotmail_864ac067c425a161@live.com on behalf of David Armstrong <daveea@email.com>

That was in December 12, 2012 and It was still not fixed as of January, 2014.

There is a way around this if you are using the small business version of Office 365, Microsoft's paid version of SkyDrive, SkyDrive Pro.

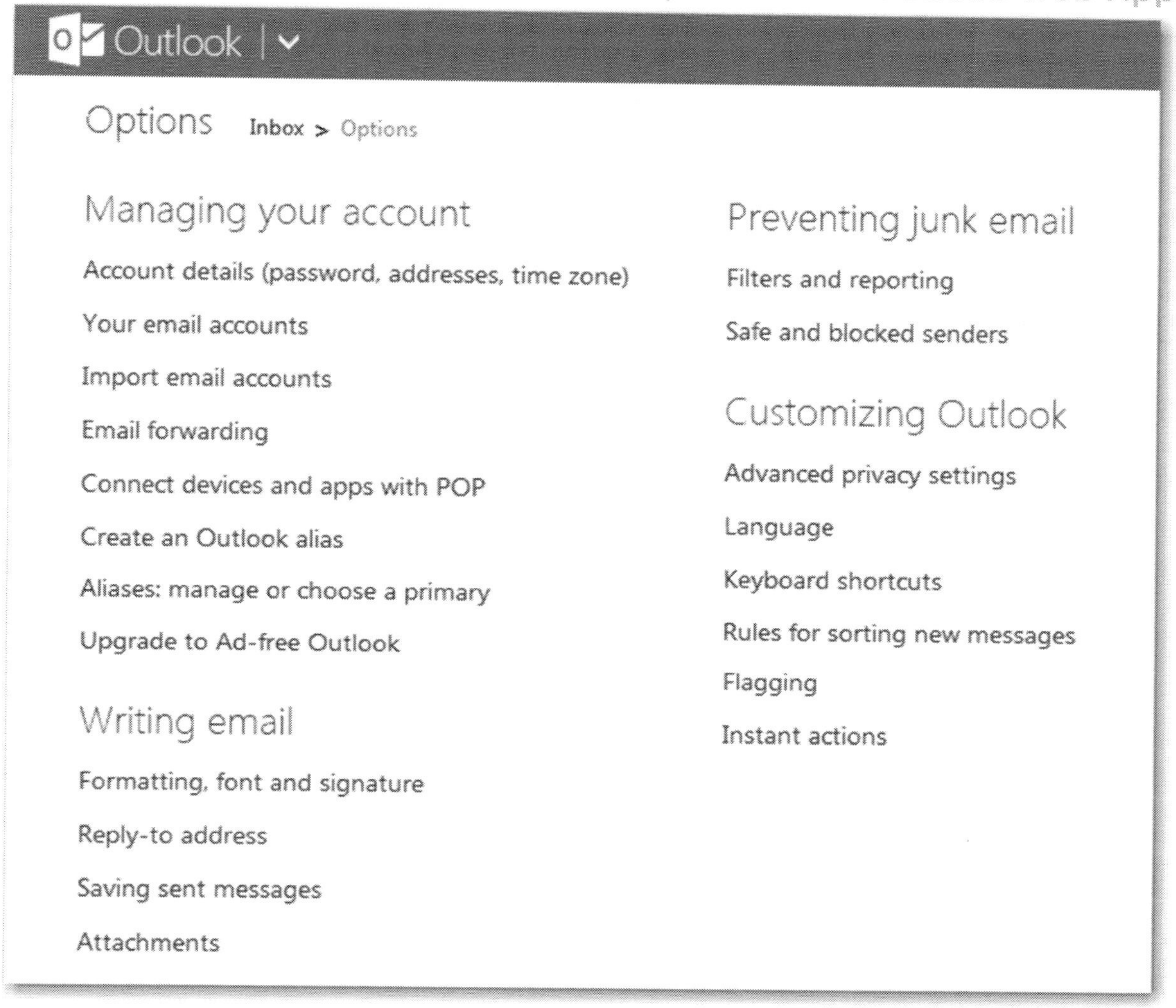

Chapter 6: The Outlook Web App

Outlook

Options Inbox > Options

Managing your account
Account details (password, addresses, time zone)
Your email accounts
Import email accounts
Email forwarding
Connect devices and apps with POP
Create an Outlook alias
Aliases: manage or choose a primary
Upgrade to Ad-free Outlook

Writing email
Formatting, font and signature
Reply-to address
Saving sent messages
Attachments

Preventing junk email
Filters and reporting
Safe and blocked senders

Customizing Outlook
Advanced privacy settings
Language
Keyboard shortcuts
Rules for sorting new messages
Flagging
Instant actions

Figure 86: Managing email settings

After turning on the reading pane to the right, we now can navigate and read email faster. We no longer have to open and close the email to see its contents (*Figure 87*).

As you can see, this looks a bit crowded on a small monitor. On a 22 inch or larger monitor, the view pane makes processing your email much easier.

Here is some valuable advice. Buy two of the biggest monitors you can afford. 27 inch monitors are well under $300. Two monitors allow you to park screens and cut and paste much quicker. The time you save when on a computer will quickly pay for the minor cost.

Once you do upsize, you will never go back. Working with a smaller single screen is like working though a porthole.

Chapter 6: The Outlook Web App

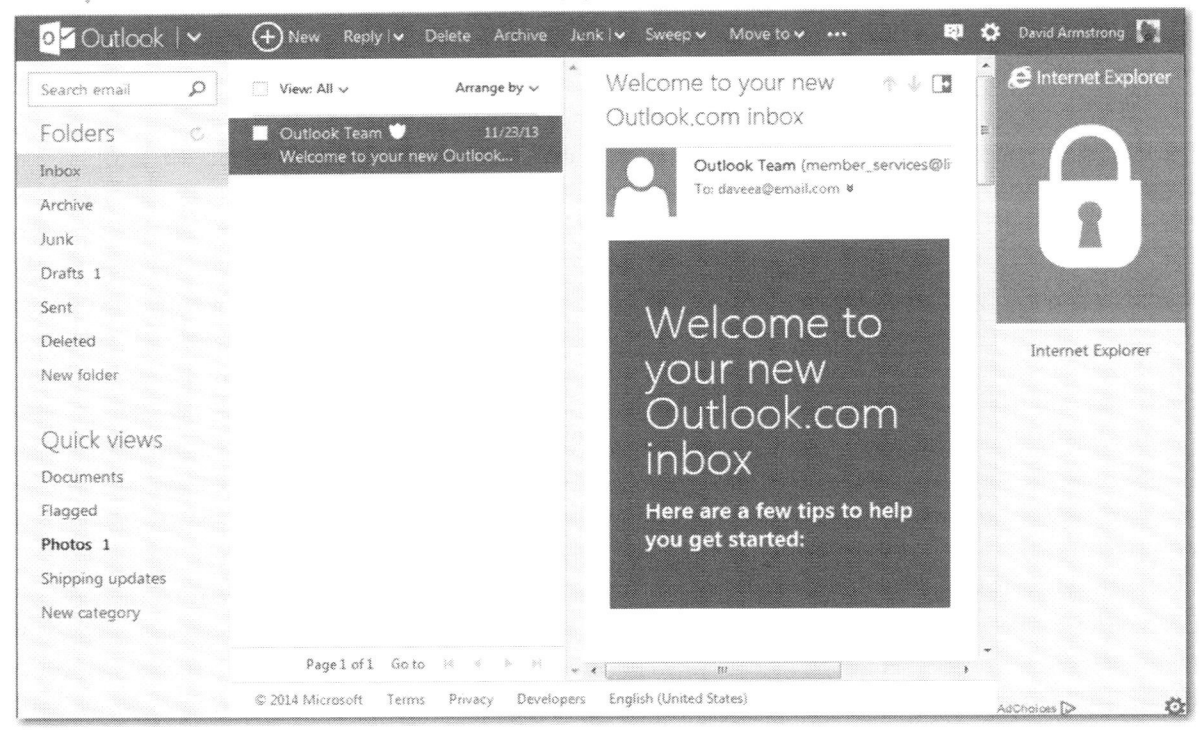

Figure 87: Email view pane

As in most SkyDrive apps, I can open my profile menu by clicking on my picture. I have indicated that I am available for chat messaging. If you are on a public computer, remember to sign out. You may need to sign out before you sign into one of your staff's account. Sign out effects all SkyDrive applications.

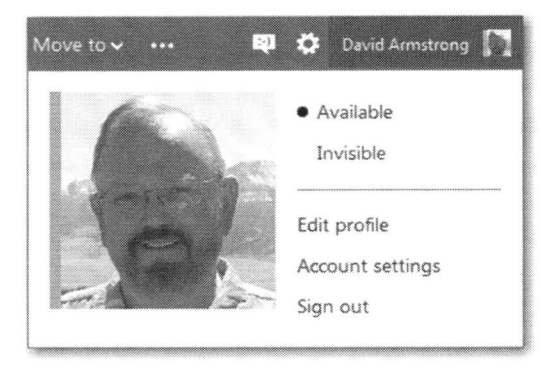

Figure 88: Profile settings

Often, you want to work with multiple emails. Check the small box to the emails you wish to group and then place your cursor over an email and pause. A menu pops up allowing you several choices dealing with groups of checked emails (*Figure 89*).

Chapter 6: The Outlook Web App

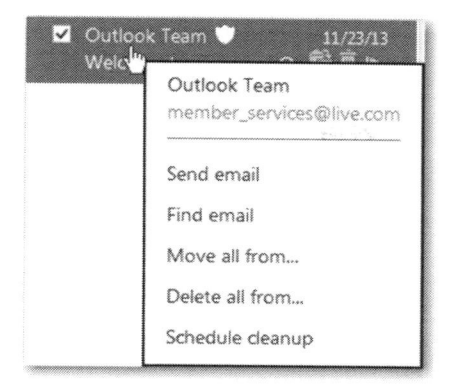

Figure 89: Email context menu via right-click

Click the **Go to** link at the bottom (*Figure 90*), and you are offered a calendar (*Figure 91*). Choose a date and you jump to that date in your list of emails. Useful, if you sort by date received, which is the default.

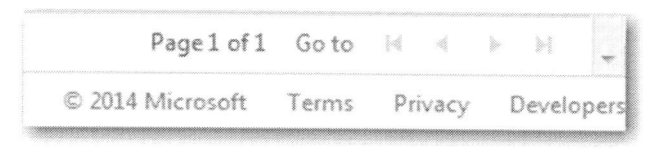

Figure 90: Go to link to a calendar

Figure 91: Filtering email list by date

There is more to be discovered and I invite you to spend time checking out the different menus and choices. There is a lot of redundancy and a right click on an object may give you the same menus we discussed throughout this section.

Creating New Email

Let's explore how you create a new email. We start with the **New** link at the top of the page (*Figure 92*).

Chapter 6: The Outlook Web App

Figure 92: Click the New button

This opens the new email screen (*Figure 93*).

Step by step, you need to:

1. Pick one or more recipients. Click on the **To**, **Cc** or **Bcc** links. All emails must have a **To** address. **Cc** sends copies to other addresses and **Bcc** sends copies, but does not reveal the other recipient's addresses.
2. Add a subject. Keep this short and interesting, as many read or delete based upon the subject.
3. Add the subject content.

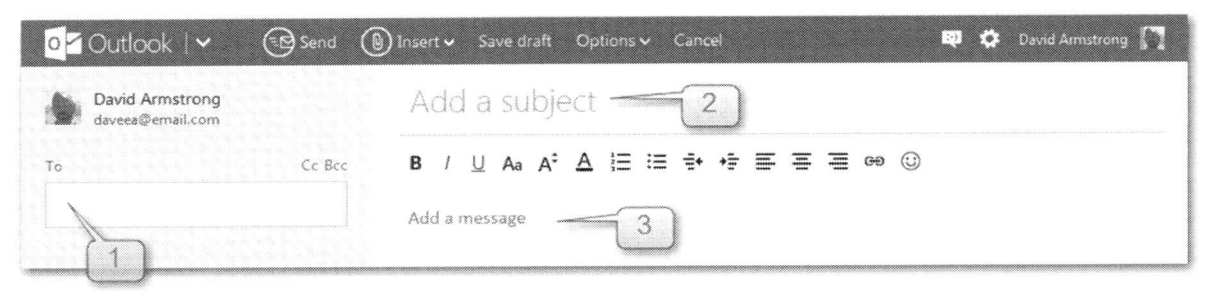

Figure 93: Steps in creating a new email

When you click on the **To**, **Cc** or **Bcc** links, you open the contact's pick box and list (*Figure 94*).

Start typing the email address. If have them in your contact list, or type part of their name, matching candidates will show up.

Chapter 6: The Outlook Web App

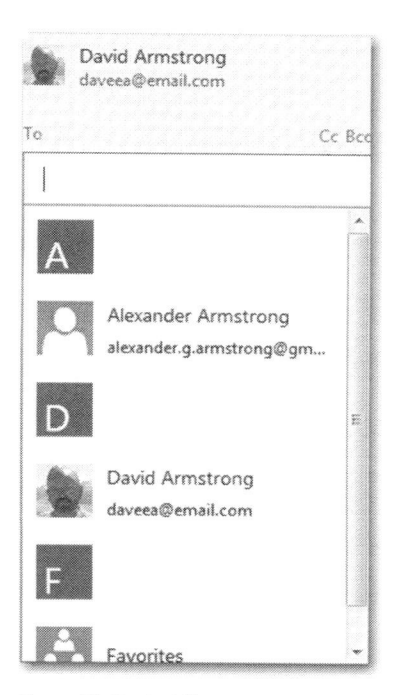

Figure 94: Contact list

Repeat the process for additional names. If you have a group of names you use often, you might create a group, as we later discuss in the section on contacts.

Add a subject and body to complete the email. A simple completed email is seen in (*Figure 95*).

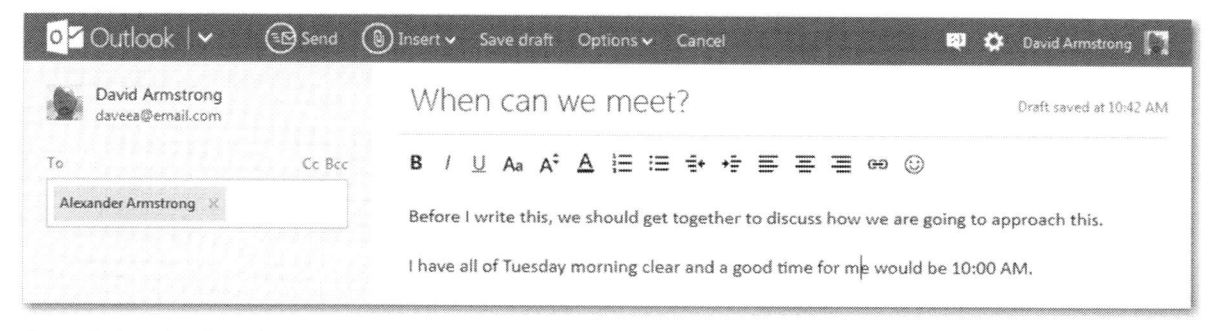

Figure 95: Completed email message

Let's explore the menu above a new email.

Chapter 6: The Outlook Web App

Figure 96: Adding attachments

- You can optionally attach a file to the email. This choice opens a file find window.

  You can paste a picture into the body of the email. However, you will need a picture in the clipboard before you can insert.

- You can add a link to a SkyDrive document you wish to share.

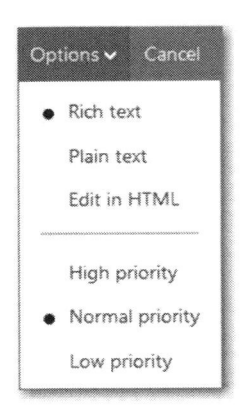

Figure 97: Setting options and priority

Most email is created as Rich text. This is Microsoft's name for HTML based email. It allows you to format text to dress up the look of your email.

Plain text offers no such formatting. It is usually only used in high-security situations. Most SPAM is sent in plain text, so a plain text email may be trapped as SPAM.

You can optionally assign a high or low priority to your emails.

The **Edit in HTML** choice in (*Figure 97*) allows you to edit the underlying HTML code. While most of you will not want to learn how to code HTML, it does give you complete control over how the email will look.

In (*Figure 98*), you see my simple email in the HTML view. The only actual HTML tags are break tags, <br>, that insert spaces between the lines of the email.

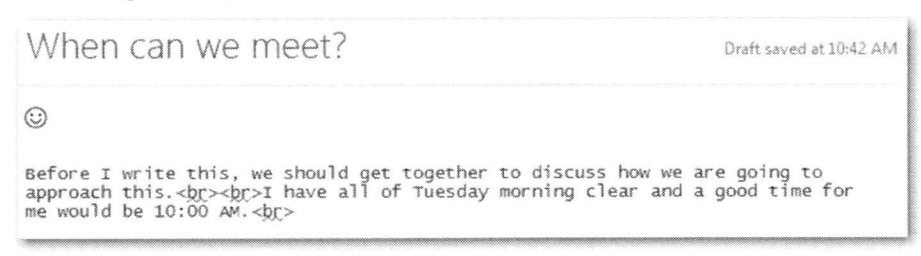

Figure 98: The email in a HTML view

In the HTML sample you see in (*Figure 99*), we see a more complex version of HTML email. This is how that beautiful, commercial email is created. If you want to try your hand there are many HTML editors, many free. WizHTMLEditor is free. You can pick up a copy from http://www.wizbrother.com/htmleditor/ (*Figure 101*).

After creating your email in the HTML editor, copy the HTML and paste it into the HTML view of your email.

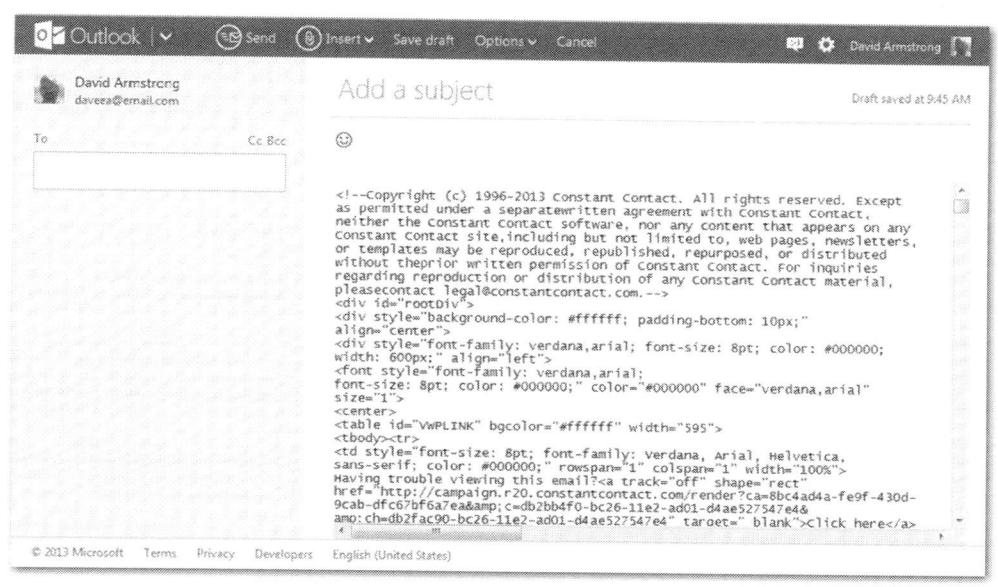

Figure 99: A complex email in HTML view

Switching back to the Rich text view, we see how your recipient sees the email (*Figure 100*).

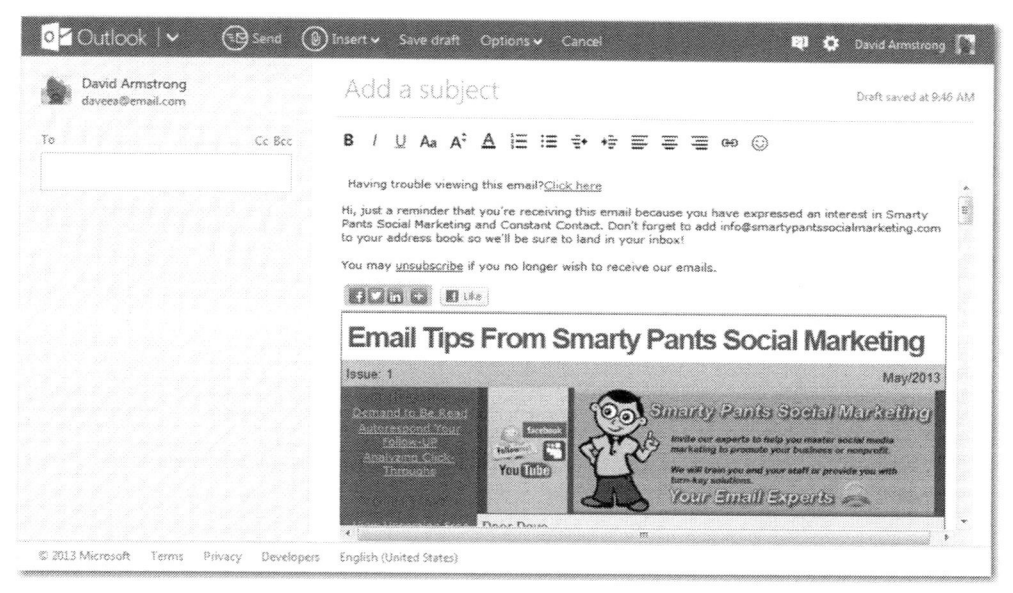

Figure 100: The complex email in rich text view

Chapter 6: The Outlook Web App

As mentioned earlier, if you decide to create a complex HTML email, you may wish to use an HTML editor. There are also many free email templates on the web you can use as a start point. Check here: http://freemailtemplates.com/.

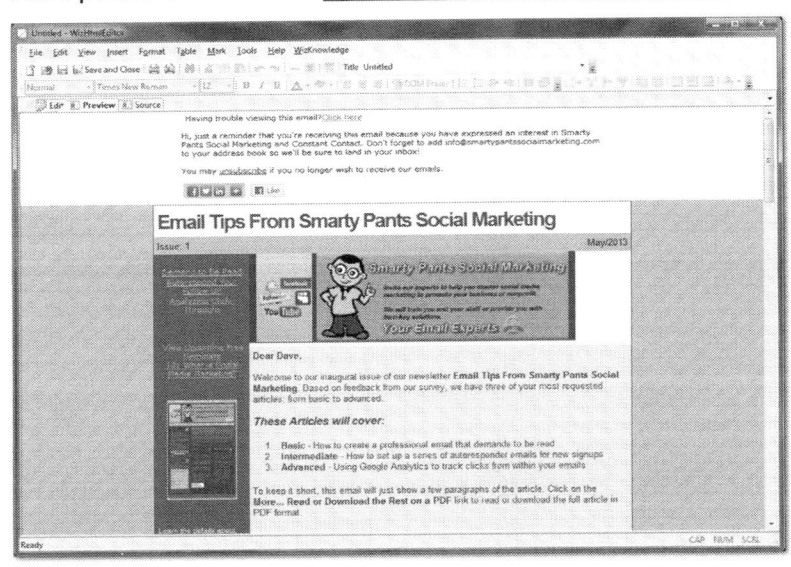

Figure 101: The free WizHTMLEditor

You can dress up any email with images. If you want to send the images as a file, you could just attach. Using HTML, you could also insert a link to the image into the message. As we saw earlier (*Figure 96*), we could insert an image directly into the email at the position of the cursor.

Navigate to the location of the image file, select and click OK (*Figure 102*). If needed, right-click the picture to select the size as a percentage of the original, from 25% to 200%.

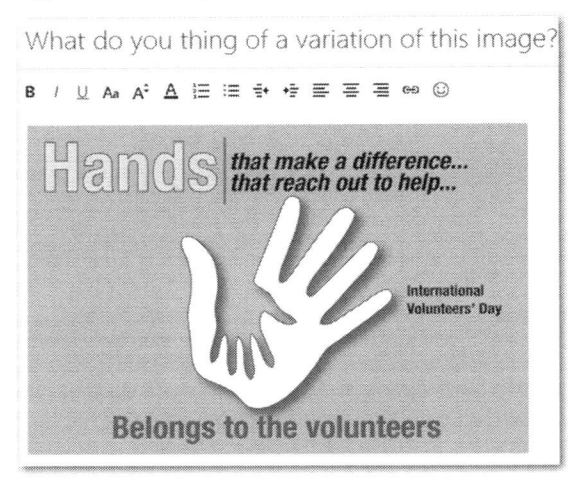

Figure 102: Embedding an image

Depending on how the receiving email client treats pictures, they may or may not see the images. If not, there usually is a link or button they can click to permit images to appear. (*Figure 103*) shows how the email looks in desktop Outlook.

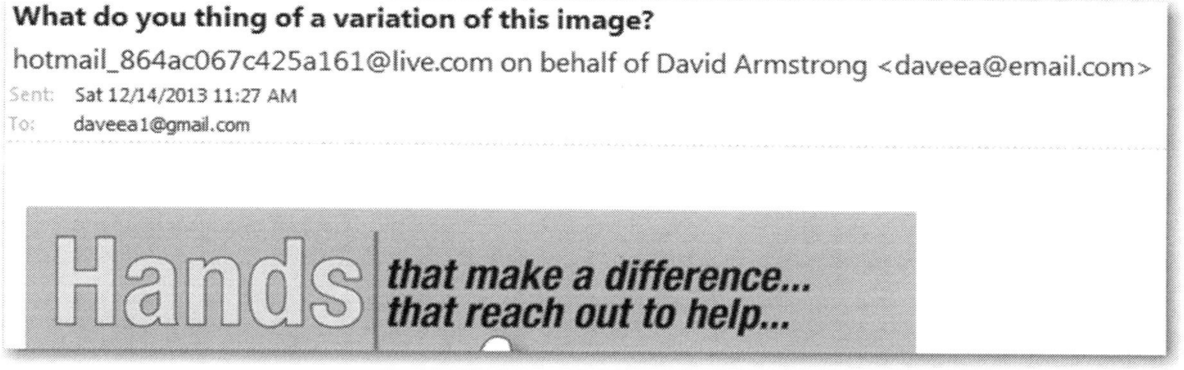

Figure 103: Issue of return address shown

Using Outlook People (Contacts)

For some unexplained reason, Microsoft changed the name contacts to people. Since all other email clients such as Gmail, Yahoo mail and the desktop version of Outlook 2013 call them contacts, I will continue using that term.

Uploading Your Existing Contacts

A new signup for Outlook.com will have no contacts. While you can send email by typing in any email address, you may want to populate the contact list with most of the names and email addresses you already have.

To do this you need to:

1. Export your list from whatever other sources you have. These could come from Gmail, Yahoo or, in my case, from my desktop version of Outlook. If given a choice when you export, choose a CSV type file. This file can be imported into OWA and is a default for most export wizards. Go to the help files for the software currently holding your list and look for export. You can open this file in Excel for editing before you import (*Figure 104*).
2. You will then import that csv file into OWA as we discuss near (*Figure 106*).

Chapter 6: The Outlook Web App

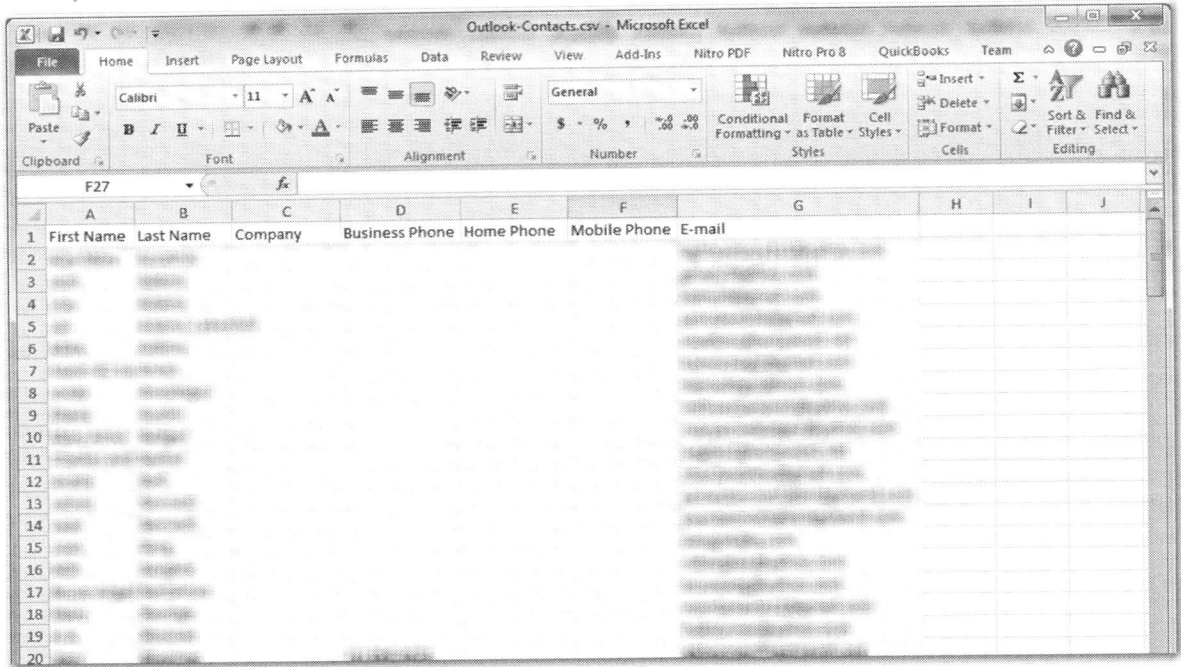

Figure 104: An Excel view of a CSV file

Let's take a tour of the contacts opening page (*Figure 105*).

1. In time, you may have a large list of contacts. It is helpful to search for them by name. Any part of the name narrows the list. Typing Arm brings up all the Armstrongs as well as Armsteads, etc.
2. While you can sort several ways, the default and usually the most useful is alphabetical.
3. You can quickly import contacts from most of the major social media sites. There is no guarantee that they will have meaningful addresses, and you will need to sign into (once) the other sites and give permission for OWA to access them.
4. You can use the **Import from file** link to read the csv file discussed earlier. We will discuss that next (*Figure 106*).
5. The **New** link allows you to add a new contact or a new group. If adding a group, you can then add existing contacts to that group.
6. The **Manage** link helps us clean up our contacts list.
7. We can use the gear icon to change the sort order, filter and display of contacts.

Chapter 6: The Outlook Web App

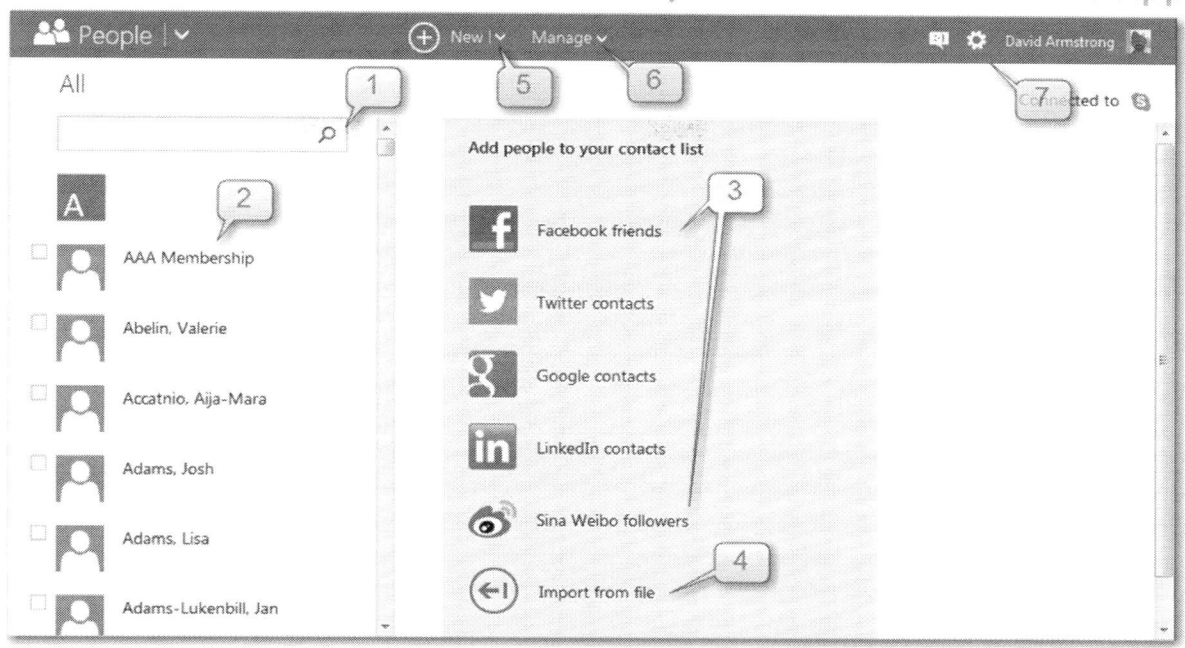

Figure 105: The main contact screen

Clicking the **Import from file** link at the bottom of the main page opens the File Upload window (*Figure 106*). We need to browse our hard drive and find the CSV file we discussed earlier.

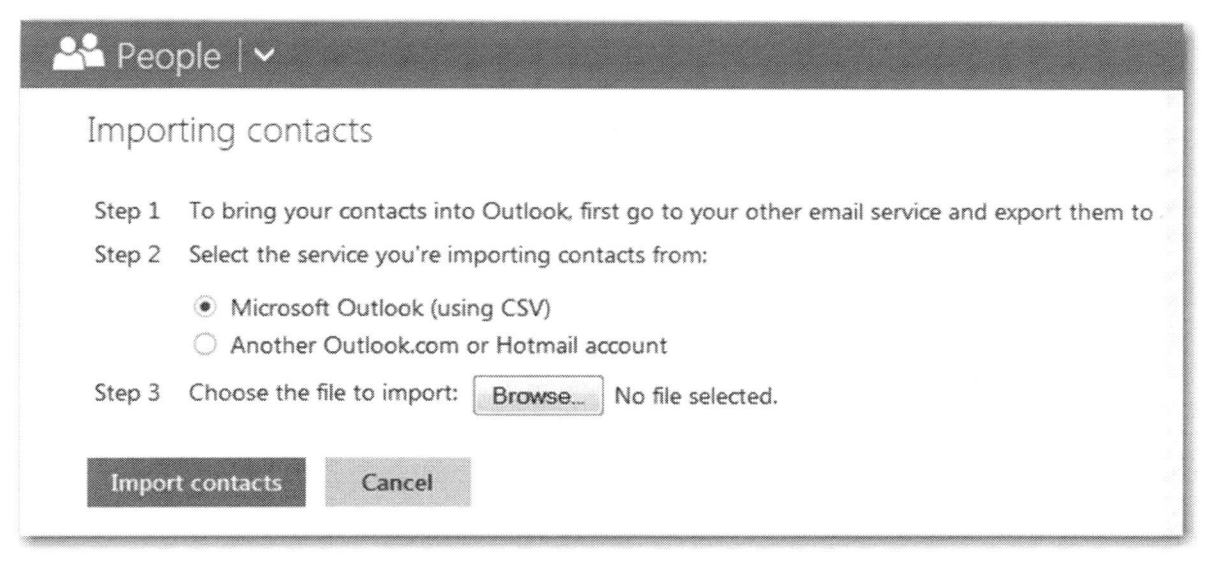

Figure 106: Picking a file to import

Use the **File Upload** window to navigate to the file you exported. Select the file and click the **Open** button (*Figure 107*).

Chapter 6: The Outlook Web App

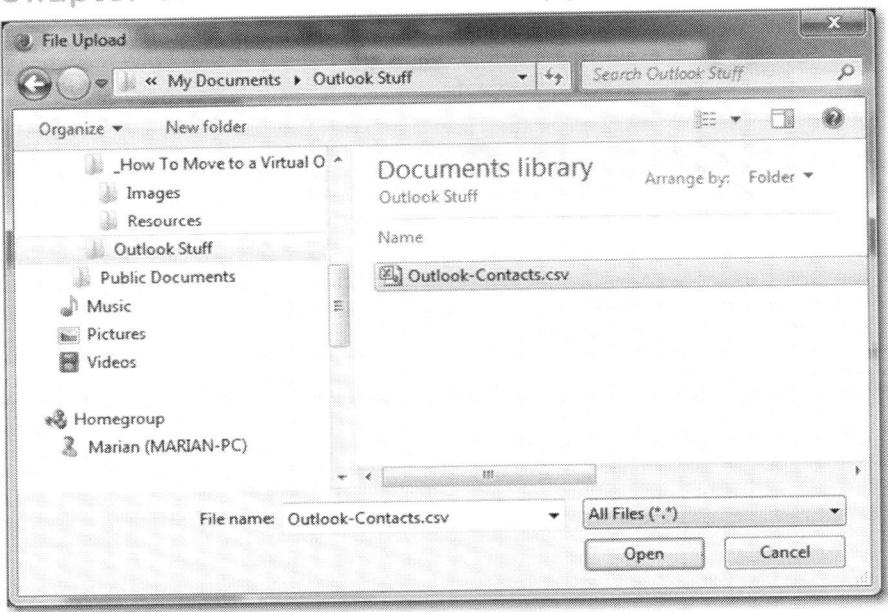

Figure 107: Locating the csv file

Step 3 will then show the name of the file. Mine was called **Outlook-Contacts.csv.** Click the **Import contacts** button to start the upload (*Figure 108*).

Figure 108: File selected, ready to import

You may have duplicates depending on how many sources you used as sources for your contacts. Menu choices **Manage->Clean up contacts** show all duplicates. You can select the ones you wish to clean up. **Clean up** merges the two or more selected duplicates.

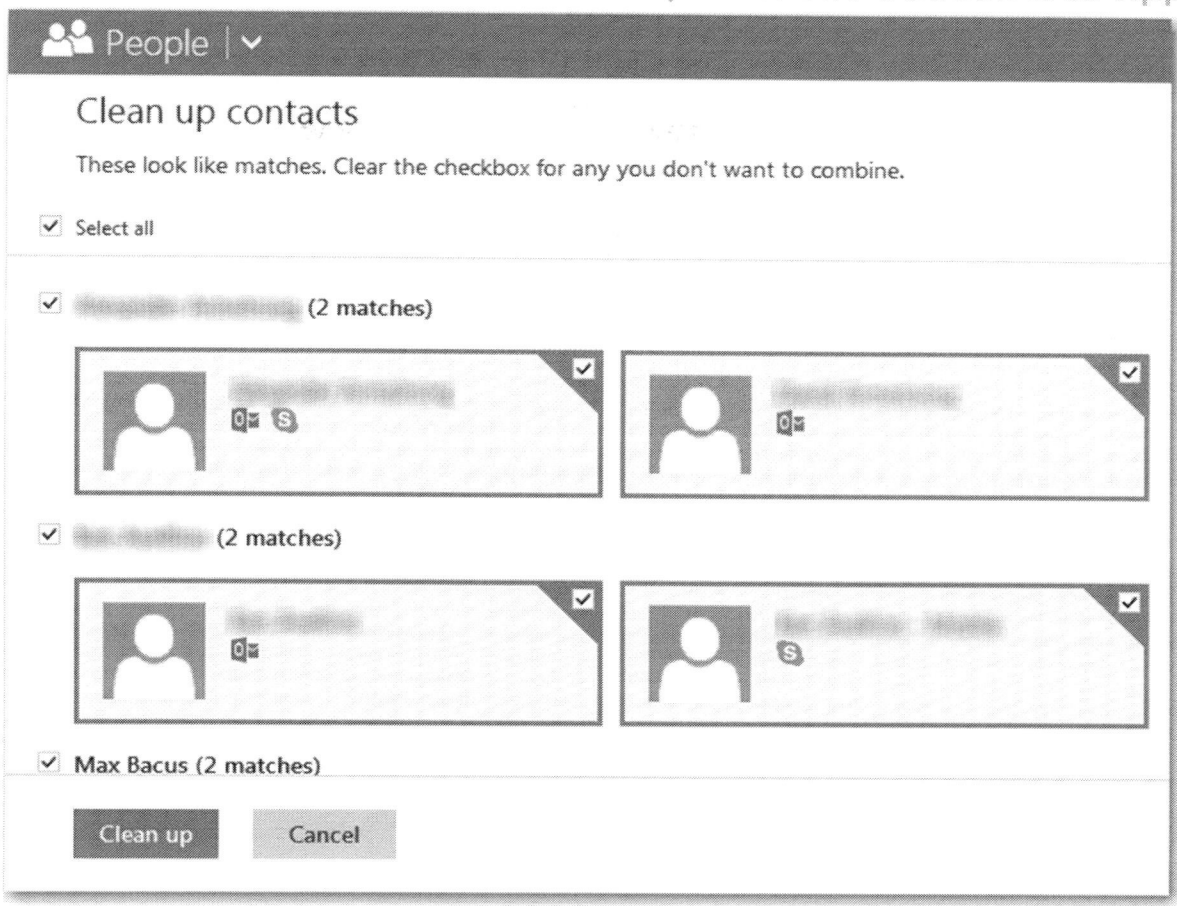

Figure 109: Cleaning up duplicate contacts

You have a menu at the top of the contacts screen (*Figure 110*).

Figure 110: The contacts menu bar

Chapter 6: The Outlook Web App

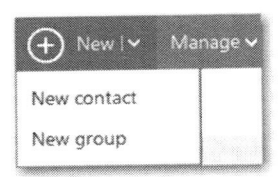

Figure 111: Adding a new contact or group

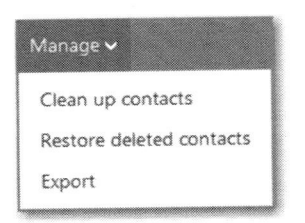

Figure 112: Cleaning up your contact list or export

If you send emails to the same group of contacts on a regular basis, you might consider adding them all to a named group. You then just send to the group and the OWA copies the message to everyone. Put the group name in the Bcc section to avoid giving everyone the full list of names.

The **Manage** dropdown allows you to clean up and manage your list of contacts. As you see in (*Figure 109*), you can find and eliminate duplicate contact records.

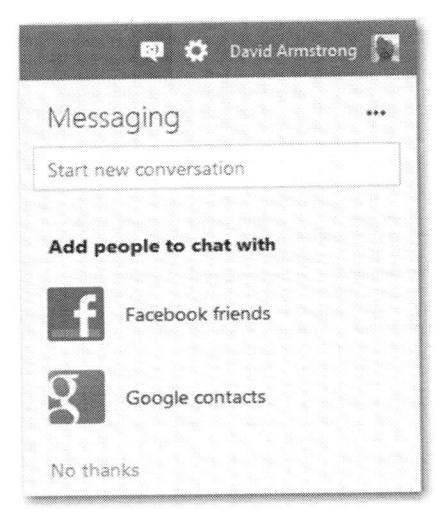

Figure 113: Messaging contacts in your list

Messaging between staff is critical to running a virtual office. All screens get to the messaging panel with a single click.

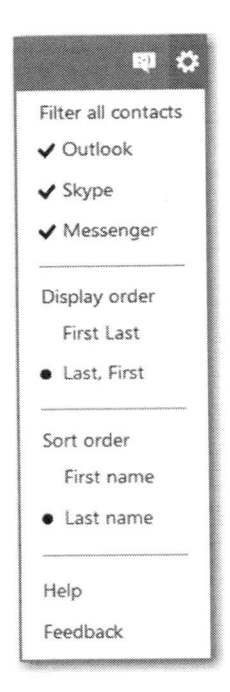

Figure 114: Sorting and filtering contacts

You can rearrange the order and the way contacts are listed.

After importing, check a few contacts to see if the information you have imported matches your expectations (*Figure 115*).

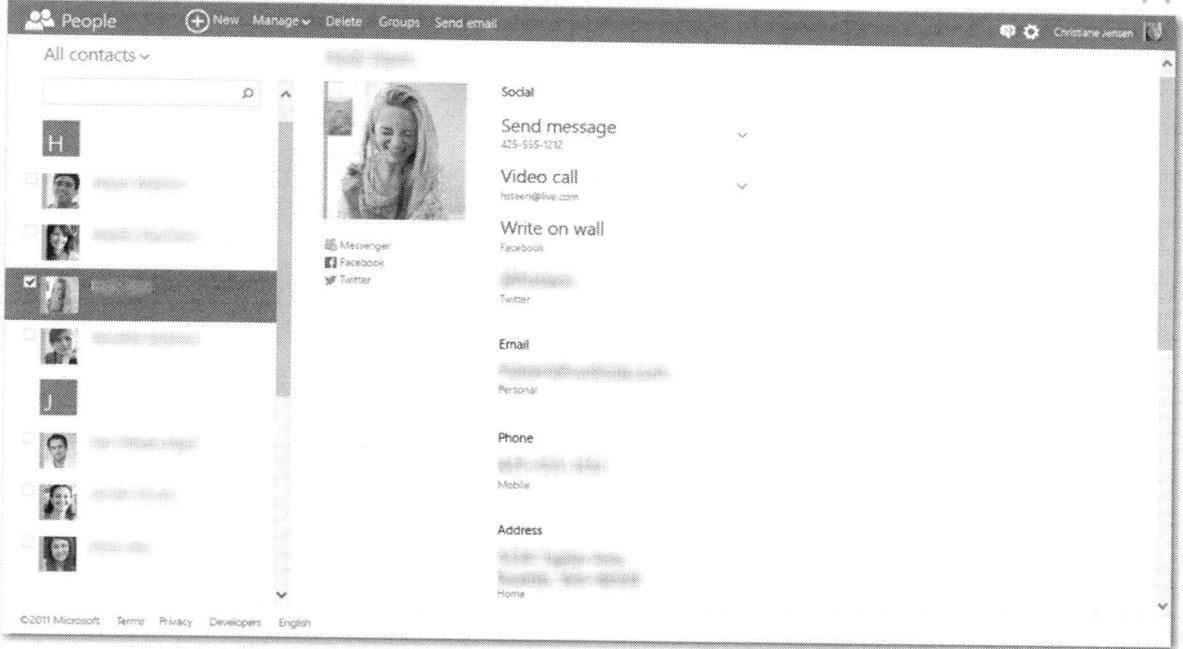

Figure 115: An individual contact's record

Let's look at adding a new contact. From the link at the top of the page, choose **New->New contact** (*Figure 116*).

Chapter 6: The Outlook Web App

Figure 116: Adding a new contact's basic information

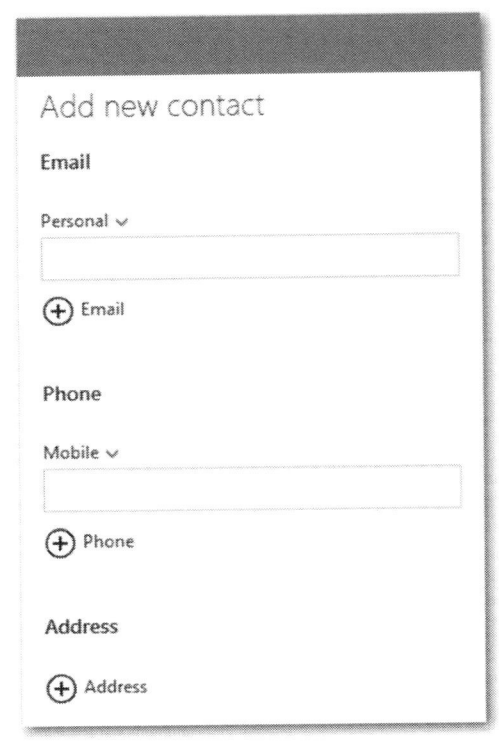

Figure 117: Adding additional emails, phone numbers and addresses

All contacts must have a name. If this is a business, I suggest you give your primary contact's name and use their business name in the Company field. Clicking the + icon allows you to add other forms of their names, such as **Nickname**.

You can add multiple emails, if needed. Same with phones, which you will want to tag as Mobile, Home, Work, etc.

You can add multiple addresses, also.

Optionally, at the bottom of the fields, you can add such things as birthdays, anniversaries, spouse name and other information (*Figure 118*).

Chapter 6: The Outlook Web App

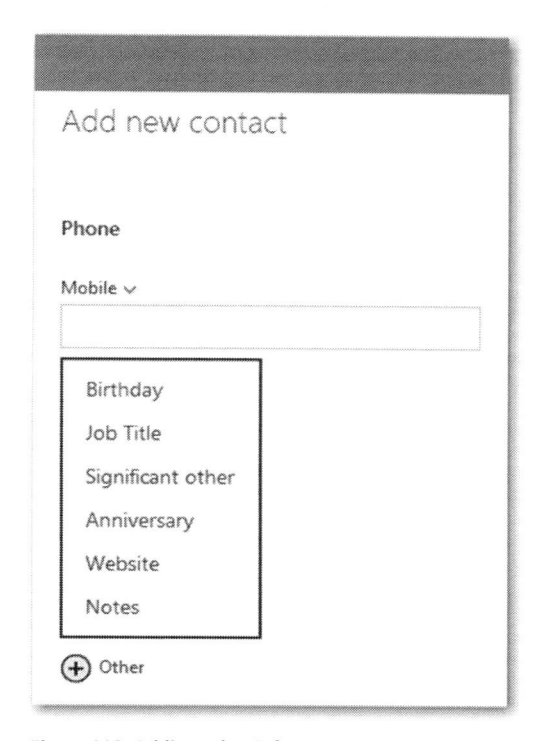

Figure 118: Adding other information

Skype Calling

We will cover Skype in detail later in its own chapter. However, if you have a Skype account and you link it to SkyDrive, you can call contacts from the contact screen (*Figure 119*).

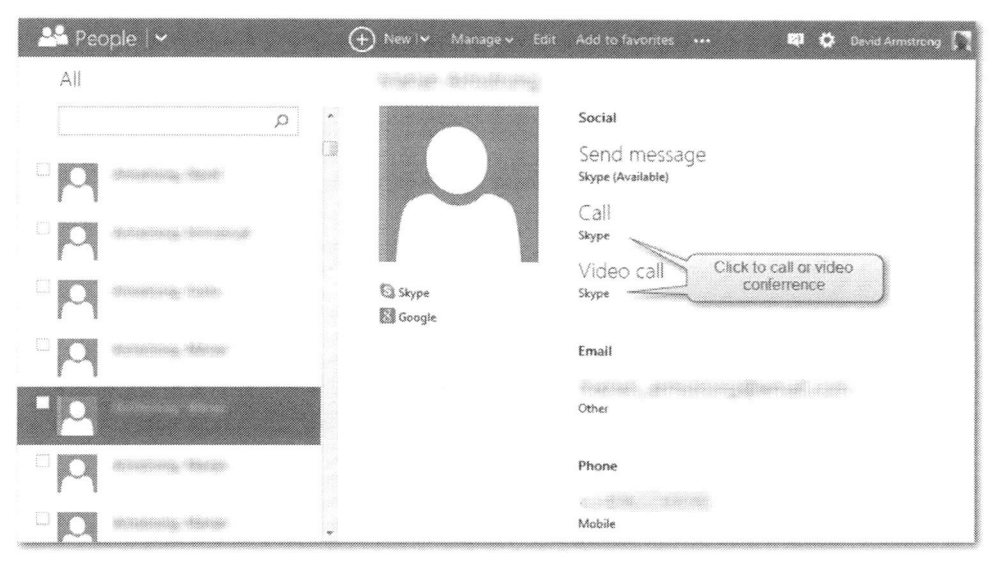

Figure 119: Calling and video with Skype

Once the call starts, you will see the dialing screen (*Figure 120*). If they have a video camera, click on the video button. You can mute the call and add text messaging.

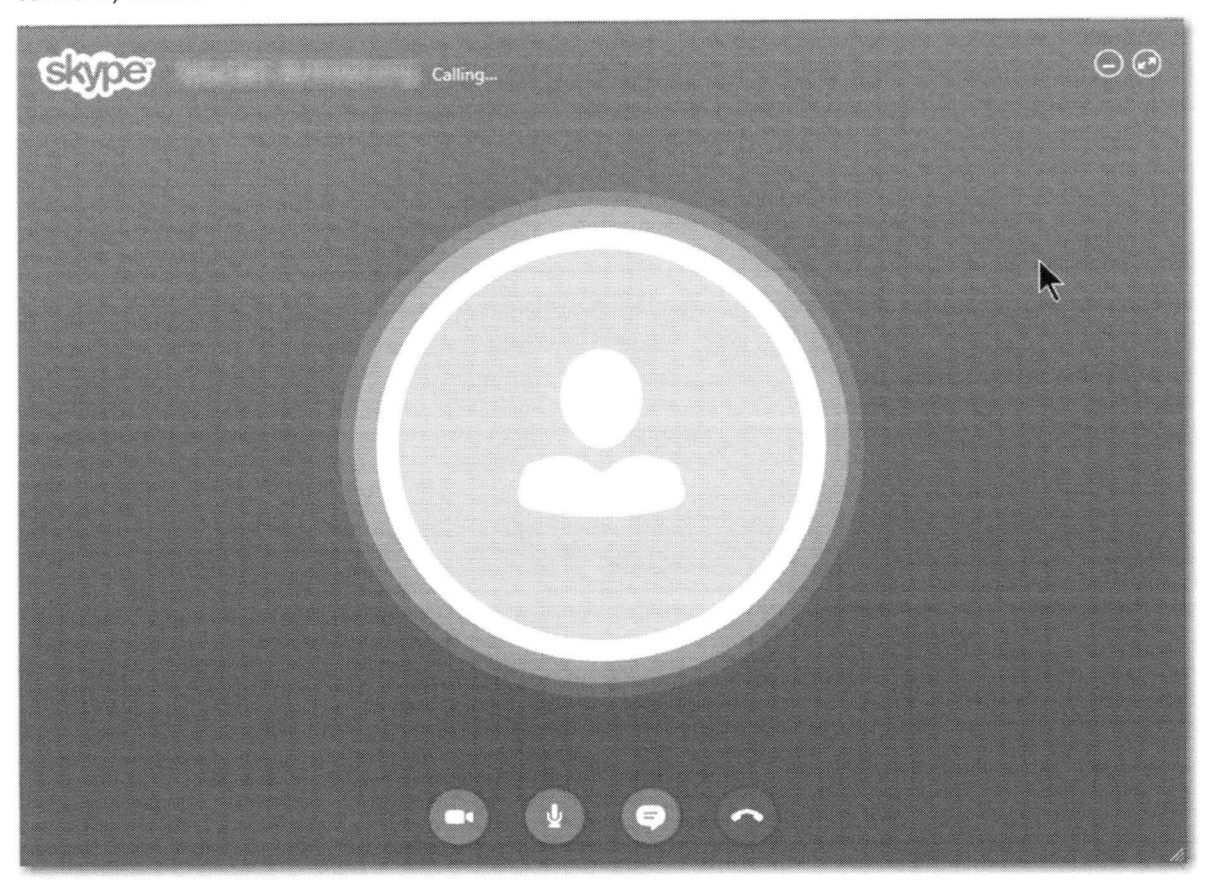

Figure 120: Skype calling screen

Using Outlook Calendar

The last app in Outlook Web Application (OWA) is the calendar. It is integrated with Outlook and allows you to plan meetings and send email invitations which they can RSVP.

This is patterned after the calendar in desktop Outlook and is similar in use.

Main Screen and Month View

The opening screen, by default, is a month view (*Figure 121*).

Let's take a high level tour of the screen:
1. Each cell represents a day and you can paginate months with the double arrows.
2. Today is marked in a different color (gray) and allows you to see what is on your schedule today. Once you add your location, you also get a mini weather report in the cell.

3. You can add a **New** event by first selecting the day and then clicking the **+ New** link at the top of the page. We will look at a new event later.
4. You can Import all the events from other calendars; useful, if you are moving to OWA's calendar.
5. **Share** your calendar with others in your virtual office. You might want an assistant to manage your emails when you are not available, on your behalf.
6. Filter your calendars, assuming you have more than one.
7. Open weekly or daily views of your calendar.
8. Most holidays for your region, can be added or removed.

Figure 121: Calendar's main screen

There are several dropdown menus we can use.

Chapter 6: The Outlook Web App

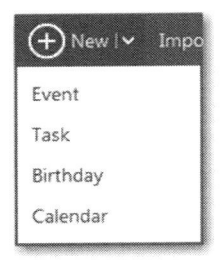

Figure 122: The calendar's New menu

Figure 123: Sharing your calendar with others

The New menu allows us to add a new event, task, birthday and even a new calendar. You might want a business and personal calendar, for example.

All staff might share the viewing of their calendars free time, locations, titles of events, etc. This would make planning a meeting much easier.

As you will see, (*Figure 125*), you have control over how others see and optionally use it.

Most calendars can save all of their events and task in an ICS type file. Here is a link to Wikipedia discussing an ICS file, http://en.wikipedia.org/wiki/ICalendar. Check your other calendar's documentation on how to export or create an ICS file.

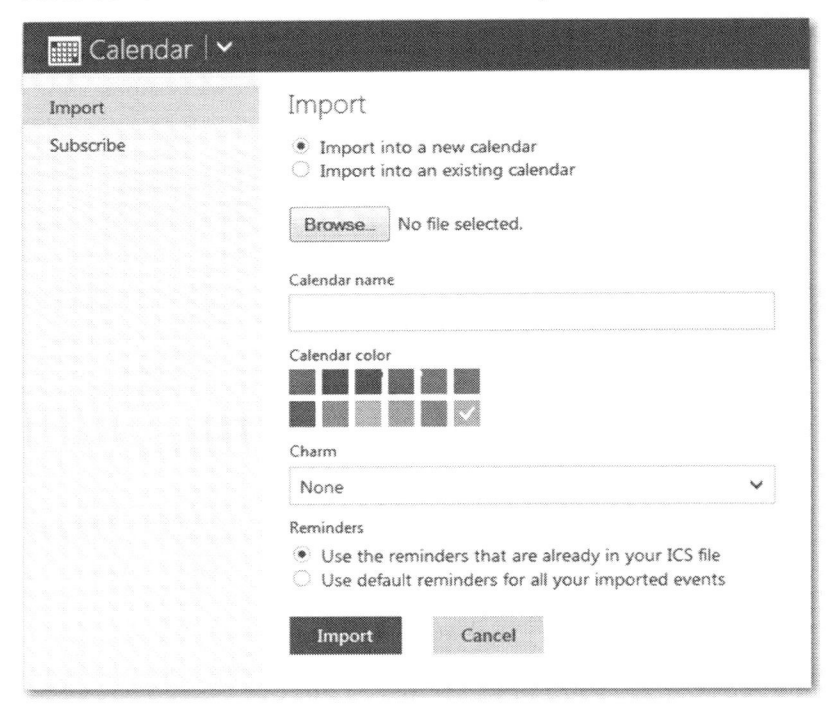

Figure 124: Importing other calendars

You probably want to share some calendar information, if others depend on your schedule. You may even want to create a calendar for your conference room and give everyone the ability to update it.

If you are very busy, you might want to allow someone else to help manage your calendar.

In (*Figure 125*), you see that you have the ability to add contacts and limit their ability to assist with your calendar.

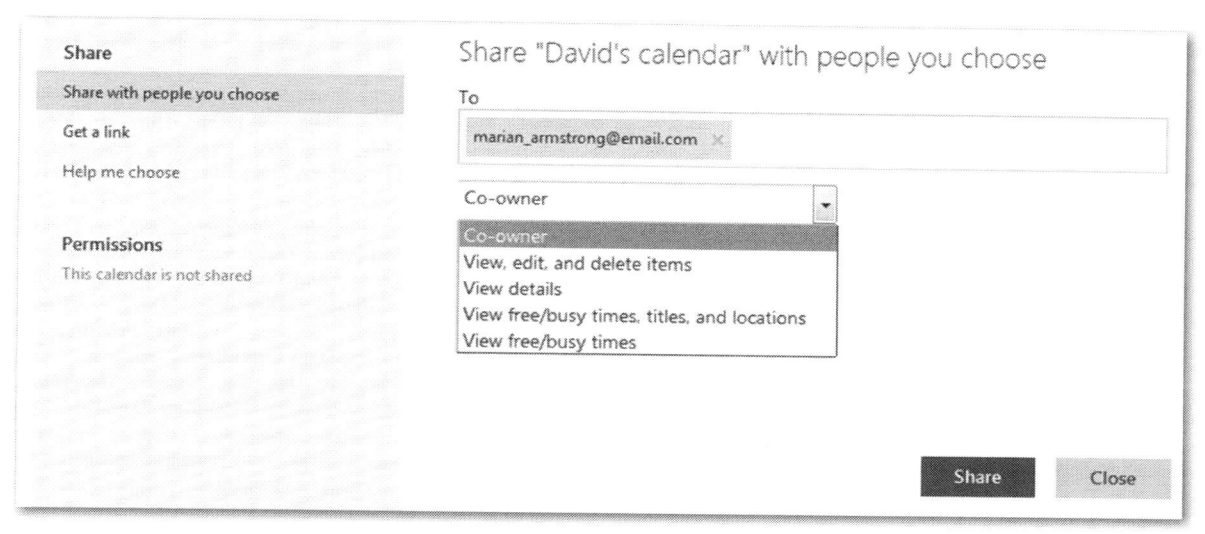

Figure 125: Sharing your calendar

Quickly change the calendar views. We will look at the different calendars a little later.

The gear icon allows you to turn on or off any of your various calendars.

As you see (*Figure 126 and* Figure 127), you can set system-wide calendar options.

Chapter 6: The Outlook Web App

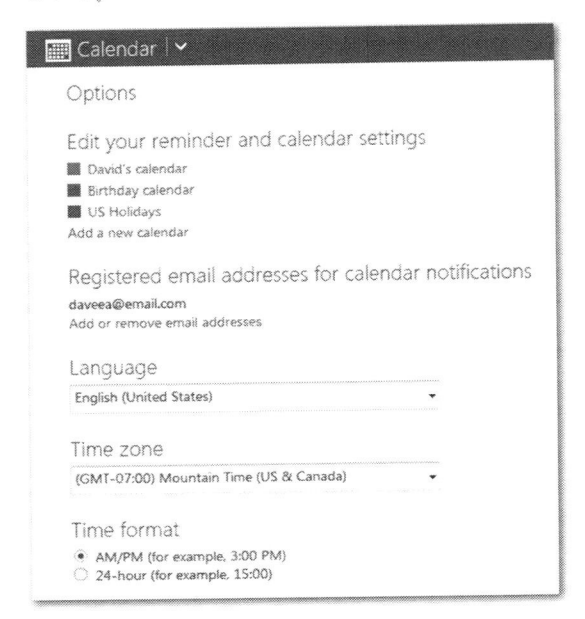

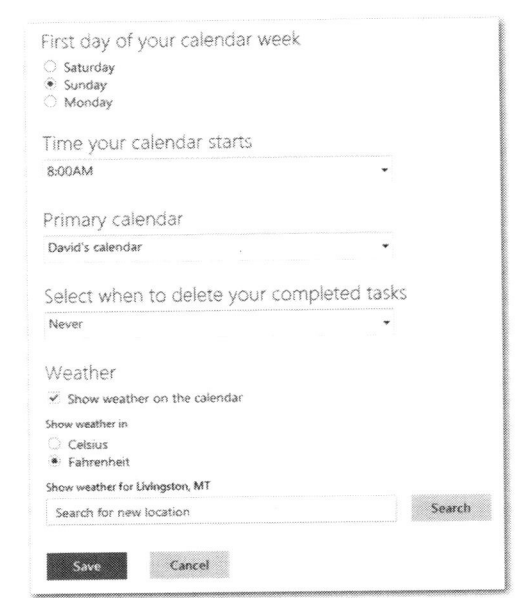

Figure 126: View/Edit calendar options

Figure 127: View/Edit calendar options (continued)

In the week view, you get a good view of events this week. You can edit and move these events. Some are all day events, but that does not mean you cannot double-book your time (*Figure 128*).

Notice, that Thursday morning has overlapping events.

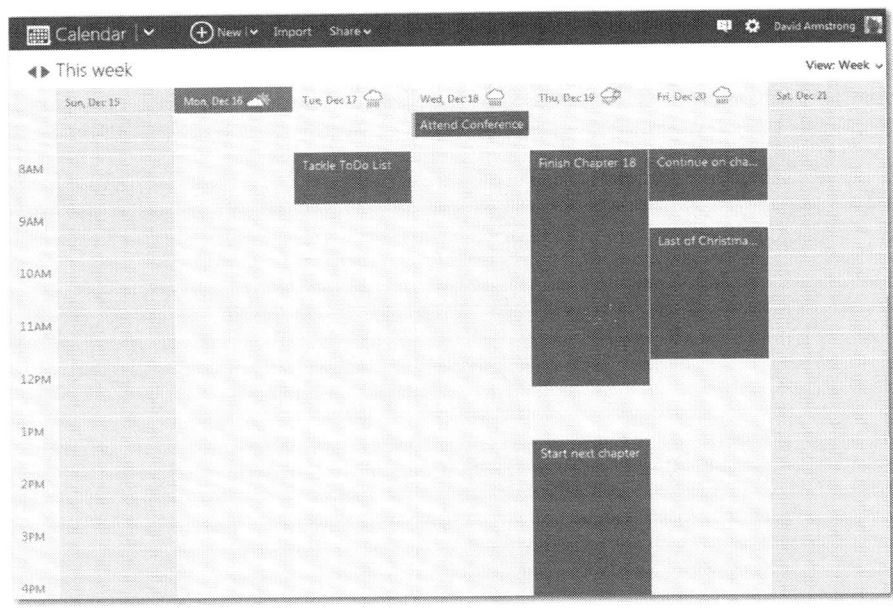

Figure 128: Week view of your calendar

Chapter 6: The Outlook Web App

The day view shows today's events by default. (*Figure 129*) shows Thursday's schedule.

Figure 129: Daily view of your calendar

When I am planning my week, my favorite view is the **Agenda** view (*Figure 130*). It shows all upcoming events in chronological order.

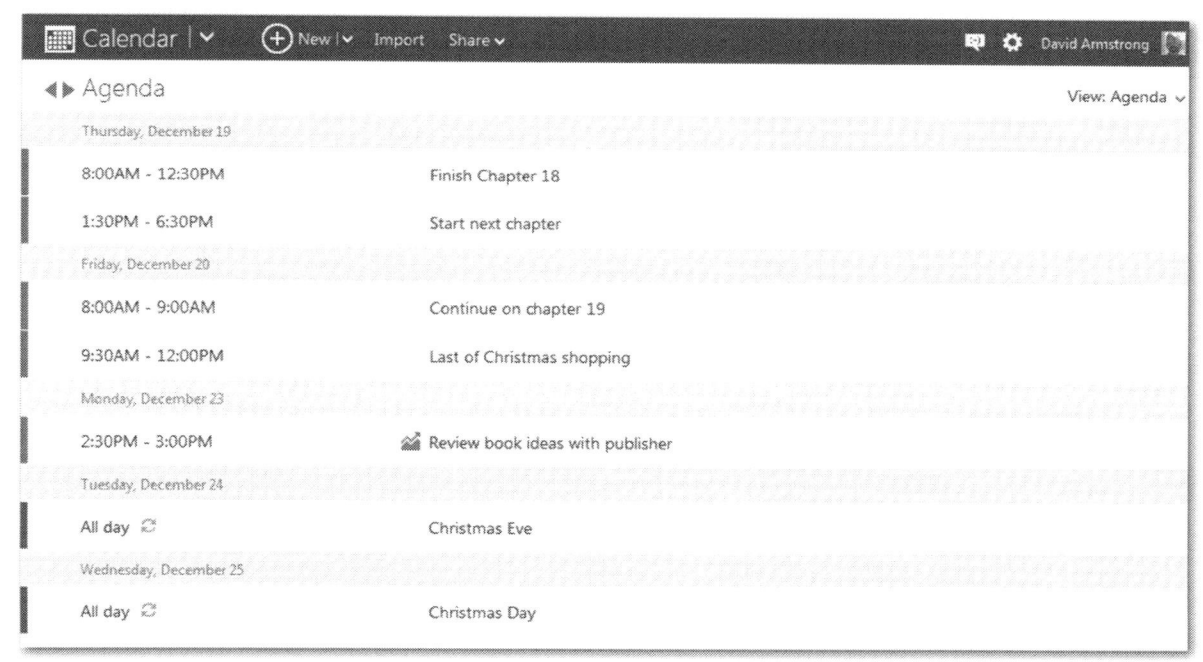

Figure 130: Agenda view of your calendar

How to Move Your Expensive Office to the Free Cloud

93

Chapter 6: The Outlook Web App

Task are similar to events in that they can be time sensitive with completion dates, etc. However, they linger until you mark them as completed (*Figure 131*).

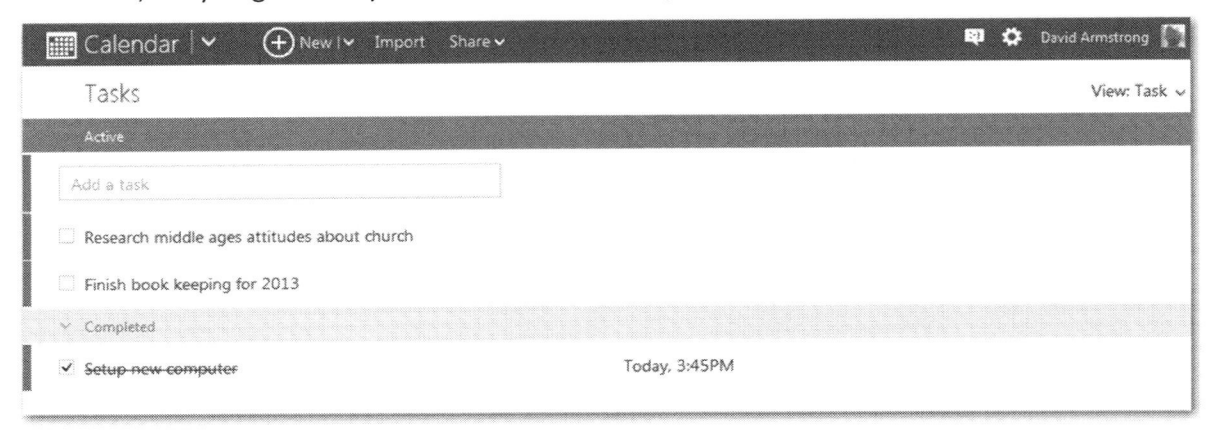

Figure 131: Calendar's task view

After adding a task, you can double-click it to add more details. You might add a due date and change priority to **High** (*Figure 132*).

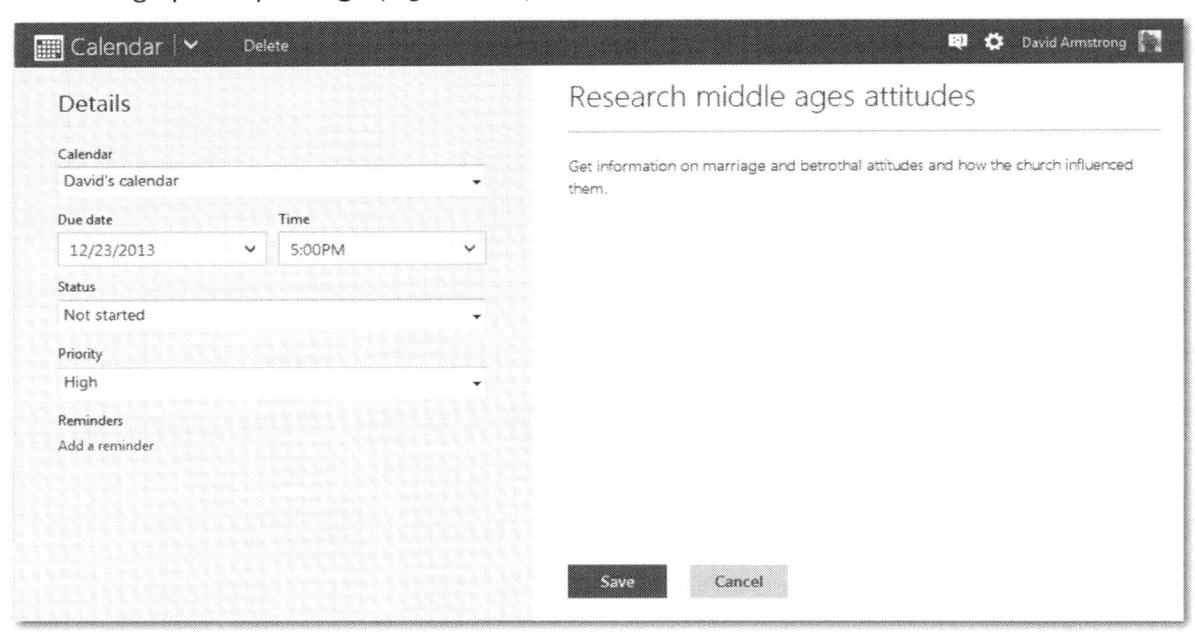

Figure 132: Task details

Adding a New Appointment

Adding a new appointment has many options, the most important is the date and time, of course.

Let's tour the screen shown (*Figure 133*):

How to Move Your Expensive Office to the Free Cloud

1. By default, this is the date that has the focus in the calendar. To change it, you can use the dropdown to open a mini calendar to pick a date. There is also a time picker dropdown.
2. How long is the event? The default is one hour, but you can set any timespan including a custom one.

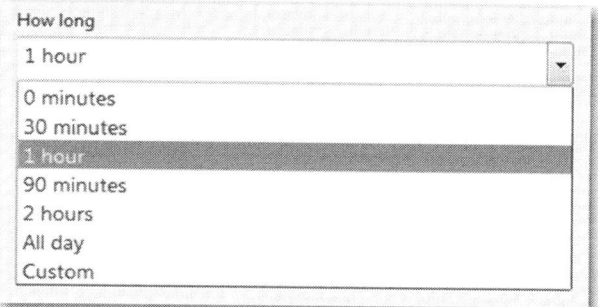

    ```
    How long
    [ 1 hour                    ▼ ]
    0 minutes
    30 minutes
    1 hour
    90 minutes
    2 hours
    All day
    Custom
    ```

3. Where is the meeting being held? Your office? Virtual?
4. Whose calendar do we want this on? Personal, business or Private or someone else's?
5. Does the event reoccur? The default is once, but you can choose other options. For example, the event might occur every Thursday. Here are some of the options:

    ```
    How often
    [ Once                      ▼ ]
    Once
    Daily
    Weekly
    Monthly
    Yearly
    ```

6. **Charms** are optional. You can assign a small icon, and later it helps you scan all appointments looking for that icon.

7. Do you want notification? Calendar can send an email, and you can give the notification a certain time to alert you.

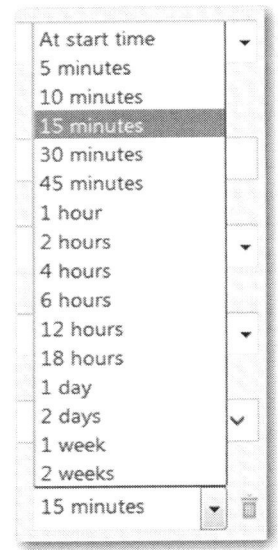

8. You can tag the event as being **Busy**, **Tentative**, **Free** or **Away**.

9. Optionally, you can mark the event as **Private**. Only you, looking at your own calendar, will see it, even if your calendar is shared.
10. Add a title that will show on the calendars. Keep it short.
11. Add a description, including telephone numbers or other details needed for the event.

Chapter 6: The Outlook Web App

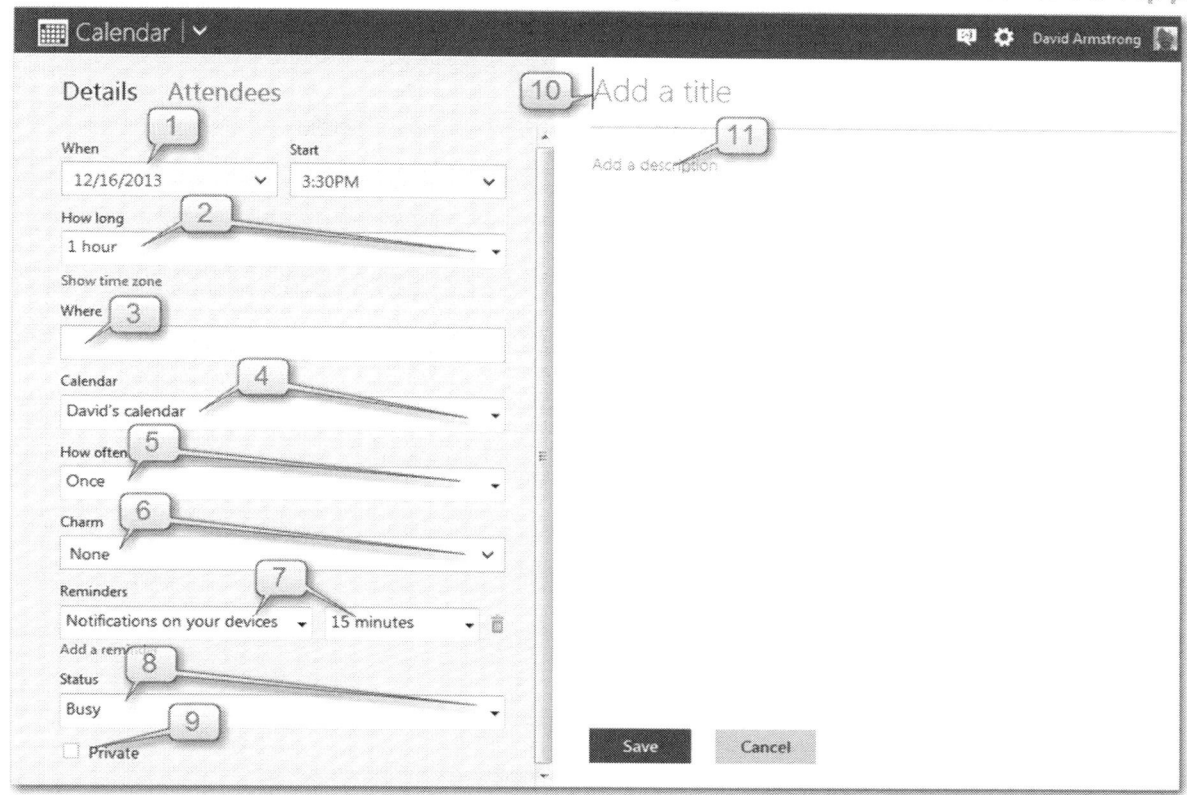

Figure 133: Adding details to an event

Here is an example of a completed event (*Figure 134*).

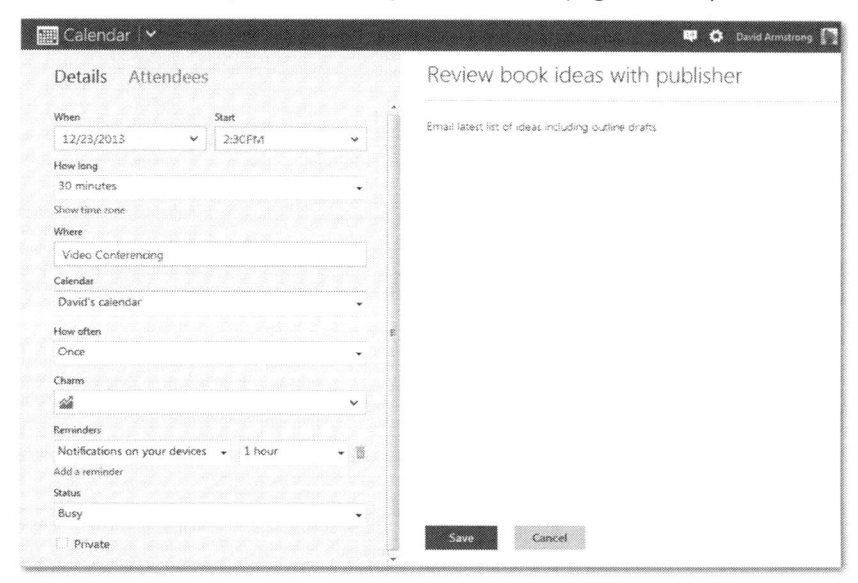

Figure 134: A completed event

Chapter 6: The Outlook Web App

Often, you will need to reschedule an event. Click the event on any of the calendars to open a quick edit (*Figure 135*). The **View details** link opens the full edit screen.

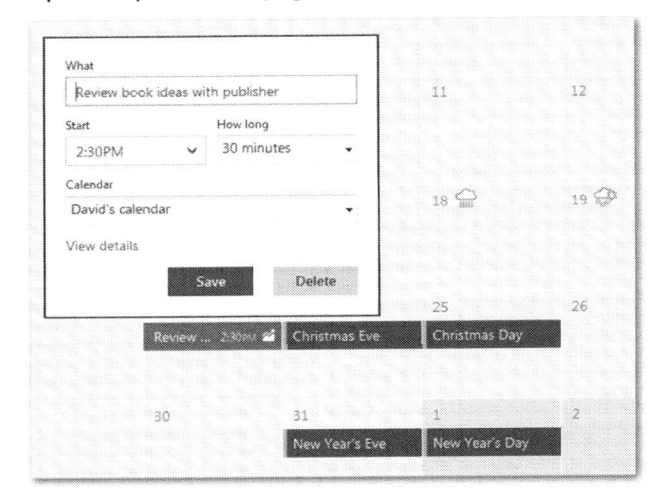

Figure 135: Quick editing of an event

Google docs

Chapter 7: Using Google Docs and Drive

In this chapter, we are going to learn how to use Google Drive which contains several office productivity applications that are similar to Microsoft's SkyDrive. Google Drive offers 15GB of free space, in which, you can store any file, in addition, to the office applications. Google has now renamed Google Docs to Google Drive. I use both interchangeably.

We will first get a high level view of the service and discuss free vs. paid. The paid versions provide some useful administrative tools, but for most businesses the free versions work fine.

We then look at each of the individual applications in a step-by-step manner. If you are familiar with Microsoft Office, these are the equivalent of Word, Excel and PowerPoint. We will look at Forms you can create to collect data. The data is automatically loaded into a spreadsheet. Forms might collect new emails in response to an email campaign or you can use to create a survey.

Google Drive offers great collaboration tools. Several people can be working on the same document in real time, seeing each other's changes.

We will learn how to use Gmail, Google's world class email client. We will also tour how to use instant messaging for brief, nonintrusive communication between your staff.

Businesses need full featured calendars that can be shared to keep everything and everyone on track. Google Calendars do that and more. They also work on tablets and smartphones so you can always be connected.

Google Hangouts is Google's answer to Microsoft's Skype. Calls or conferencing between computers are free. You can call land lines in the US and Canada at no charge. You can purchase credits to call overseas at very reasonable rates.

In the last section of the chapter, we look at the enterprise version of Google Drive.

Chapter 7: Using Google Docs and Drive

Understanding Google Docs and Google Drive

Google has built a great business by giving away very useful applications and tools. They make their money selling ad space on their search results and other applications such as Gmail. They also have a successful store, Google Play, similar to Amazon in that it sells movies, books, music, magazines and Android applications.

They give us tools that make the virtual office possible. Businesses live on documents. We create letters, plan with spreadsheets and communicate ideas with overhead presentations. We need to collect data using forms and we need to store that data and perhaps use it for analysis. Understand that these are all web based and you will need a web browser to access them. Google does have a Google Drive app that you can download to have local access by way of a special folder.

To use Google Drive and the contained Google Applications, you first need to go to http://google.com to sign up. You will pick a Gmail email address and a password. This single sign-in gives you access to all of Google's applications. It also writes a cookie that identifies you as you move between products. That is very convenient and is safe as long as you remember to log out, if you access Google on a public computer.

Google gives you 15GB of free space to store any document you might create and any other file you wish to upload. You can make folders to organize your mp3 music, images PDFs and other documents. They also give you free Apple and Android applications that allow you to access your files on tablets and smartphones. This offers a great way to move files from one device to another.

Here is what you see when you access Google Drive. It is called your dashboard. We will explore it in more detail later (*Figure 136*).

Chapter 7: Using Google Docs and Drive

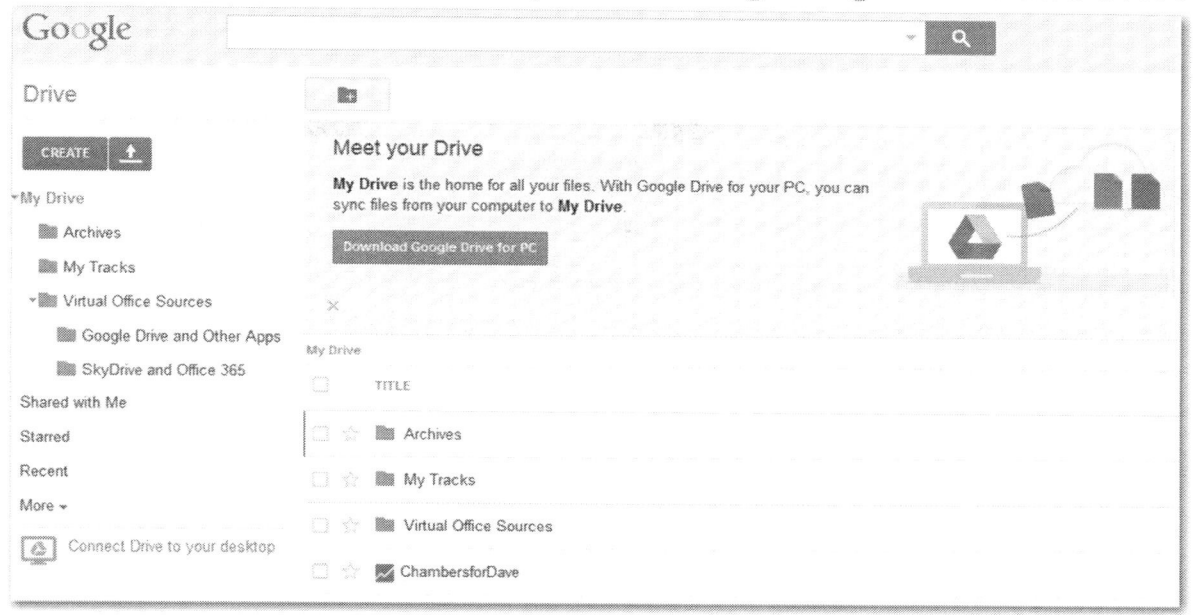

Figure 136: The Google Drive Dashboard

Google Desktop Drive

From the dashboard, click the **Download Google Drive for PC** button (*Figure 137*). This probably says something a little different if you have an Apple computer. Regardless, download and double click the file to install on your computer.

Figure 137: Download the Google desktop drive app

Once installed, you will have a new folder in your favorites at the top of Windows Explorer (*Figure 138*). This folder is linked in real time to your online, cloud based Google Drive. Any files you copy or drag into the folder will show up on your online Google Drive and any files you create online will show up here. It automatically syncs the two locations.

As mentioned, similar applications for your phone or tablet can make this connection.

Chapter 7: Using Google Docs and Drive

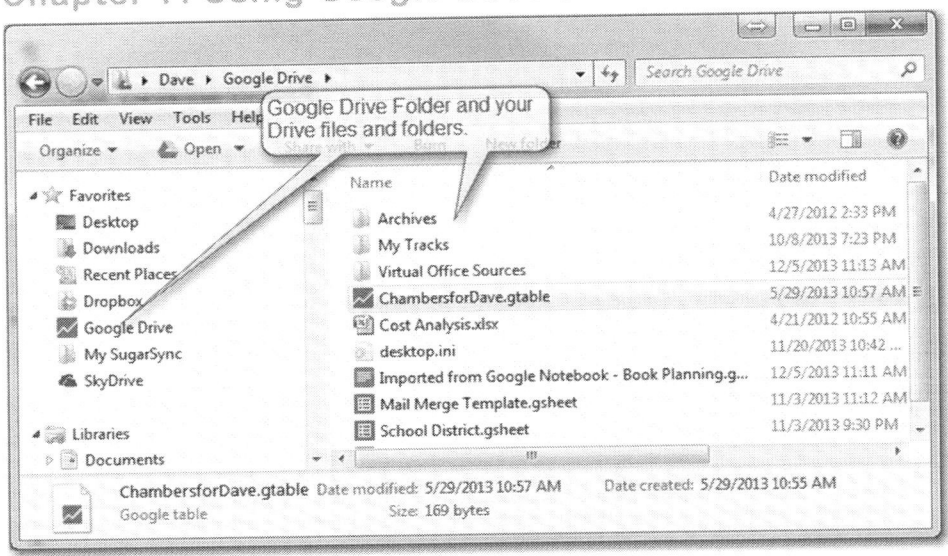

Figure 138: Your local folder linked to Google Drive

If you study the icons in your Google Drive folder (*Figure 138*), you will see differences. Some represent folders in Goggle Drive. Double-click and they open like any other folder. One file, **Cost Analysis.xlsx** is a spreadsheet created in Microsoft's desktop Excel program. The other blue and green square icons indicate documents that were created in the web version of Google Drive using a browser.

If we double click **Cost Analysis.xlsx**, it opens in our local copy of Office Excel. I am using Google Drive just for the storage of that file. I could convert it into a Google Spreadsheet file if I needed to edit it within Google Drive online.

School District.gsheet is a native Google Drive online file. I created it from my browser within Google Drive. There is no local or desktop app that can open it. However, if I double-click on its icon it opens in the browser just as if I had opened from my dashboard. Double-click and see this (*Figure 139*).

Figure 139: A Google Spreadsheet opened from the desktop folder

After adding files, either in the folder or web, it may take a few minutes for everything to sync. This is especially true if you upload large files for storage. Any file you have placed in Google Drive is available to you from any device that has a browser and Internet access.

Google Docs

While Google Docs are similar to Microsoft's Office's, they do not have all of the MS Office applications. Office was first introduced in 1990, 24 years ago (in 2014). The current Office Suite is the 15th generation of Office. Additionally, there are many things you can do in a desktop application you simply cannot do in a web based one. Google Docs are not as rich and full featured as Office desktop applications.

However, the core functionality is there and will satisfy 98% of the tasks for which most of us use Microsoft Office. If you have Microsoft Office installed and you need the missing functionality, first create the document Microsoft application and then upload and convert into Google's format.

If you have a lot of Microsoft Office documents and you wish to abandon using desktop Office and instead only use Google Drive, you can upload and convert them into Google's format. Realize that you may lose some functionality, such as macros and any VBA programming (automation) in the original document. While you can convert them back into Office format by downloading them as a Microsoft Office file, this round trip conversion does not restore the missing original features and, sometimes, formatting. You might want to back up the Office created originals in another folder on Google Drive before converting.

What applications are missing?

If you purchased Microsoft Office, the applications you get vary according to the edition you purchased. The free starter version you get on a new computer contains only three apps: Word, Excel and PowerPoint. These are the same as you get on Google Drive. The Professional Plus Office suite contains 10 applications.

Missing from Google, are the Microsoft applications **OneNote**, **Outlook**, although Gmail works as well, if not better, **Publisher**, **Access**, **InfoPath**, **Lync** and **SharePoint Workspace**. While all of these missing applications are sometimes useful, the question is, "Do you use them?" The core applications in Google Drive are the workhorses for most offices and may do well enough.

Understanding the Google Drive Dashboard

A single screen, the Google Drive Dashboard, gives you access to all of your files and folders (*Figure 140*).

It also allows you to:

- Create new files.

Chapter 7: Using Google Docs and Drive

- Organize your files into single or multiple folders.
- Share files with others for collaboration.
- Make files private or public. You can send a link to a public file to anyone.
- Delete, and if necessary, recover any file.
- You can give access to all or part of your desktop to anyone else such as an assistant. Control access anyway you wish.

The Desktop is your gateway to all of Google Drive's functionality.

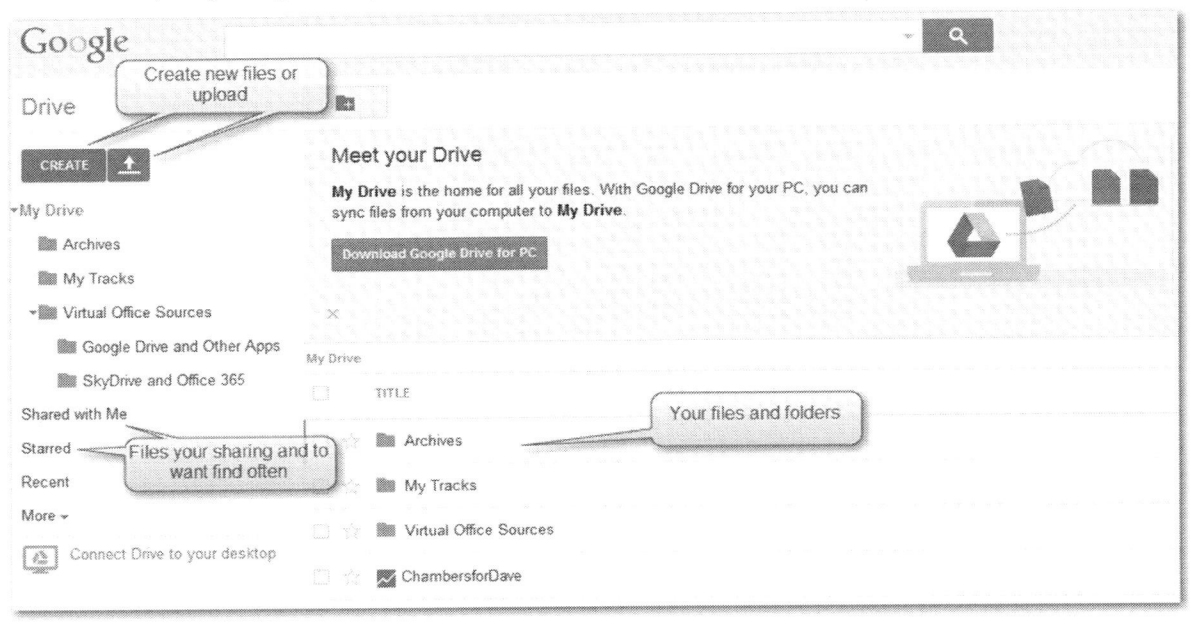

Figure 140: The major functions of the Desktop

You can also switch to a grid view of your files and folders (*Figure 141*).

Chapter 7: Using Google Docs and Drive

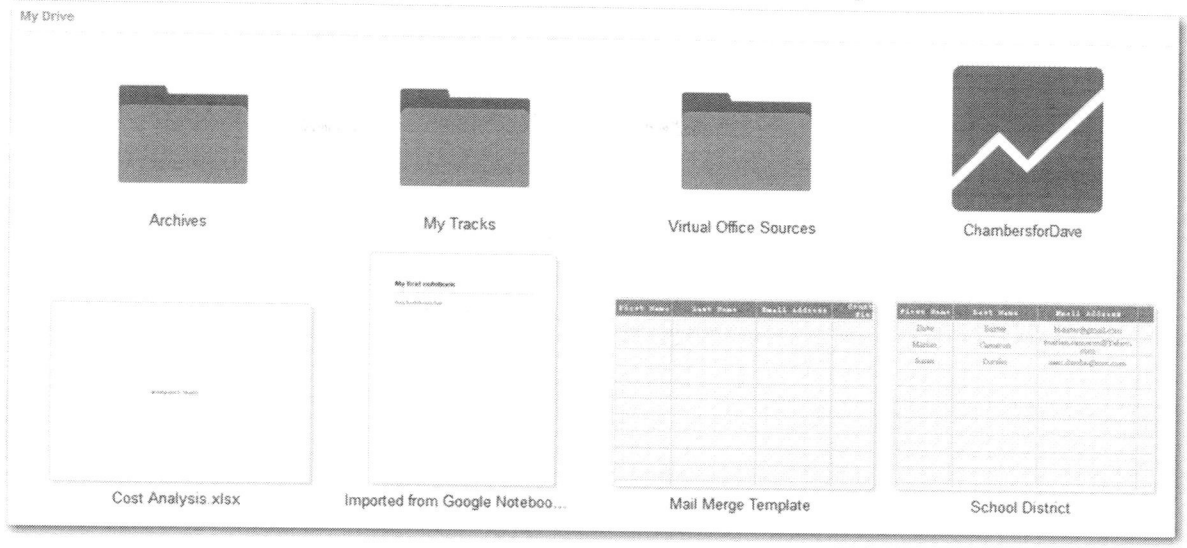

Figure 141: The grid view of your files and folders

There are a few settings you may need to check (*Figure 142*). Time zones become important if you work across them. You reach your setting by clicking the small gear icon in the upper right. Some settings, not shown, would force all Office Word, Excel and PowerPoint files you upload to be automatically converted. Great idea if you have several thousand. You can toggle this on or off.

Figure 142: General dashboard settings

How to Move Your Expensive Office to the Free Cloud

105

Chapter 7: Using Google Docs and Drive

Google Templates and Add-Ons

There are hundreds of templates and add on features you can use with Google Drive. To see these you click the **Create** button and choose **Connect more apps** (*Figure 143*).

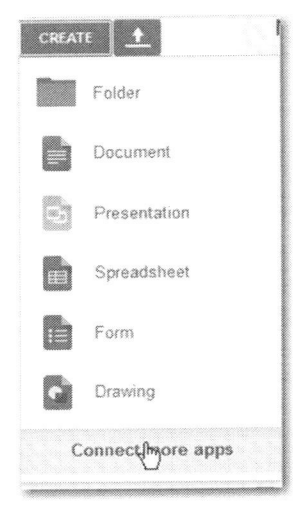

Figure 143: Adding add on apps to Drive

These apps enhance Google Drive. For example, free faxing sounds like a good idea. I can click on the **HelloFax** icon (*Figure 144*) to see the details and many times a video explaining what this add on does and why I would want it.

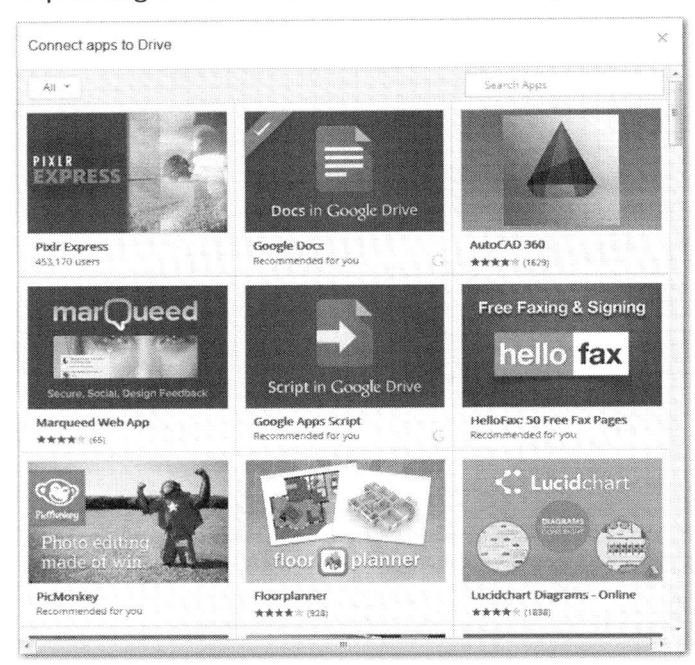

Figure 144: The first page of the many add on programs for Google Drive

Clicking the icon, opens the details screen (*Figure 145*). It seems the 50 free faxes apply only if you sign up for the HelloFax service as a new customer. However, create a fax in Document, signing and the sending it sounds great. They even email you incoming faxes.

I know little about HelloFax and am not promoting them, but there are some very interesting extensions, or add on applications, for Google Drive.

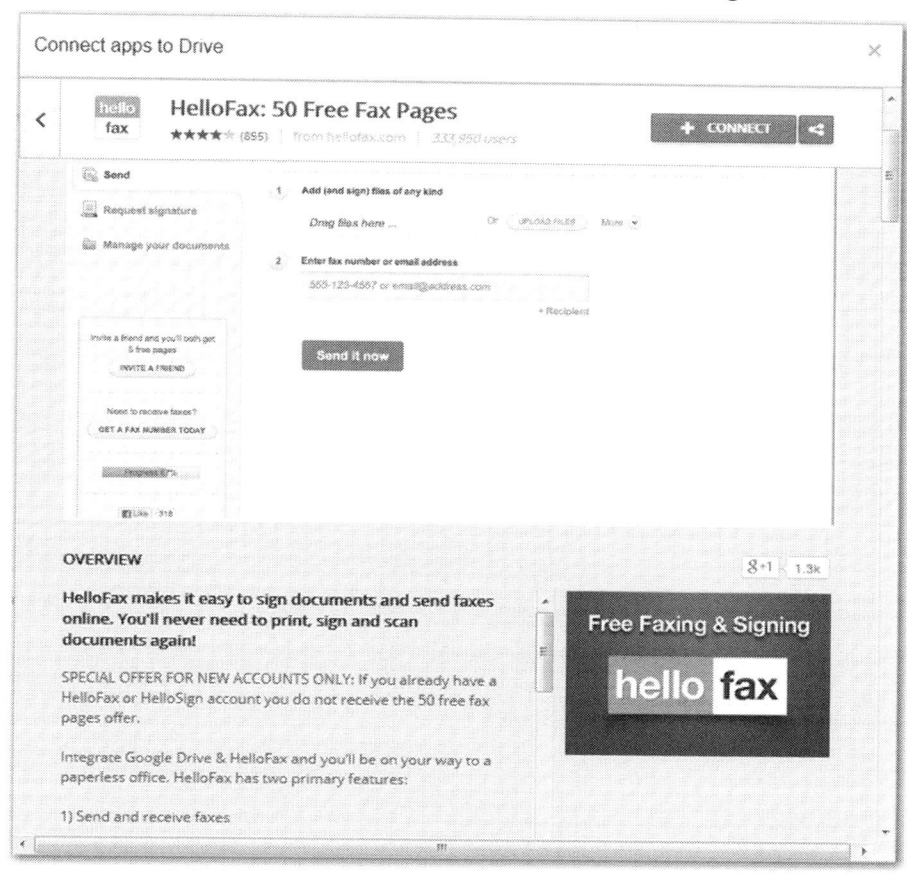

Figure 145: Details on the HelloFax application

Using Document

Document is Google's version of Microsoft Word and emulates most of the menus and techniques. You start by clicking the **Create** button in the upper left and then choosing **Document** (*Figure 146*).

Chapter 7: Using Google Docs and Drive

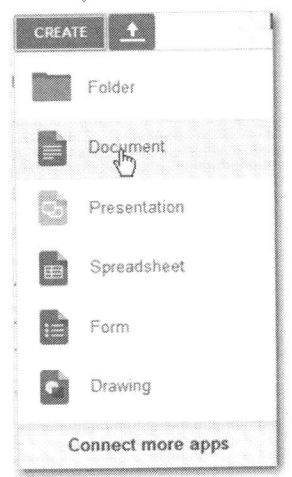

Figure 146: Opening a new document

Creating a New Document

This will open a new document page (*Figure 147*).

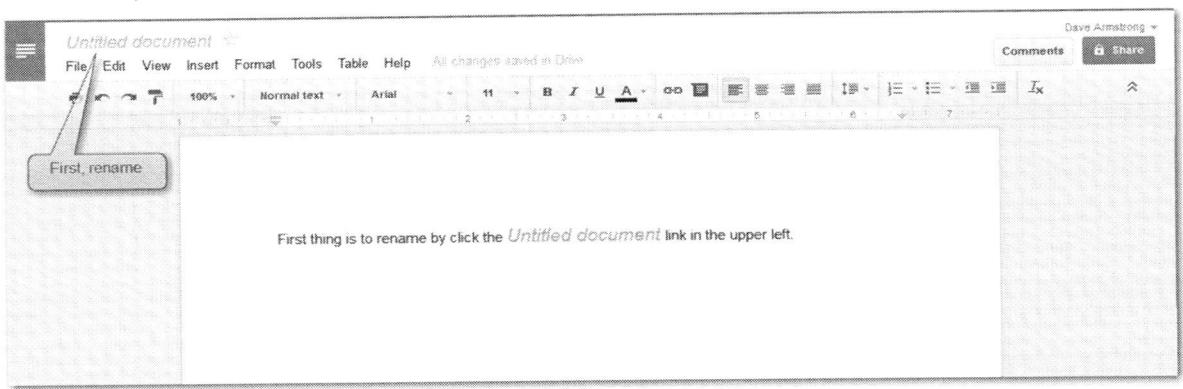

Figure 147: A newly opened Google Document

First, give your document a meaningful name. You do not have to explicitly save it, as Goggle Drive automatically saves every few seconds. However, you still have undo and can revert to any previous versions.

Notice, the formatting bar. It is almost identical to the one in Word. One useful feature that Word does not have is the **Paint Format**. Highlight the text that contains the formatting you want to copy and then select the **Paint Format** button. Then drag over the new text and replace its formatting with what you originally selected.

Like Word, Document has a set of styles (*Figure 148*). When possible, use these instead of direct formatting. While the selection of styles is limited compared to Word's styles, they do an adequate job for most documents.

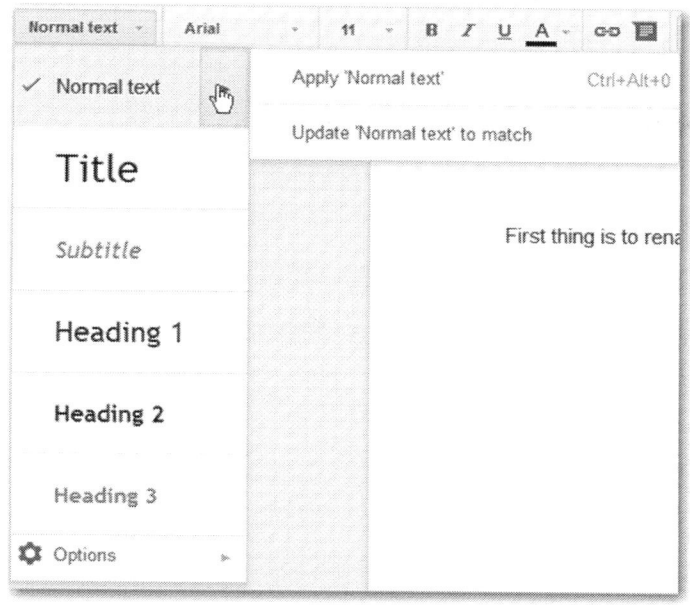

Figure 148: Built in styles that you can modify

This book cannot teach word processing in any real depth and I am assuming you have previously created a word processor document. Google Documents is a close copy of Microsoft's Word. If you already know Word, you will feel very comfortable. If not, any basic, entry level book will get you up to speed.

Most undo and redo, text formatting, alignment, linking and insertion can be done from the toolbar at the top of the screen (*Figure 149*).

The Document Toolbar

Figure 149: The Document toolbar

More depth and more choices reside in the dropdown menus above the toolbar. While we need not drill down into every menu choice, let's explore the menus and their features.

The Document Menus

Chapter 7: Using Google Docs and Drive

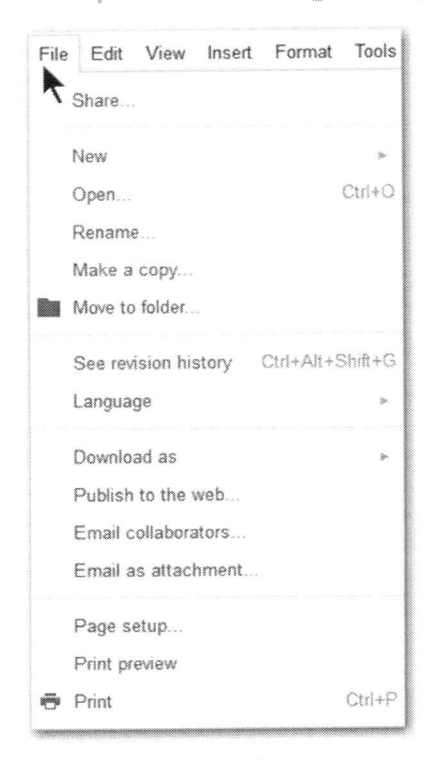

Figure 150: Document's File menu

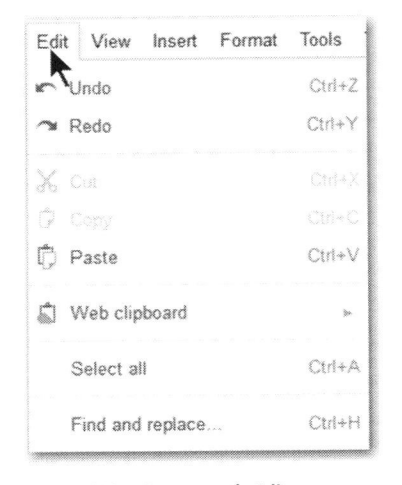

Figure 152: t Document's Edit menu

The **File** menu is almost the same on all of the Google Drive Apps. You can **Share** with others. We will cover sharing and collaboration in another topic below. You can **Rename** or move to another folder. You can **Email** and change the **Page setup.**

Use **See revision history** to see all previous changes by you or others. You can revert to any previous version.

While you can do most editing from the toolbar, the **Edit** menu gives you access to the keyboard shortcuts. You can also **Find and replace** or just find. You can select any text and save it to the **Web clipboard** and you can save multiple snippets. Later, when you need the text, you can select one of these snippets to paste.

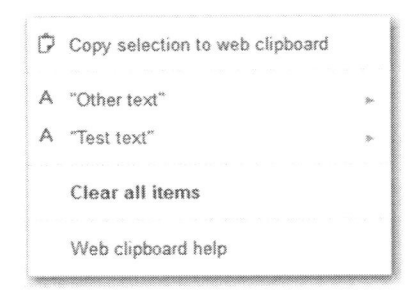

Figure 153: Document's Web clipboard with two snippets

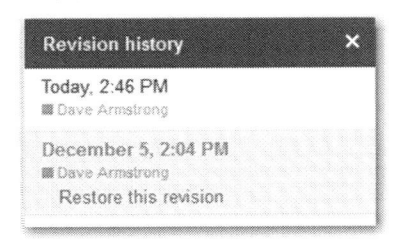

Figure 151: Revision history

How to Move Your Expensive Office to the Free Cloud
110

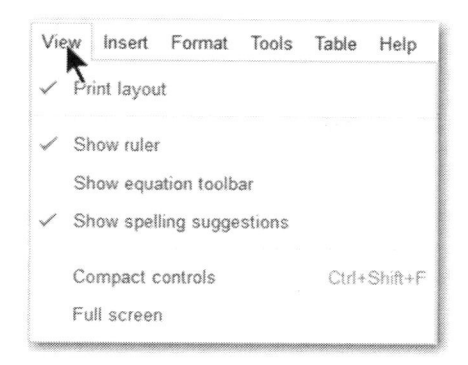

Figure 154: Document's View menu

The **View** menu can turn on or off the **Show spelling suggestions**. You can also hide the menus at the top with **Compact controls** to gain a little more space. **Full screen** eliminates the browser, menus and toolbar to give you even more space. The esc key returns to regular view.

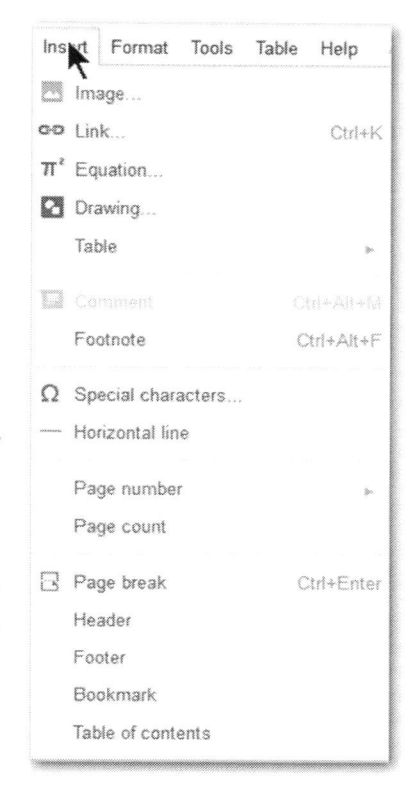

Figure 155: Document's Insert menu

The **Insert** menu allows you to insert an **Image**, web **Link**, math **Equation**, a previously drawing created in the Google app **Draw** or a **Table**. Add a **Page number**, **Page break**, a **Header** or **Footer** and even a **Table of contents**.

Almost anything you do with the Microsoft Word insert menu, is here.

Chapter 7: Using Google Docs and Drive

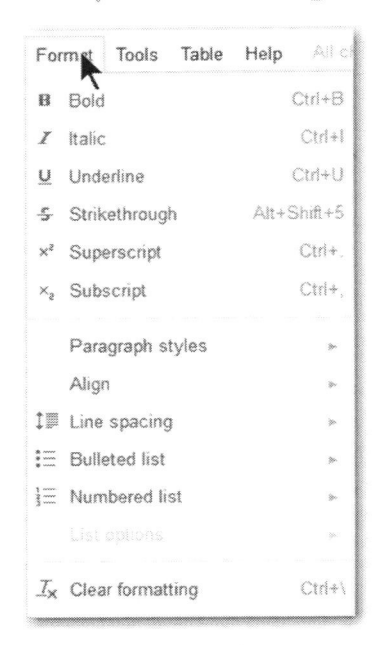

Figure 156: T Document's Format menu

Most formatting can be done with the toolbar. However, the **Format** menu gives you more choices in some instances, plus, it helps you learn the keyboard shortcuts.

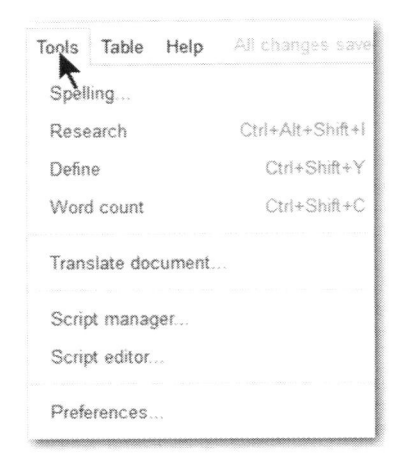

Figure 157: Document's Tools menu

The **Tools** menu is similar to the other Google Docs. You can check your document's **Spelling**, **Research** the web without leaving the document and you can insert anything found. Look up spelling and meaning in the **Define** option, as well as, a thesaurus. **Translate document** can produce some humorous translations, but is in most cases, understandable. You can program new features in Docs, if you know the JavaScript language using Script editor.

Chapter 7: Using Google Docs and Drive

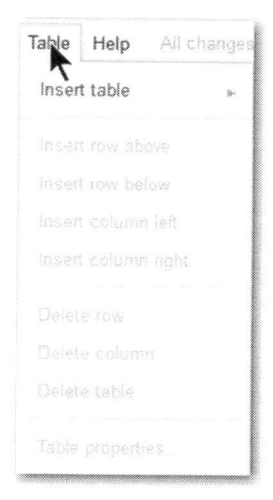

Figure 158: Document's Table menu

The **Table** menu allows you to insert and then format and edit a table.

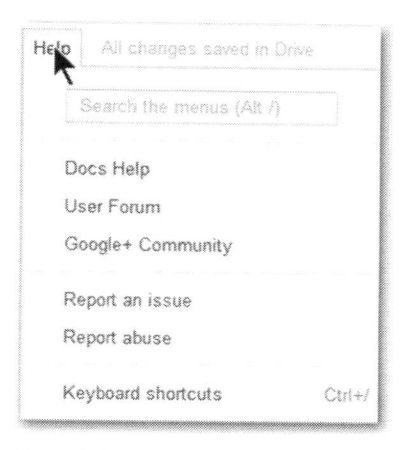

Figure 159: Document's Help menu

The **Help** menu provides excellent web based help. There is also a **User Forum** and **Google+ Community** where you can post questions and search for similar questions others have asked in the past.

If you use Documents a lot, it is worth learning the many **Keyboard Shortcuts**.

Click the small blue square icon in the top left to return to Google Drive. The file is automatically saved.

Using Presentation

Google Presentations is similar to Microsoft's PowerPoint without some of the advanced bells and whistles. Unlike Office's desktop version, you do not have to carry your slides with you as they are web based. Just connect to your Google Drive and start the slide show from any computer.

Creating a new Presentation

To create a new Presentation, click the Red **Create** button in the upper left and select **Presentation**. The first screen asks you to pick a template. Notice, that by default the presentation will be wide screen. You need to think about what kind of computer screen you will use. Older screens probably have a 4:3 ratio. If you do not like any of these templates, you can Import others (*Figure 160*).

Chapter 7: Using Google Docs and Drive

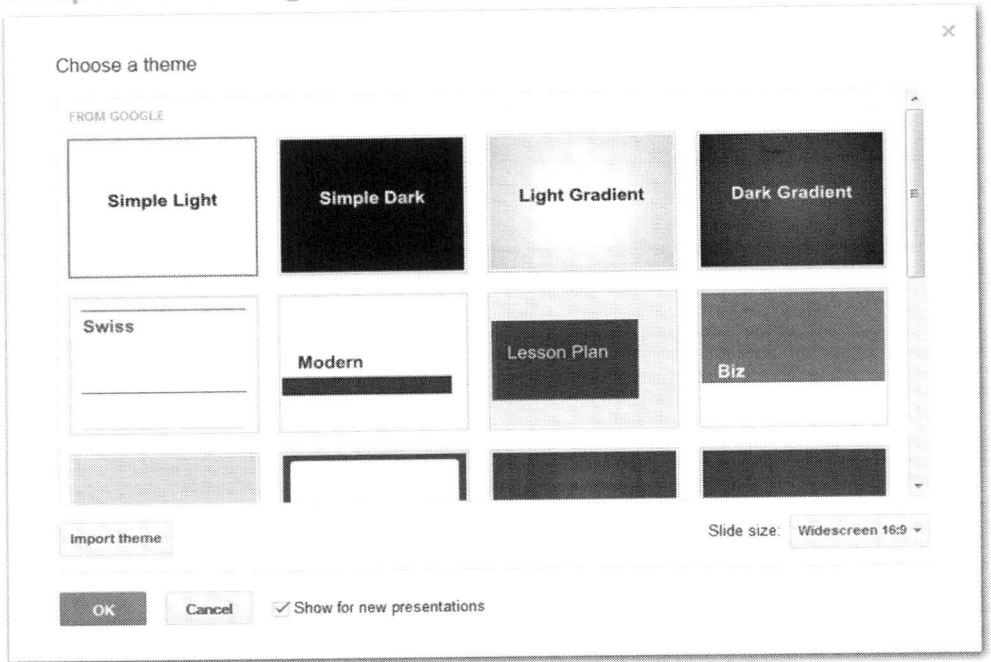

Figure 160: Pick a theme

You can turn this pick theme window off, if you want to start from scratch. Picking the **Lesson Plan** theme, my new Presentation screen opens (*Figure 161*).

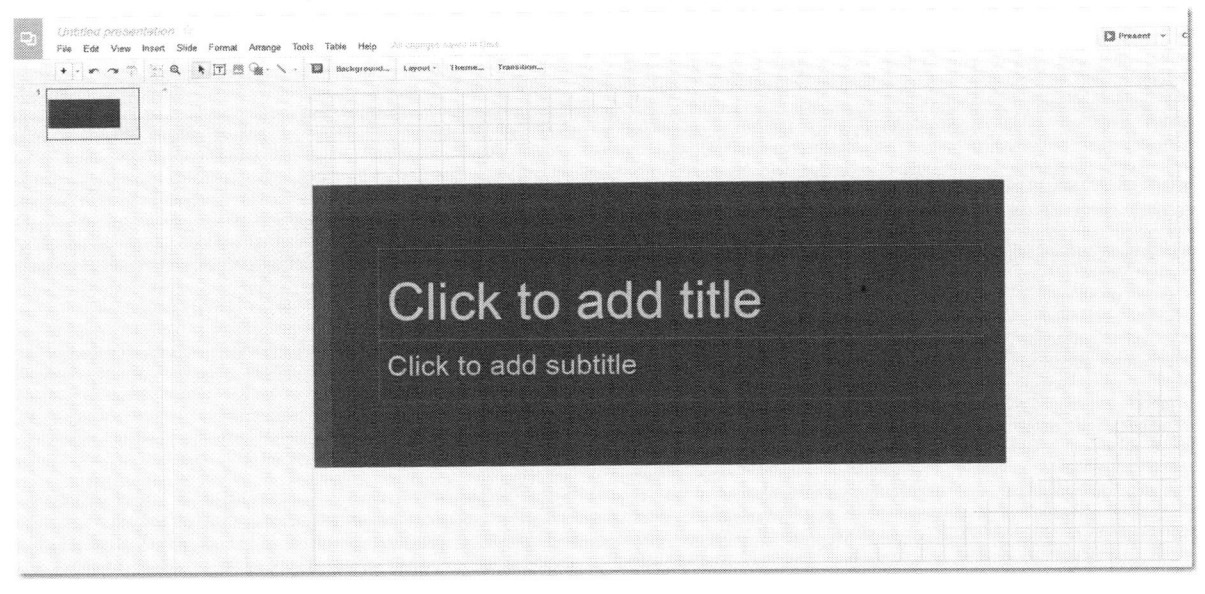

Figure 161: A start screen for a new presentation

If you are familiar with Microsoft's PowerPoint, you should feel at home. This is a title slide. Using the Insert menu, I could add new slides with a different format such as an interior slide.

Using the column on the left, you can rearrange the order of the slides or select a slide for deletion or duplication. Click once in the built-in text boxes and type to change content. You can also insert pictures, shapes and lines. You can assign different speeds of the transitions between slides and, at an any time, you can **Present** to test how the slides look full screen.

Clicking **Present** launches a separate browser window full screen and the slide show plays (*Figure 162*).

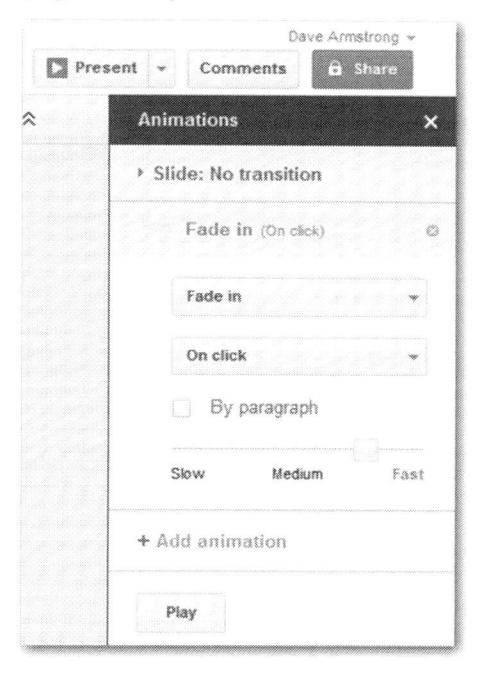

Figure 162: Changing animations and testing by clicking Present

As usual, Google presentation has copied Microsoft's PowerPoint. Any entry level book on PowerPoint, will get you up to speed.

Most slide layouts, do and undo, formatting and insertion can be done from the toolbar at the top of the screen (*Figure 163*).

The Presentation Toolbar

Chapter 7: Using Google Docs and Drive

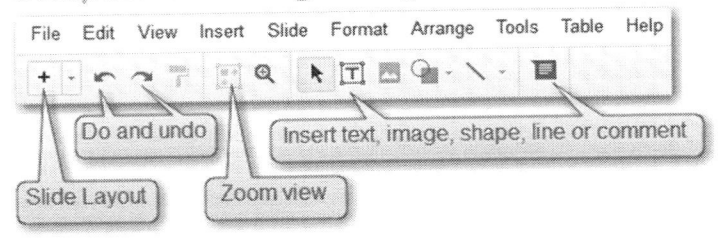

Figure 163: The Presentation tool bar

The Presentation Menus

More depth and more choices reside in the dropdown menus above the toolbar. Here is a high level view of the menus and their features.

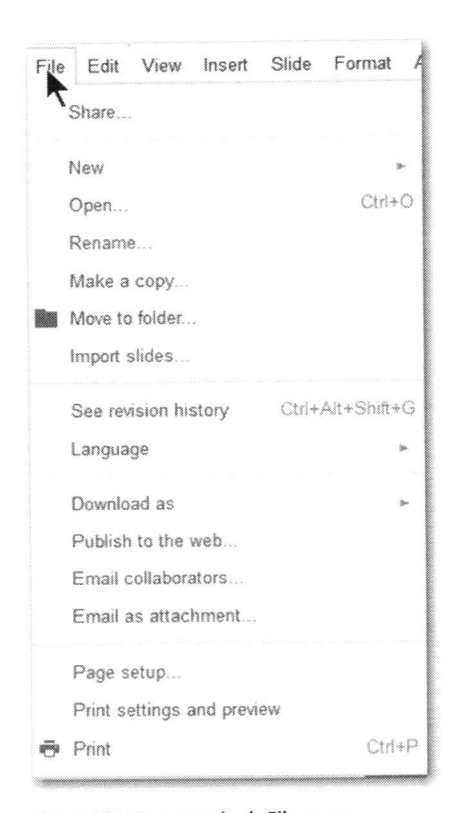

Figure 164: Presentation's File menu

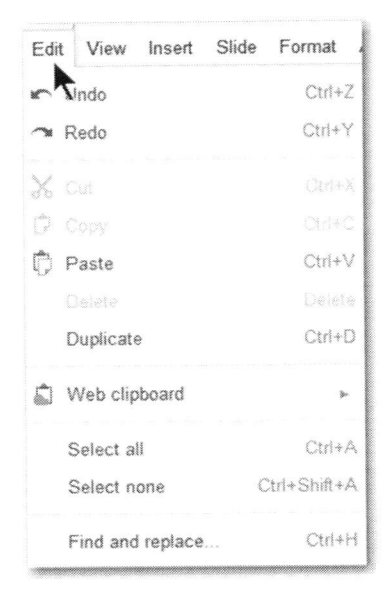

Figure 165: Presentation's Edit menu

Edit allows you to **Undo** and **Redo**. It allows you to select and **Duplicate** any object on the slide. You can **Find and replace** or just **Find** text.

The **File** menu allows you to **Share**, **Make a copy** and **Move to folders**. You can also **Download** into different formats, as well as, **Print**. You can **Import slides** from Microsoft's PowerPoint. Send a link to anyone that will start the slide show full screen.

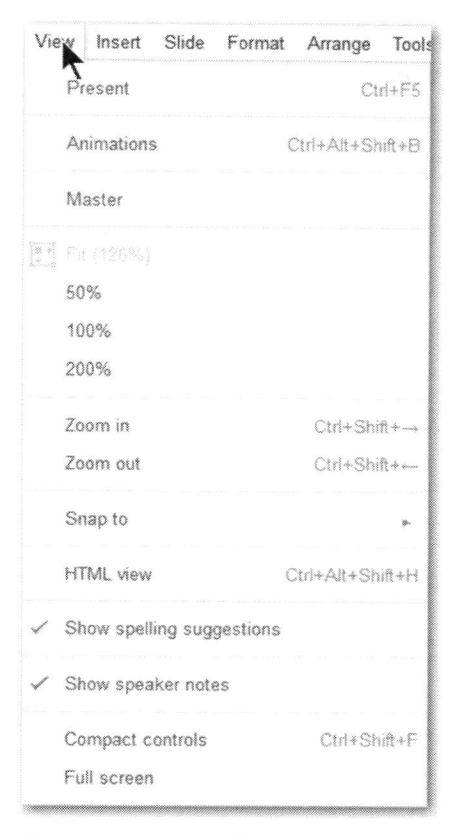

Figure 166: Presentation's View menu

In the **View** menu, use the **Zoom** features to enlarge or shrink your viewing area. You can turn on a **Snap to** a grid that helps align objects. **Html view** shows all slides as a web page.

You can toggle on or off spelling suggestions and speaker notes.

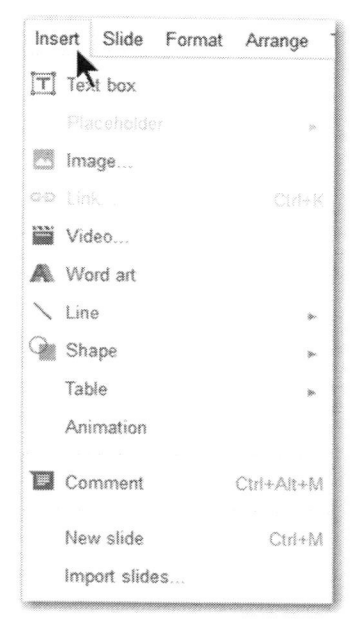

Figure 167: Presentation's Insert menu

Use the **Insert** menu to add an **Image**, **Text Box**, web **Link**, fancy text with **Word art**, a **Shape**, **Line** or **Table**.

Comments are notes about corrections or suggestions. These are great when you are planning or collaborating. They remain hidden when presenting and can be toggled on or off anytime.

Chapter 7: Using Google Docs and Drive

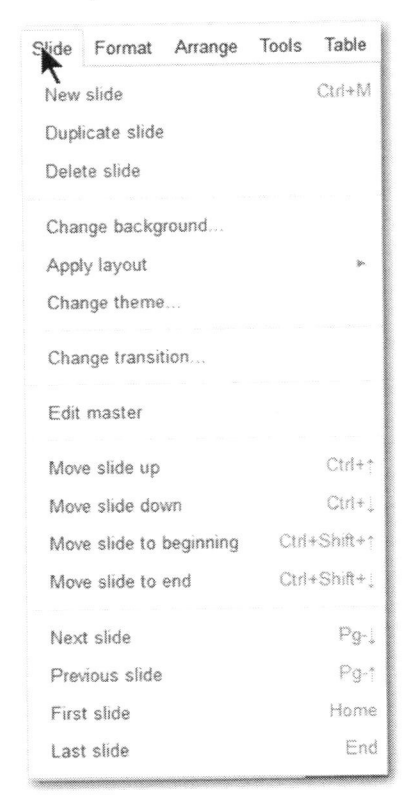

Figure 168: Presentation's Slide menu

While you can use drag and drop to rearrange slices, the **Slide** menu gives you more choices. It reveals the most common keyboard shortcuts you can use to speed up development.

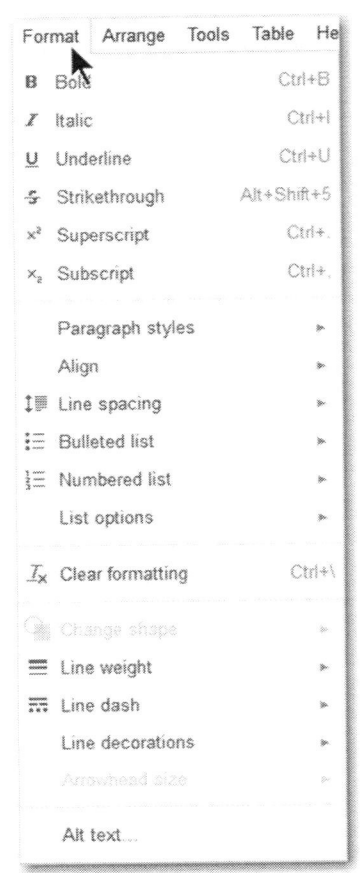

Figure 169: Presentation's Format menu

After selecting text or object, the **Format** menu allows you to format that selection. While some of these formatting options are on the tool bar, this menu gives you more choices.

Chapter 7: Using Google Docs and Drive

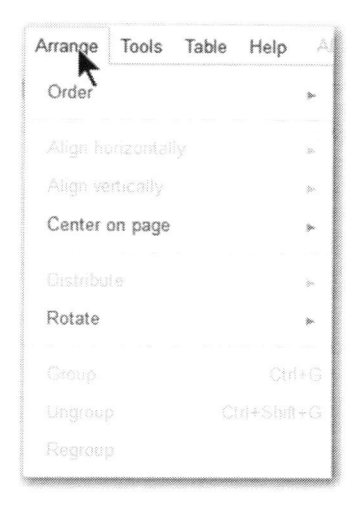

Figure 170: Presentation's Arrange menu

Figure 171: Presentation's Tools menu

We usually drag and drop items onto a slide. Once there, the **Arrange** menu allows you to precisely align the objects. You can rotate the object, make a group of objects equidistant from each other and bind objects into a **Group** to preserve their relative layout.

The **Tools** menu allows you to check **Spelling**, open a sidebar to **Research** and search the web for images, videos, quotes and citations. Once found, you can insert them into your slide. After selecting a text term, the **Define** menu opens a dictionary and thesaurus.

Preferences open an automatic substitution list. You can add to the list of substitution. Type (a) and © is substituted. Add your initials and substitute your spelled out name.

Chapter 7: Using Google Docs and Drive

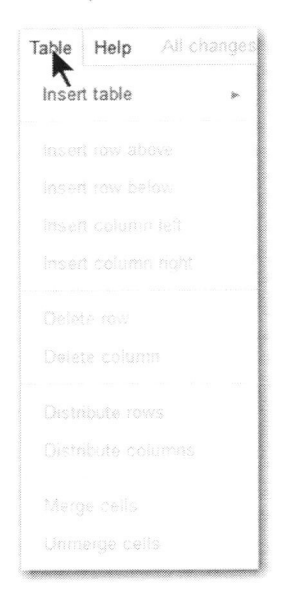

Figure 172: Presentation's Table menu

The **Table** menu allows you to first insert a table with a given number of rows and columns. You then can insert rows and columns or merge cells.

Figure 173: Presentation's Help menu

The **Help** menu provides excellent web based help. There is a **User Forum** and **Google+ Community** where you can post questions and search for similar questions others have asked in the past.

If you use presentation a lot, it is worth learning the many **Keyboard Shortcuts**. Keeping your fingers on a keyboard rather than reaching for a mouse, saves a lot of time and energy.

Using Spreadsheet

If you are familiar with Excel, you should feel right at home. The formatting features are the same as the other Google Drive apps. You have a neat border tool if you like to draw boxes around content. You can insert charts, sort and filter the data that shows up.

Creating a New Spreadsheet

You create a new Spreadsheet by selecting the **Create** button and then choosing **Spreadsheet**. It opens to look like what you see in (*Figure 174*).

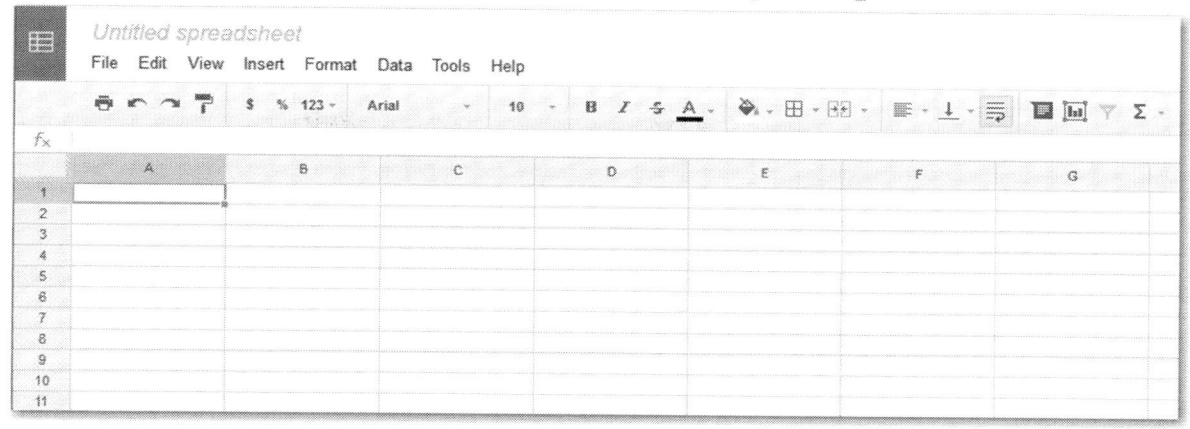

Figure 174: A new spreadsheet

The formulas echo Excel's methods. For example, enter an equal symbol followed by references to other cells mixed with operators such as +, - *, etc. (*Figure 175*).

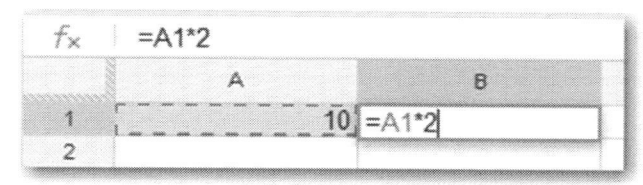

Figure 175: Adding a formula

This book is not a manual on how spreadsheets work. There are plenty of good books that teach how to create that mixture of literal data that you enter and formulas that manipulate the data. Spreadsheets are powerful tools for calculating raw data into a meaningful state.

The good news is that Google has copied the leading spreadsheet, Microsoft's Excel. Any entry level book on Excel will help you understand Google's Spreadsheet.

The Spreadsheet Toolbar

Most undo and redo, formatting, alignment and insertion can be done from the toolbar at the top of the screen (*Figure 176*).

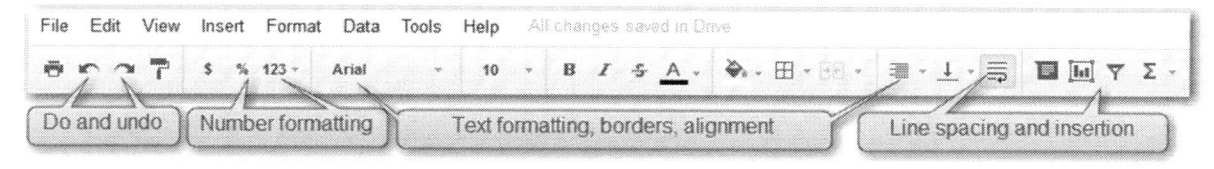

Figure 176: Spreadsheet's toolbar

The Spreadsheet Menus

Chapter 7: Using Google Docs and Drive

More depth and more choices reside in the dropdown menus above the toolbar. While we will not drill down into each menu choice, here is a high level view of the menus and their features (*Figure 177* through Figure *186*).

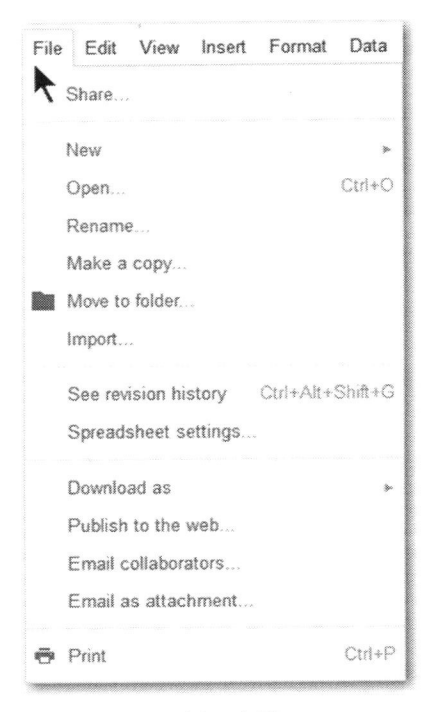

Figure 177: Spreadsheet's File menu

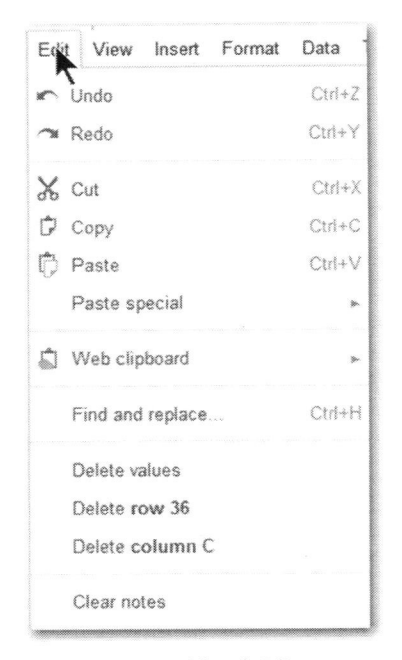

Figure 179: Spreadsheet's Edit menu

The **File** menu is almost the same on all of the Google Drive Apps. You can **Share** with others. You can **Rename** or move to another folder. You can **Email** and change the **Page setup.**

Use **See revision history** to see all previous changes by you or others. You can revert to any previous version.

While you can do most editing from the toolbar, the **Edit** menu gives you access to the keyboard shortcuts. You can **Find and replace** or just find. You can save text snippets to the **Web clipboard.** Later, when you need the text, you can select one of these snippets to paste.

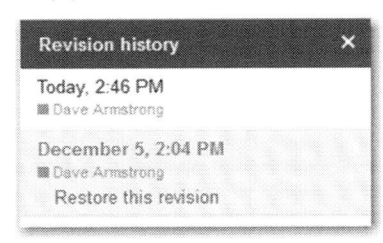

Figure 178: Spreadsheet's Revision history

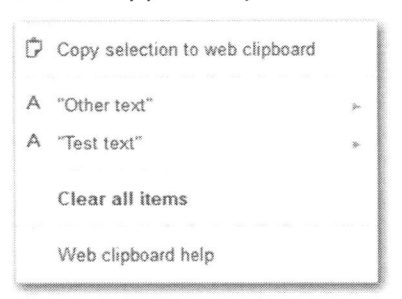

Figure 180: Spreadsheet's Web clipboard

You can **Delete Row**s, **Column**s or **Values**.

Chapter 7: Using Google Docs and Drive

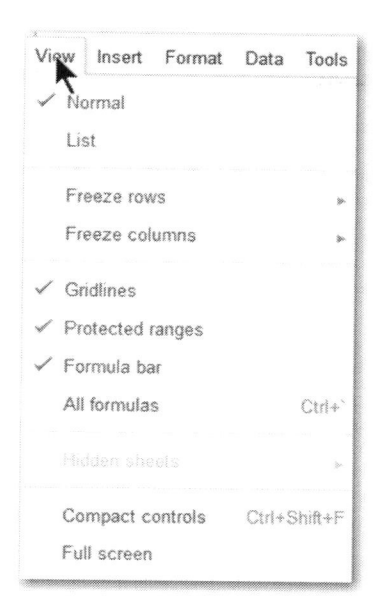

Figure 181: Spreadsheet's View menu

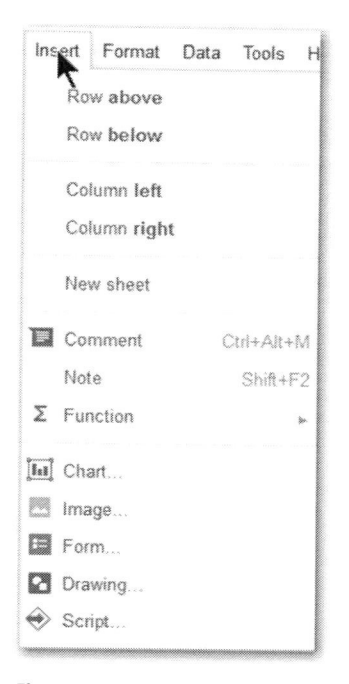

Figure 182: Spreadsheet's Insert menu

The **View** menu can **Freeze rows** or **columns**, great for scrolling spreadsheets. You can hide the menus at the top with Compact controls to gain a little more space. **Full screen** eliminates the browser, menus and toolbar to give you even more space. The Esc key returns to regular view.

You can toggle on or off the **Gridlines**, **Protected ranges** and a special **Formula bar** that helps in creating formulas.

Normally, you just see the results of formulas, but if you toggle on **All formulas,** you see the all formulas in their individual cells.

The **Insert** menu allows you to insert a **Function**, **Chart**, **Image and Form** for entering data**,** or a **Drawing** previously created in another Google app **Draw**. You can add rows and columns.

Almost anything you do with the Microsoft Excel insert menu, is here.

Chapter 7: Using Google Docs and Drive

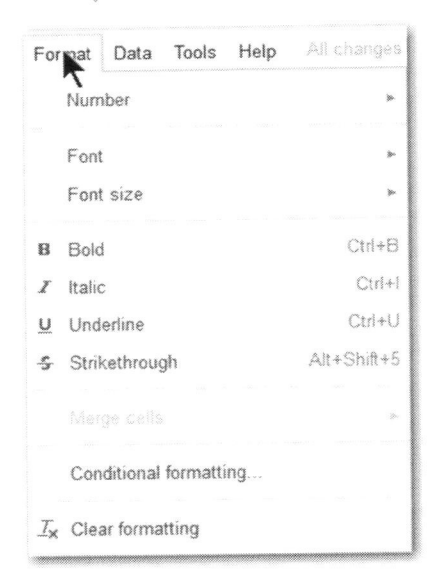

Figure 183: Spreadsheet's Format menu

While most formatting can be done with the toolbar, the **Format** menu gives you more choices in some instances, plus, it helps you learn the keyboard shortcuts.

Conditional formatting can change formatting based on a value. For example, negative numbers could be made red.

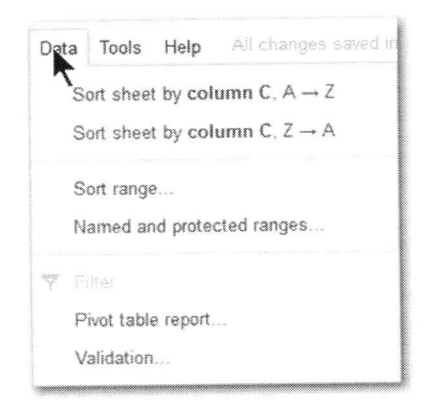

Figure 184: Spreadsheet's Data menu

Sorting is the main feature of the Data menu. However, you can create validation rules with messages prompting correct values, i.e., "Please enter a number between 1 and 10" when a user enters "Dave".

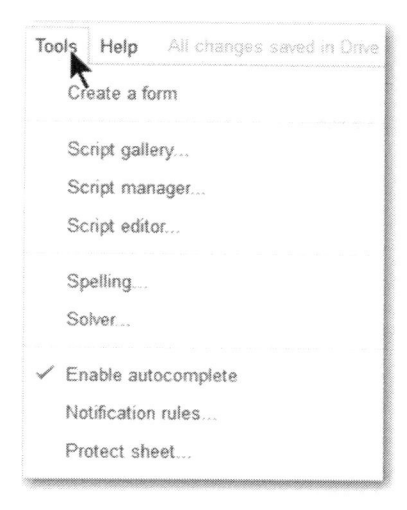

Figure 185: Spreadsheet's Tools menu

The **Tools** menu is similar to the other Google Docs. You can create a form that will collect data, more later when we study forms. You can Look up spelling and meaning, as well as, a thesaurus. Solver can help you set rules for cell automation, i.e., "Don't show 0.00 in empty cells."

Using the **Script editor**, you can program new features in Docs, if you know the JavaScript Languages.

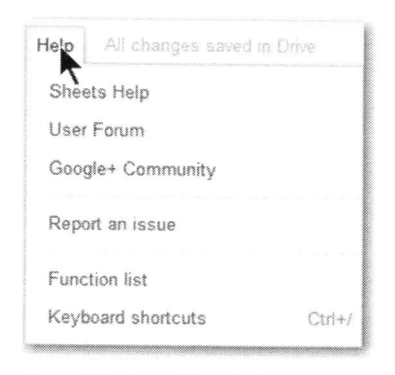

Figure 186: Spreadsheet's Help menu

The **Help** menu provides excellent web based help. There is a **User Forum** and **Google+ Community** where you can post questions and search for similar questions others have asked in the past.

Find a bug? **Report an issue** tells Google.

If you use Google Spreadsheets a lot, it is worth learning the many **Keyboard Shortcuts**.

Collaborating using Google Docs

Two or more people can be working on the same document at the same time. Each can see the other's modifications within seconds of the change they make. It could get a little confusing if several try to work on the exact same text, but it makes collaborative documents possible.

Sharing the Google Doc

Use the menu choices **File->Share...** Note, that we will use pointing arrow (->) to describe a series of menu choices. It means choose this menu first->then this one. Seeing the three periods after a choice, means that it will open a dialog or another screen which you will need to configure.

Here is the share screen (*Figure 187*).

Chapter 7: Using Google Docs and Drive

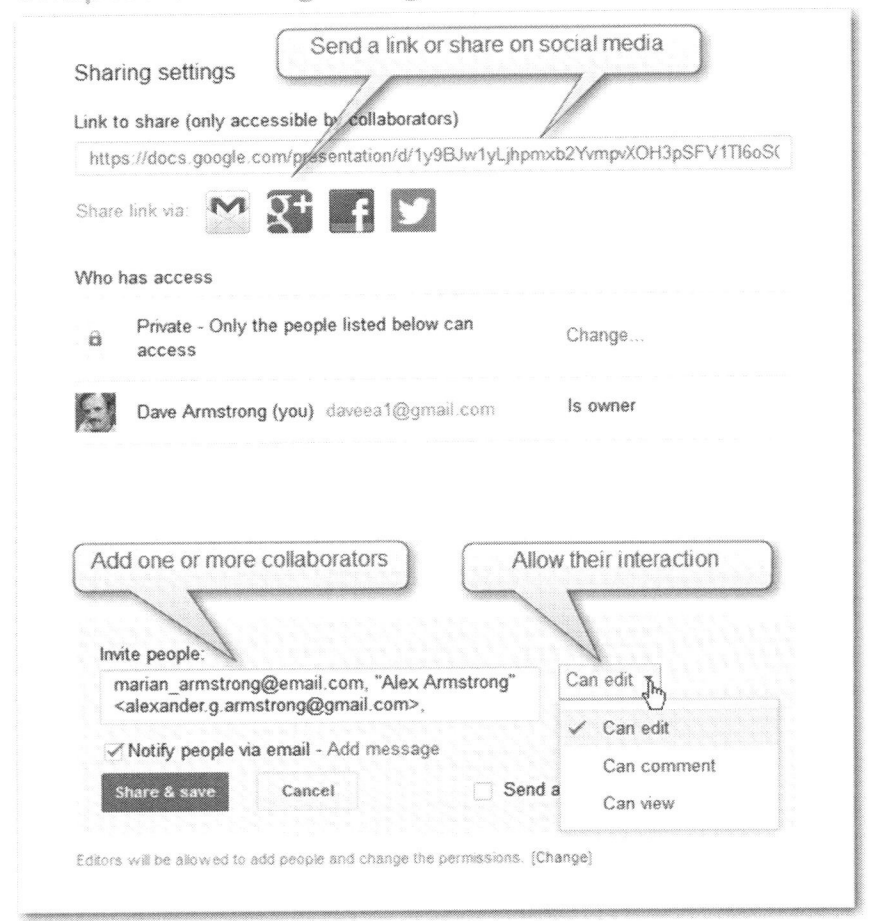

Figure 187: Sharing window

Notice, that you could change access to public and send the link to anyone you wish to view the document. They cannot make changes. You can also share the link by Google+, Facebook, and Twitter or open a Gmail message with the link embedded.

However, to give others the ability to edit the documents, you need to add their email addresses in the **Invite people** box. They do not have to be Gmail addresses, although, if they are, there are some advantages, as you will see.

In the **Can edit** dropdown, decide how they have access. To collaborate in editing, choose **Can edit,** the default.

You have the option to add a short message, telling them what the email is about. You might want to send a message to yourself, so as to have a copy of what they received. Notice in (*Figure 188*), we have added a day and time, **Tuesday at 10:00**.

Chapter 7: Using Google Docs and Drive

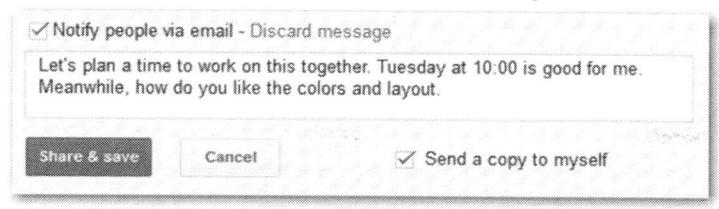

Figure 188: Adding an email note to the link

After the invitation is sent, the **Who has access** section changes to include all of the collaborator invitees. You now can reconsider what each invitee can do. Changing one of them to view, only might be an important decision (*Figure 189*).

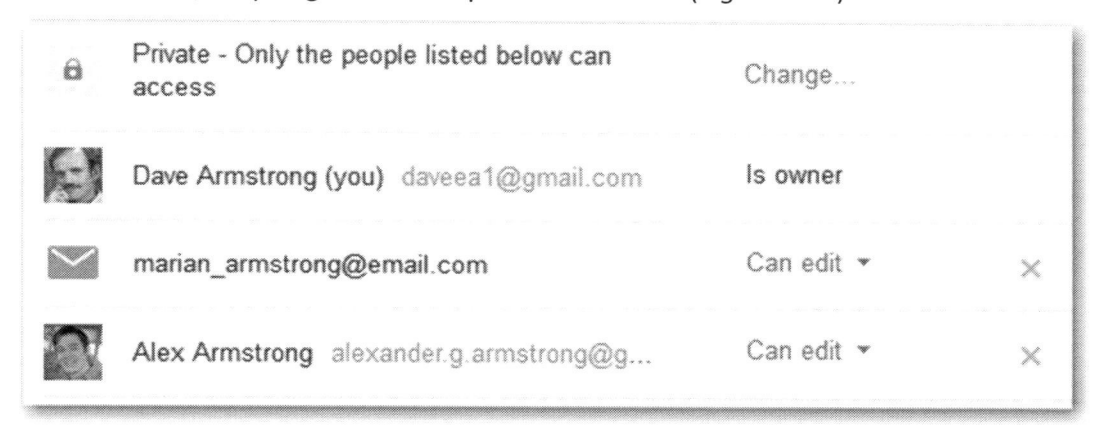

Figure 189: This document's collaborators

When the email arrives in Gmail, it finds the **Tuesday at 10:00** text and assumes it might be a calendar entry and will open up my Google Calendar to next Tuesday's date at the 10:00 slot. When Tuesday, at 10:00 arrives, I can open my calendar, click the link **Proto Presentation**, the presentation's name, and join the others in the collaboration (*Figure 190*).

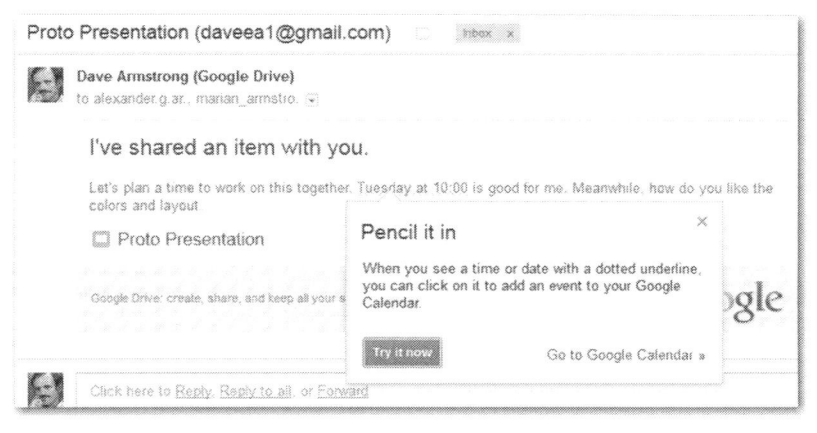

Figure 190: Gmail's version of the email sent

Chapter 7: Using Google Docs and Drive

Here is the same email seen in Microsoft's Outlook 2010. Outlook does not guess that there may be an appointment suggestion in the text, but you could drag the email to my Outlook calendar (*Figure 191*).

Figure 191: Outlook's version of the email sent

Page Setup and Printing Files

The menus **File->Page setup...** opens the **Page setup** screen that allows you to adjust your **Orientation**, **Paper size**, **Margins** and even the page's background color. It might be a good idea to set these at the beginning of the Document's creation, as doing so later may rearrange your content (*Figure 192*).

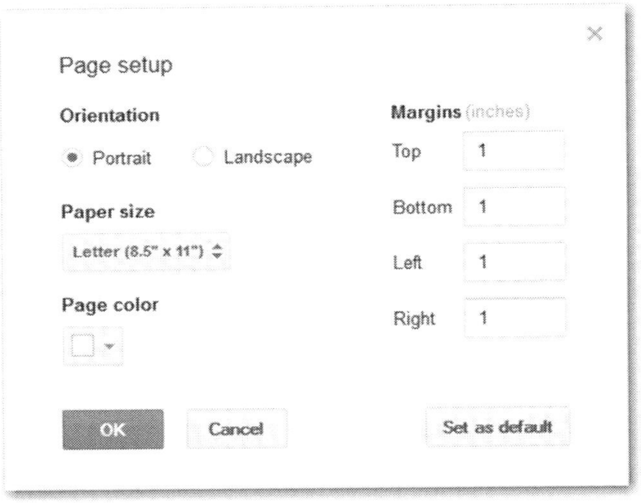

Figure 192: Setting the page setup

When you are ready to print, the menu choices **File->Print...** will open this screen which will allow you to pick a printer (*Figure 193*). Note, that you could save it as a PDF file back into your Google Drive and could then simply email it to anyone, including an HP ePrint printer that has been configured to receive email and print it's attachment. We will discuss printing using **Google cloud print** later in the chapter devoted to remote printing over the Internet.

Figure 193: Printing window

Want to see exactly what it will look like before printing? The menu choices **File->Print preview** will show a representation of what it will look like printed (*Figure 194*). If you have multiple pages, you can select any page(s) from the column on the left to print just those pages.

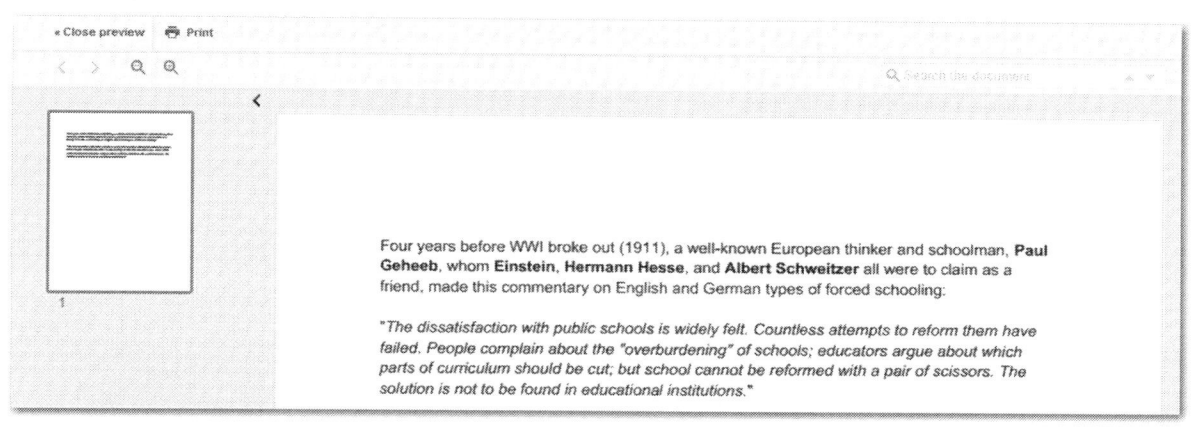

Figure 194: Printing preview

Using Form

On Google's help page for Forms, it says "*Google Forms is a useful tool to help you plan events, send a survey, give students a quiz, or collect other information in an easy,*

Chapter 7: Using Google Docs and Drive

streamlined way. A Google form can be connected to a Google spreadsheet. If a spreadsheet is linked to the form, responses will automatically be sent to the spreadsheet. Otherwise, users can view them on the "Summary of Responses" page accessible from the Responses menu."

Let me add, Google Form is a great way to collect email addresses. Additionally, you can answer the question, "What do your customers really want?" A survey will tell you in detail. If you wish, the survey answers can be stored in a Google Spreadsheet. Google will even give an analytic page with charts and a timeline of responses. Start by clicking the red **Create** button and selecting **Form**.

The opening screen has the link **Learn more,** if you want to view the step-by-step help files. Click **Get started** to open the form designer page (*Figure 195*).

Picking a From Template

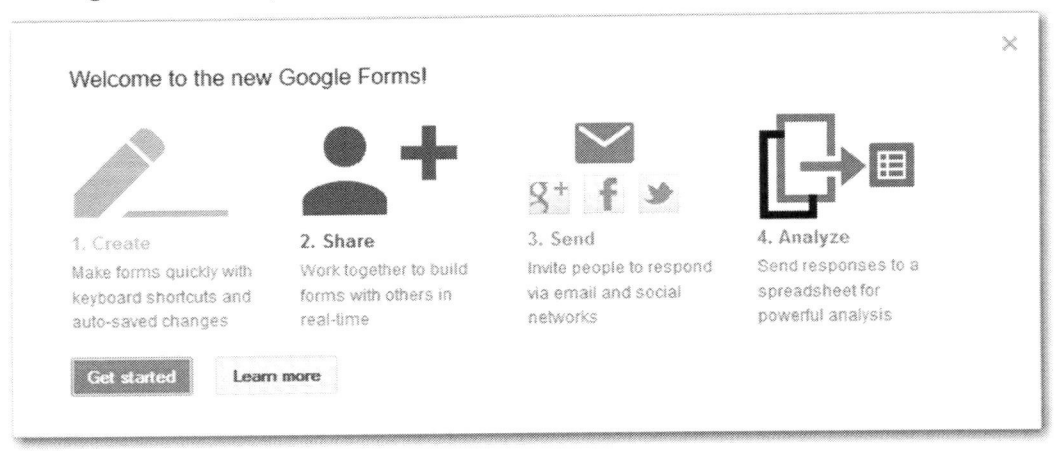

Figure 195: Form's welcome screen

To begin, we pick one of the many themes to dress the survey up. After naming the survey and picking a theme, click OK (*Figure 196*).

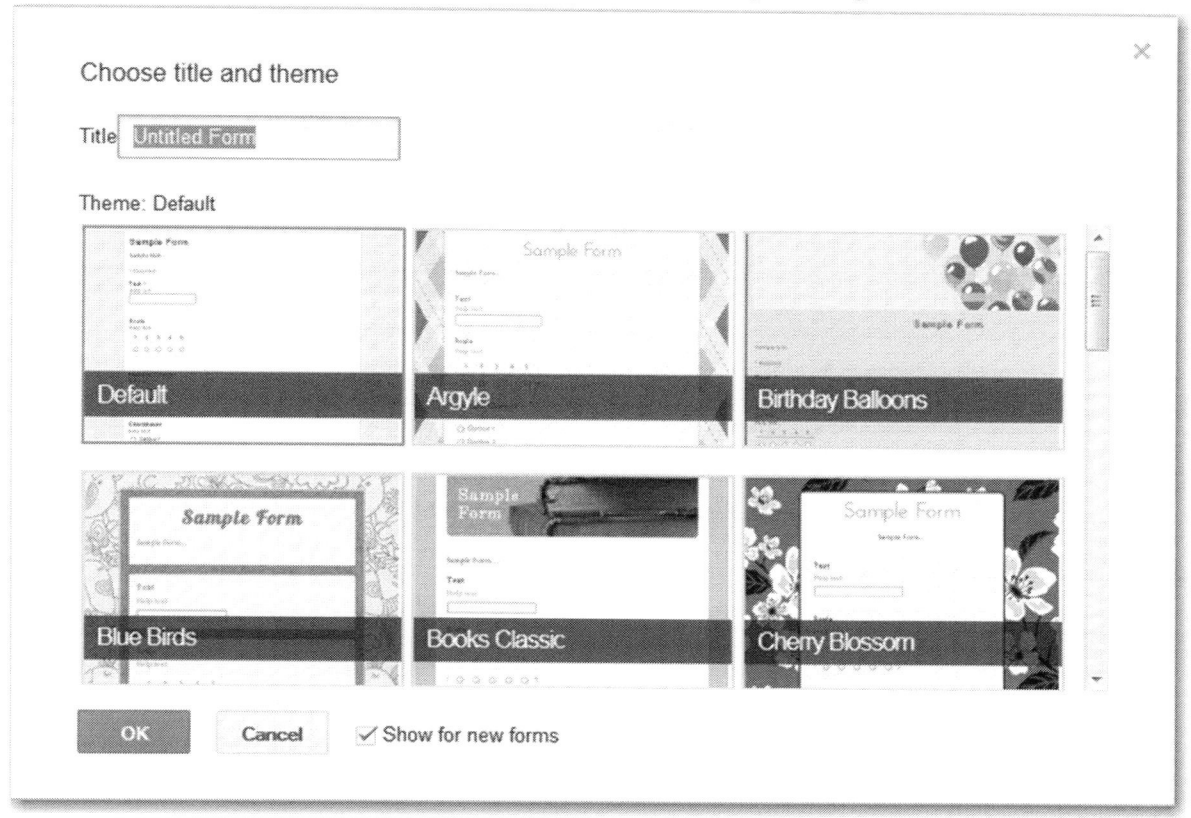

Figure 196: Pick a Form's template

Like most Google Docs, there is a toolbar with the most common editing choices (*Figure 197*).

The Form Toolbar

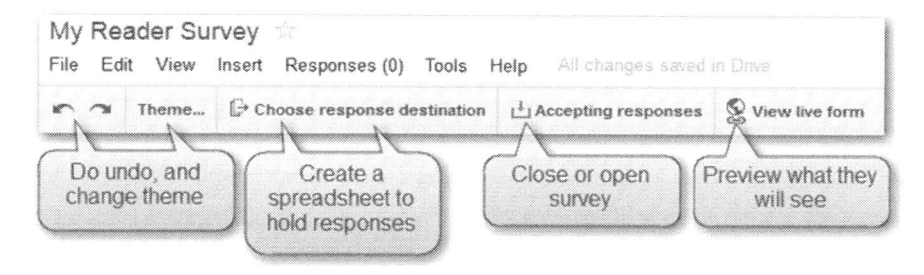

Figure 197: Form's toolbar

Google tries to put the most common feature needs on this toolbar. They have done a good job, as; you rarely have to use the menus. The first thing you do use the menus for, is to learn the keyboard shortcuts. You will find them a real timesaver, as you can keep your fingers on the keyboard. Having started with computers when everything was done from the keyboard, I still prefer using them.

Chapter 7: Using Google Docs and Drive

The Form Menus

The menus give us more choices and reveal the most important keyboard shortcuts (*Figure 198* through *Figure 206*).

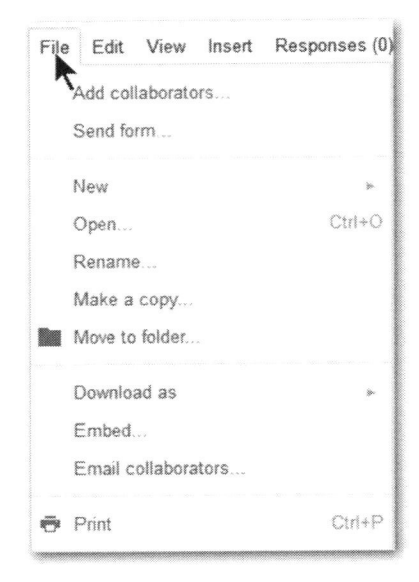

Figure 198: Form's File menu

This **File** menu looks almost identical to the other Google Docs. You can share by choosing **Add Collaborators**: you can **Send the Form**, **Rename**, **Make a Copy**, **Download as** in many downloaded formats.

You can embed this form in any page. If you have a website, adding a survey to one of its pages is a great way to engage visitors.

Figure 199: Form's embed code

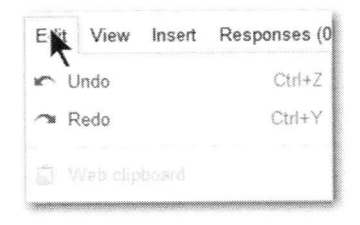

Figure 200: Form's Edit menu

The **Edit** menu only has **Undo** and **Redo** and the **Web clipboard**. Learn to use the keyboard shortcuts **Ctrl+Z** and **Crtl+Y** as it is much faster and your hands do not leave the keyboard.

You can select any text and save it to the **Web clipboard.** It can hold multiple items. Later, when you need the text, you can select one of these snippets to paste.

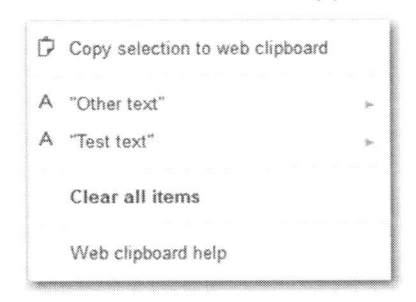

Figure 201: Form's Web clipboard with two snippets

Chapter 7: Using Google Docs and Drive

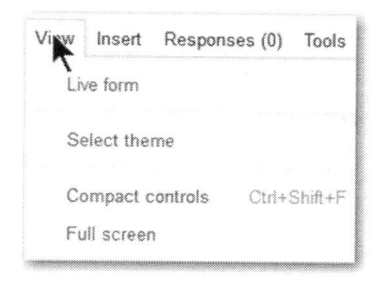

Figure 202: Form's View menu

Use the **View** menu to see what the form looks like to users and change the theme.

You can gain a little more screen real-estate by hiding the menus and toolbar.

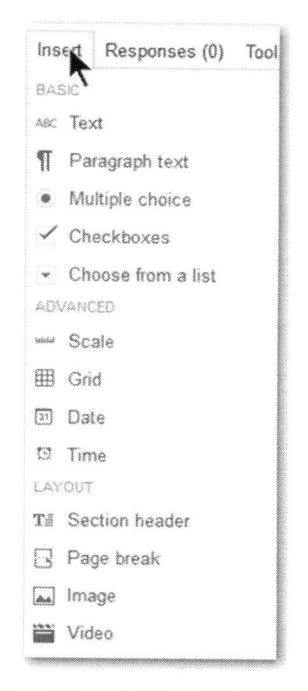

Figure 203: Form's Insert menu

You can **Insert** new differing types of questions such as free form **Text**, **Multiple choice**, **Checkboxes** and **Choose from a** (dropdown) **list**. You can group the questions together with a **Section header**, and a **Page break** to paginate between questions. You might, also, add an **Image** or **Video**.

Chapter 7: Using Google Docs and Drive

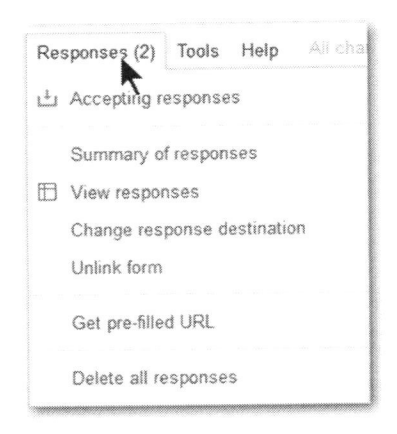

Figure 204: Form's Responses menu

Figure 205: Form's Tools menu

Unless you are a programmer, you will not need the **Script editor** or **Script manager**. In the hands of a skilled JavaScript programmer, you can build custom applications from Google Docs.

In the **Responses** menu, you can toggle the survey on or off. You can close or end a survey by creating a date and time to end the survey.

You can see a **Summary of responses** as a graphic analysis with charts and timelines or **View responses** in the attached spreadsheet. You can link and **Unlink** the spreadsheet and **Delete all responses,** if you want to reuse the survey.

Keyboard Tips

Learn keyboard shortcuts to really increase your productivity. Every time you move from the keyboard to the mouse, your mind has to reprogram your muscles. This increases both mental and physical exhaustion. As you use the menus, note and learn the keyboard shortcuts next to the most popular features.

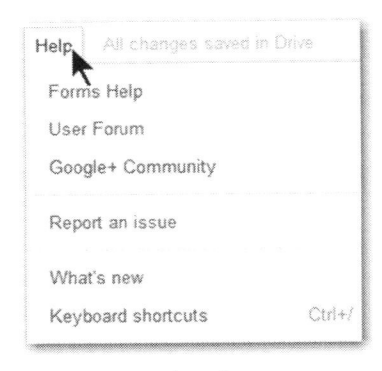

Figure 206: Form's Help Menu

The **Help** menu takes you to the web based help files from Google. There is also a **User Forum** and **Goggle+ Community** where you can ask and answer questions from others.

Creating Your First Survey Form

Let's create a form. After choosing a template, you get to the form creation page *(Figure 207)*.

By default, your first question is a **Multiple choice**, the most common type of question. This can be as simple as a Yes or No or it can have any reasonable number of choices. In programming parlance, these are called radio buttons. Only one out of the group can be checked. All choices are mutually exclusive.

The **Help Text** labeled box allows you to give a hint or add help to the question. For example, you might say "Choose only one answer" in a **Multiple choice** type question.

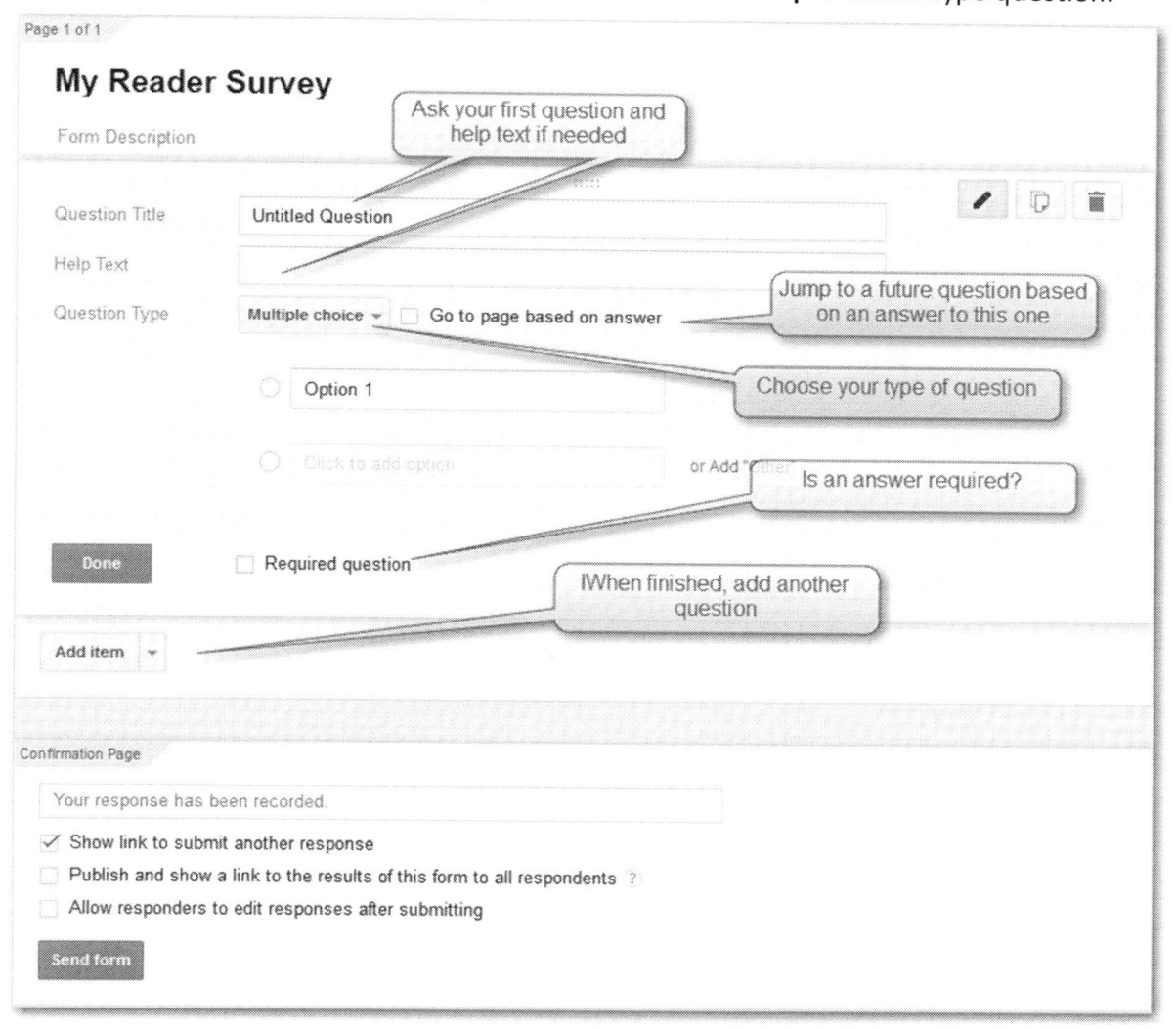

Figure 207: The new Forms screen

Notice, you can branch to another question based on an answer. For example, if they say they have no children, there is no point asking them how many, their names and ages.

Chapter 7: Using Google Docs and Drive

You can go to the page/question following the unnecessary questions. Do this branching after all of the questions are in place as it is then easier to visualize how the branching questions should work.

In (*Figure 208*), you can see my first question. I want to know how much they have completed in reading my book. I want it categorized in defined bands: **Less than 25%, About 50%,** etc. My hint (**Help Text**) suggests they use these bands. If they want to be more precise or just comment, I have added an **Other** choice with an accompanying text box. While text input is not as easy to quantify as the multiple choice, you might get better insight from this ad hoc textual input.

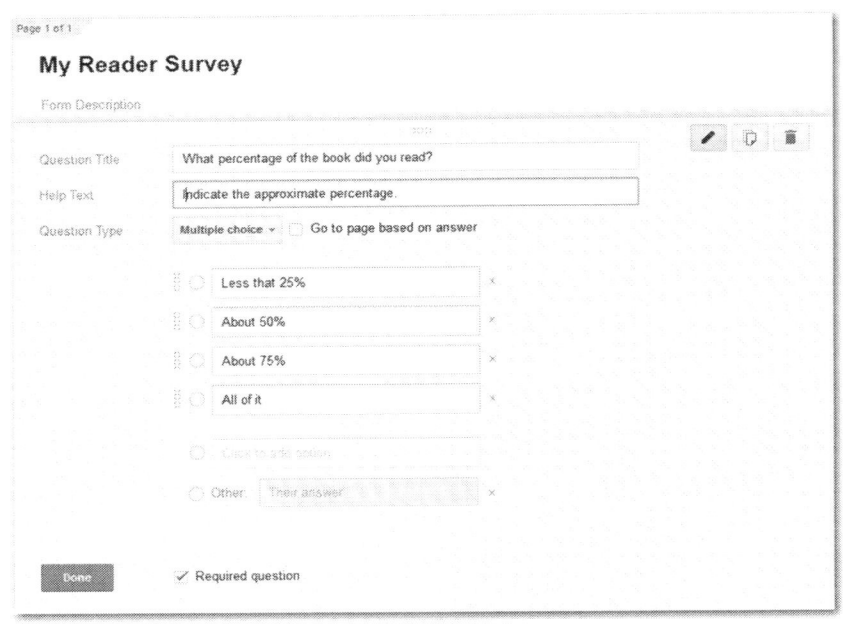

Figure 208: My first Form question

My second question wants to know how they read books. I might use this information to decide where to put my next effort. Should I skip printing a book, as most of my readers use Kindles (*Figure 209*)?

In this case, they may read on different devices, so I give them a list of checkboxes. They can select all or any combination of them. Also, note that I want the questions to always be answered, so I checked the **Required question** checkbox at the bottom of the question. Only use the required question option when there will always be an answer of some type. For example, all people probably read paper books.

Figure 209: My second Checkboxes question

Here are my two questions, as the user will see them. I clicked the **View live form** button and checked a few answers as an illustration. My actual answers are recorded in the spreadsheet when I click the **Submit** button. I can easily delete my test responses out before I publish the survey (*Figure 210*).

By inserting page breaks between questions, or groups of questions, we provide pagination to the survey. Long surveys need pagination, otherwise, the single web page becomes too long requiring a lot of scrolling. Any survey with more than 5 questions would benefit for page breaks.

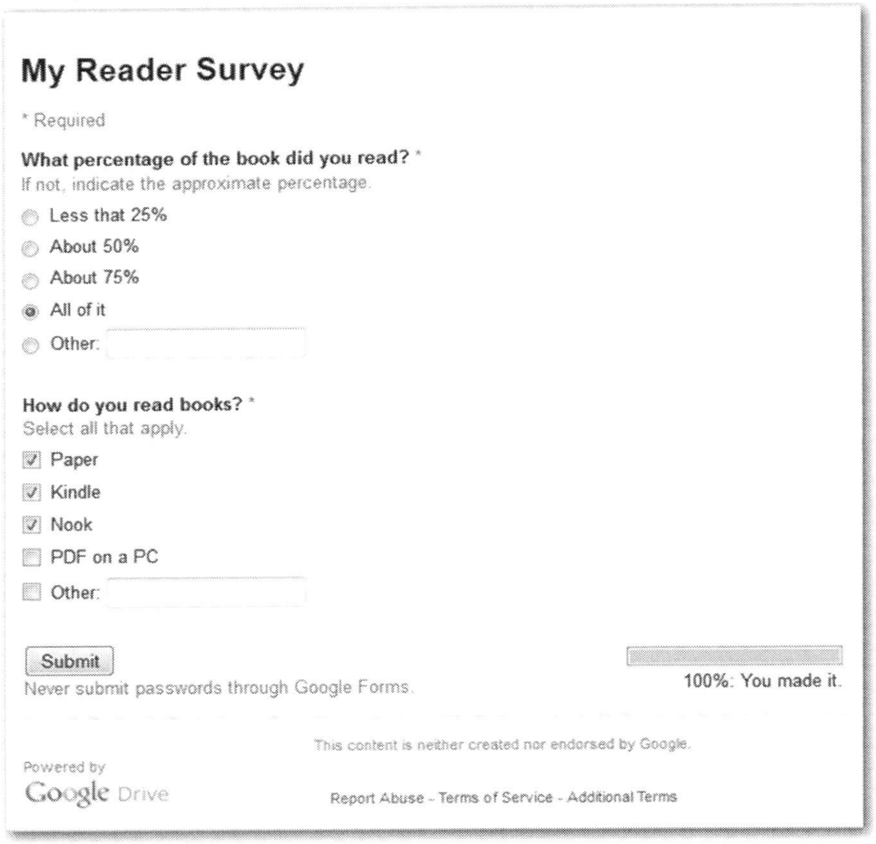

Chapter 7: Using Google Docs and Drive

My Reader Survey

* Required

What percentage of the book did you read? *
If not, indicate the approximate percentage.
- ○ Less that 25%
- ○ About 50%
- ○ About 75%
- ⦿ All of it
- ○ Other: _____

How do you read books? *
Select all that apply.
- ☑ Paper
- ☑ Kindle
- ☑ Nook
- ☐ PDF on a PC
- ☐ Other: _____

[Submit]
Never submit passwords through Google Forms.

100%: You made it.

This content is neither created nor endorsed by Google.

Powered by
Google Drive   Report Abuse - Terms of Service - Additional Terms

Figure 210: Previewing the form survey

Before we actually send the form off, we need to attach it to a spreadsheet. While you can attach the responses to any existing sheet, the easiest way is to click the menus **Responses->Change response destination**.

You can give the spreadsheet a new name, but the default is the name of the Form plus (Responses) (*Figure 211*).

Figure 211: Attaching a spreadsheet to collect data

While Google provides some basic analytics, you might gain more insight working with the responses in the spreadsheet using charts, averages, minimums, maximums and means. There are four different standard deviations to choose from, for example. The spreadsheets provide the raw data in a tabular form, but you can massage that data into meaningful insights into the results of the survey.

All spreadsheet documents are actually spreadsheet books (Microsoft's terminology), so you could choose a single book type Spreadsheet with a sheet just from that survey. This would group all of your survey sheets together into a single document.

Sending or Embedding Your Form

When you feel ready, you can click the **Send form** button to open the **Send form** screen (*Figure 212*).

Here are some of your options:

- If you just want to put a link on your website, you can copy the **Link to share**.
- To actually embed the code for the form within your website, click the **Embed** button and copy the code. Add this to a page at your site. This somewhat hides the fact that you are sending them off to Google.
- You can post the link to your Google+, Facebook or Twitter.
- You can send the form and link to any email you add into the **Send form via email** box. As we will see, how they can respond to the survey depends on how they get their email.
- If you are still in the design phase and you want to collaborate with others on the design, click the **Add collaborators** link at the bottom of the window. When ready, click the green **Send** button at the bottom.

Chapter 7: Using Google Docs and Drive

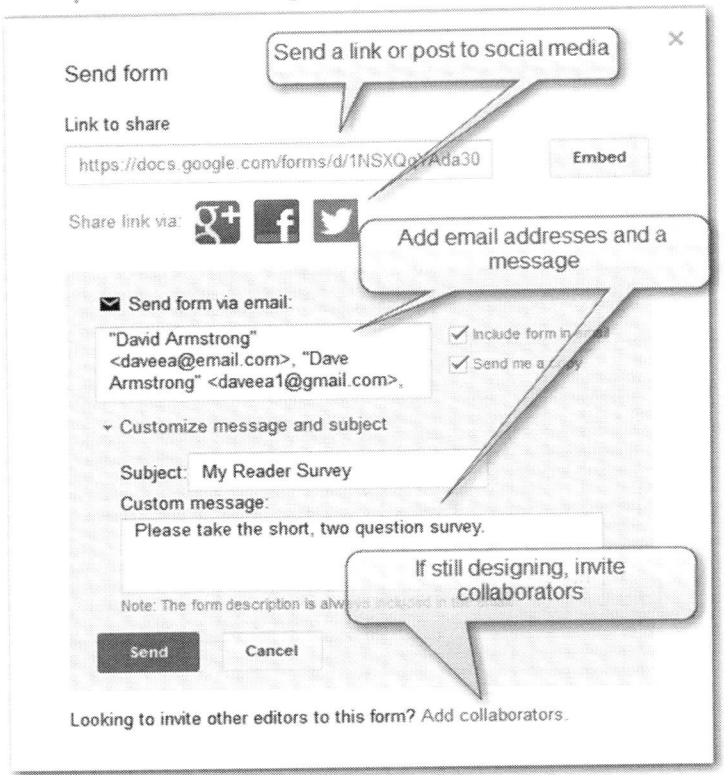

Figure 212: Sending the survey

Here is what the survey request looks like in my Gmail. Since Gmail is web based, I can take the survey right from the email, if all of the questions are on the same page as you see here. If you paginate the survey using page breaks, you will move off to the web version when you click next page (*Figure 213*).

We could, of course, just click the link near the top of the email to start on a web page instead of my email.

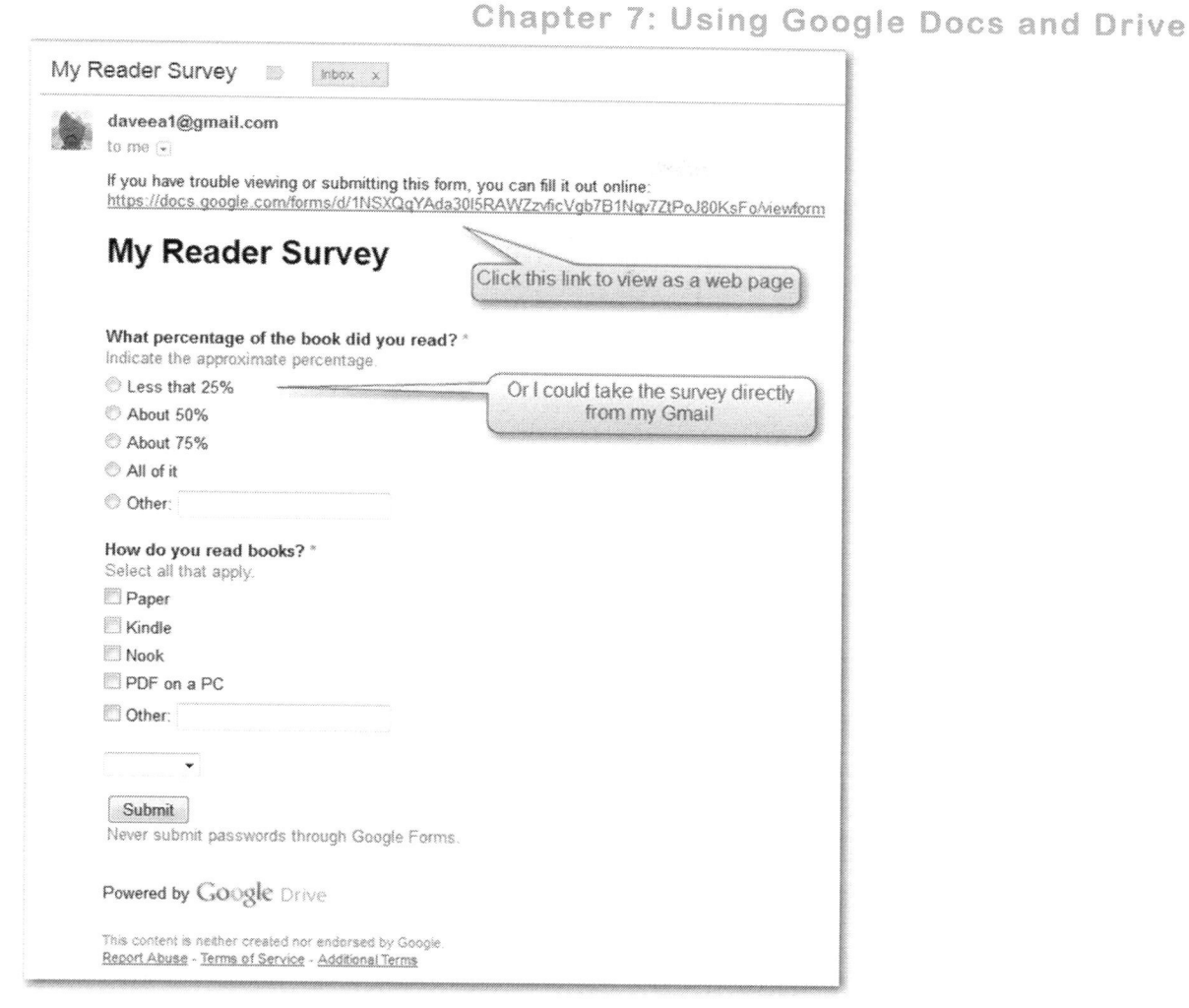

Figure 213: The survey in Gmail

Desktop email clients limit what email can do. For example, this is what the email looks like in my desktop Outlook client. Only the link works. While I can see some indication of the survey questions, I cannot click them. To take the survey, I will have to click the link to a web based version (*Figure 214*).

Chapter 7: Using Google Docs and Drive

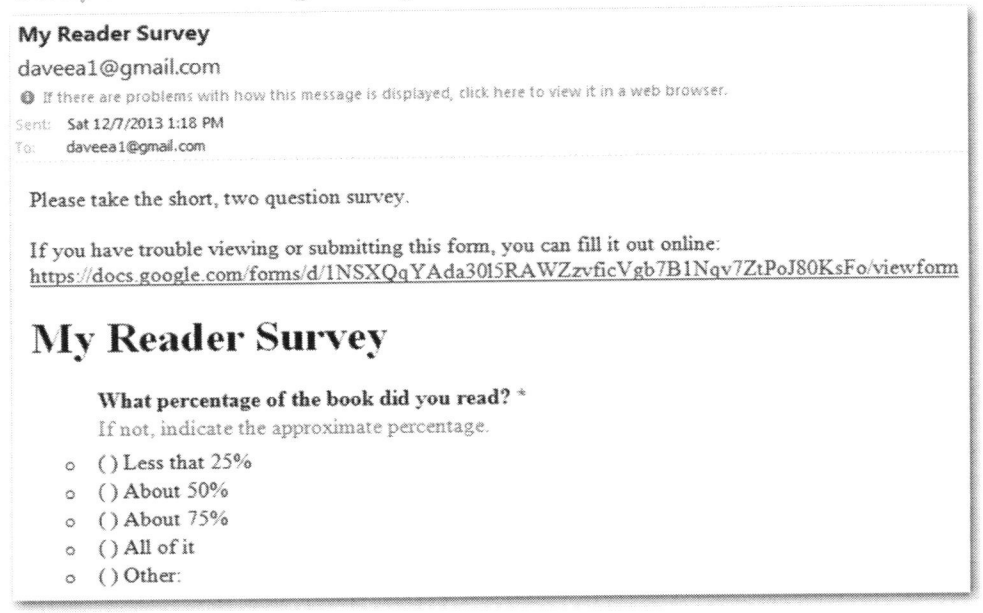

My Reader Survey
daveea1@gmail.com
If there are problems with how this message is displayed, click here to view it in a web browser.
Sent: Sat 12/7/2013 1:18 PM
To: daveea1@gmail.com

Please take the short, two question survey.

If you have trouble viewing or submitting this form, you can fill it out online:
https://docs.google.com/forms/d/1NSXQqYAda3OI5RAWZzvficVgb7B1Nqv7ZtPoJ80KsFo/viewform

My Reader Survey

What percentage of the book did you read? *
If not, indicate the approximate percentage.

- ( ) Less that 25%
- ( ) About 50%
- ( ) About 75%
- ( ) All of it
- ( ) Other:

Figure 214: The survey in Outlook

Regardless, of how users take the survey, at the end they see a screen with several options. The choices vary according to how I configured the survey when designing it, but in this case, they can see all possible responses. They can go back and edit and, since we allow it, they can take the survey again (*Figure 215*).

Ever the master marketer, Google invites the survey participant to **create your own form**. Eventually, Google will assimilate us all.

My Reader Survey
Your response has been recorded.

See previous responses
Edit your response
Submit another response

Create your own form   Google Drive

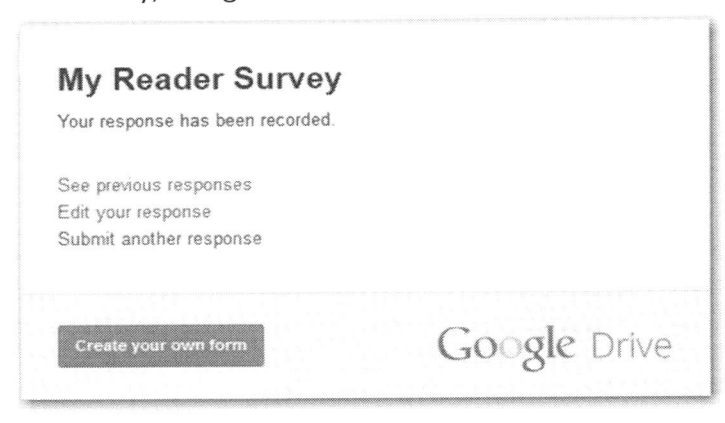

Figure 215: The survey completion page

Viewing the Response Analytics

If they click the **See previous responses** link, they see survey analytics (*Figure 216*). I have only had two responses, but much is revealed. Over a few days, I can see a pie chart showing the percentages of each choice. With checkboxes, I can see a bar chart showing choice accumulations.

At the bottom, I can see a timeline of when surveys were taken.

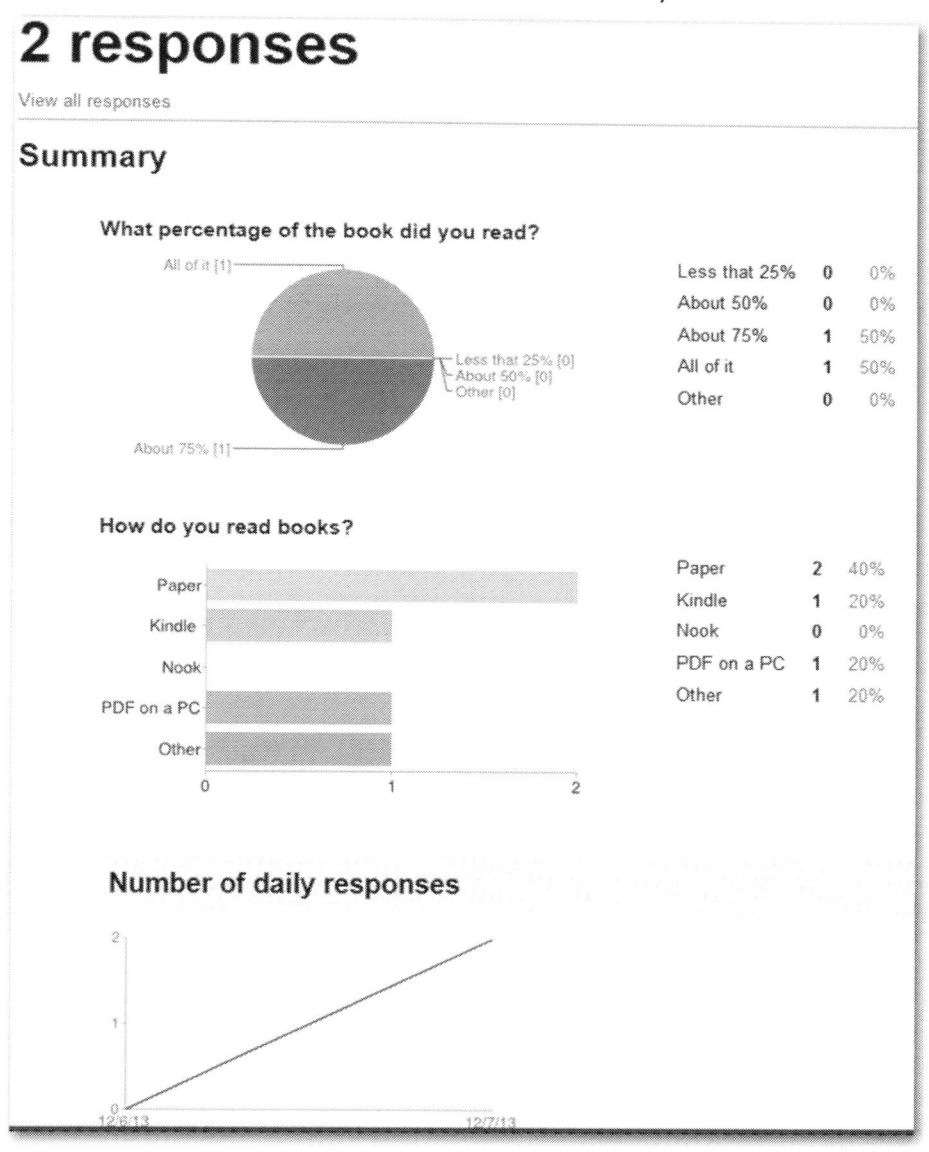

Figure 216: Survey analytics

Chapter 7: Using Google Docs and Drive

I can check the details of the answers in the spreadsheet created for me. Each survey is added into a row and the columns are the individual questions. In the **How do you read books?** Column, I have another entry of **Kindle PC**. This respondent is reading Kindle books on Amazon's downloadable reader for PCs and he added that into the other text box (*Figure 217*).

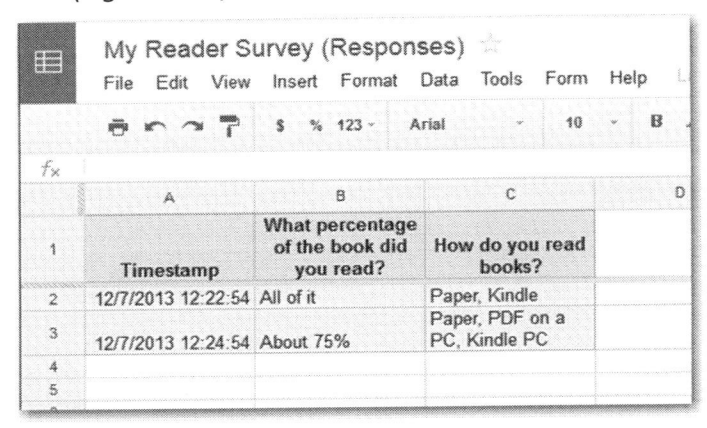

Figure 217: The survey spreadsheet

Chapter 8: Using Gmail and Google Docs Automation

Google has automation you can add to any of the Google Docs. However, it is not for the faint of heart. The scripting language they use to add automation is JavaScript. The good news is that other programmers have created many excellent automation scripts you can use without any programming on your part.

You will need to know enough to understand where these scripts are located and how to use them. The example we use here is a very useful one. We are going to add names and email addresses to a spreadsheet and then email each name on the list. This will not have the sophistication of a full featured email service provider, such as Constant Contact, but it will let you blast a customized email to many people with just a few clicks.

Copying a Prepared Spreadsheet for Names and Email Addresses

We can create a list using a Google spreadsheet. To do so you will have to have a Google, and thus, Gmail account. You only need to sign up once. It is free and it is easy. To sign up, go to google.com and create a new account. If you already have a Google account, you need only to remember your Gmail address and password.

Here is what we will do in this section:

1. Go into Gmail and create a draft email with special place mark holder fields that when merged will have information specific to that recipient, such as their name.
2. We will then use a Google Docs spreadsheet which we will provide to hold the individuals to which you wish to send emails.
3. Lastly, we will merge and send a personalized email to each row in the spreadsheet. We will have a saved copy of the spreadsheet if we want to send a new group of emails later.

Chapter 8: Using Gmail and Google Docs Automation

Acquiring the Sample Spreadsheet

I have prepared a copy of the spreadsheet discussed below. You will need to add that to your Google Drive before you can try it out. Before you can copy the spreadsheet, you must have a Google Account, of course. You need to carefully type http://goo.gl/8cmYMO into your browser. Use the exact case. If you are reading this as an eBook (Kindle, Nook, Sony reader or PDF), just click the URL link. Regardless, you should then see this (*Figure 218*):

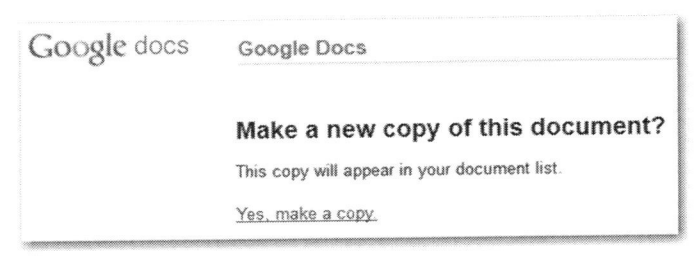

Figure 218: Copying the custom spreadsheet into your Google docs

Click the **Yes, make a copy** link and a copy of the spreadsheet will appear in your Google docs. This will add the spreadsheet to your Google docs and open it in your browser (*Figure 219*).

This spreadsheet has custom automation that merges your data with an email. We have modified the fields to fit our task better, but the script and programming came from Amit Agarwal, a very talented individual. Type (case sensitive) or click on this link to see his video if you want a more detailed explanation. http://goo.gl/sFHlo3.

Figure 219: Your copy of the custom spreadsheet

Now, you need to start adding the information you have collected. The field headers are self-explanatory. It is important you do not delete any of the header fields in row 1. Start adding your info in row 2.

We will add just three rows to demo our example. Leave the Mail Merge Status field empty (*Figure 220*).

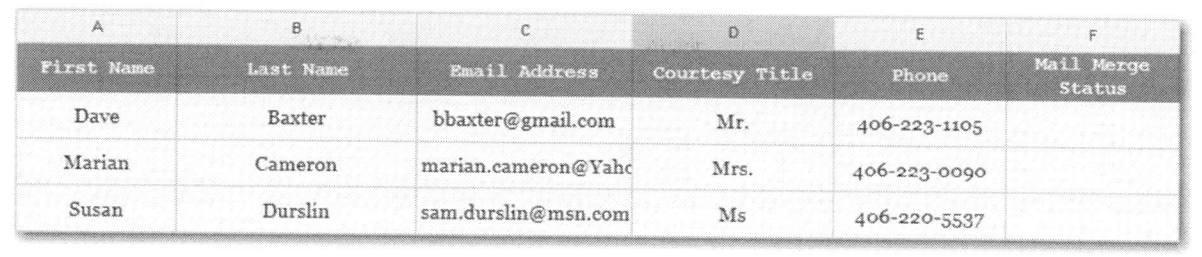

A	B	C	D	E	F
First Name	Last Name	Email Address	Courtesy Title	Phone	Mail Merge Status
Dave	Baxter	bbaxter@gmail.com	Mr.	406-223-1105	
Marian	Cameron	marian.cameron@Yahoo	Mrs.	406-223-0090	
Susan	Durslin	sam.durslin@msn.com	Ms	406-220-5537	

Figure 220: Add the information from your Google search

Creating Your Email Template

Most modern browsers have tabs. Open a new tab and go to your Gmail account. Click the compose button in the upper right. Do not fill in the **To** email section as the merge will do that.

Understanding the Merge Fields

Notice, in the figure below that we have placed three place mark fields that will be filed by the merge. Each starts with a dollar sign followed by a percent and the end of the field ends with another percent. The format is **$%Inserted Field%.** This will tell the merge what field to match with when the merge occurs (*Figure 221*).

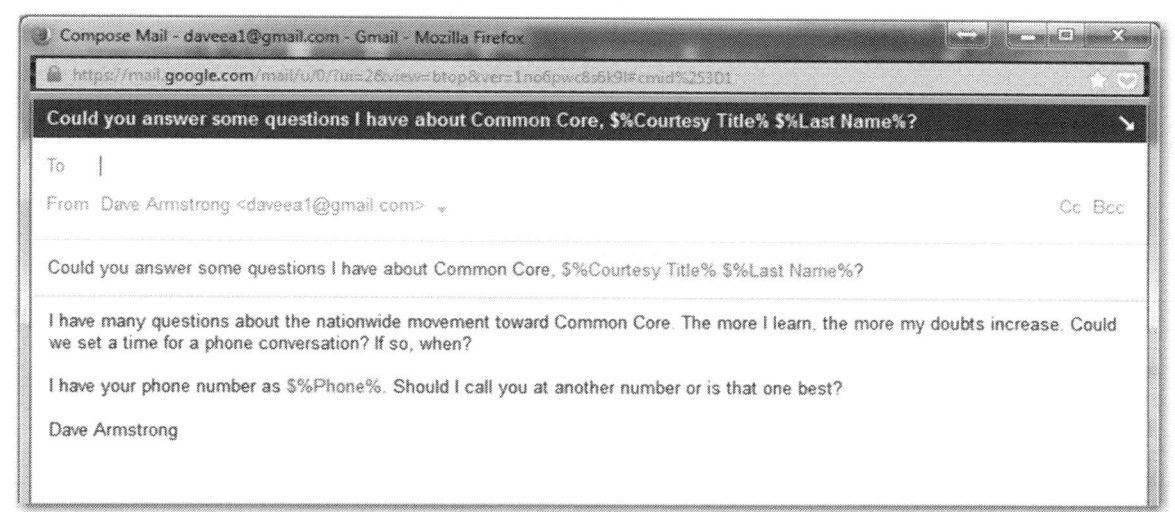

Figure 221: A simple email with field place mark holders

Any field name you have in the first row of the spreadsheet can be a field name within the email by using this prefix ($%) and suffix (%). Once you have the email setup, just close it. It will automatically save as a draft or template email. Do not send it!

Merging Your Email List

Return to your spreadsheet. If you left it open in one of your browser's tabs, just click the tab. Click the **Mail Merge** menu at the top and click **Start Mail Merge** (*Figure 222*). Be careful you do **NOT** choose **Clear Canvas** (Reset) or you will remove your data.

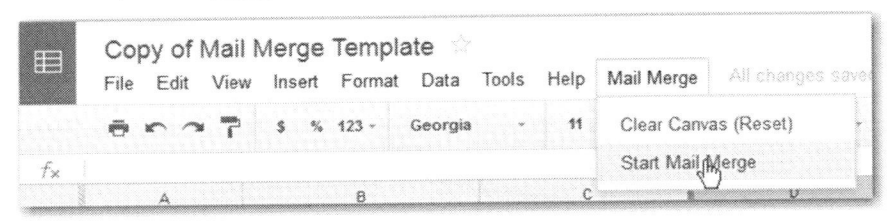

Figure 222: Starting the mail merge process

Giving Permission for the Script to Run

The first time you run the mail merge you will have to authorize the process. On the first popup dialog, click **OK** (*Figure 223*).

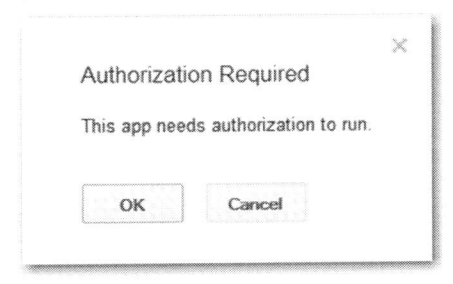

Figure 223: Click OK to start the authorization process

Clicking **OK** opens another pop up screen warning you that this app, Google spreadsheet, wants to manage your email and run a script in the spreadsheet. Click **Accept** (*Figure 224*).

Chapter 8: Using Gmail and Google Docs Automation

Figure 224: This tells you what apps will be affected by the merge

This created no mail merge, it just told security it is ok to merge. You will now have to choose the menus **Mail Merge** and then **Start Mail Merge** again.

This opens the dialog you see in (*Figure 225*). Click the dropdown arrow and select the template we made earlier. You may have several, if you have previous drafts.

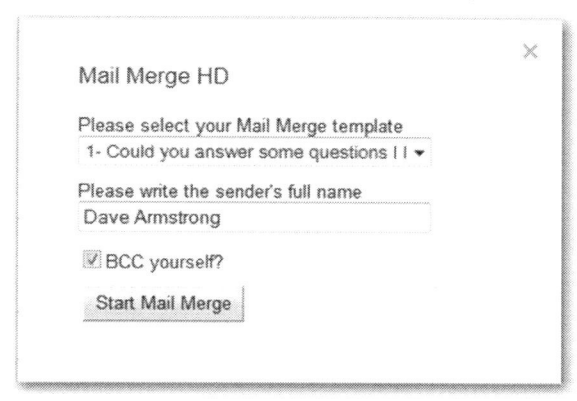

Figure 225: Pick your template, add you name and BCC yourself

Add the name you wish to use as the sender's name in the email and always send a **BCC** to yourself. By checking the BCC checkbox, you will get a completed email similar to the ones you have sent to everyone.

Chapter 8: Using Gmail and Google Docs Automation

Running the Mail Merge

You will briefly see a notification that the merge is running. After completion, a few seconds, you will notice that the **Mail Merge Status** column will now have **EMAIL_SENT** in each of the rows that were successfully merged (*Figure 226*).

Should you add new rows later and want to send just the new ones, this **EMAIL_SENT** flag will prevent the resending the email to them. Should you want to resend some or all emails, delete all of the **EMAIL_SENT** flags. Drag over them and hit the delete key.

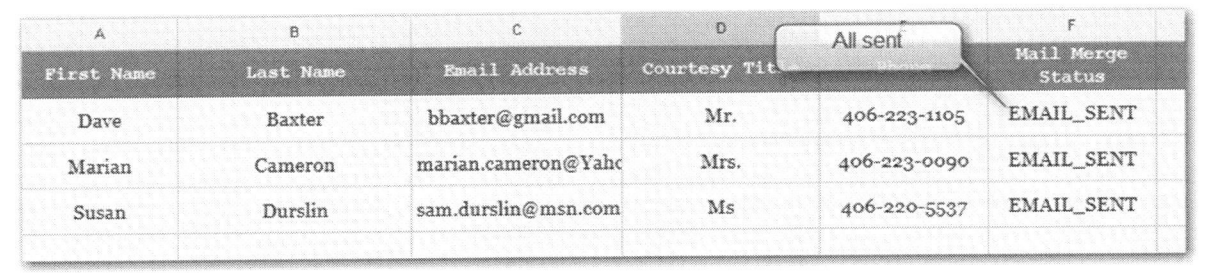

A	B	C	D	E	F
First Name	Last Name	Email Address	Courtesy Title		Mail Merge Status
Dave	Baxter	bbaxter@gmail.com	Mr.	406-223-1105	EMAIL_SENT
Marian	Cameron	marian.cameron@Yaho	Mrs.	406-223-0090	EMAIL_SENT
Susan	Durslin	sam.durslin@msn.com	Ms	406-220-5537	EMAIL_SENT

Figure 226: Each row with EMAIL_SENT was successful

Checking Your Results

Returning to your Gmail, you should see your BCC copy of the email in your Inbox (*Figure 227*).

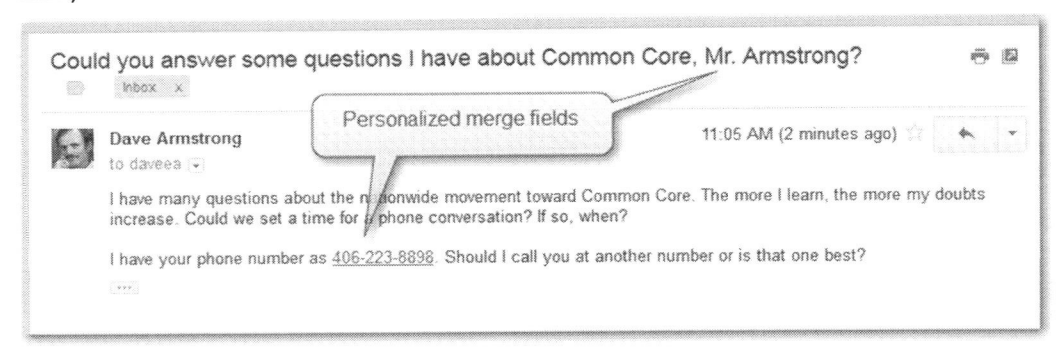

Figure 227: Email with inserted merge data

You can look into your **Sent** folder to see all of the other emails sent.

Getting Back to Your Email Template and Spreadsheet

The merge spreadsheet automatically saves, but at some point you will want to return to use it again. To do so, we need to find our draft/template, if we need to edit it. If you go back to Gmail, click the **Drafts** folder on the left and you will see something like this. Click the subject line to reopen, and edit if necessary (*Figure 228*).

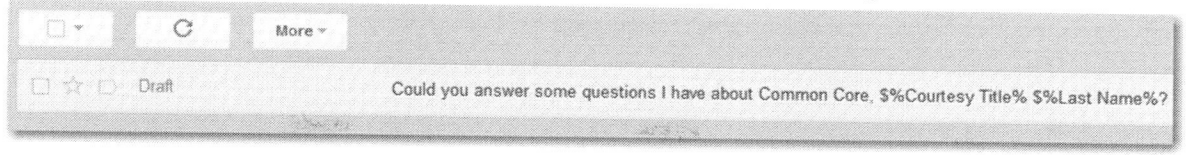

Chapter 8: Using Gmail and Google Docs Automation

Figure 228: You email template is in your Draft folder

To get back to your spreadsheet, go to http://docs.google.com and, if necessary, sign in with your Gmail address and password. You may not have to sign in as Google stores your information in a cookie on your computer. Regardless, you will see something like this (*Figure 229*):

Figure 229: Your list of documents and saved files

If you want to give the spreadsheet a more meaningful name, select it by clicking the small box to the left of the **Copy of Mail Merge Template** and the selecting **Rename...** from the dropdown **More** menu (*Figure 230*).

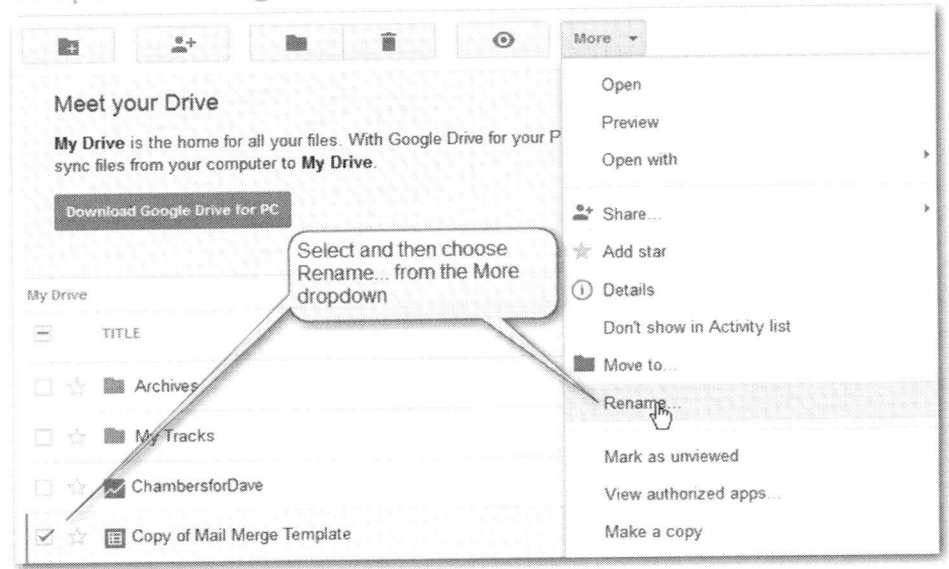

Chapter 8: Using Gmail and Google Docs Automation

Figure 230: Using the Rename feature

Type a meaningful name and click OK (*Figure 231*).

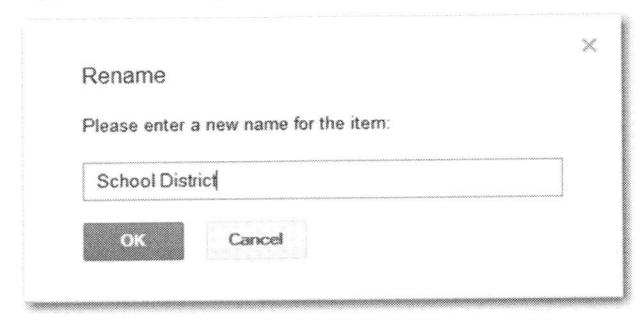

Figure 231: Add a meaningful name

Warning, Gmail is Watching!

Don't overdue the number of emails you send at one time. Google freaks when they see a lot of emails going out in a short period of time. They will warn you not to use Gmail for SPAM. If you send more than 100 emails at a time they will warn you and if you send more than 500 emails within a 24 hour period, they will lock you out of your account for a day. Keep it up and they will permanently ban you from Gmail.

Use common sense and spread them out over a few days, if you have a lot of names.

How Google Docs Scripting Works

Google allows you to add automation to any of their office products. Some people call these macros, as they can do a series of steps so you do not have to do them manually. They can do much more in the hands of a JavaScript programmer. By now you should

Chapter 8: Using Gmail and Google Docs Automation

have the spreadsheet mentioned above. Let explore how the Mail Merge menu got there and what it does when used (*Figure 232*).

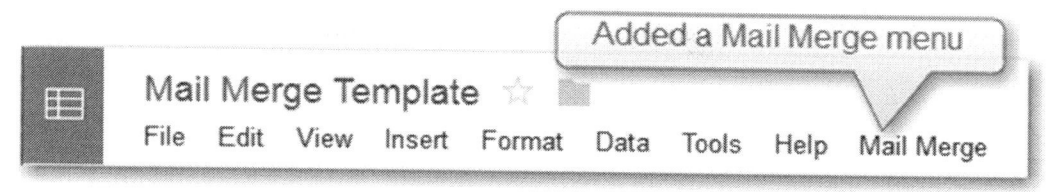

Figure 232: A script added a new menu

Clicking the menus **Tools->Script manager**…, opens a list of all the functions that were programmed into the spreadsheet (*Figure 233*).

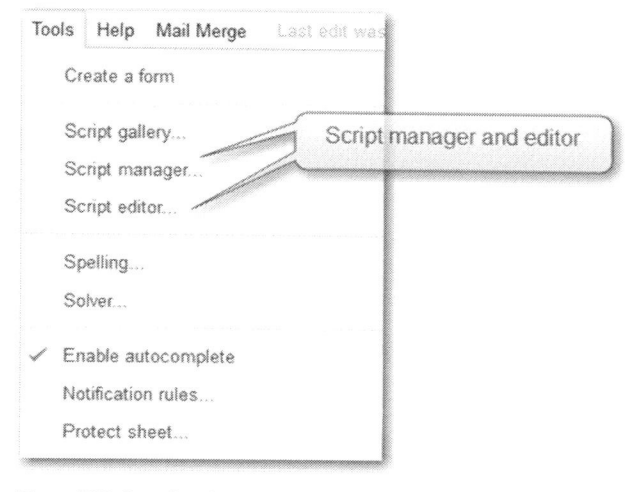

Figure 233: Opening the Script manager…

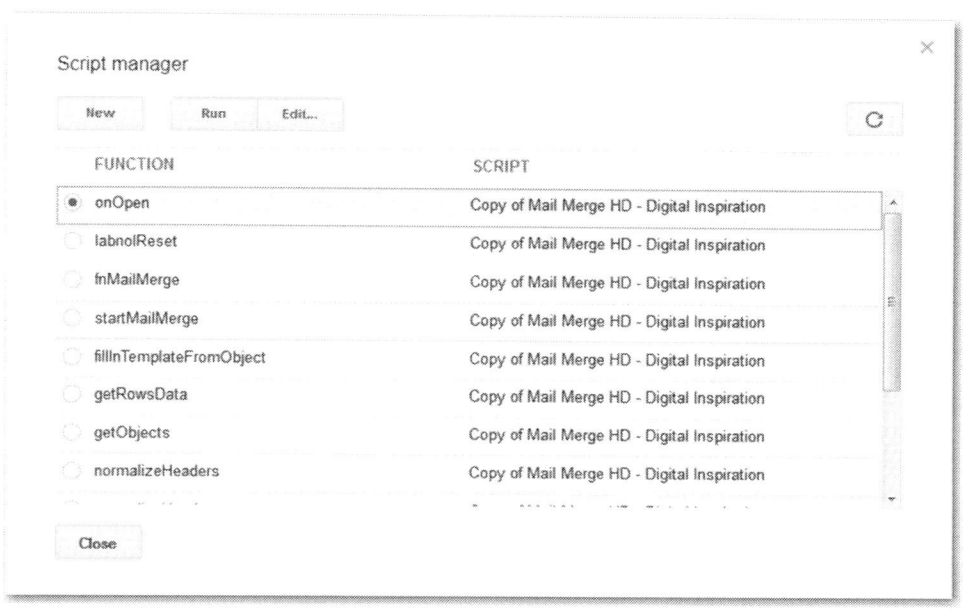

Chapter 8: Using Gmail and Google Docs Automation

Clicking the menus **Tools->Editor**, opens the script editor which is where you would create and test the JavaScript (*Figure 234*).

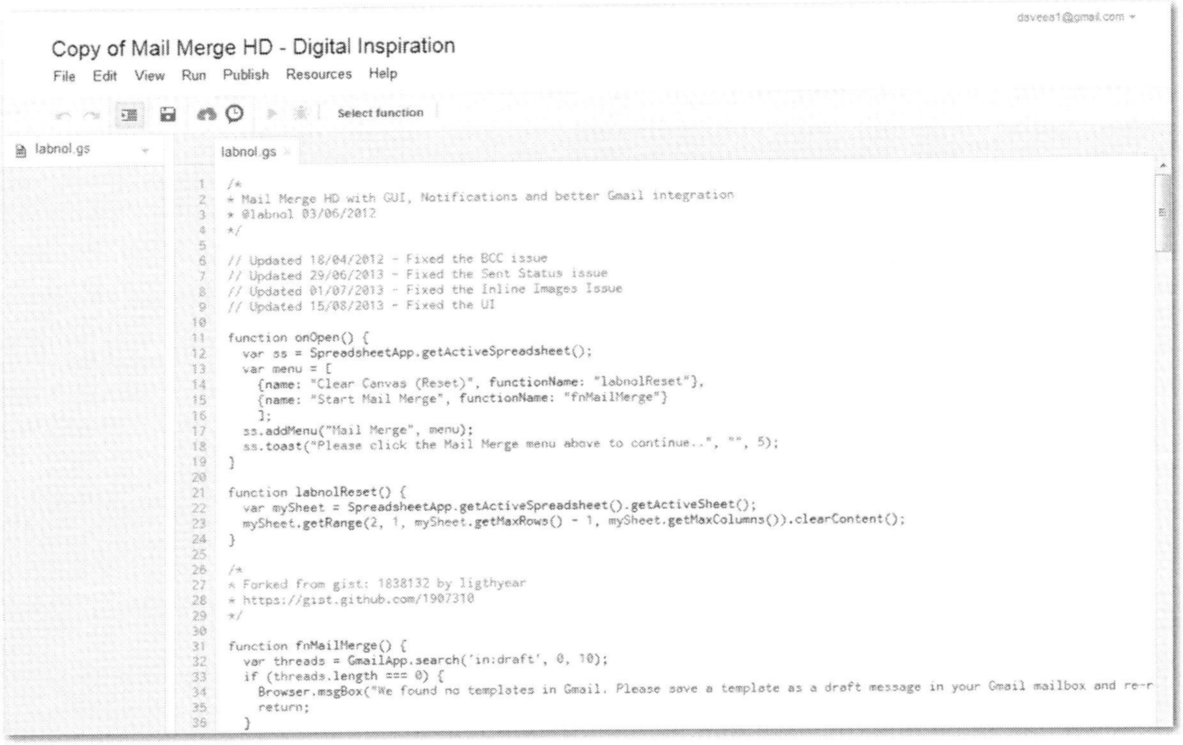

Figure 234: The JavaScript editor

Analyzing a Google Doc's Script

You really do not want to become a programmer unless that is your business, however, I will describe a small part of the code just to give you some idea of what is going on. This code adds a new menu (Mail Merge) and then adds two sub menus (Clear Canvas (Reset) and Start Mail Merge).

1. Create a function called onOpen

```
function onOpen() {
```

2. Create a variable called ss that points to the current active spreadsheet.

```
var ss = SpreadsheetApp.getActiveSpreadsheet();
```

3. Create a variable called menu that has the two sub menus. Notice that they are mapped to two functions that clear the canvas (labnolReset) or start the mail merge (fnMailMerge).

```
var menu = [
{name: "Clear Canvas (Reset)", functionName: "labnolReset"},
```

Chapter 8: Using Gmail and Google Docs Automation

```
{name: "Start Mail Merge", functionName: "fnMailMerge"}];
```

4. We then add a new parent menu called Mail Merge and add the menus we created above to it.

```
ss.addMenu("Mail Merge", menu);
```

5. Lastly, we cause a slide up box that tells the user the click the Mail Merge menu at the top to continue. It stays up only for 5 seconds.

```
ss.toast("Please click the Mail Merge menu above to
continue..", "", 5); }
```

The good news is that there are many excellent scripts available for free that you can use.

The menu choices, **Tools->Script gallery...,** opens an extensive list. Click the Info link to get more information and, optionally, install. Some have **Help page** links (*Figure 235*).

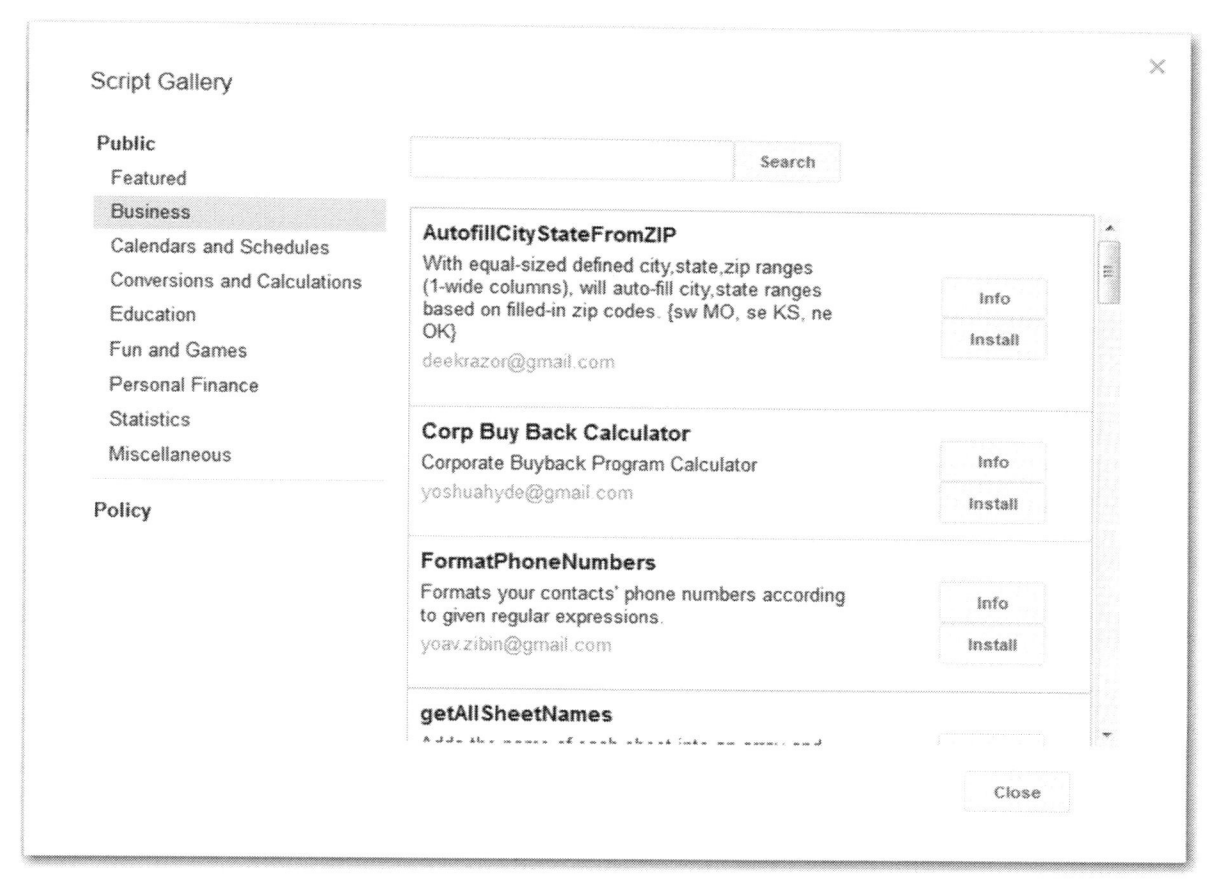

Figure 235: Add-ins from the script gallery

Chapter 8: Using Gmail and Google Docs Automation

You can click on the info button to see more details on a gallery script. For example, this script used a zip code entry to fill in the city and state. This would not only speed entry, but would insure accuracy.

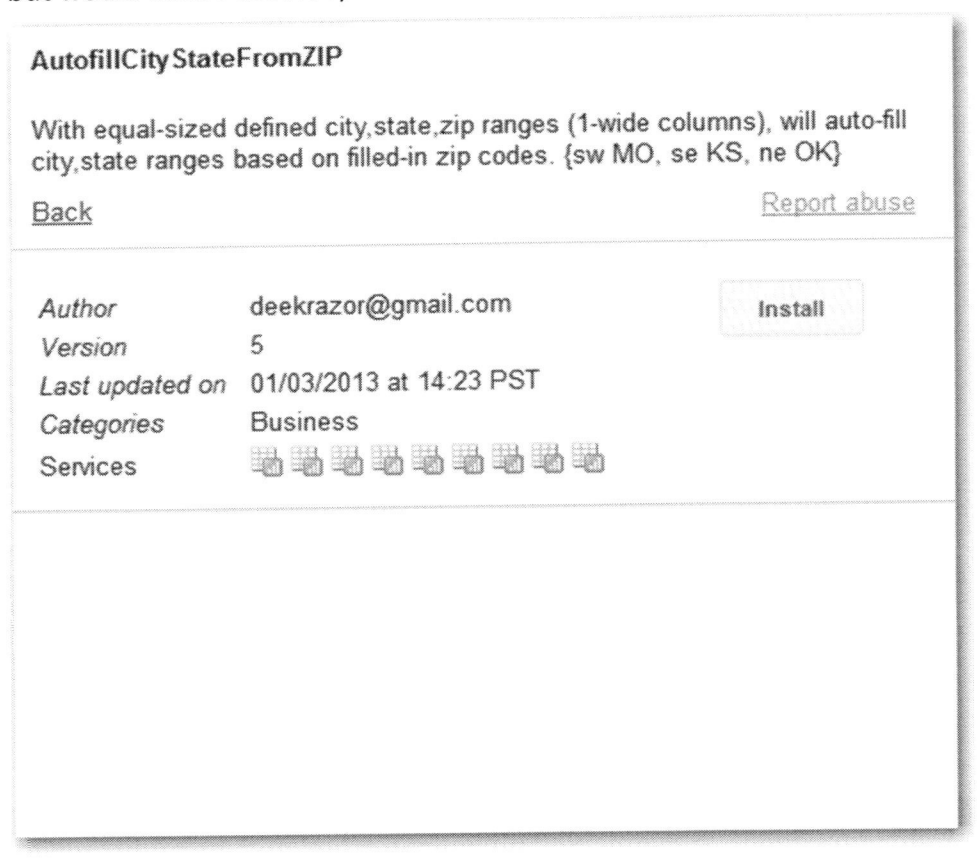

AutofillCityStateFromZIP

With equal-sized defined city,state,zip ranges (1-wide columns), will auto-fill city,state ranges based on filled-in zip codes. {sw MO, se KS, ne OK}

Back   Report abuse

Author	deekrazor@gmail.com	Install
Version	5	
Last updated on	01/03/2013 at 14:23 PST	
Categories	Business	
Services		

Chapter 9: Using Gmail and Hangouts

In this section, we are going to take a tour of Google's very popular email client, Gmail. It has as many users as all the other web based email clients combined, 425 million as of June, 2012. On an average day, about 10,000 people sign up.

Gmail Main Screen

Gmail integrates with Google Calendar which is very useful. When you receive an email with a calendar file attached, a single click adds it to your calendar. We will cover calendar in the next section.

Let's tour the main features of Gmail (*Figure 236*):

1. You would need to click the COMPOSE button to create a new email.
2. You are currently in the Inbox folder and you can see all of the emails within it.
3. There are other folders which help you segment your emails into groups.
4. As we will see later, you can place a phone call or start a video call if you sign up for the free Google Hangouts.
5. You can apply a star to an individual email. There are several colors to use to visually tag your emails for further action.
6. Gmail has a rich set of settings which you can explore by clicking the gear icon.
7. If you have large amounts of email, search is very handy and it searches all folders.
8. The group of icons in the upper right, allows you to jump to other Google applications.
9. You can initiate chat with any of your contacts, think fellow employees. There are, also, Gadgets that you can add that make Gmail more useful.

Chapter 9: Using Gmail and Hangouts

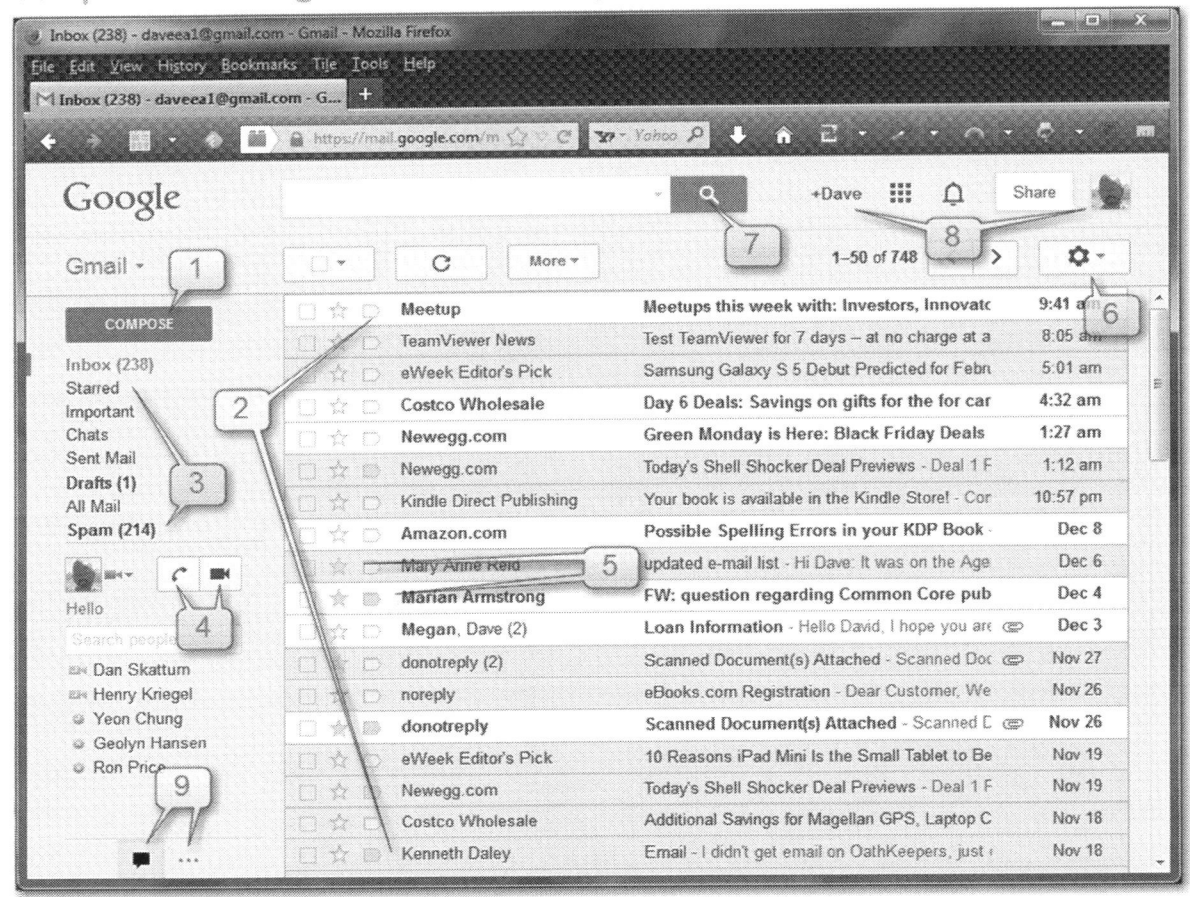

Figure 236: Gmail's main screen

Let's explore the icon menus in 8 above. The +Dave opens your Google+ social media page. This is Google's version of Facebook. While not really a virtual office business tool, you could connect to just your employees so they might share business information.

Like Facebook, these social sites are the virtual equivalent of a group's collective memory. Obviously, you need to make it a hard and fast rule that only your staff are in the circle. We will not explore Google+ in this book. However, there are many books and videos teaching you the details.

Chapter 9: Using Gmail and Hangouts

Google+ has a simple opening screen (*Figure 237*).

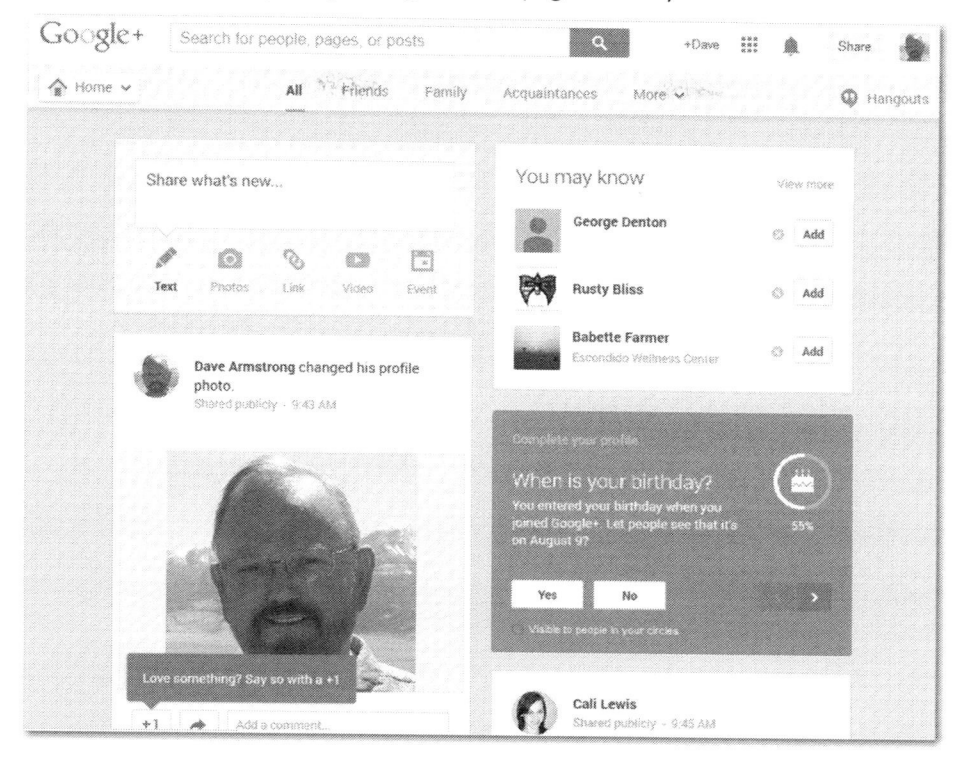

Figure 237: You Google+ opening screen

Use the grid icon to open a menu of all of Google's services. This lets you quickly jump to your Drive, Calendar, etc. (*Figure 238*).

Figure 238: Quickly jump to other Google Programs

Chapter 9: Using Gmail and Hangouts

Occasionally, Google will send you notifications. Click the bell icon and then on one of the items to see the details (*Figure 239*).

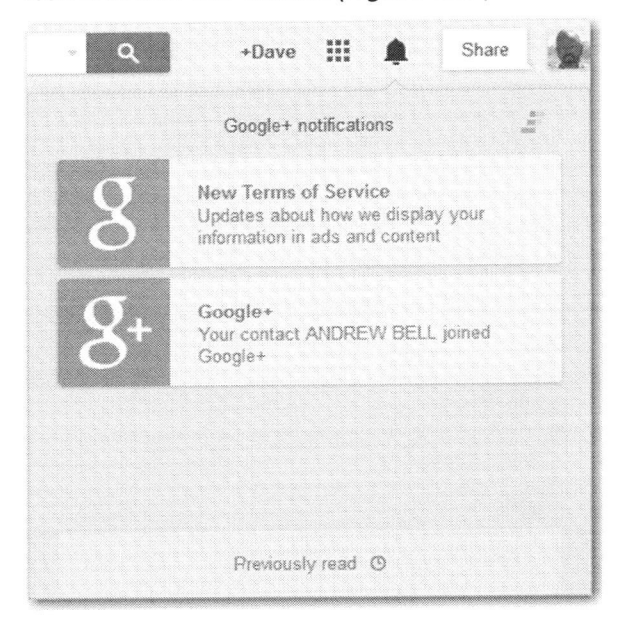

Figure 239: Google's notifications menu

The **Share** button allows you to post a message, photo, hyperlink, video or an event to your Google+ page (*Figure 240*).

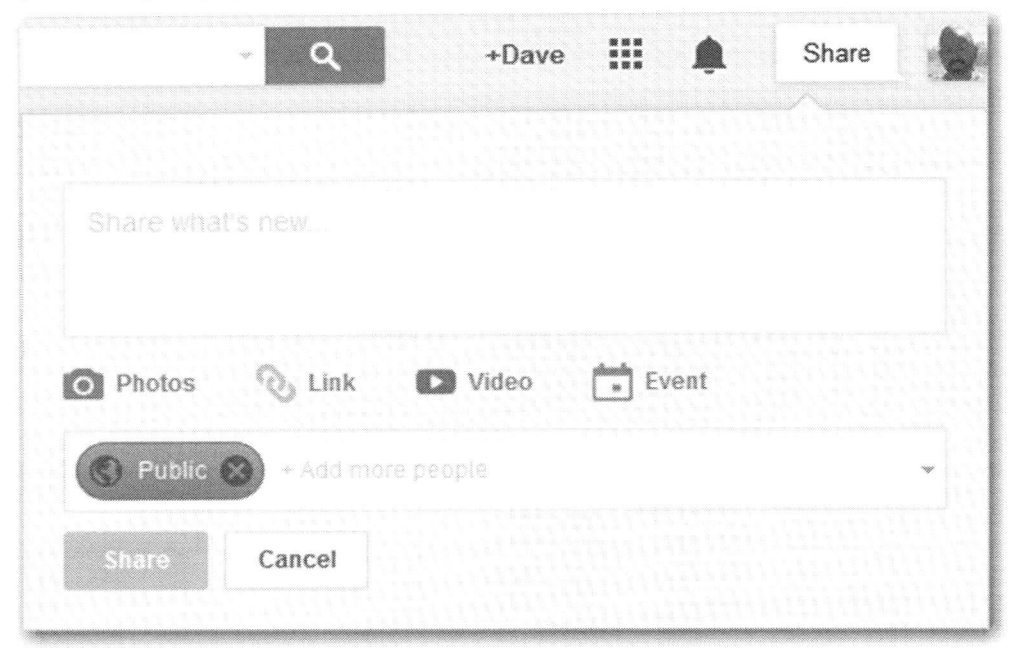

Figure 240: Posting to your Google+ page

The last icon, your profile picture, if you uploaded one, opens access to your profile. It allows you to **Sign out**, which is necessary if you have more than one account or want to log into another's account (*Figure 241*).

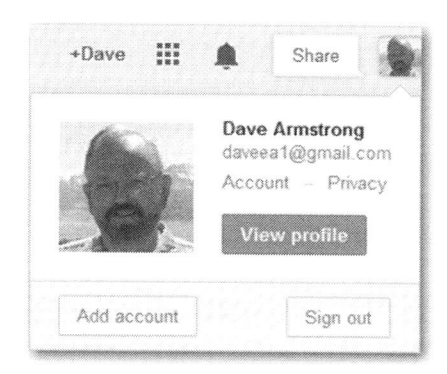

Figure 241: Access your profile or Sign out

The **Add account** button allows you to sign into another Gmail account. However, be aware, that Google uses a cookie to store your account information. Log into another account and you will have to log out and then back into your original account. The only way you can work with two accounts at the same time, is to use different browsers, as browsers do not share cookies (*Figure 242*).

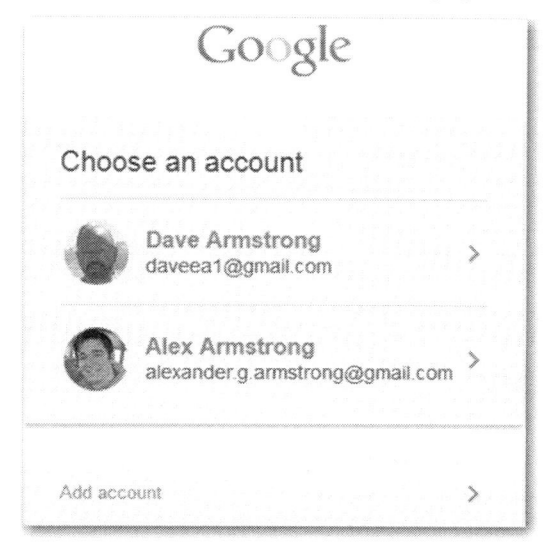

Figure 242: Switching accounts

Gmail remembers these switches and the next time you open your face icon, you see the other account (*Figure 242*). You may want to use this method to open your employee's business Gmail account to check for compliance. It is a common business practice to have

Chapter 9: Using Gmail and Hangouts

full access to accounts that are a part of your business. Make sure your staff knows you will be checking their Google Drive and Gmail regularly (*Figure 243*).

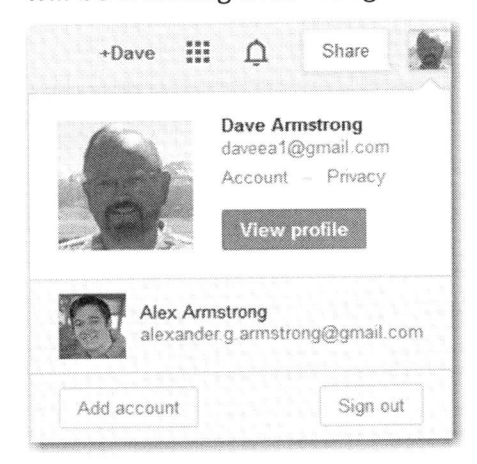

Figure 243: Can now use to have quick access to other Gmail accounts

Using Gmail Setting to Collect All of your Email

You can configure Gmail to collect email from all of your accounts. Gmail becomes the one email to rule them all, in that, all your email funnels into your Gmail account. Add the Gmail app to your phone or tablet and you see all emails while on the go.

To start, click the **gear icon**->Settings (*Figure 244*).

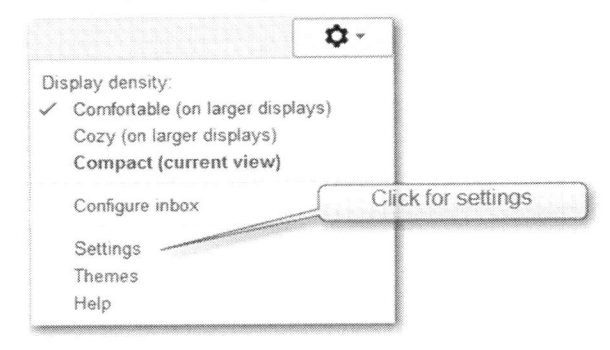

Figure 244: Opening Gmail settings

Click the **Accounts** link at the top (*Figure 245*).

Figure 245: Selecting the Accounts group

Then the **Add a POP3 mail account you own** (*Figure 246*).

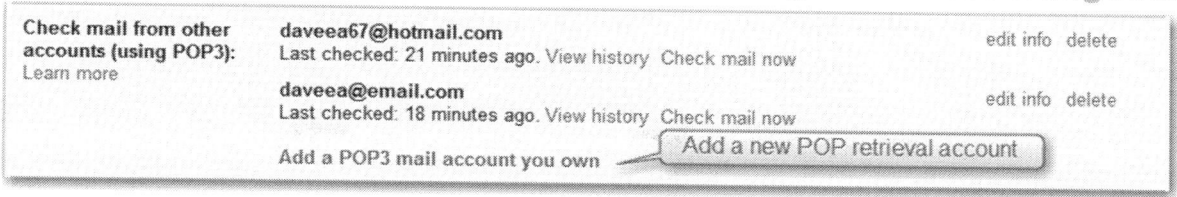

Figure 246: Adding a new POP account

Enter the email of the account you are trying to collect (*Figure 247*).

Figure 247: Adding your email address

Add you username, password and POP server address.

Figure 248: Completing the connection info

Letting Your Assistant Access Your Gmail

You can delegate access to your Gmail to another person so they can read, send, and delete messages on your behalf. For example, you could delegate your business Gmail access to your assistant. The delegate can also access your contacts by clicking the Contacts link. Clicking the **To**, **Cc**, or **Bcc** links in the mail compose window, will also bring up your contacts.

Chapter 9: Using Gmail and Hangouts

You won't be able to give anyone permission to change your account password or account settings, or chat on your behalf. You can give limited access for up to 10 users *(Figure 249 and Figure 250)*.

Here's how:

1. Click the gear in the top right.
2. Select **Settings.**
3. Select the **Accounts** tab/link.
4. Under **Grant access to your account,** click the **Add another account** link.

Figure 249: Giving others limited access to your account

5. Enter the email address of the person you'd like to access your account and click **Next Step**. Remember, you can only enter a Gmail address.

Figure 250: Adding them with their Gmail address

6. You'll see a confirmation message. Click **Send email** to grant access if you're sure.
7. The delegate will receive a verification email explaining that you've granted access to them.

After the delegate confirms this request, it may take up to 30 minutes for the verification process to be completed. To see if the delegate has confirmed access to your account, look at the Accounts tab in Settings.

Any messages someone else sends from your account, will have your name listed, in addition, to the other person's name, so they'll show the sender as: Your Name (sent by Delegate).

There are many features you might use under **Settings**. I could write a small book, if I explained of all them. For example, I use the POP setting to collect all my email from several different email accounts into my Gmail. You are telling Gmail to go to the other email servers and pick up your email.

Managing Your Gmail Folders

Let's look at how you manage your email. While, I earlier said, that you organize your email into folders, it is not an exact analogy to your desktop PC's version of folders. In Gmail, an email can be in several folders at the same time. The folders are actually tags that group the emails. For example, you might have a folder for all emails that come in from an important customer. However, in one of those emails, you added a star. You could find the email in the customer's folder and in the **Starred** folder. Delete the customer's folder and it does not delete the email as it is still in the **Starred** folder.

While you can add any number of folders, there are some built in (*Figure 251*):

- **Inbox** - All new email shows up here.
- **Starred -** You can add a star to any email as a way of making it stand out. This folder shows only Starred emails.
- **Important -** If Gmail sees you have a lot of emails exchanged with this person, it assumes that the emails are **Important** and places a copy in this folder.
- **Chats** - If you use the chat features of Gmail, all of your chat conversations will be in this folder.
- **Sent Mail** - Email you have sent.
- **Drafts** - These can be templates. You might use them to respond to common questions or inquiries.
- **All Mail** - Lose an email? This view of your email shows all that is not considered Spam.
- **Spam -** Google's spam filters are very good, but not perfect. You could just delete it all, but a spam catch could be an important false positive. We will discuss next.
- **Trash -** Delete anything but spam and it goes to trash. If you accidently delete an important email, you can restore from **Trash**.

Chapter 9: Using Gmail and Hangouts

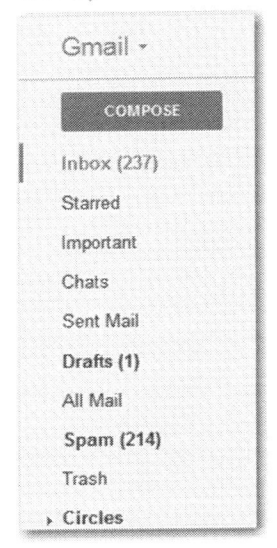

Figure 251: Your Gmail folder list

A single click of the **Delete all spam messages now** link will delete all of your spam older than 30 days (*Figure 252*). However, this is risky as some of the emails Google counts as spam may be important to you. I suggest you, at least, look at what you are deleting and rescue any important emails.

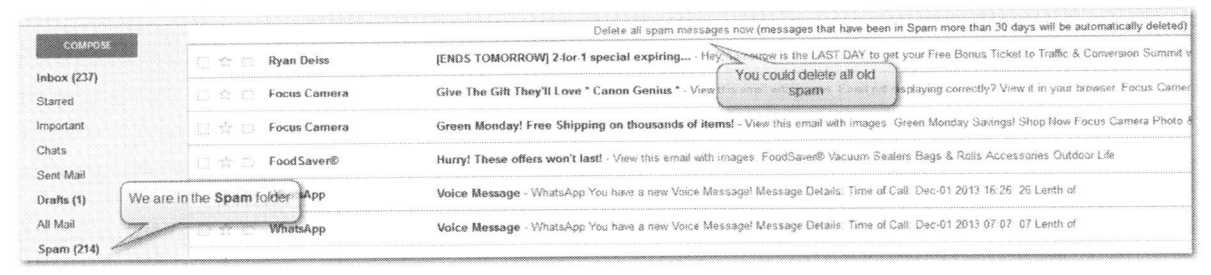

Figure 252: A list of your probable spam

Checking Your Spam Folder for False Positives

A safe assumption is that a vast majority of email in the folder is spam. Start by checking the checkbox at the top to select that entire page of emails (*Figure 253*). Now, scroll down looking for any false positives. If found, deselect them. When all of the emails are selected and not selected, click the **Delete forever** button. These are not moved to the trash and cannot be recalled.

A new page of spam candidates will appear, if there are more. At the top, are the ones from the previous page you wish to keep. Select each and click the **Not spam** button. You have options to move the rescued email into a folder. By default, they go back to your Inbox. Repeat this process until your spam folder is empty.

Chapter 9: Using Gmail and Hangouts

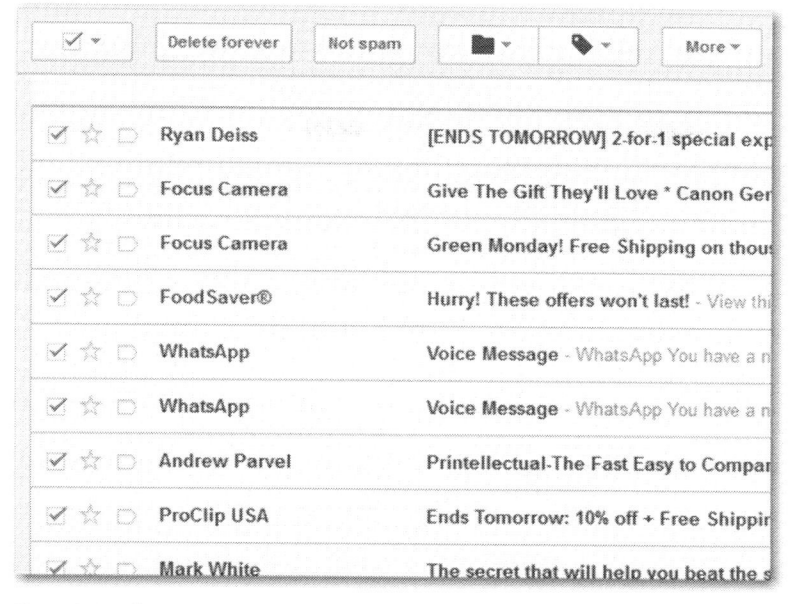

Figure 253: All spam emails selected

Composing a New Email

When I click the red COMPOSE button in the upper left, I open the compose screen (*Figure 254*).

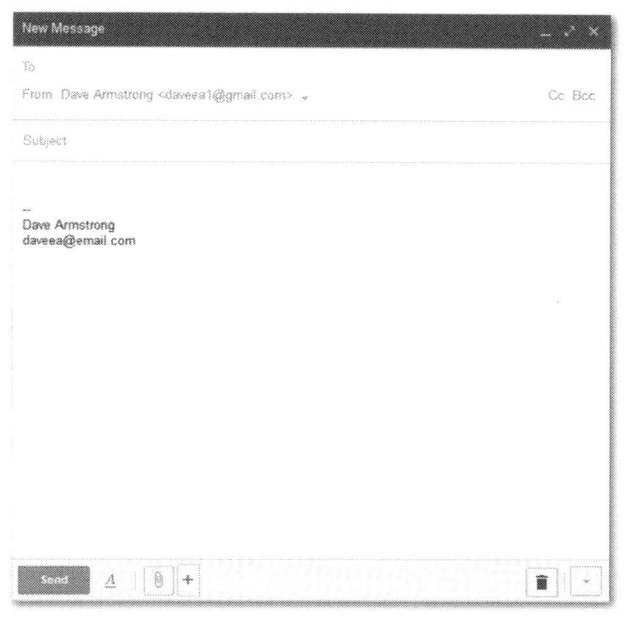

Figure 254: Creating a new message

Chapter 9: Using Gmail and Hangouts

Double-clicking on the **To** link of the new email screen, brings up a list of your contacts (*Figure 255*). If you have a large list, you might want to use search to narrow the visible list down.

If you wish, you can use this contact selection screen to create a group. This might be to all of your employees. The next time you want to broadcast an email to all employees, the named group would show in the contacts and will be a choice.

Figure 255: A list of your contacts

Move your mouse pointer over the bottom of the email and the insert menu appears (*Figure 256*).

Figure 256: Fade in insert menu

Left to right, the choices allow you to:

- Apply formatting to select text.
- Attach a file.
- Insert files using Drive.
- Attach money, if you have enrolled in Google Wallet.
- Insert images.
- Insert a link.
- Insert an emoticon.
- Insert an invitation.
- Discard, using the trashcan icon.

Chapter 9: Using Gmail and Hangouts

- Open a dropdown with several options (*Figure 257*).

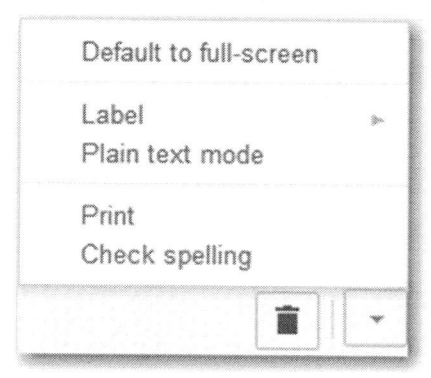

Figure 257: Menu of email choices

Click the **Send** button when the email is ready to send.

Using Contacts in Gmail

An important part of Gmail is your contacts. To get there, click the down arrow next to Gmail in the upper left and select Contacts (*Figure 258*).

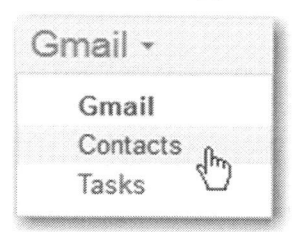

Figure 258: Moving to Contacts

Note that the screen layout is similar to Gmail.

Here is a quick overview:

1. Use the **NEW CONTACT** button to add new contacts.
2. Groups of **My Contacts** I have added or imported.
3. **Circles** from my Google+ application.
4. To add a **New Group** or **Import Contacts** from Excel and CSV files.
5. I can chat, dial on phone or start a video meeting, if one of my contacts has a video camera and is available.
6. I can see where my contacts come from and what group they are in.

Chapter 9: Using Gmail and Hangouts

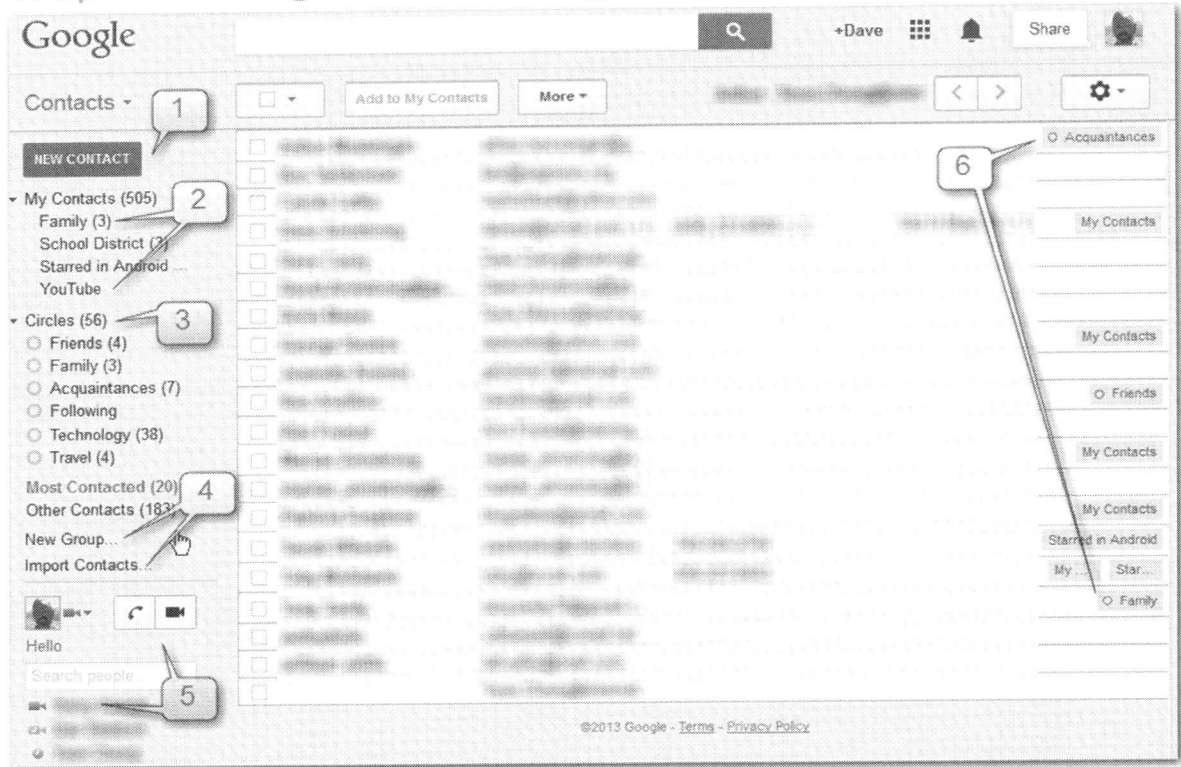

Figure 259: Main Contact screen

Adding Contacts

I have filled in some of the basic information on a new client (*Figure 260*). If you put in an existing Gmail address, it will add the information it has in that profile. While the Contacts list is by no means a CRM or a Customer Relationship Management system, it can be a quick source of your client's or staff's information.

Chapter 9: Using Gmail and Hangouts

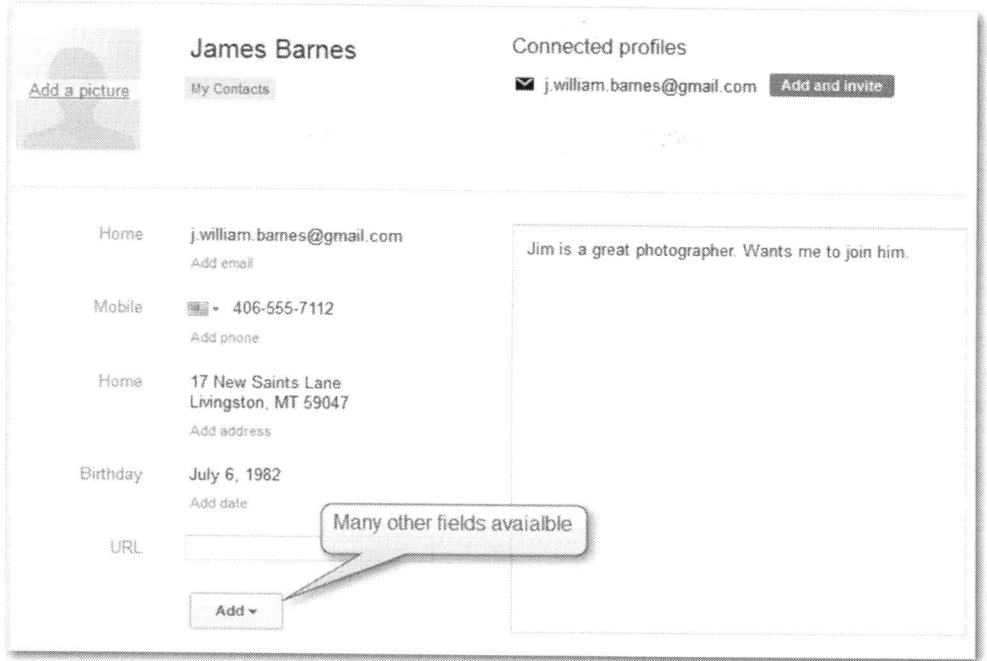

Figure 260: Basic new contact entry screen

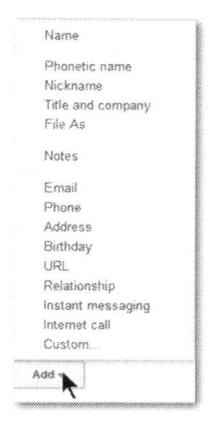

Figure 261: Optional fields you can add for more contact information

There are optional fields you can add to a contact's record. As you see, you can store fairly complete data in Google Contacts (*Figure 261*).

The more complete the data you have, the more you will be able to build a relationship with the contact. Record and then call on their birthday, for example. You can extend with custom fields, if you wish.

Using Google Tasks in Gmail

Use Google Tasks to keep track of the things you need to do. You can create lists of items, set due dates and notes, and even add Gmail messages directly to Tasks. At any time from either Gmail or Contacts, you can open **Task.**

How to Move Your Expensive Office to the Free Cloud

171

Chapter 9: Using Gmail and Hangouts

To get started, click the down arrow next to **Gmail** or **Contacts** in the top left corner of your Gmail/Contacts page, then choose **Tasks**. A new task pop-up will appear allowing you to enter a new task (*Figure 262*).

To enter tasks, click in the **Tasks** window and start typing. Once you've typed in a task, press 'Enter' to create another task, or use the + button at the bottom of your list.

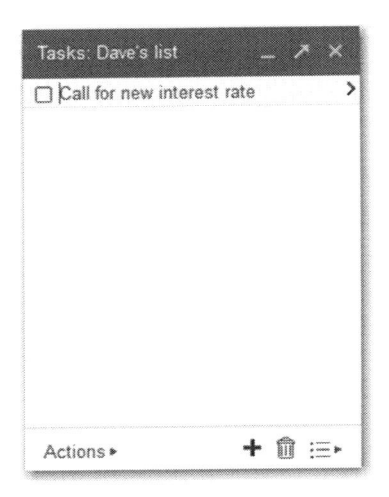

Figure 262: Adding a new undated task

Click the right pointing arrow head to the right of the task (>) to add a date and more details. This will open the detail view of the task (*Figure 263*).

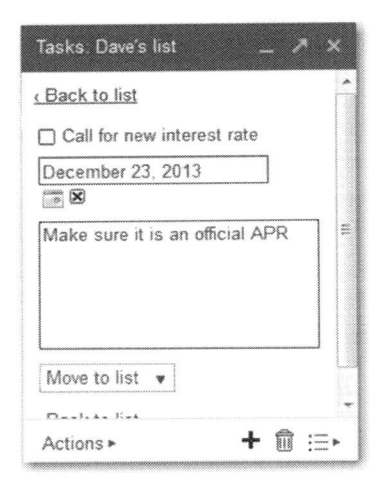

Figure 263: Adding a completion or due date and note

Here are some of the options available in Google Tasks:

- Create a task about a Gmail message using the keyboard shortcut Shift + T, or by choosing **Add to Tasks** from the **More** menu above your Gmail conversation.
- Switch between existing lists or create new ones using the list icon in the bottom right corner.

- Create "subtasks" by using Tab to indent them, and Shift + Tab to move them back.
- Move tasks by grabbing them to the left of the check mark and dragging them up and down.
- Add new tasks to the middle of a list by clicking at the beginning or end of an existing task and pressing Enter.
- Check off Tasks when you're done, and use **Actions** > **Clear completed** to hide them. Don't worry, you can still view them later!
- Print your tasks by clicking **Actions** and selecting **Print task list**.

Using Hangouts to Make Text Messaging, Phone and Video Calls

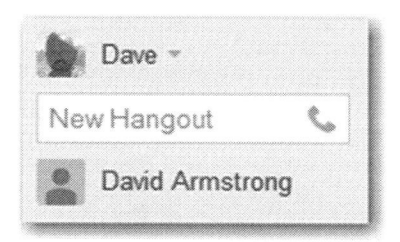

Figure 264: Use Hangouts to communicate with others

Hangouts is Google's latest version of what was called Google Talk. It is available from Gmail and Google+ on the web and anytime from within Google's Chrome browser. They provide apps for Apple and Android tablets and phones. You can locate the Hangout feature in the lower left of the Contacts screen (*Figure 264*).

You will need to sign up separately for Hangouts. Unlike most Google applications. Use the same Gmail address and password. They provide a free phone number in your area code for incoming calls. You can route that number to other numbers so that an incoming call is transferred to the other phones. My apologies to Lord of the Ring fans, but you get, "***One number to rule them all!***"

You can call anywhere in the United States and Canada for free. You can call overseas for about 2 cents a minute.

If you are at Gmail or Contacts, type the name, phone number or email into the **New Hangout** text.

This opens a new browser screen *(Figure 265)*. You will see a similar screen in the video section which is next.

Since this is a call to an older flip phone, you can see the video button in red at the top has a line through it indicating the phone is not capable of video.

If you need them, you can open other Google apps using the buttons on the left.

Chapter 9: Using Gmail and Hangouts

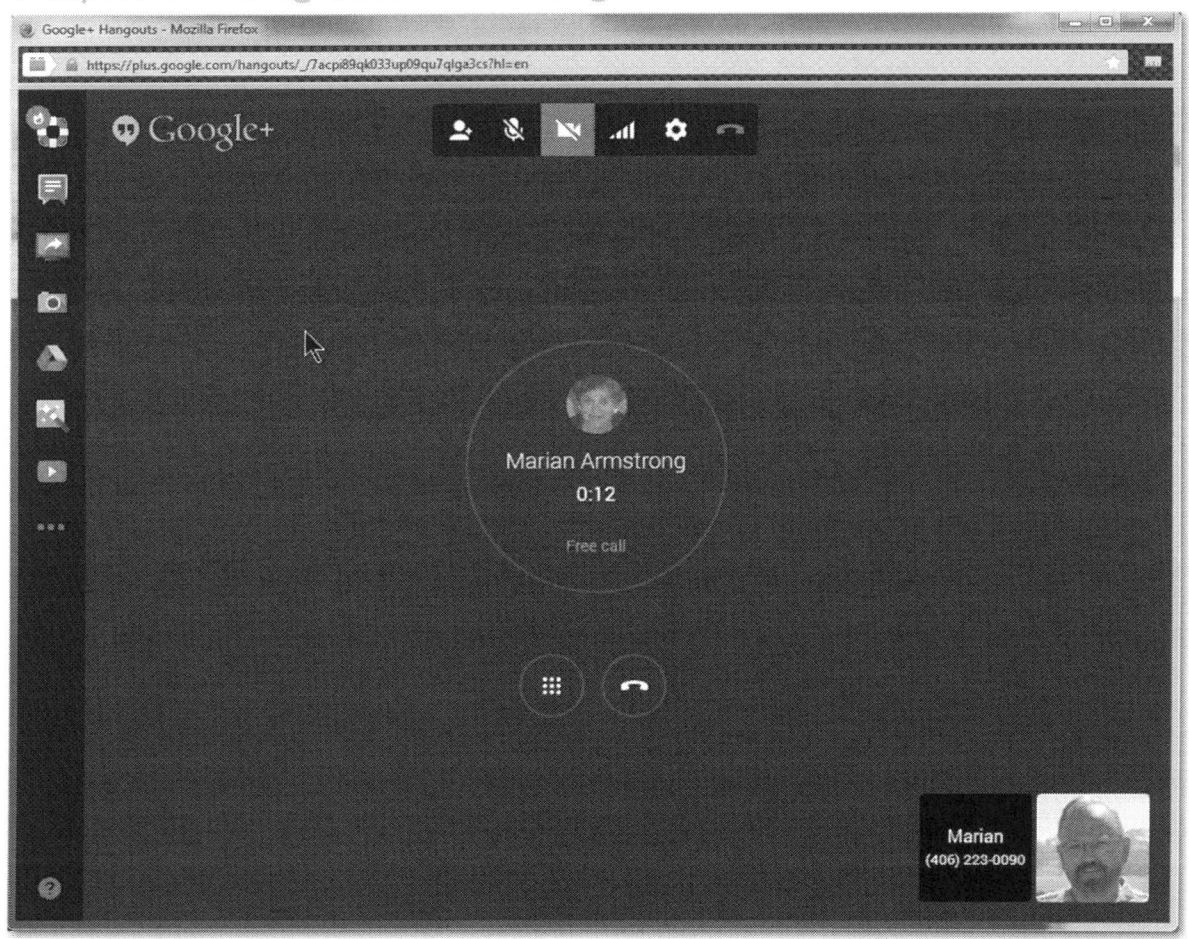

Figure 265: Talking on Hangouts

Video calling

While you can call a phone number from the video screen, video conferencing only occurs when the person at the other end is using Hangouts. Notice, that during a call, you can chat, share your screen, show images and share your Google Drive.

Video calling opens another web page full screen (*Figure 266*).

Chapter 9: Using Gmail and Hangouts

Figure 266: Ready to invite people

If you add telephone numbers, you will not get video unless they are using a smart phone with the Hangouts app installed. Add a Gmail address and you should be able to initiate a video call, if the other person has signed up for Hangouts and has a computer or smartphone (*Figure 267*).

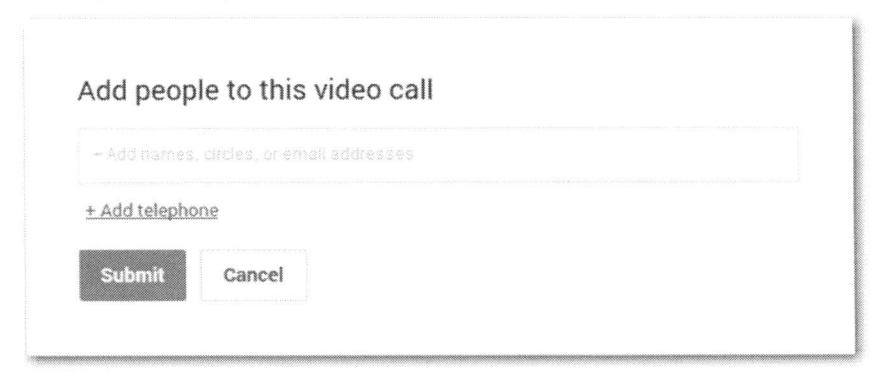

Figure 267: Add Gmail Addresses for video, phone numbers for voice

If you do type a phone number and the person is in Contacts, you can pick from a list with just a partial number (*Figure 268*).

How to Move Your Expensive Office to the Free Cloud

175

Chapter 9: Using Gmail and Hangouts

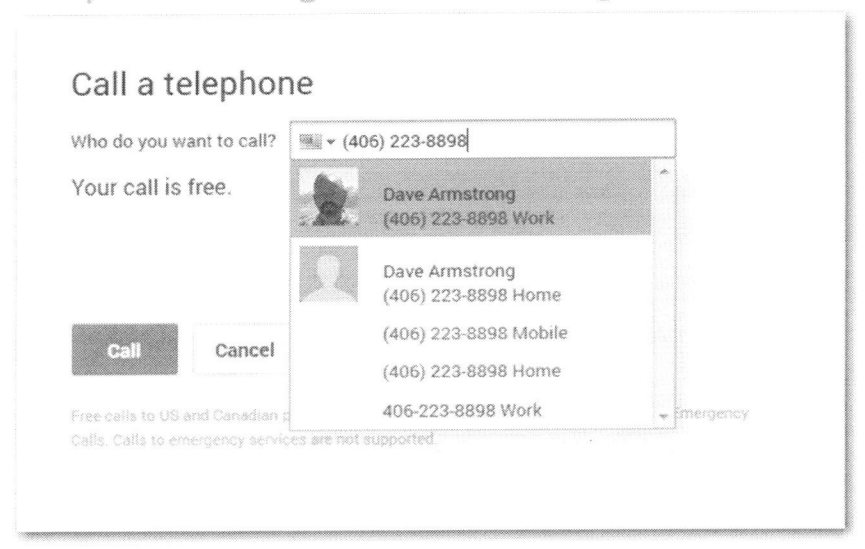

Figure 268: Suggested phone numbers from your contacts

I did manage to connect to myself on my Android smart phone, Hangouts PC to Hangouts phone. You see your image in the lower right and the person on the other end, full screen.

This is what I look like after writing a long chapter, such as this one.

I know this is a long chapter, but whether you want a true virtual office or just better communication from the desk, Google has a lot to offer and it is free for small businesses.

How to Move Your Expensive Office to the Free Cloud

Chapter 10: Using Google Calendar

The Main Screen

Google gives you an integrated calendar. It can send and receive events via Gmail. It has **Day**, **Week**, **Month**, **7Days** and **Agenda** views.

Let's take a high level tour (*Figure 269*):

1. Use the **CREATE** event button to create a new event.
2. You can have more than one calendar and can share a calendar with an assistant that has limited access. He or she can make or move appointments, for example. You might even have a calendar for some resource such as a conference or meeting room. You would share that calendar with all staff so they could book the room.
3. Today is always shown as a default date for a new event.
4. Events show up on the proscribed date in time order.
5. You can change views from the default of **Month** to any of the other views.
6. You can see your task list.
7. You can quickly jump to any date before you add an event. You can also do this from within the add event screen.
8. You may also see birthdays, holidays and other predefined events.

Chapter 10: Using Google Calendar

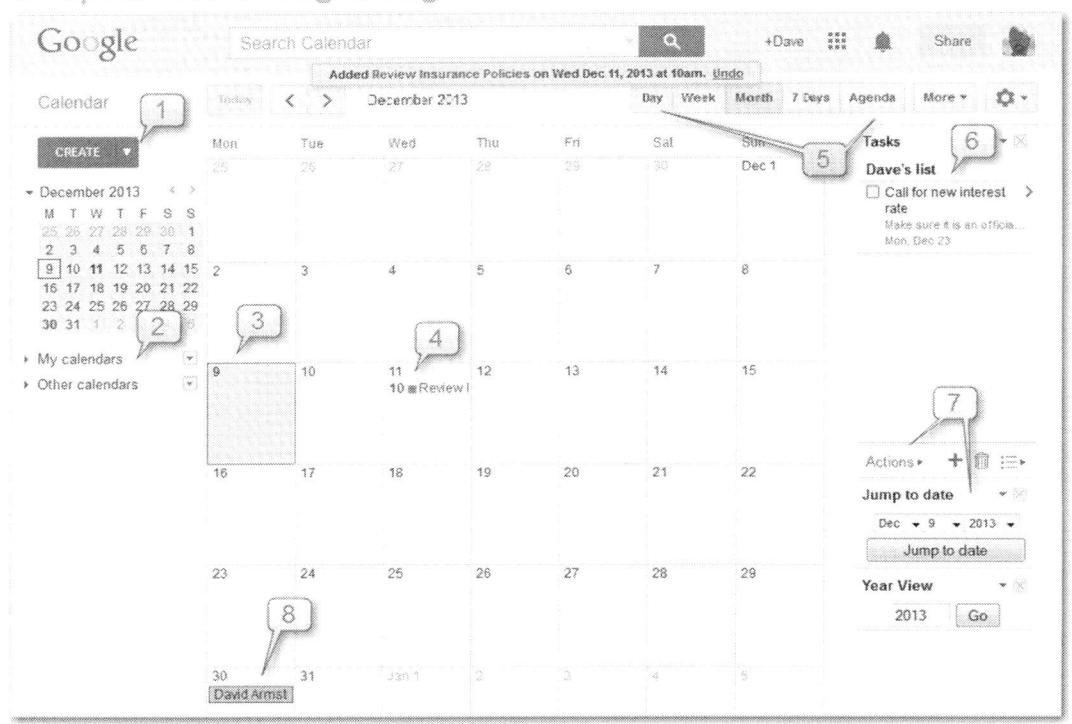

Figure 269: Calendar's main screen

Month, Week, Day and Agenda Calendar Views

Looking at the day view, we see an existing appointment between 10 and 11 am (*Figure 270*). Click a timeslot and you can add a new appointment. If you need to add more information, click the **Edit event>>** link or double click to open the detail view.

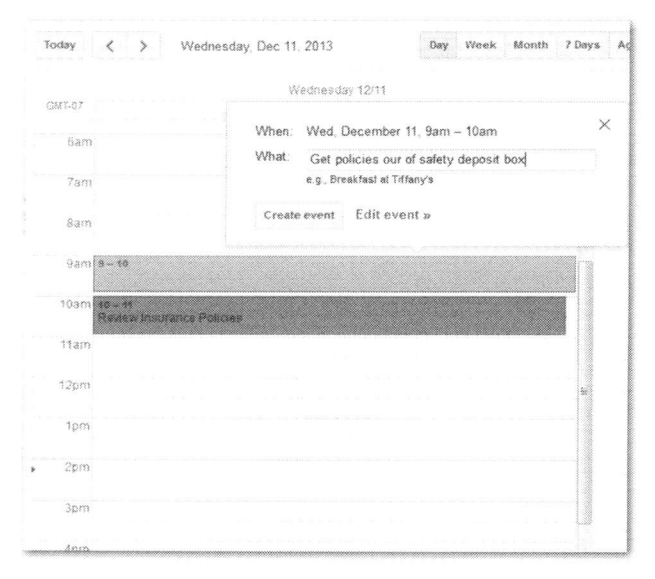

Figure 270: A day view

Chapter 10: Using Google Calendar

In the week view, you see the appointment(s) you have for the current week (*Figure 271*). Again, you can click or double-click to add an event.

Figure 271: A week view

The **Agenda** view shows all upcoming events in chronological order (*Figure 272*). I usually start with the agenda view, as it gives me a contextual view of my near future.

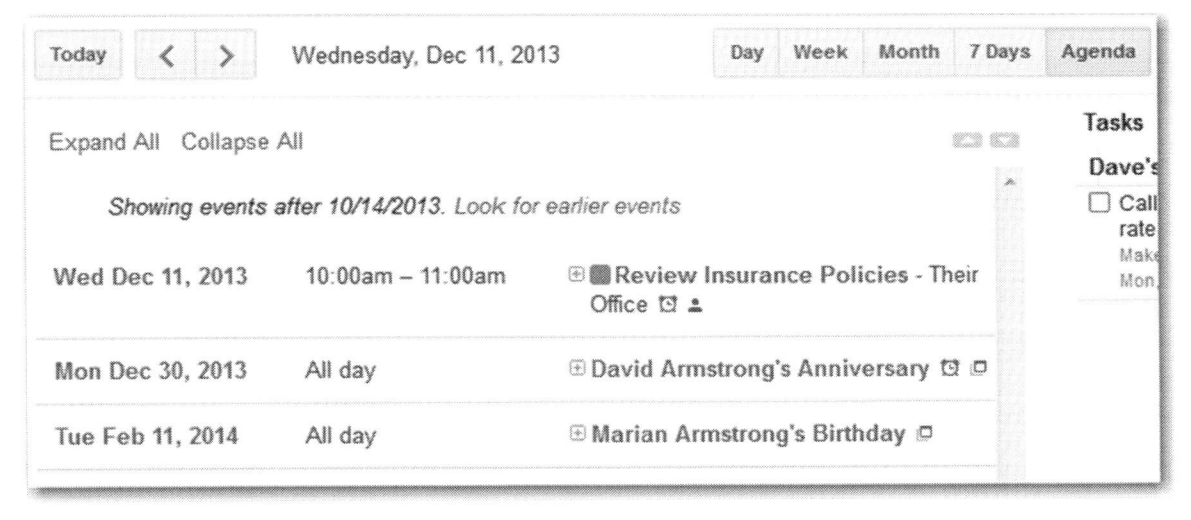

Figure 272: The Agenda view showing all upcoming events

How to Move Your Expensive Office to the Free Cloud

Chapter 10: Using Google Calendar

Annual Calendar View

You can also see an annual calendar by clicking the **Go** button in the **View year** box in the lower right of the screen (*Figure 273*).

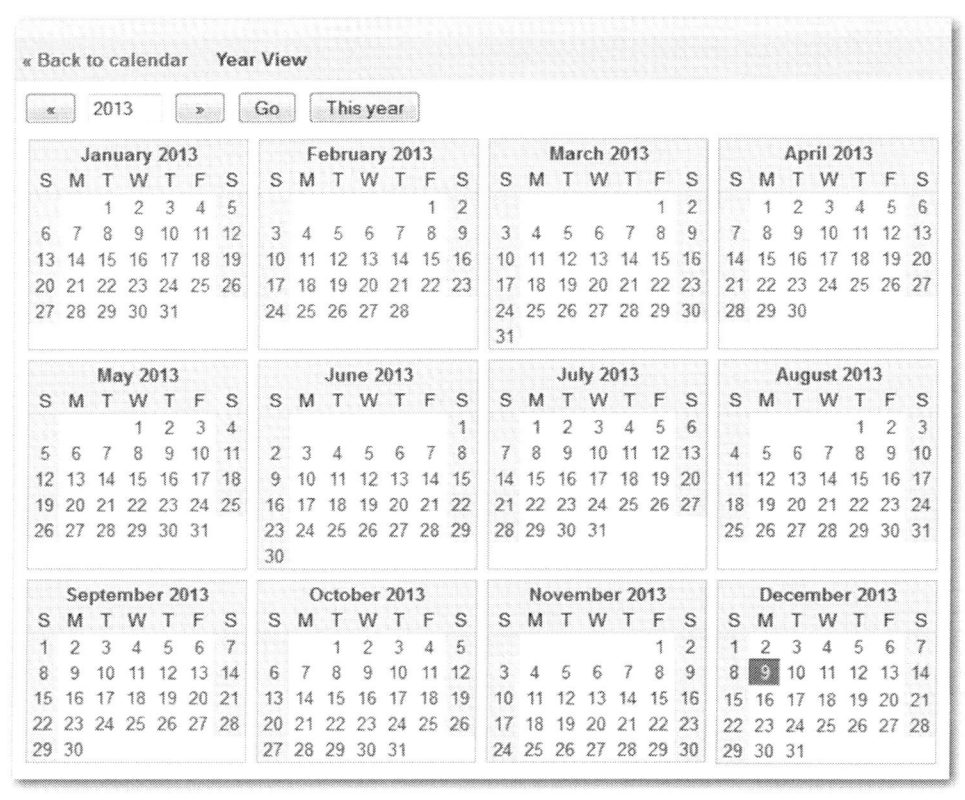

Figure 273: The full Year View

Chapter 10: Using Google Calendar

The sidebar menu shows the create button. Below it is a calendar with live links to the days. Click any day on the calendar to jump to that day (*Figure 274*).

Below the calendar, you can access any of your alternate calendars. Keep a calendar for business that your staff can see and keep a personal one private for just your use.

Figure 274: Sidebar menu

Adding a New Event

In the create a new appointment details screen, there are many choices, so let's step through the main decisions you will need to make (*Figure 275*):

1. Give a meaningful name and decide if the event is **All day** or timed. If repeating, check the **Repeat...** box and describe the manner of the repeating. If out of your **Time Zone**, indicate the other time zone. This is great, if you are on a trip.
2. Where will the event take place? No entry can be assumed from your office, such as a phone call.
3. Whose calendar should this be on? The default is yours, but if you share calendars, you can place it on another's.
4. Add a short **Description**, if you feel it is necessary to jog your memory.
5. Some like to color code their events.
6. Should the Calendar show you as busy during that time? You might want to be available if an important call comes in. Also, is the event **Public** or **Private**? Private events do not show, even if your calendar is public.
7. Want to add a guest? You can email invitations to others you wish to attend. Depending on how they receive emails, they will have an attached invite. They can accept or reject the invitation. All they have to do is double-click to accept and add the event into their calendar.
8. What controls over the scheduled events do you want to give others? With your permission, they can **Modify event**, **Invite others** or **See Guest list** of other attendees.

Chapter 10: Using Google Calendar

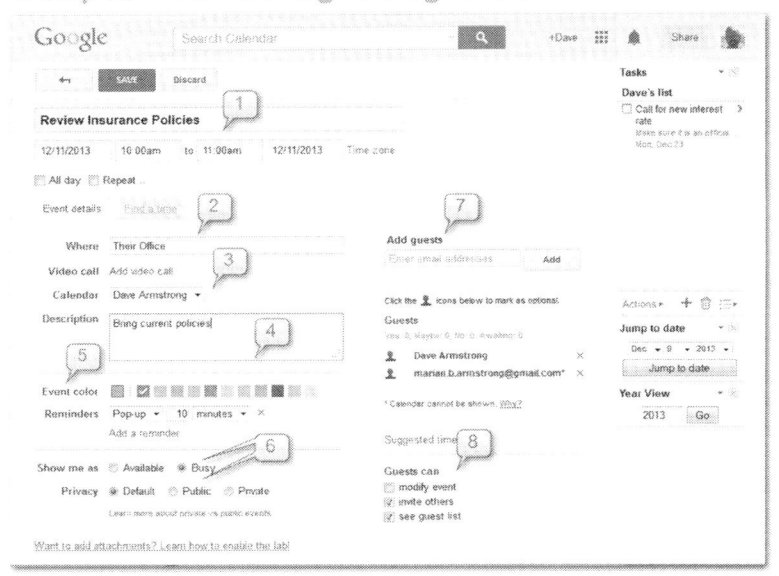

Figure 275: Creating a new appointment

There is more to Gmail, but this should help you get a good start.

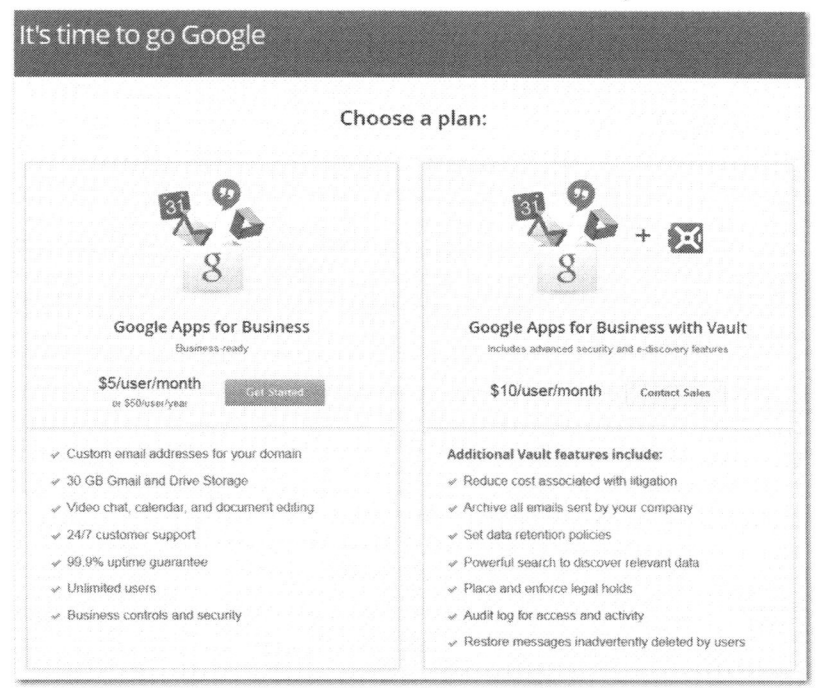

276: Google paid plans

Google Docs in the Enterprise

Google adds some nice features for their paid service. While the free applications work just fine whether you are a business or not, for $5, per user, per month, or $50 a year, you get:

- **More storage.** Instead of 15, you get 30 GB per user.
- **Custom email address.** Instead of daveea1@gmail.com, you get one tied to your domain, such as david.e.armstrong@smartypantssocialmarketing.com. However, you can change the **From** address in Gmail to a domain based name on a personal account, whether or not, you have the paid service.
- **Unlimited users.** Meaning a user can have any number of different email addresses.
- **Business controls** that offer an admin tool for managing user account, Drive documents and security.
- **24/7 customer support** that includes phone and email.
- **99.99% uptime guarantee.**

For $10 a month, per person, you can upgrade to Google Apps for Business with Vault. This gives you in addition:

- Business-critical data archiving.
    - Set data retention policies to archive business-critical information, such as Gmail messages, attachments and chat logs.
- Data retrieval for investigation.
    - Meet your data preservation obligation for litigation and investigation by enforcing legal holds.
- Company-wide data discovery and export.
    - Search for all user data across the domain, filter for relevance and export.

If you are a legal or finance business, this may be a better choice as you have special legal retention obligations.

Chapter 11: Google Cloud Print

Even in the virtual world, there is still a need for paper. You may have documents destined for snail mail that need signatures. You may need a staff member to markup a printout before a meeting. In the old workspace, you would print to the appropriate printer, walk over and retrieve the paper document.

Most printer manufactures now produce printers that can be accessed over the internet. Hewlett-Packard (HP) has their ePrint line, which we will look at later. Epson has their Remote Print software.

However, there are a lot of old printers that are not capable of connecting directly to the Internet. I have several and am not ready to replace them. Google can route to the new Internet capable printers, but they also have the ability to connect to any printer that is connected to any computer on the Internet. When you are ready to get started, go to http://www.google.com/landing/cloudprint/ (*Figure 277*).

Quoting Google, "*Google Cloud Print is a new technology that connects your printers to the web. Using Google Cloud Print, you can make your home and work printers available to you and anyone you choose, from the applications you use every day. Google Cloud Print works on your phone, tablet, Chrome device, PC, and any other web-connected device you want to print from*".

Chapter 11: Google Cloud Print

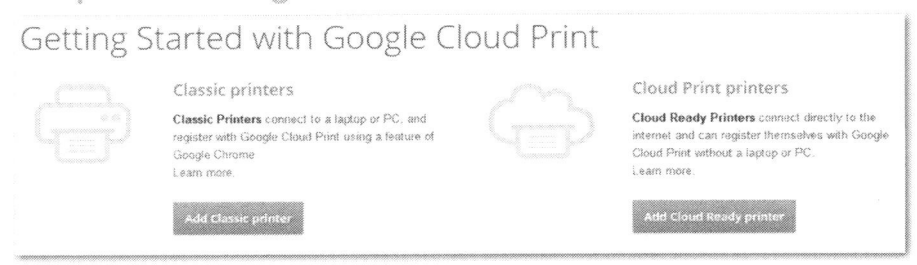

Figure 277: Connecting to your printer over the internet

Hooking Up a Classic Printer

Your first step, is to register your local printer with Google and you MUST use Google's own browser, Chrome, for this. If you do not have it installed, you will need to first download and install.

http://goo.gl/02agLu

1. Open your Chrome browser and click the Chrome menu button, , on the browser toolbar.
2. Select **Settings**.
3. Find the **Google Cloud Print** section and click the **Manage** button (*Figure 278*).

Figure 278: Click Manage to add a printer

4. If you do not see your printer, click the **Add printer** button (*Figure 279*).

Chapter 11: Google Cloud Print

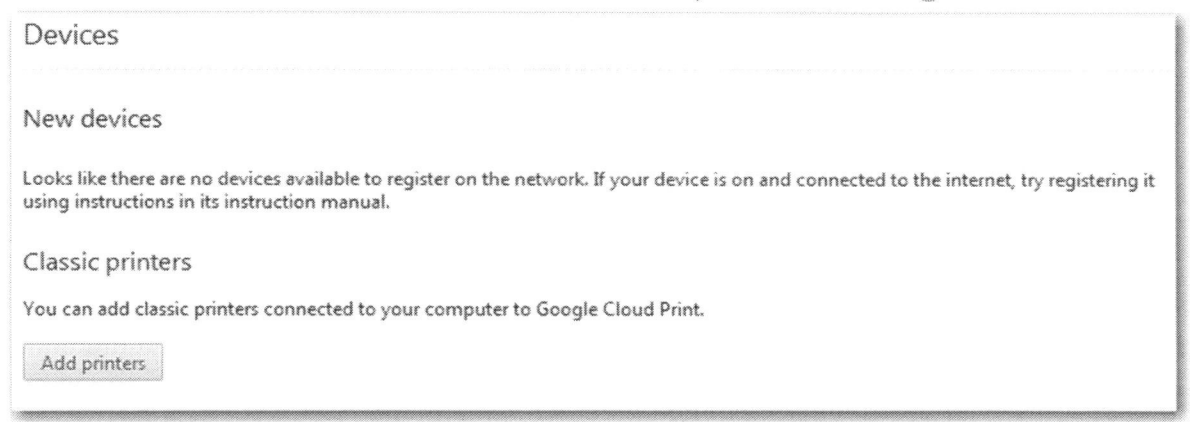

Figure 279: Add classic printers

You will probably have to sign into your Google account (*Figure 280*).

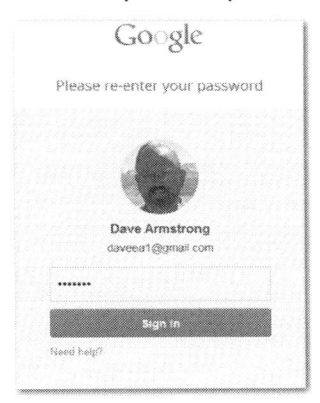

Figure 280: Sign into Google

The **Printers to register** screen will list all of the printers Google thinks are attached to your computer. Select the printer or printers you wish to register and click the **Add printer(s)** button (*Figure 281*).

Chapter 11: Google Cloud Print

Figure 281: Picking printers to register for Google's cloud print service

If all goes well, you will get a **Thanks, you're ready to go!** Dialog (*Figure 282*).

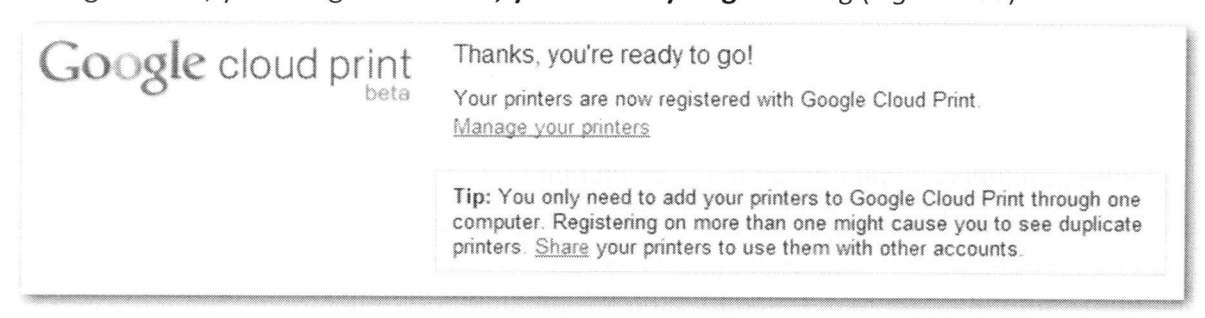

Figure 282: Registering successful

Getting to Your Registered Printer

You are half way there. You now need to have a way of printing to the registered printer. There are a lot of applications listed at this link for printing from browsers, tablets and smart phones and PCs, including Macs.

Chapter 11: Google Cloud Print

http://www.google.com/cloudprint/learn/apps.html

Scroll down to the Google Cloud Printer for Windows. Click on the Google Cloud Print Windows Driver link (*Figure 283*).

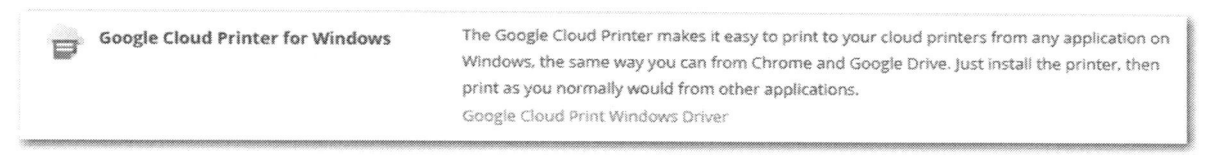

Figure 283: Downloading the Google cloud printer driver

On the download screen, Google shows how the new printer driver might look. Click the **Download Google Cloud Printer** button (*Figure 284*).

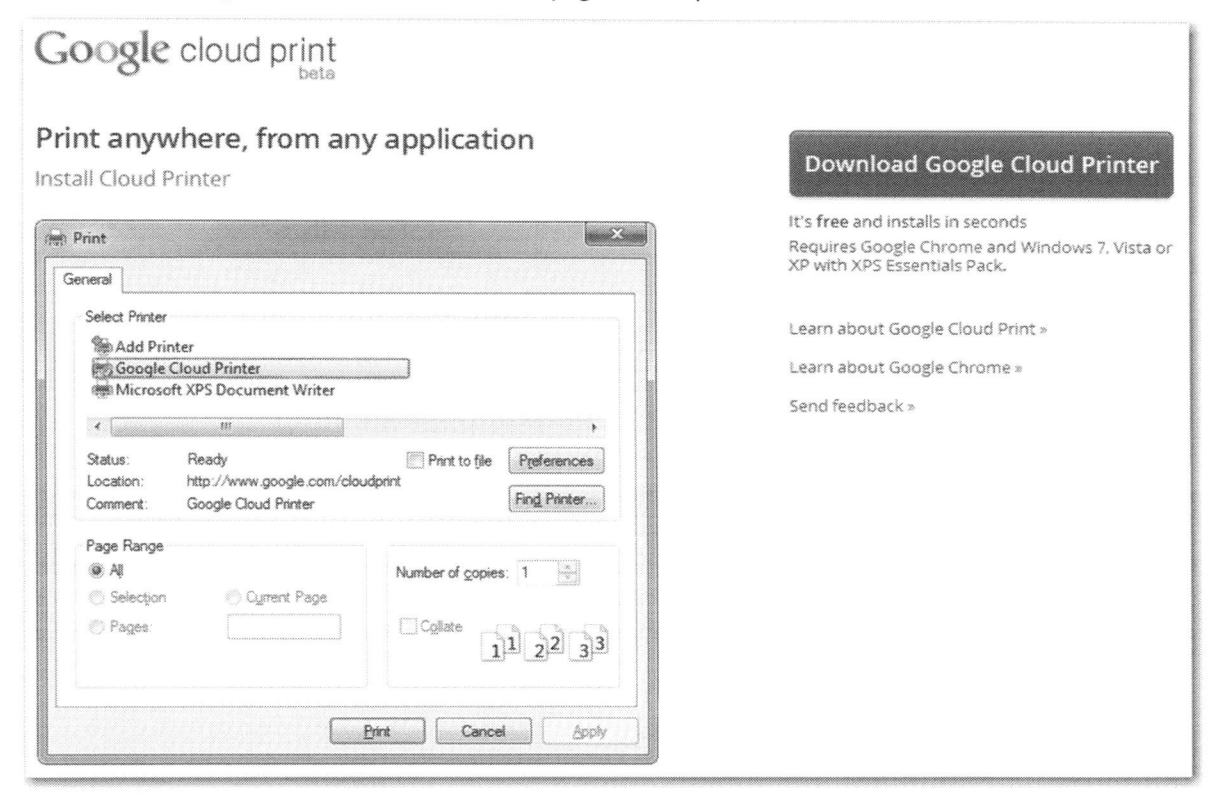

Figure 284: Downloading the cloud printer driver

Accept Google's terms of service (*Figure 285*).

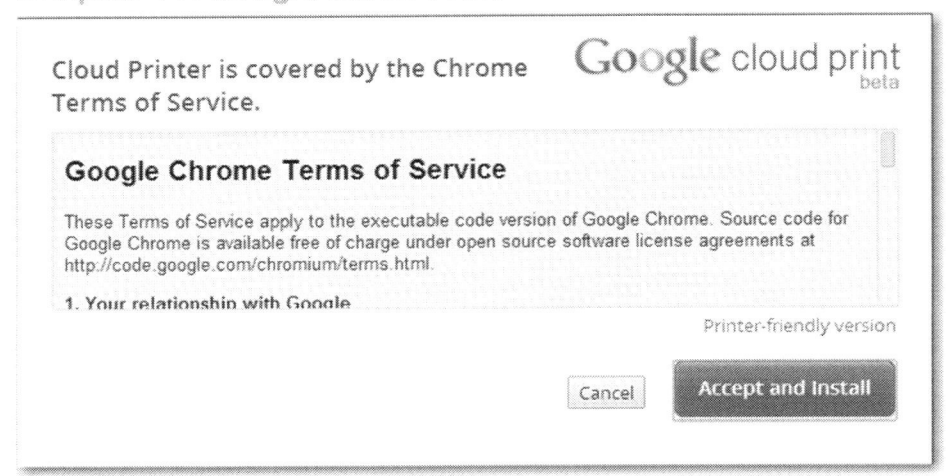

Figure 285: Google's terms of service

As with any download, save the file and when the download completes, find and double-click it. Click on the **Run** button to install. (*Figure 286*)

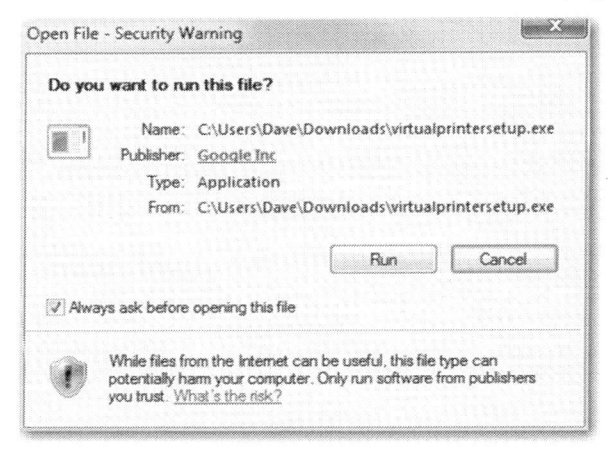

Figure 286: Install the printer driver

The next time you print, you will have a new printer choice. It will be called **Google Cloud Printer** and will be listed with the other printer drivers installed on your computer (*Figure 287*).

Chapter 11: Google Cloud Print

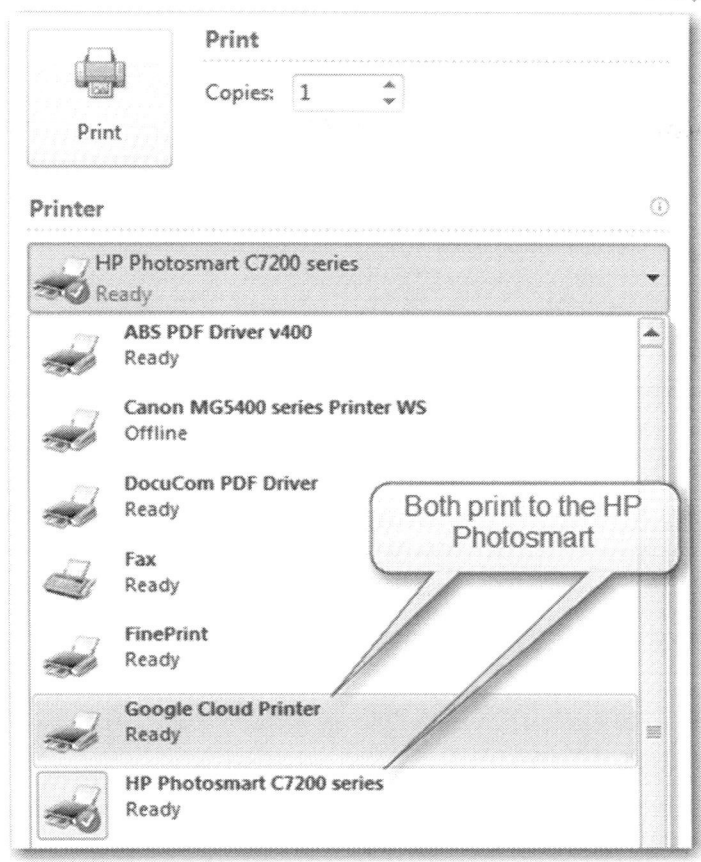

Figure 287: Your new Google Cloud Printer driver

If you usually print from your computer, this Google printer driver is all you need.

Each of your staff will need to register and connect to their printers. Your staff, then need to share their printers with other staff. Each will have to have a Goggle Gmail address and password.

Sharing Your Printers

Follow these steps to manage your printer's sharing permissions:

1. Visit the Google Cloud Print management page at https://www.google.com/cloudprint#jobs.
2. Click the Printers on the left side.
3. Select the printer that you want to share.
4. Click the Share button.

Chapter 11: Google Cloud Print

[screenshot: Google Cloud Printer sharing settings dialog showing Private, Dave Armstrong (daveea1@gmail.com) Owner, Invite people field with marian.b.armstrong@gmail.com, Can print, Share/Close buttons]

5. When you share printers, you'll share printer names, so choose a descriptive name when setting up your printer for the first time.
6. In the dialog that appears, enter the email address for the person or Google Group you want to share with.
7. Click **Share.**

Your colleague will receive an email notification. To disable sharing, follow the steps above to open the Sharing dialog for the printer and edit the user list.

Hooking up a Cloud Reader Printer

Most new printers have a wireless connection mode. They can connect to your computer without the need of a USB cable. Most, but not all, can be accessed across the Internet. You can print from anywhere you have an Internet connection.

You can connect from a PC or Mac, but also from most mobile devices. The printer manufacturers provide free apps that enable printing.

As an example, HP has Internet enabled most of their printers under the ePrint series. When you set up the printer, you choose wireless access and, as part of the setup you enable ePrint. You then print a sheet that shows the setup parameters and one of those values is an email address. It might look like **myprinter@hpeprint.com**. To print to the printer across the Internet, you attach the file to be printed and email it to that email address.

Google Cloud Print goes one better. You can register the printer by its email address, but Google bypasses the need for an email with attachment and prints directly. Google eliminates the need to email.

From the opening screen, we saw in (*Figure 277*), click the Add Cloud Ready printer button (*Figure 288*). You will go to this page. http://goo.gl/uFTwzE.

Chapter 11: Google Cloud Print

Figure 288: Adding a cloud ready printer

On the next page, pick your brand of printer on the left. It is important to get the right brand as each one has very different ways of connecting. Once the brand is selected, click the link at the bottom. Most listed printers just have a link to more detailed instructions (*Figure 289*).

Figure 289: Picking your printer brand

Chapter 11: Google Cloud Print

Take the setup parameter page you printed when you enabled ePrint in the setup of the printer. It will have the email address assigned by HP. Enter the first part of that email address. This allows Google to find the printer when you try to print.

Figure 290: Enter the email address to your ePrint printer

You will still need a printer driver that represents the printer and you, also, need to share so other staff can print to it.

Lastly, there is an alternative to printing directly. You could print to a PDF, attach the PDF to an email and send. They then open the PDF and print. This takes more time and requires effort on both you and their part. While setting up remote printing takes a few steps and a little time, it saves a lot of time in the long run.

Chapter 12: Using Zoho CRM

What is Zoho

Zoho earned its success as an easy to use, relatively inexpensive CRM or customer relationship manager. If you are new to CRM, the software allows you to track customers, prospects and leads. You can schedule follow-up, record phone calls and emails sent. At any time, you can see all interactions and notes you have generated on that person or contact.

There are many players in the virtual cloud based CRM. Most are extensive with many add-ons to integrate with other apps and extend the functionality of the core system. Some of the big players are Salesforce.com, Microsoft Dynamics CRM, and Oracle's RightNow Web Experience. While these are enterprise level apps and may be great for large companies, they are too expensive and overkill for small to medium-sized businesses.

Why the mention of CRM? While we have looked at Google and Microsoft free cloud based storage and applications, none of them offer a way to track the activities of individual contacts. I could search for all emails sent to a contact in both Gmail and Outlook web application, but I cannot see the contact information at the same time without opening another browser tab and opening the contact. If I make a phone call, I have no place to add a note about the discussion.

While CRM is the main product of Zoho, they have added many other applications, including a suite of office productivity products. All of these products are integrated with the CRM. This table shows the matching products.

Chapter 12: Using Zoho CRM

Microsoft	Google	Zoho
Word	Document	Writer
Excel	Spreadsheet	Sheet
PowerPoint	Presentation	Show
Outlook Web App	Gmail	MailMagnet
Skype, Lync	Chat	Chat
Skype, Lync	Video meetings	Zoho Meeting

Zoho has a plethora of products, including specialized products, such as Invoicing and recruiting. To be consistent with this book's purpose, we are going to cover only two: CRM and Zoho Docs.

However, it would not be fair to Zoho to not, at least mention these specialized products. All are integrated with CRM so you can see invoices or email campaigns from the contact's or lead's screen.

I am quoting Zoho descriptions. Here are some other Zoho products:

Campaigns

"To make this communication process easy, you need the perfect harmony between your CRM system and your email marketing software. Zoho offers this solution by connecting your Zoho Campaigns and Zoho CRM accounts and lets you reach out to your leads, prospects and customers with ease. You can also measure the effectiveness of your efforts - all from within your CRM account." Zoho also gives you instant response tracking."

Mail

"You can even receive notification and reply to customer emails within CRM, saving you the time and hassle of toggling back and forth between applications. With MailMagnet for Zoho CRM there's no gap between what's said and what needs to be done. Nothing falls through the cracks, and everything is stored and organized for easy, instant access."

Chat

"A sales rep might want to quickly check some technical information with his pre-sales/technical-sales counterpart. Or maybe he is checking for availability. Or the sales rep might want to check with his manager about approval for some special deal. These are the kinds of situations that the instant messaging in Zoho CRM addresses."

Invoice

"Zoho Invoice is the easiest way to invoice your customers. It helps create, send and manage your invoices online. Using Zoho Invoice you can track customer payments and also accept online payments from customers."

Zoho will print snail mail invoices for you and your customers can pay online using PayPal or Google Checkout.

Meeting

"Meet online, provide product demos, sales presentations, online training, team meetings and much more anywhere at any time. Just sign up for Zoho Meeting and conduct unlimited number of meetings with your customers, clients and team members. Collaborate globally, reduce travel time & cost, increase turn over, and grow your business smarter."

Creator

"Use our intuitive and feature-rich platform to build your custom database applications. Just write your business rules and let the software handle deployment and hosting. You can create your own forms/tables afresh or import data from standard formats (.xls .csv .mdb) and get your database application online within minutes, really!"

Recruit

"Zoho Recruit is an easy-to-use Applicant Tracking System and Recruitment Software that helps staffing agencies and recruiting departments track job openings, resumes, candidates and contacts more quickly and efficiently. Zoho Recruit allows you to spend less time on the process and more time on what you do best: getting the right candidate."

Projects

"Professional service firms, and other project-based companies will find our Zoho CRM and Zoho Projects integration very useful in their daily lives. The Zoho Projects integration allows Zoho CRM customers to plan, execute and monitor customer projects right from within your CRM account."

Support — "*The integration of Zoho Support with Zoho CRM provides a platform for you to keep track of the customer tickets within your Zoho CRM account. With this integration, Sales and Marketing users can view the support tickets of individual leads, contacts and accounts in CRM.*"

Reports — "*Zoho CRM, the popular Online Customer Relationship Management system from Zoho, now has a fully featured, seamlessly integrated, advanced analytics add-on, powered by Zoho Reports. Zoho Reports makes it easy to slice and dice your Zoho CRM data the way you like. You can easily create sales funnels, know your win/loss rates, do sales predictions, gauge your sales team performance, track your KPIs (Key Performance Indicators) and do much more in a flash!!*"

LiveDesk — "*Easily embed click-to-chat capability into any, and every, space where your customers search for answers about your products or services. You have customers, they have questions, and Zoho LiveDesk effortlessly connects you, your customers and the support solutions they crave.*"

What Does CRM Cost?

Zoho is free for up to 3 users and $12 per user, per month, for the standard plan (*Figure 291*).

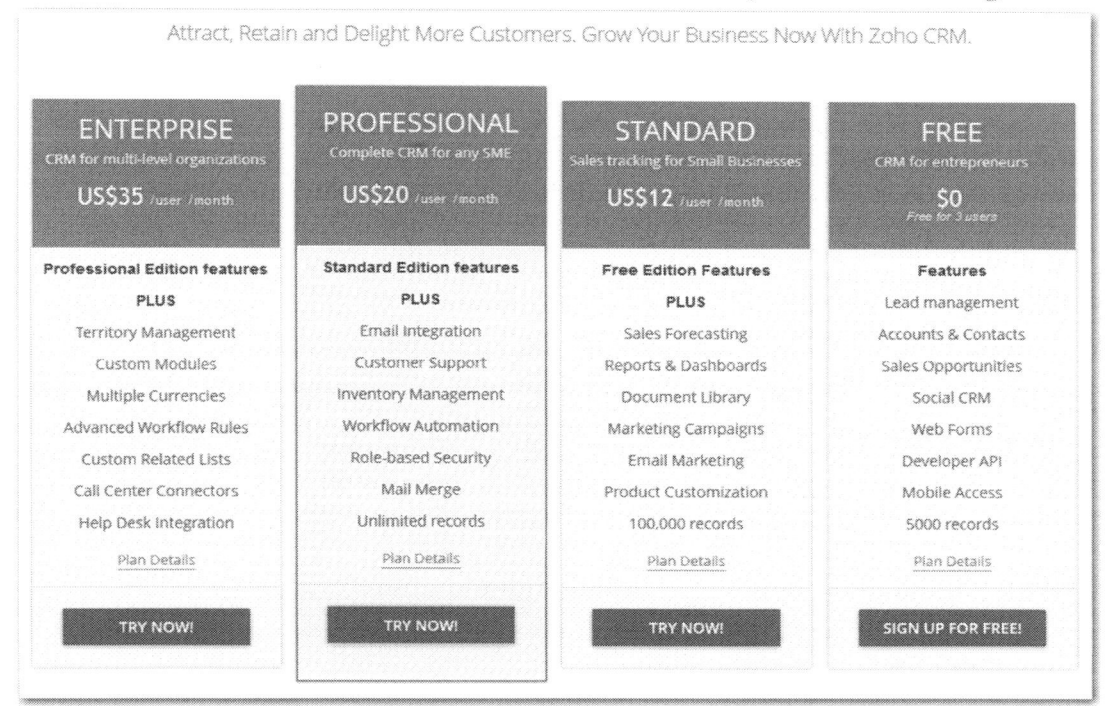

Figure 291: Zoho CRM pricing

Zoho CRM

In the real world, we have customers, prospects we are trying to move to customers and leads we would like to become prospects or customers.

We get leads from promotions or referrals. We then contact them via phone, email, social media or snail mail working to establish a relationship with them.

Our ultimate goal is to turn them into customers and then repeat business. Only a few leads are good prospects and only some of the prospects will become customers. If you have been in sales, you recognize this as the sales pipeline.

Good software models the physical world. CRM software models this relationship between your business and its lifeblood, customers. Computers and software make this far easier that the days of 3 by 5 cards or a thick Rolodex.

Zoho CRM tracks all of the stages from lead to customers and can show the sales pipeline in a graphic manner (*Figure 292*).

Chapter 12: Using Zoho CRM

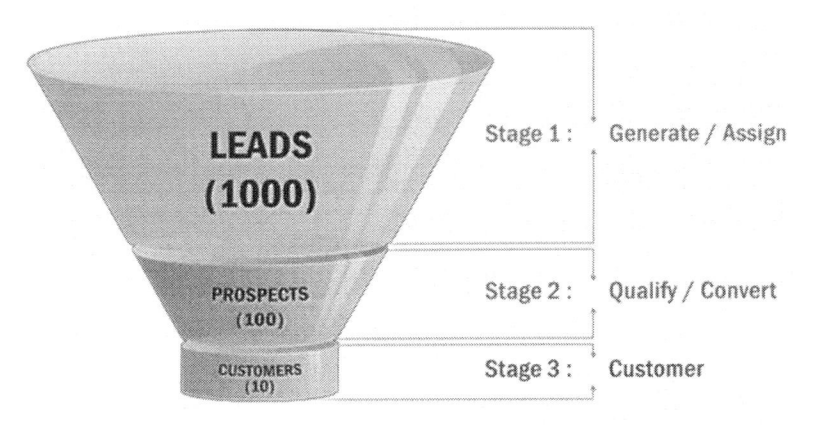

Figure 292: The sales pipeline

Your first step is signing up for Zoho CRM. If you start your evaluation with the free versions, you can have three users and up to 5,000 records. You will not need to provide a credit card for the free version and you can always upgrade, once you commit to using Zoho's CRM.

The Home/opening screen shows your main tabs of **Leads**, **Contacts**, **Accounts** and **Activities**. This is where you do most of your daily work. Further down on the page are links to some of the **Administration** features and customization of your CRM app *(Figure 293)*.

Chapter 12: Using Zoho CRM

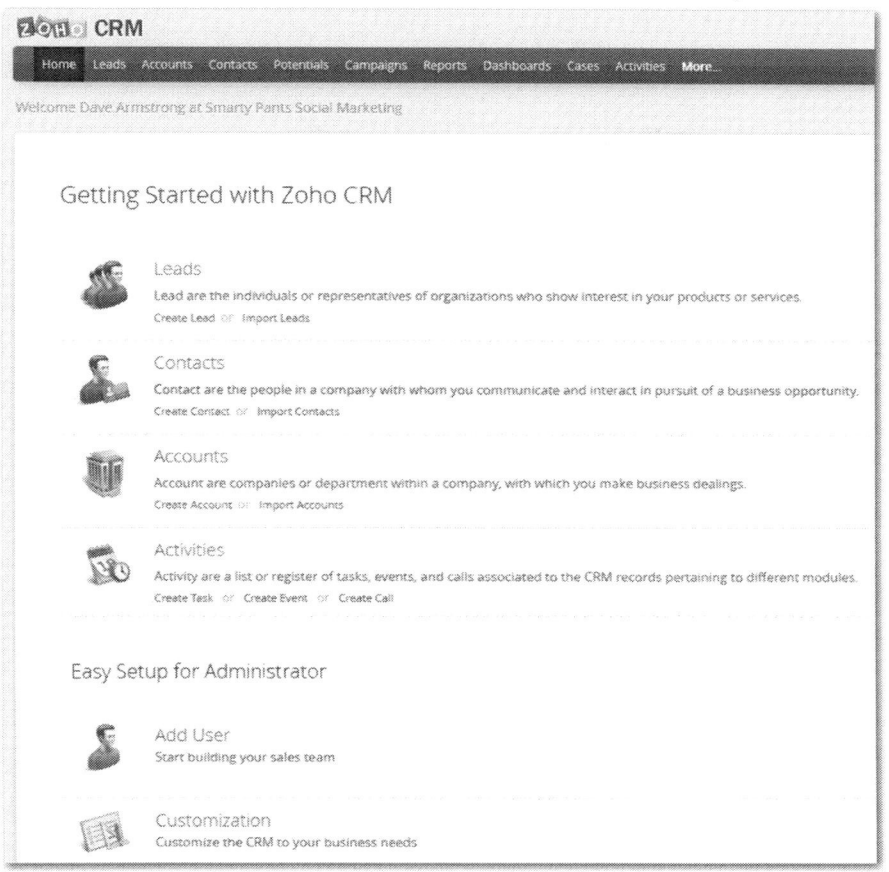

Figure 293: CRM home page

Scroll down further and you can set you time zone, pick a visual theme and upload your company Logo (*Figure 294*).

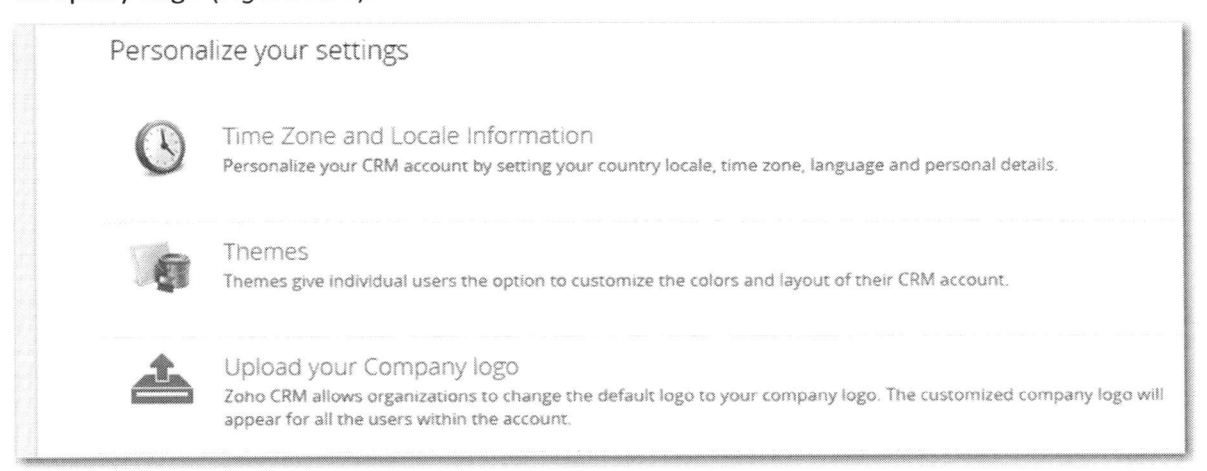

Figure 294: CRM home page (continued)

How to Move Your Expensive Office to the Free Cloud

Chapter 12: Using Zoho CRM

Notice, that you have menus across the top that give you access to the same view, such as **Leads**, **Contacts**, etc. In the rest of this CRM section, we will explore this top menu and the features they represent.

Working with Leads

All new leads start here. You can import them, if you have them in an appropriate format such as a CSV type file. You can also type them in (*Figure 295*).

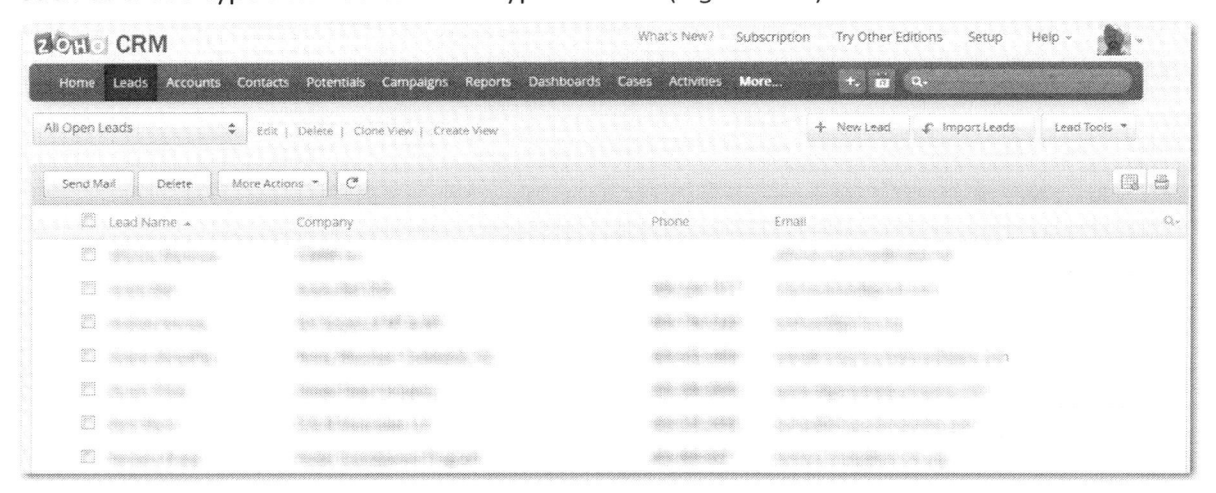

Figure 295: Leads view

> **Note**
>
> As you see in many of the images, I have blurred some of the names, addresses and phone numbers. These screen captures come from my live system and I want to protect their information.

Adding a New Lead

To add a new lead, you must click the **+ New Lead** button in the upper right to open the **Create Lead** screen (*Figure 296*).

This holds any information you might want to keep on a lead. If you wish, you can edit the page layout to remove any of the standard fields. You can add new custom fields. For example, you might want to have a spouse or office manager's information.

The only mandatory fields are the **Company** name and **Last Name**.

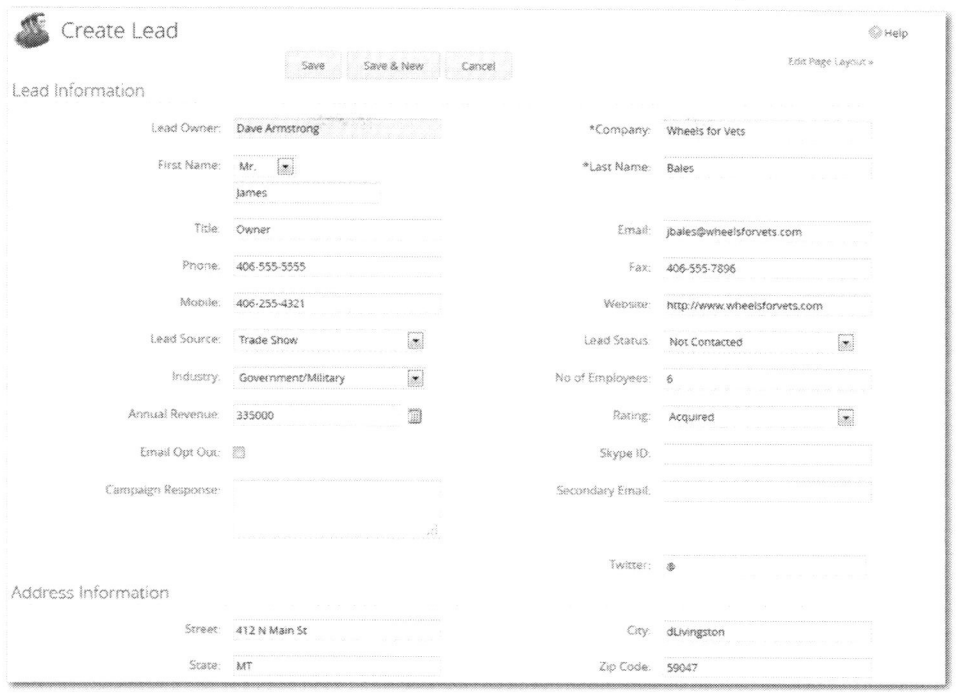

Figure 296: Adding a new lead

Once in your list, you need only click their linked name to open them up in full view (*Figure 297*). From this screen, see all activity you have had with them.

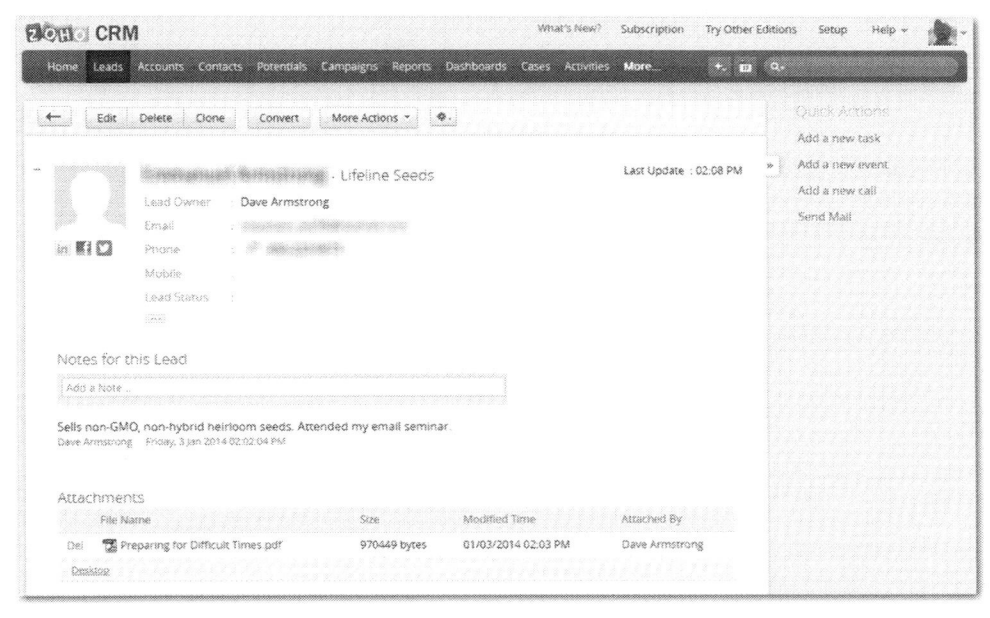

Figure 297: An individual lead

The screen is divided into several areas:

Chapter 12: Using Zoho CRM

- **Notes for this Lead** - Add any information you wish in this note section.
- **Attachments** - You can attach any file from your hard drive or Zoho Docs, which we discuss in the next segment of this chapter. This might be letters sent or, in our case, a PDF file.
- **Open Activities** - This shows pending activity such as a New Task, New Event or to Log a Call.
- **Closed Activities** - These are task completed, events that have passed or a completed log of a call.
- **Emails** - Emails sent.
- **Invited Events** - This section shows events and meetings to which you have invited the lead.
- **Campaigns** - If you do mass snail or email campaigns, this shows the interaction this lead had with those campaigns.

Emailing a Lead

Click the **Send Mail** link in the upper right of the screen below the **Emails** section to send an email. An email form opens in a new window ready for you to complete. The one I show is rather plain, but you can create attractive, HTML type templates on which you can base the email.

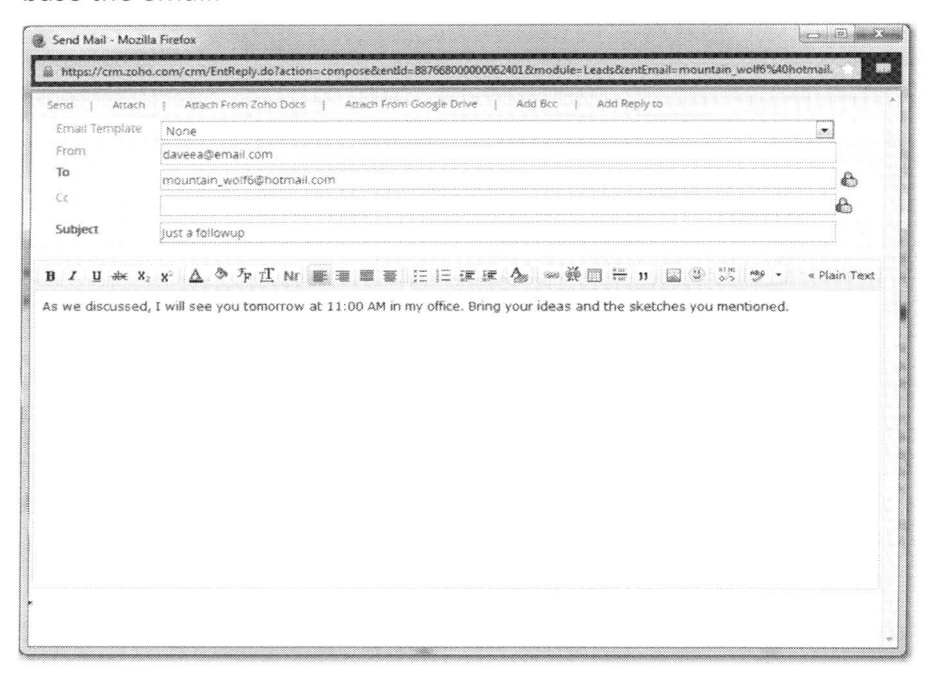

Figure 298: Sending email to a lead

Calling a Lead

Chapter 12: Using Zoho CRM

If you have Skype installed, you can call the lead by clicking on the phone icon(s) below their email address (*Figure 299*).

Figure 299: Dialing a lead or contact

While you are on the call, you can record information by clicking the **Log a Call** link in the Open Activities section or clicking the **Add a new call** link in the **Quick Actions** area in the upper right (*Figure 297*).

You can choose **Inbound** or **Outbound**, pick the **Call Purpose** and/or start the **Call Timer**. You can add the text to the **Call Results** and clicking **More Fields** will open a **Description** text area for notes. You can mark the call as **Billable,** if you are set up to track time (*Figure 300*).

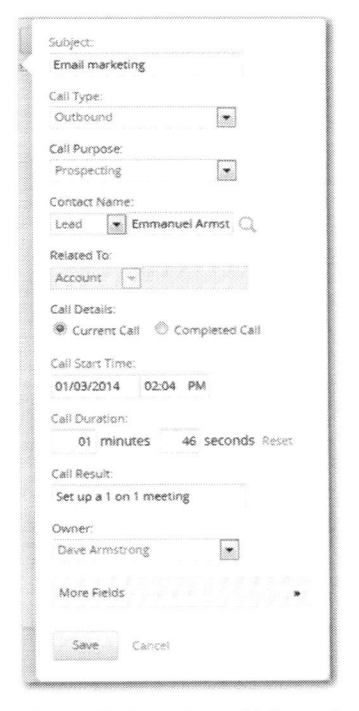

Figure 300: Recording call information

> **Note**
>
> **Have you considered recording your calls?** There are many valid reasons. You might want to review the recording to assure you have missed nothing. You may want to make and save a recording for a potential, future errors and omissions issue.
>
> If you call through Skype, there are several low cost or free add-ons that will record calls. I use Amalto, http://amolto.com/. They have a free version and, if you upgrade to the $30 per user premium version, it does video, sends automatic chat and more.
>
> Before starting, you need to check the laws of your state. Some allow all recording, some if one person knows the call is being recorded and some only if both parties know. You can, and probably should, notify that you are recording to allow someone to opt out.

Adding a Task to a Lead

Nothing ruins a growing lead relationship like a failure to follow-up on something they feel is important. Tasks can have completion dates and you can prioritize.

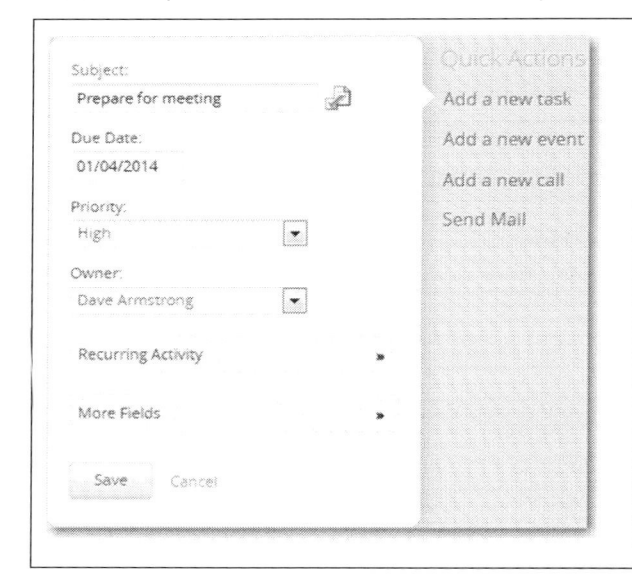

The assumed due date is today, although, you can pick a future date. You can assign a priority from **Highest** to **Lowest** with **High**, **Medium** and **Low** in-between.

You can assign the task to another by changing the Owner. If this is a **Recurring Activity**, you can change the start date and then, daily, weekly, monthly or yearly.

You, also, have **More Fields** that allow a long description.

Once saved, you can see the task either from this Lead's screen or from your activities, as you will see later.

To stay on top of your tasks, you will need to edit. Under the **Open Activities** section, you will see the new task. Click the **Edit** link to open full screen (*Figure 301*). I could change the Status to **In Progress** and later to **Completed** or **Waiting on someone else**.

Chapter 12: Using Zoho CRM

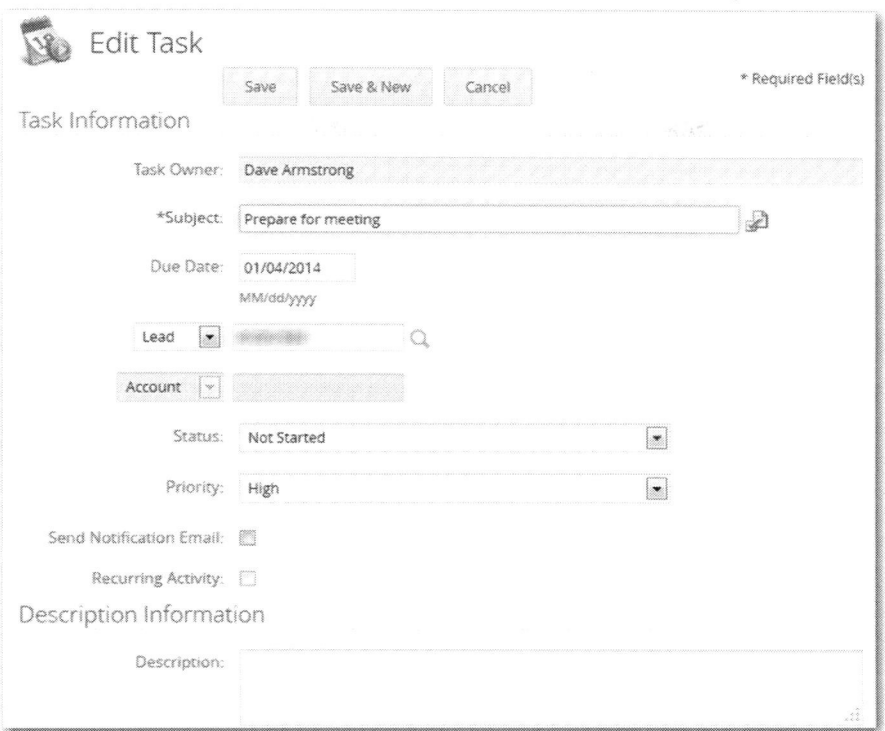

Figure 301: Editing a task

Adding an Event to a Lead

Adding an event, places that event on your calendar. You can assign a **Start DateTime** and **End DateTime**. You could change the **Owner** to another of your staff.

If this is a recurring event, you can add a date range and make it daily to yearly.

You may wish to invite others. Just add their email and the get an invitation.

More Fields gives you a description text area, a venue field (where the event is going to be held) and a send notification email field.

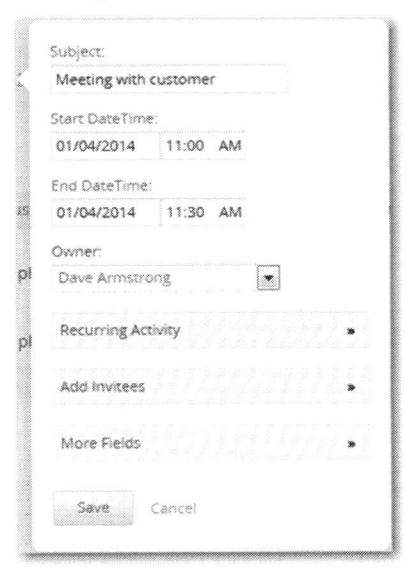

Figure 302: Adding a new Event

Editing an Lead's Event

Chapter 12: Using Zoho CRM

Click the **Edit link** to the left of the event in the **Open Activities** section of the lead screen. This opens the event full screen (*Figure 303*).

You can change the date and/or time or Venue and **Send** a **Notification Email**. Checking this sends a new email to all attendees.

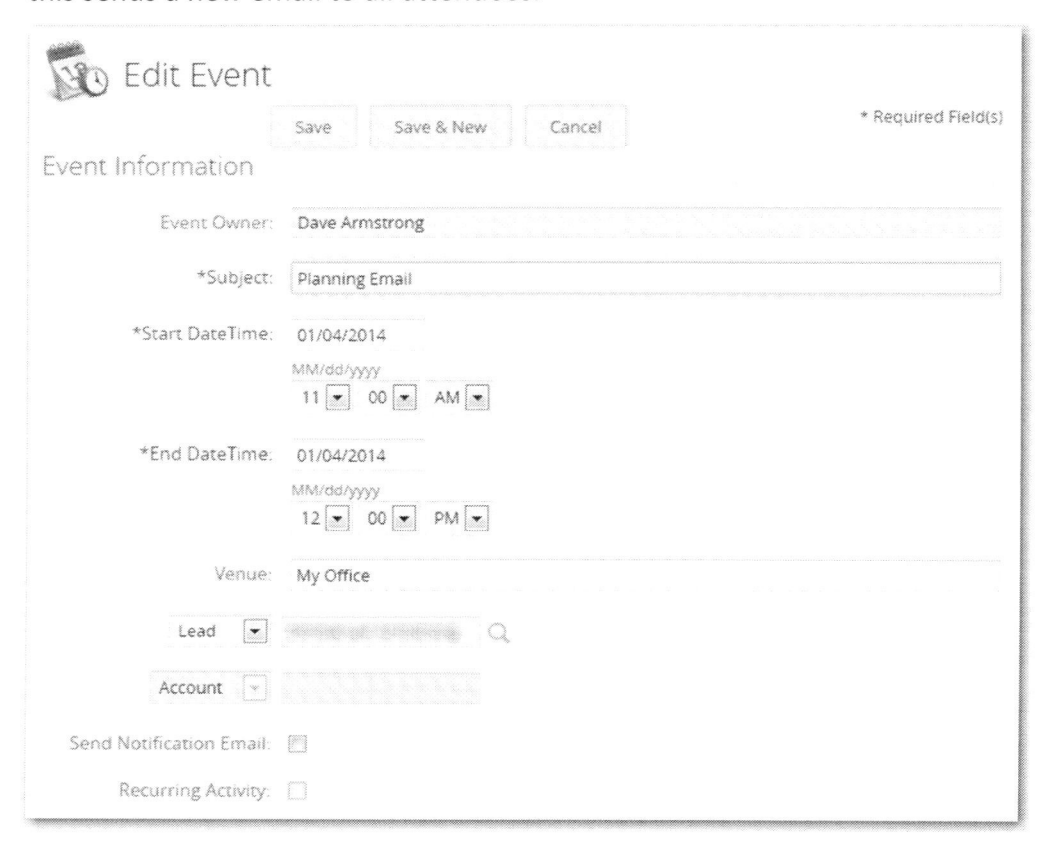

Figure 303: Editing an event

Viewing a Lead's History

All the activity with a lead is on the full page view of the lead.

You can see:

- **Open Activities** - This might be future scheduled events or uncompleted tasks.
- **Closed Activities** - This shows events from the past and phone calls made.
- **Emails** - All emails sent.
- **Invited Events** - Past events or meetings.
- **Campaigns** - Any email or promotional campaign that the lead received.

At some point, this lead becomes a contact. Remember, contacts are customers or serious prospects. You change their status by clicking the **Convert** button at the top of the screen.

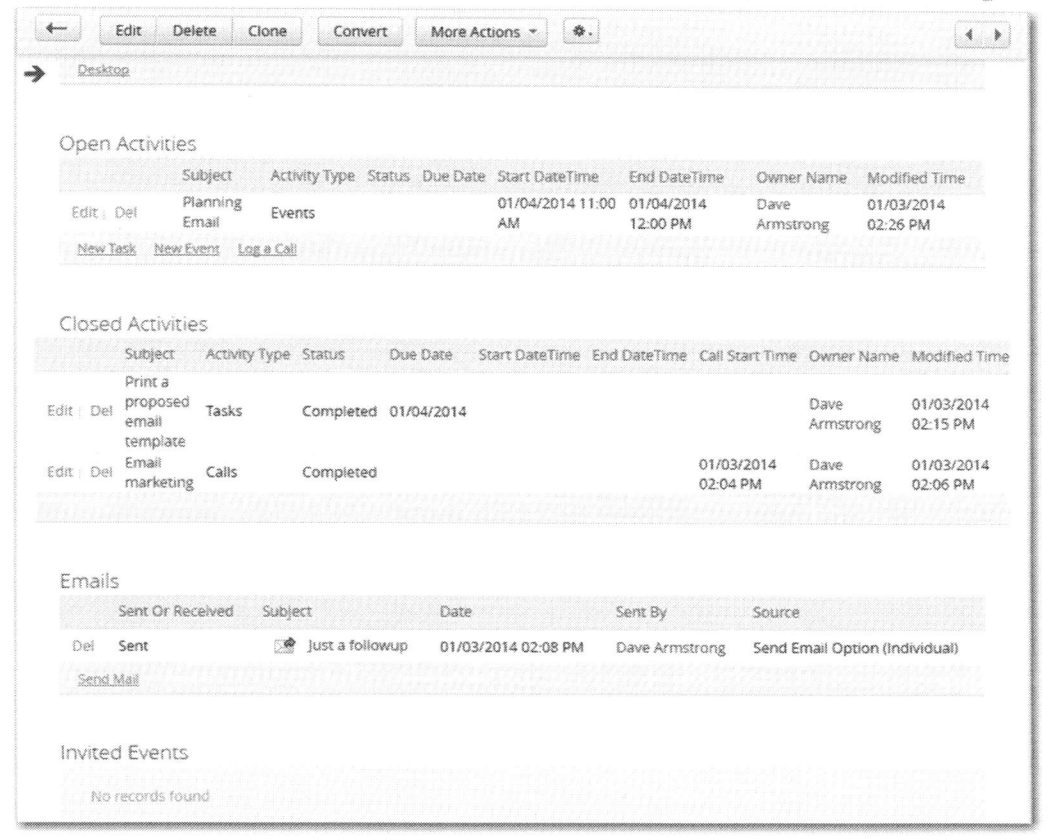

Figure 304: A leads history

Converting Leads into Contacts

Once you click the **Convert** button, you get the **Convert Lead** screen (*Figure 305*). Notice, you have the options of assigning a potential dollar amount to the new contact. You can assign a **Contact Role** such as **Decision Maker**. If you acquired this lead from one of your campaigns, you can look up or type the campaign name.

Chapter 12: Using Zoho CRM

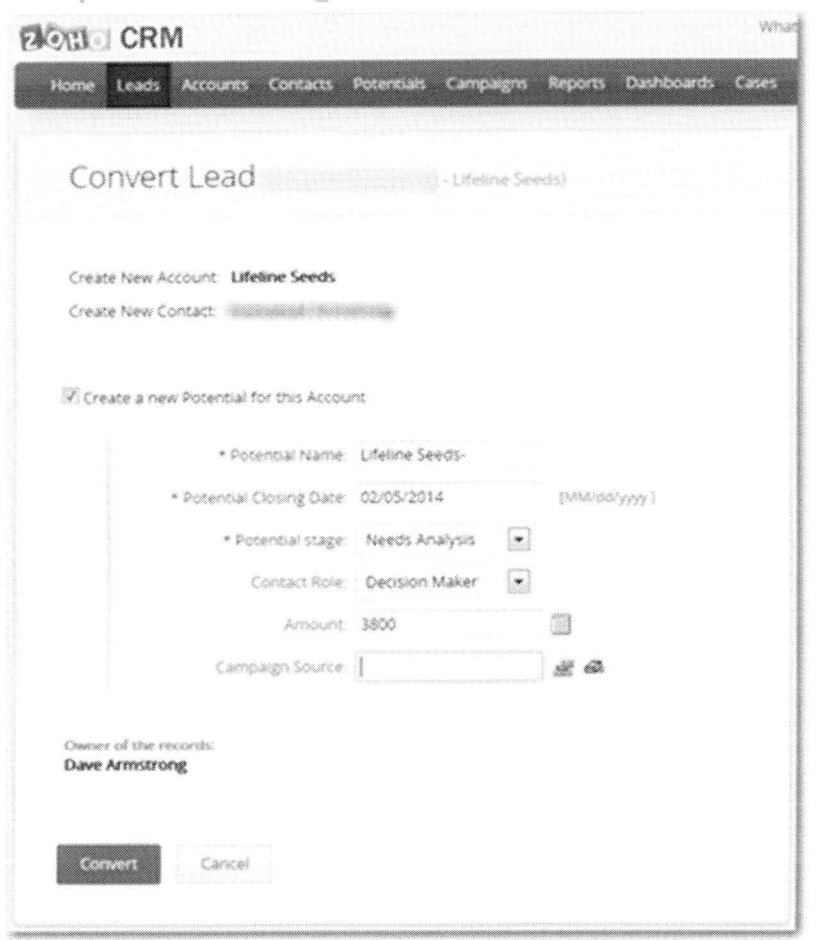

Figure 305: Convert lead screen

The Accounts List

An account is a business or entity name. If you add a business name to a lead or contact, the business name becomes the Account name. An account can have several leads or contacts that work there. Accounts are useful when thinking or working with a business vs. an individual (*Figure 306*).

Chapter 12: Using Zoho CRM

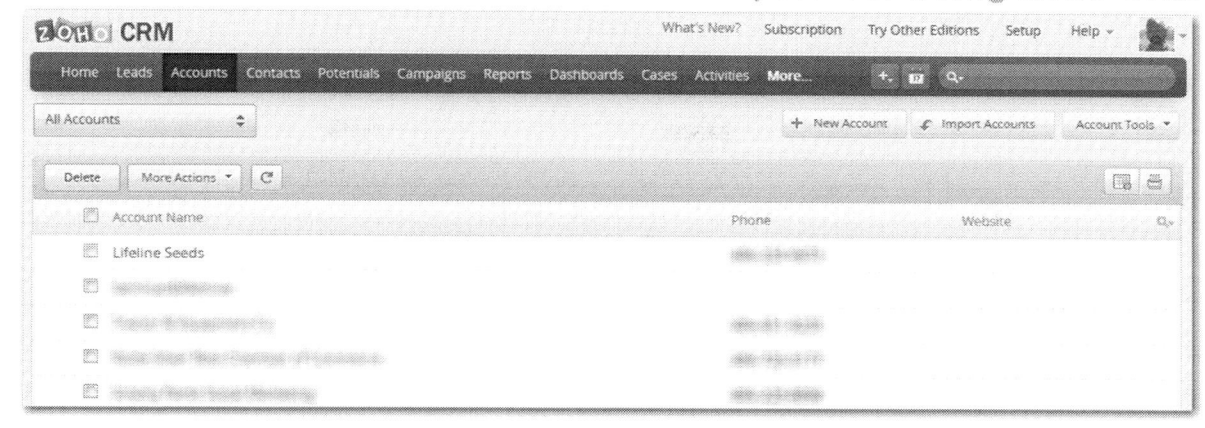

Figure 306: The Accounts list

You may want to flesh out the account information with billing and shipping addresses, account type, number of employees, etc. (*Figure 307*).

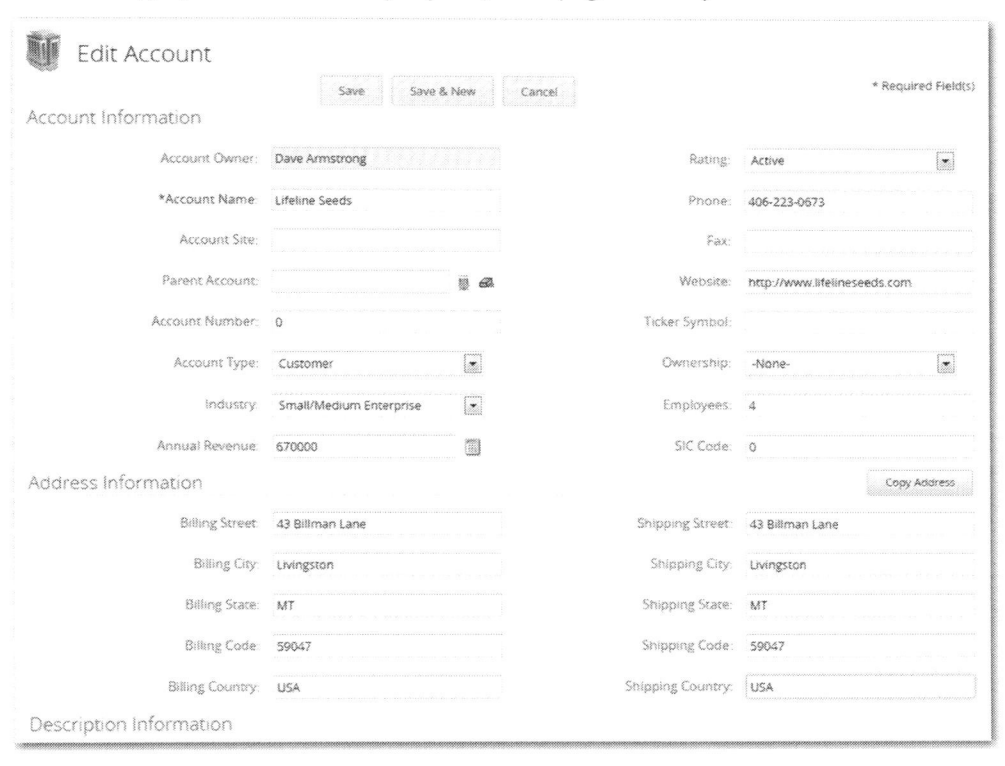

Figure 307: The edit account full screen

Chapter 12: Using Zoho CRM

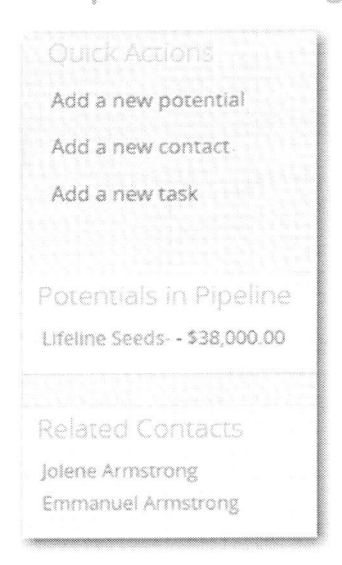

From the account view, we see the business with one or more contacts or leads (*Figure 308*).

We can add potentials. This is the amount of revenue you would expect from this account over a set period of time.

Figure 308: Contacts and potentials of this account

The Contacts List

Contacts are anyone to which you wish to track and communicate. While the list and screens are similar to leads, you probably have more interest and perhaps more information on contacts (*Figure 309*).

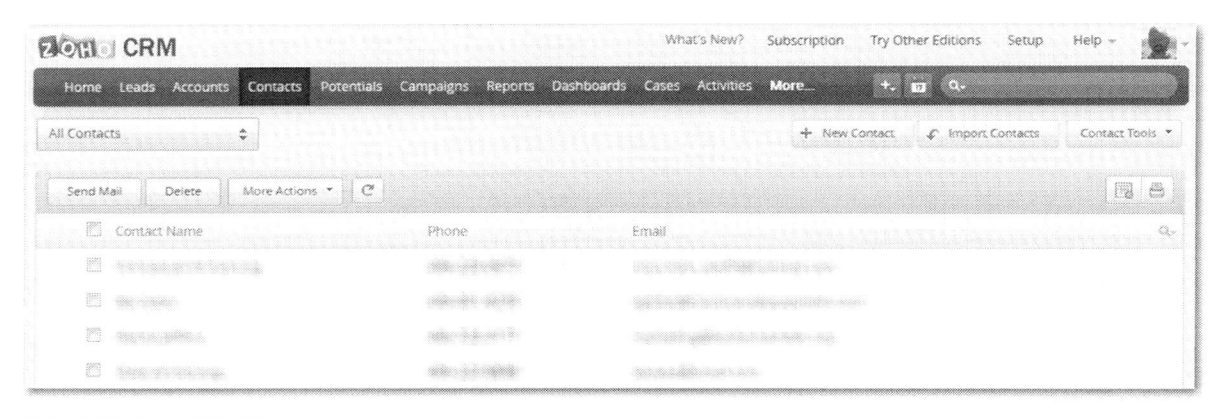

Figure 309: The contacts list

The full screen view of a contact is similar to a lead. You can send emails, make and log phone calls, add task and events. Because of the similarities, we will not cover them again with one exception. Contacts have a new section labeled **Cases**. A case is feedback from a contact requesting support. It may be a complaint, suggestions or something you need to solve to keep a happy customer. We will see how to create cases later (*Figure 310*).

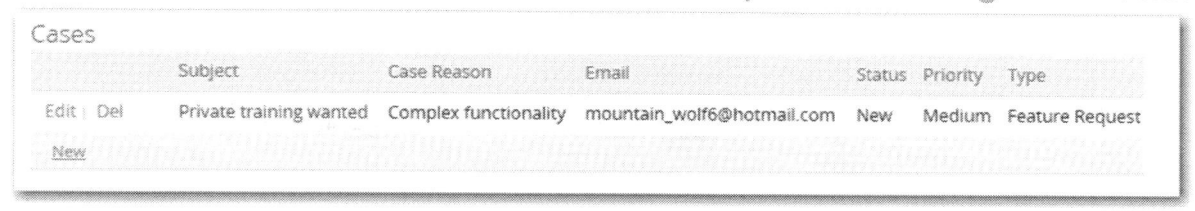

Figure 310: A contact open case

The Potential List

Potentials help you plan and estimate upcoming sales or revenue. If you use potentials, you can estimate your future revenue. If you have several salespersons, you can use the potentials as a metric to gauge their performance (*Figure 311*).

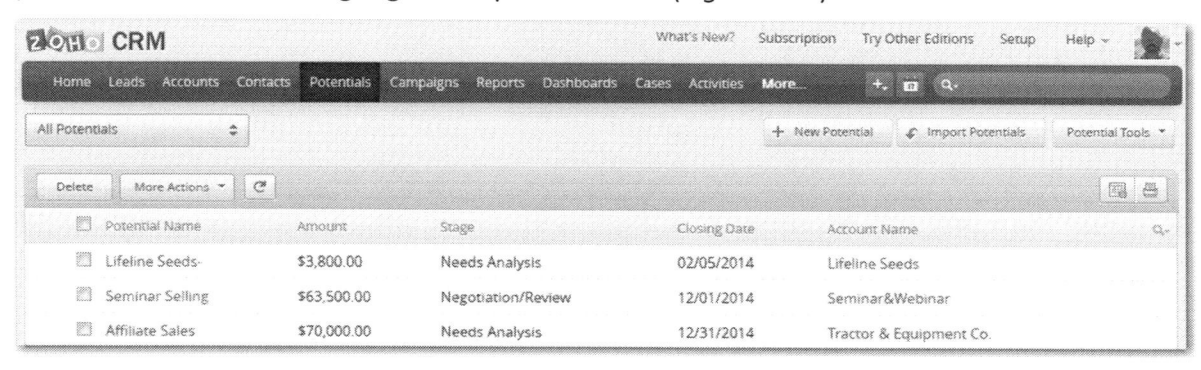

Figure 311: The potential list

While assessing potential sales starts with a good guess, you can refine the estimate as sales develop. You can assign the potential to various stages from qualification to closed (*Figure 312*).

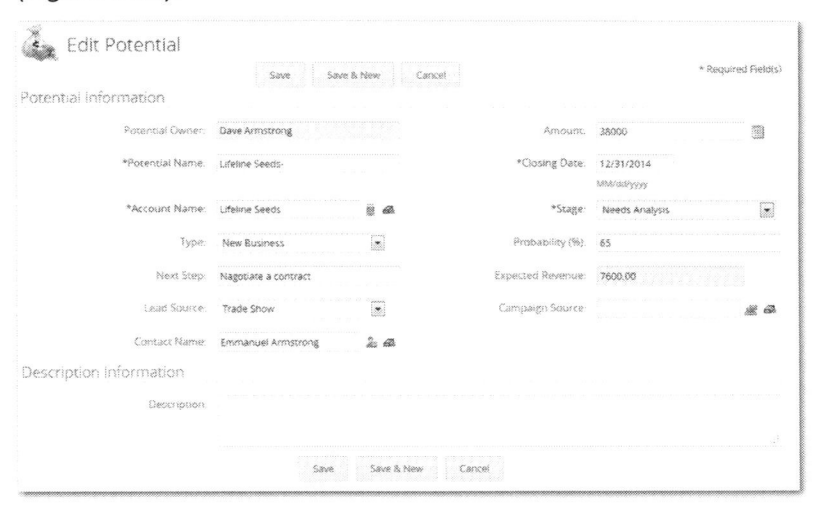

Figure 312: Editing a potential

Chapter 12: Using Zoho CRM

As the potential passes through various stages, you modify the record. When you view the potential, you can see what stage it is in and the history of the various stages (*Figure 313*).

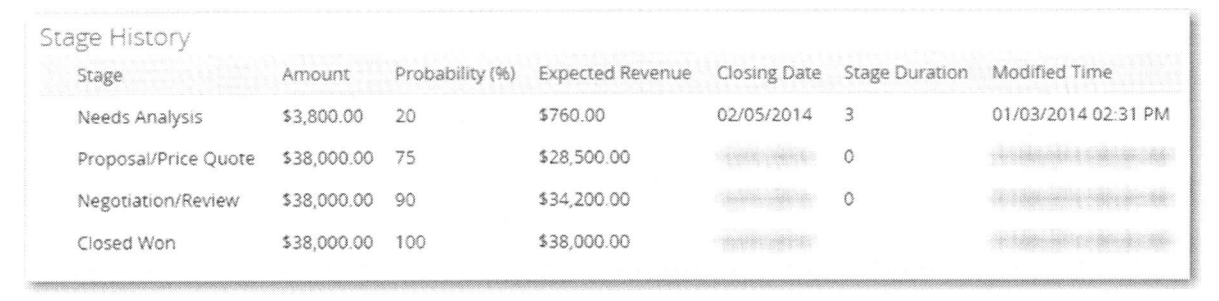

Stage History						
Stage	Amount	Probability (%)	Expected Revenue	Closing Date	Stage Duration	Modified Time
Needs Analysis	$3,800.00	20	$760.00	02/05/2014	3	01/03/2014 02:31 PM
Proposal/Price Quote	$38,000.00	75	$28,500.00		0	
Negotiation/Review	$38,000.00	90	$34,200.00		0	
Closed Won	$38,000.00	100	$38,000.00			

Figure 313: A stage history entry

For potentials to be accurate, they require maintenance in that you must review for amounts and stage changes. The payoff is you can foresee future revenues. It is worth the effort.

The Campaigns List

Campaigns are promotional in that you contact groups of leads hoping to generate interest in your products or services. They might be email, telephone or snail mail promotions. A campaign might be a seminar and would track the task needed to plan the meeting. You would schedule and track the attendees (*Figure 314*).

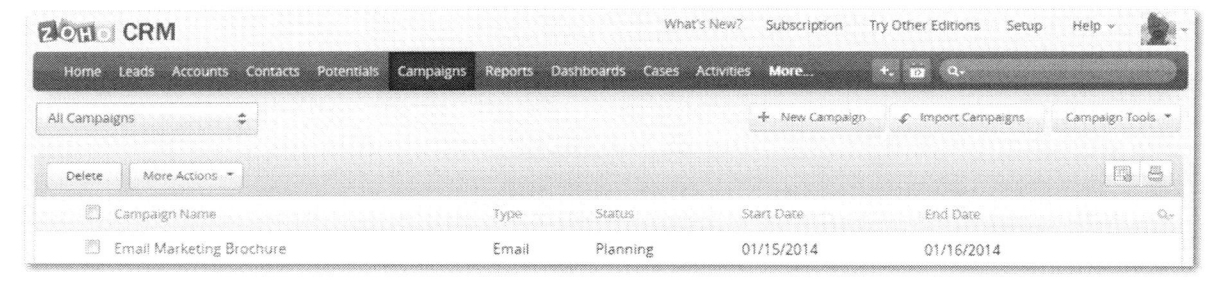

Figure 314: The campaigns list

When planning a campaign, you can (*Figure 315*):

- Give a start and end date.
- Estimate the revenue.
- Estimate the response.
- Track the budgeted and actual cost.
- Track the status of the campaign from planning to complete.

A successful campaign can be cloned and easily rerun.

Chapter 12: Using Zoho CRM

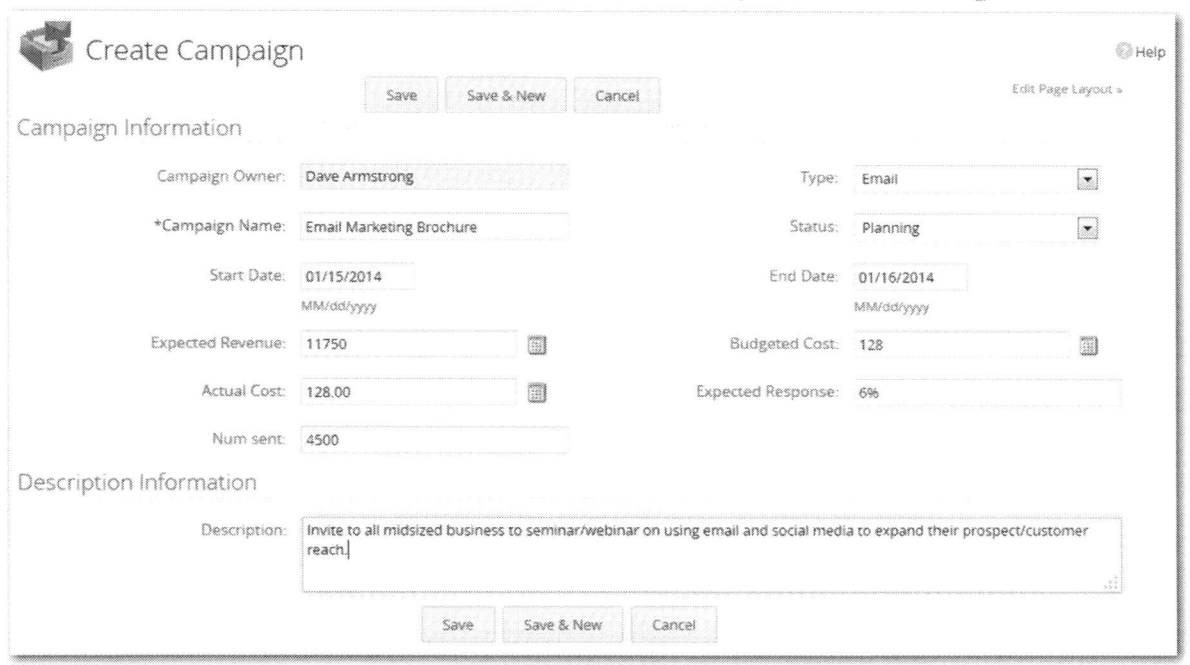

Figure 315: Create a campaign

Accessing Reports

The reports menu opens a screen of built-in and custom reports. They are grouped and can be expanded by clicking the +, - icons (*Figure 316*).

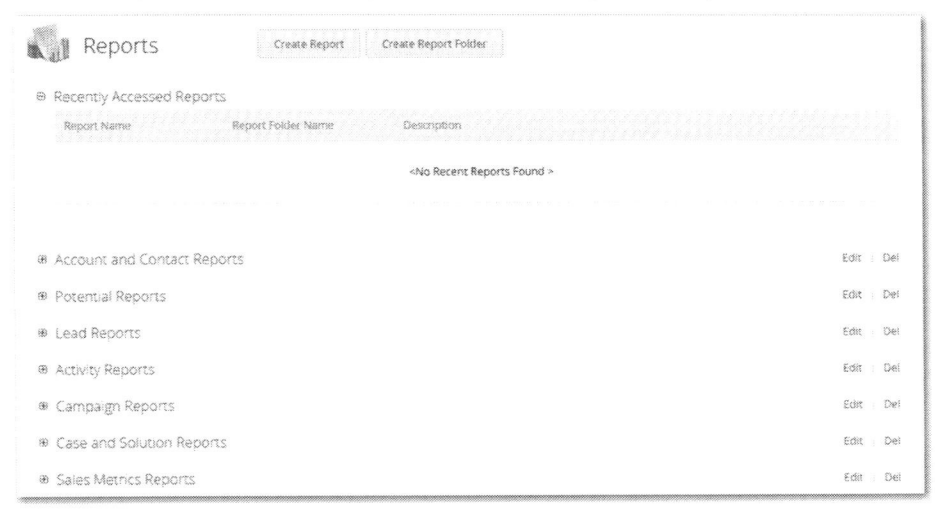

Figure 316: Getting to the reports

Once opened, the report can be customized by adding or deleting columns, and can be filtered by creation time and other fields. You can, also, sort on any column (*Figure 317*).

215

Chapter 12: Using Zoho CRM

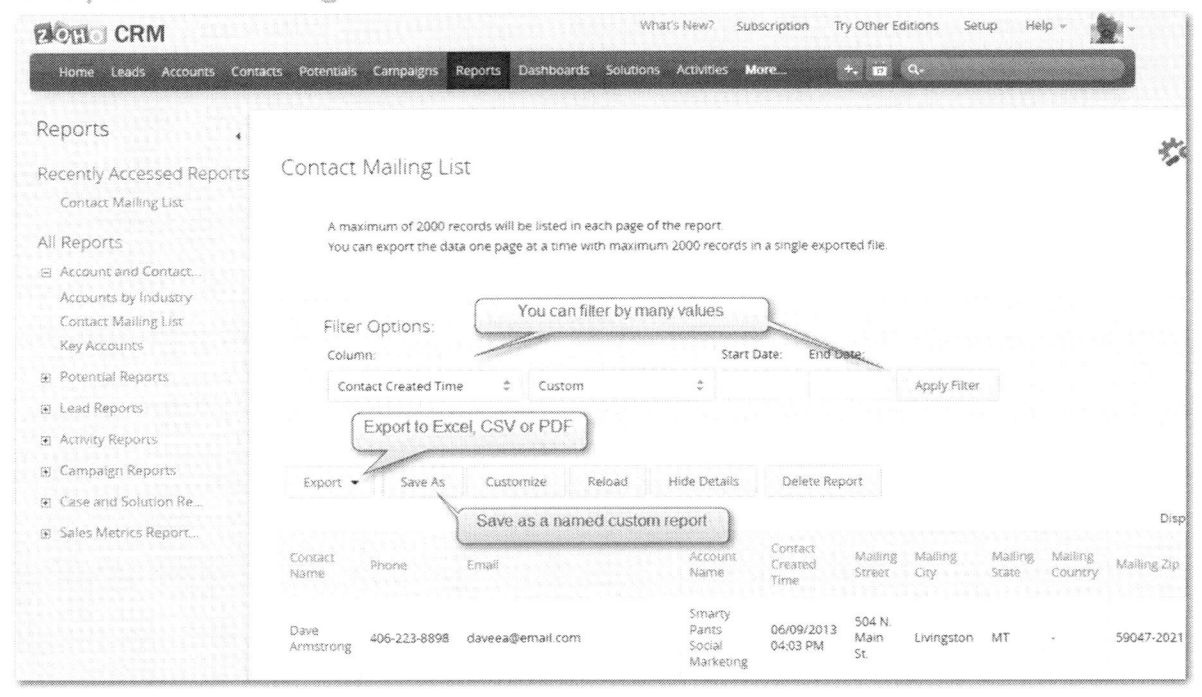

Figure 317: Customizing the report

You can customize the type of report, including reports that summarize or group values as totals or averages. Once you get the report to your liking, you can save with a new name.

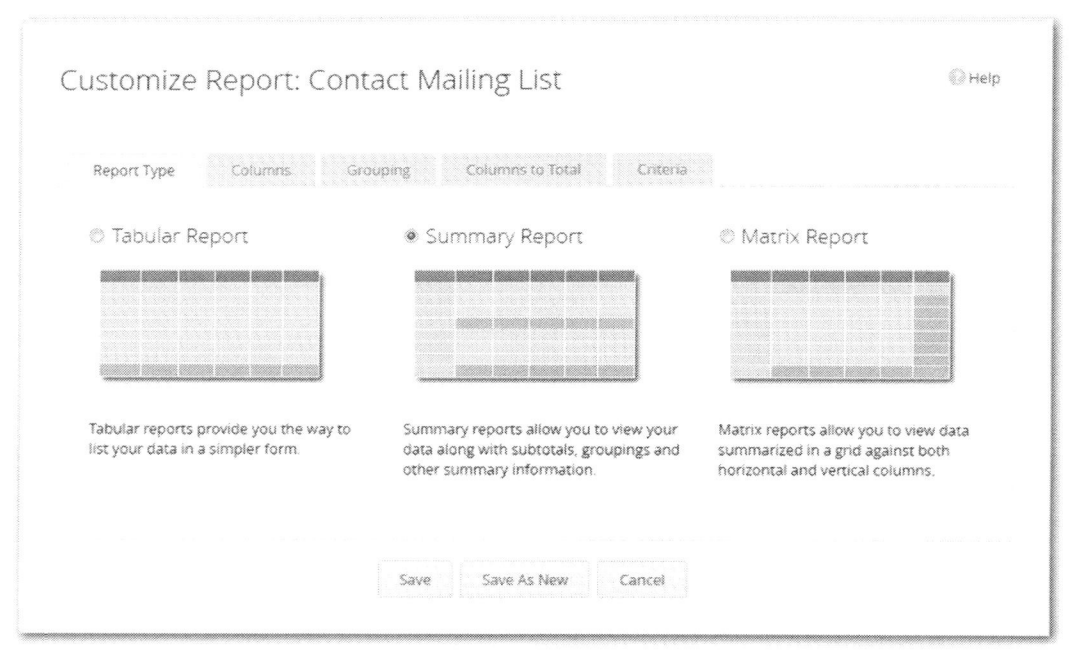

Chapter 12: Using Zoho CRM

Reports can give you valuable insight into your business and the reporting features are powerful. Zoho sells an add-on called Advanced CRM Analytics, if you really want to crunch data.

Reading Your Dashboard

They say a picture is worth a thousand words. A good graft is worth tens of thousands of numbers. Zoho provides customizable graphs and charts. At a glance, you can see how work is progressing through various pipelines and other graphs (*Figure 318*).

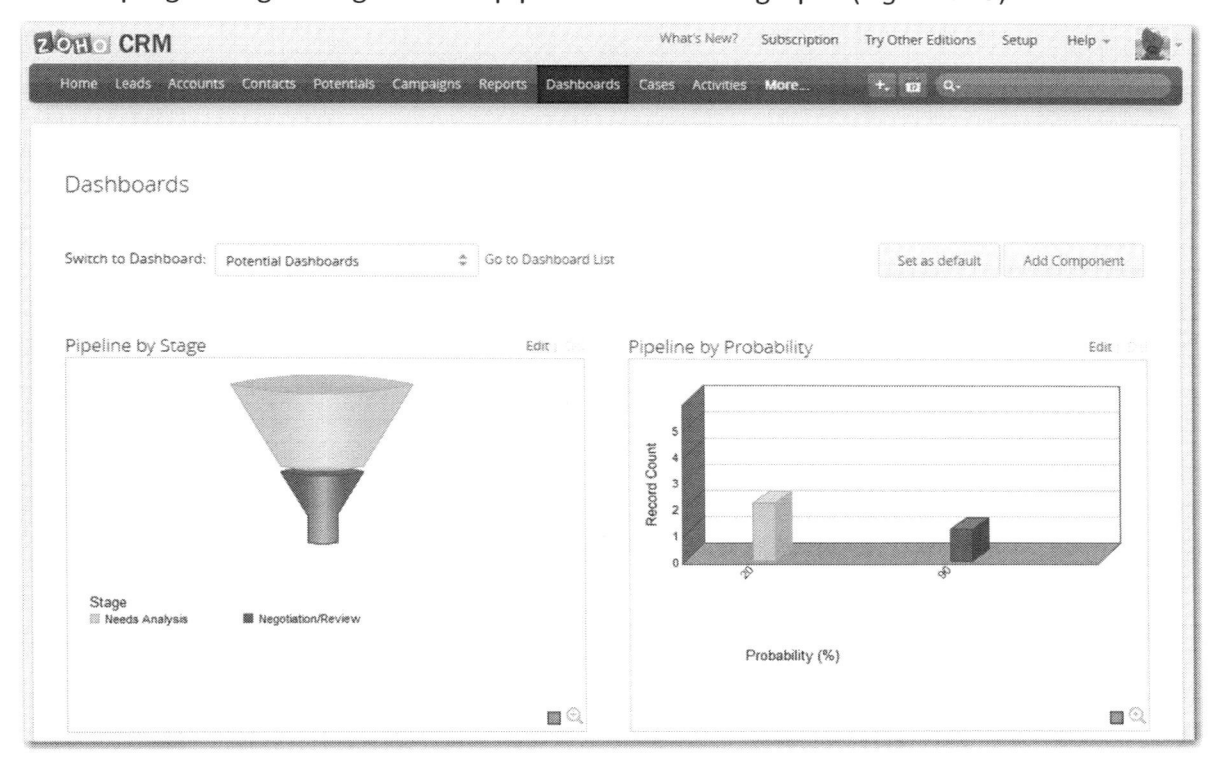

Figure 318: The dashboard

You can customize any dashboard and you can even create your own. You can add folders to keep them organized. When you open any dashboard, it updates and shows a current view of the underlying data (*Figure 319*).

Chapter 12: Using Zoho CRM

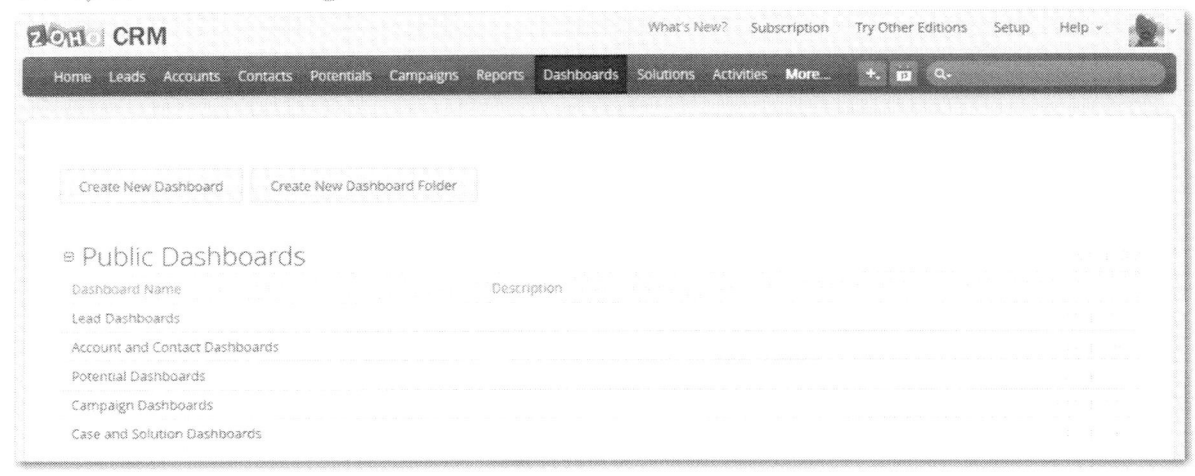

Figure 319: The dashboard list

Cases

The primary purpose of tools, like Zoho CRM, is to make sales for necessary revenue. However, the long term success comes from repeat business and to have repeat business you need happy, satisfied customers.

Even the best run businesses have occasional problems with unhappy customers. A product does not work the way the customer thinks it should. It arrives broken by the carrier. While this may be a problem, it is also an opportunity to show the customer how well you treasure their business and how you can make it right.

Client Relationship Management is more than just sales. It is a tool to help create and maintain a positive relationship. This is where case management comes in. When an issue arises, your support staff creates an open case describing the issue.

The case must be assigned to a lead or contact and can be assigned to an individual staff member. As a solution is found, that status of the case can be changed from new to escalated, to on hold, to closed. You can add comments, once a solution is found, to document (*Figure 320*).

Chapter 12: Using Zoho CRM

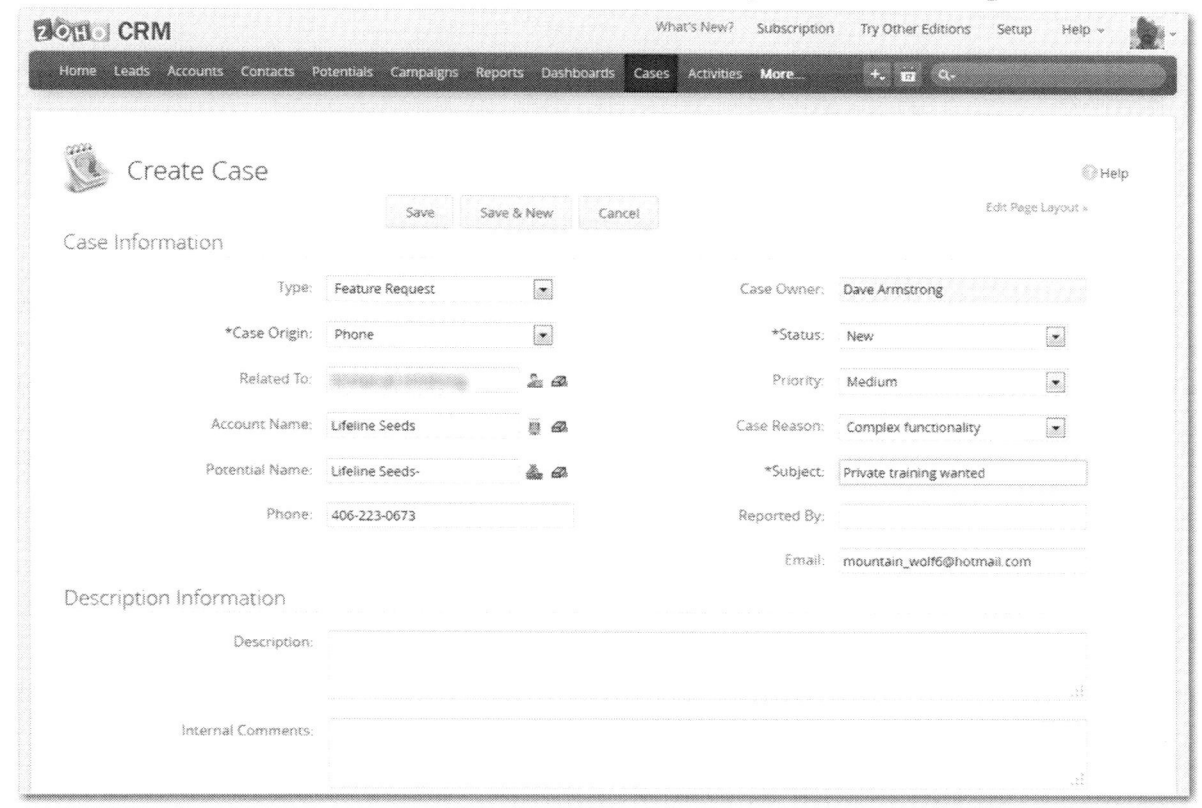

Figure 320: Creating a case

Once a case is created, it appears in the list of **Cases** (*Figure 321*).

Figure 321: The cases list

Activities

To shorten the width of the menu, Zoho placed a **More...** button that allows you to change the last menu item. You may need to click it to get to **Activities**. You can filter the list to, let's say, open activities (*Figure 322*).

Chapter 12: Using Zoho CRM

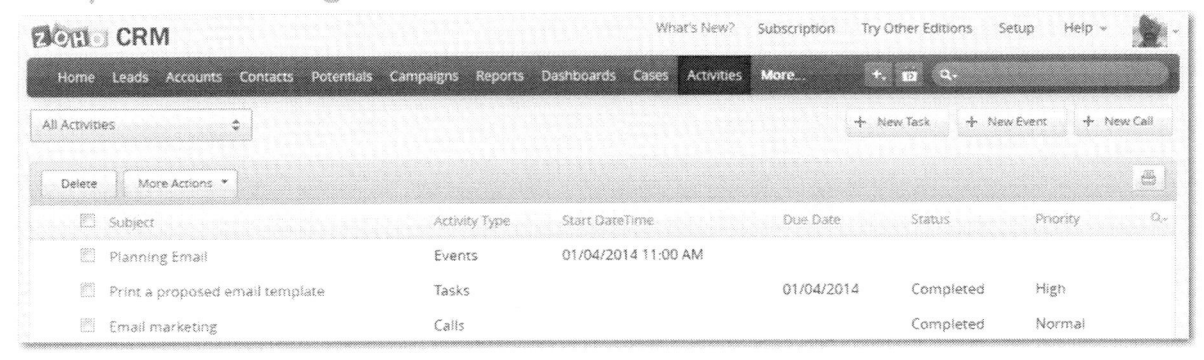

Figure 322: The activities list

You can customize and name a list showing just the view you wish to see.

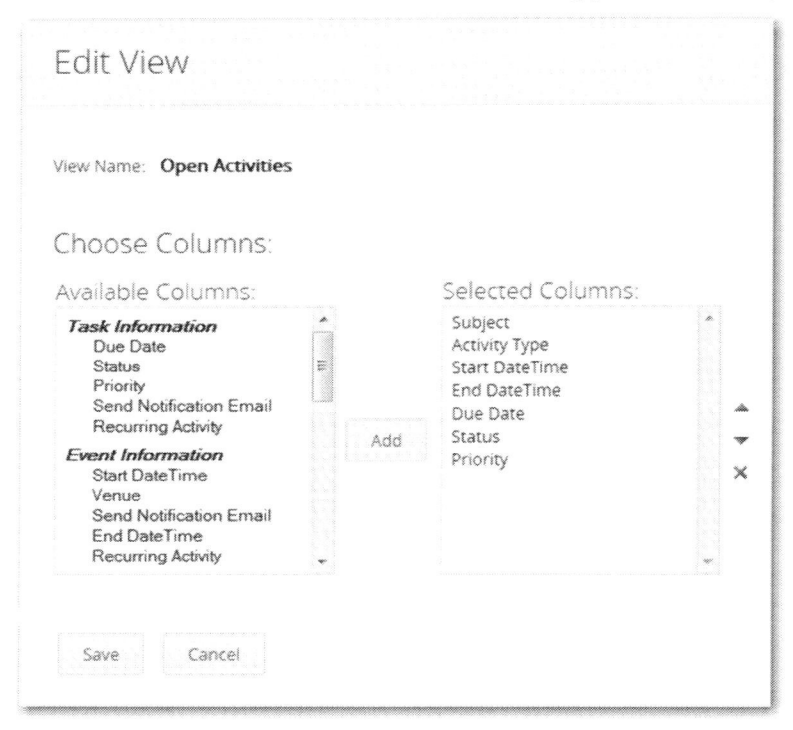

You will spend a lot of follow-up time in activities, as you review your work, as well as your staff's. As admin, you can review any staff's activity for their performance and proper use of Zoho.

Solutions

If you have ever been in support, you have solved and supported the same issue over and over. Many companies provide an FAQ (frequently asked question) page that list and answers these common questions.

Chapter 12: Using Zoho CRM

The Solutions list provides a similar function for your support staff. When a common issue is found, support creates a question/answer solution. Later, your newer support person can search this solution list rather than have to diagnose from scratch (*Figure 323*).

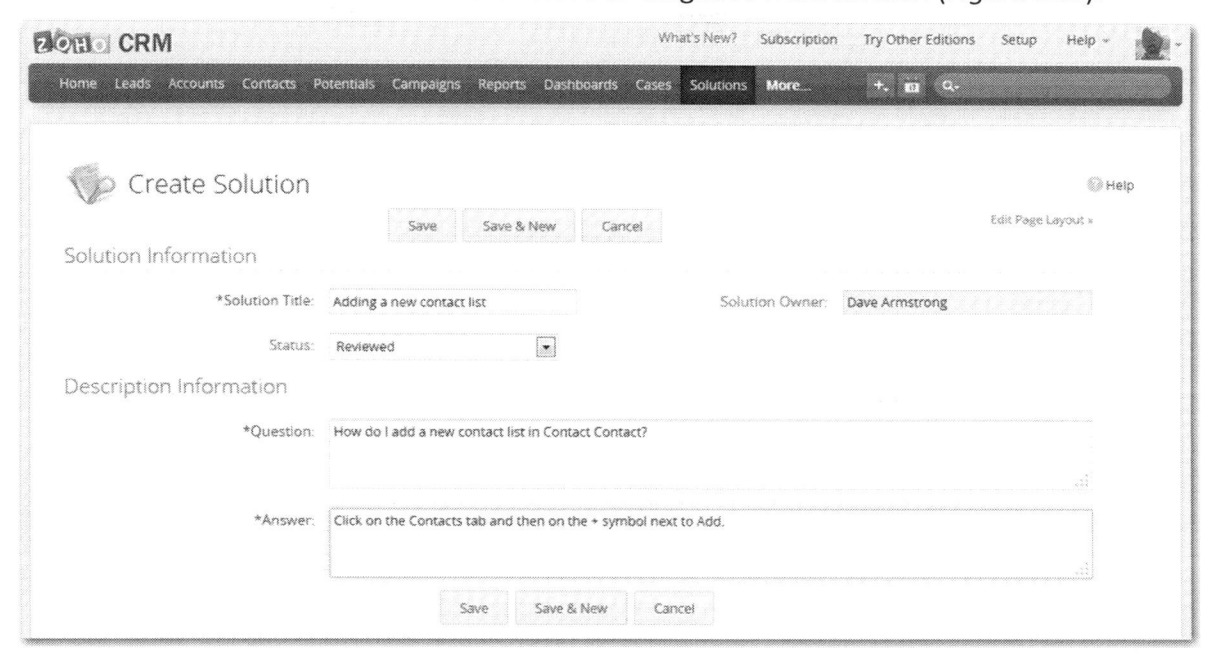

Figure 323: Creating a solution

The **Solutions** list can be filtered by several categories and you can customize the list view to show just the columns you wish (*Figure 324*).

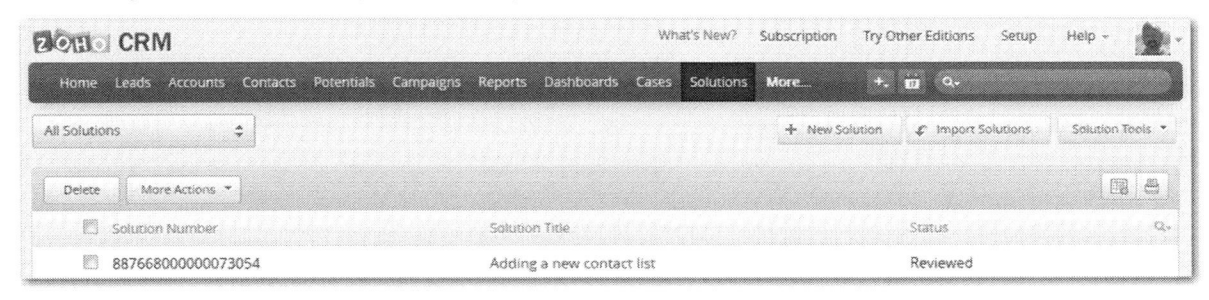

Figure 324: The solutions list

Chapter 12: Using Zoho CRM

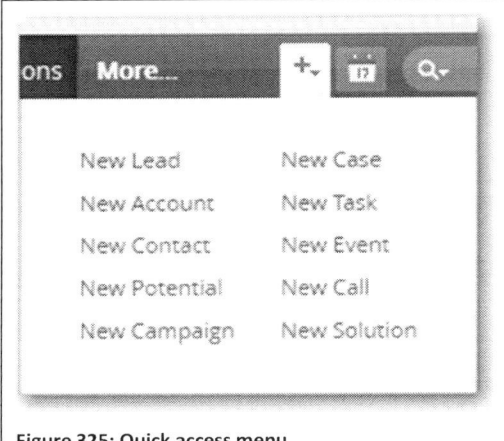

Figure 325: Quick access menu

From any screen, you can click the + tab at the top right to add new records. This is quicker than navigating to a list and then clicking the new button.

Figure 326: The built-in calendar

Clicking the calendar icon opens a quick view of the current month in your calendar. Days with activity will show in blue.

Click on any day, or one of the three icons at the bottom, to open the calendar full screen. The day view shows all events for today (*Figure 327*).

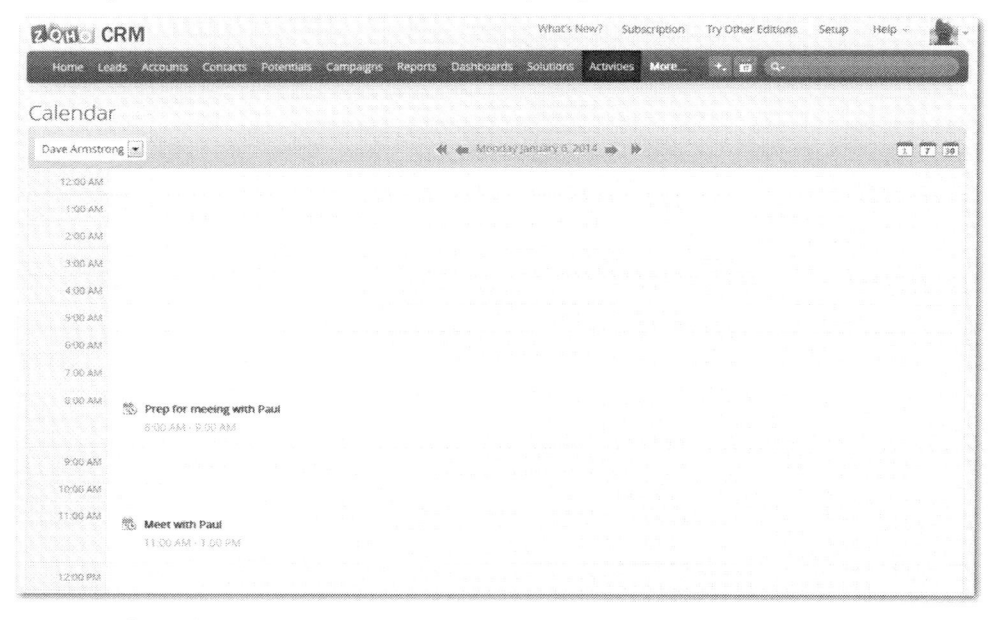

Figure 327: The week view of the calendar

The week view shows all events for the week. There is a bar view toggle that compresses the events list, if you have a busy calendar with a lot of items (*Figure 328*).

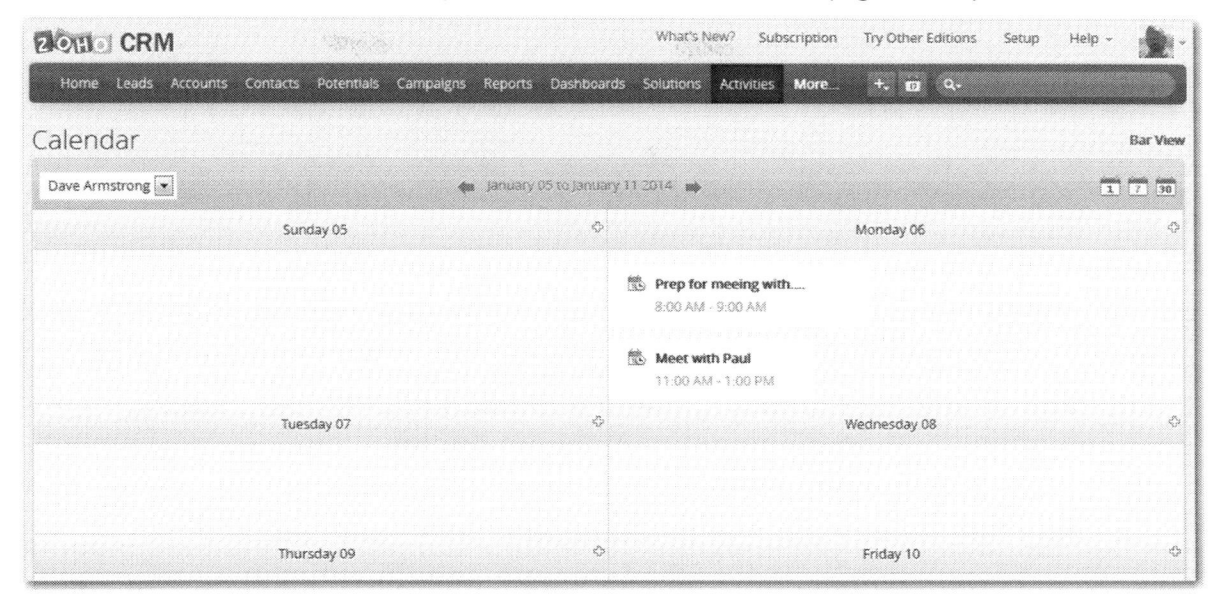

Figure 328: The week view of the calendar

The month view is useful for longer term planning. You can easily add or edit any event (*Figure 329*).

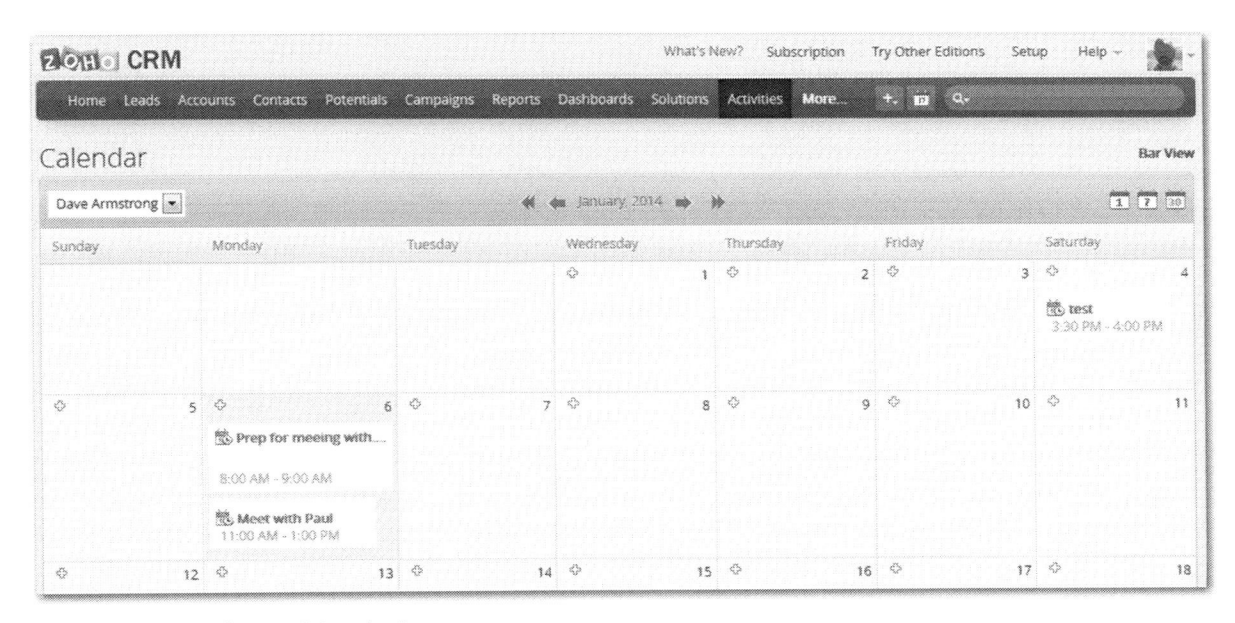

Figure 329: The month view of the calendar

Chapter 12: Using Zoho CRM

When you open or add an event, you can see other scheduled events, make notes, attach documents and invite others (*Figure 330*).

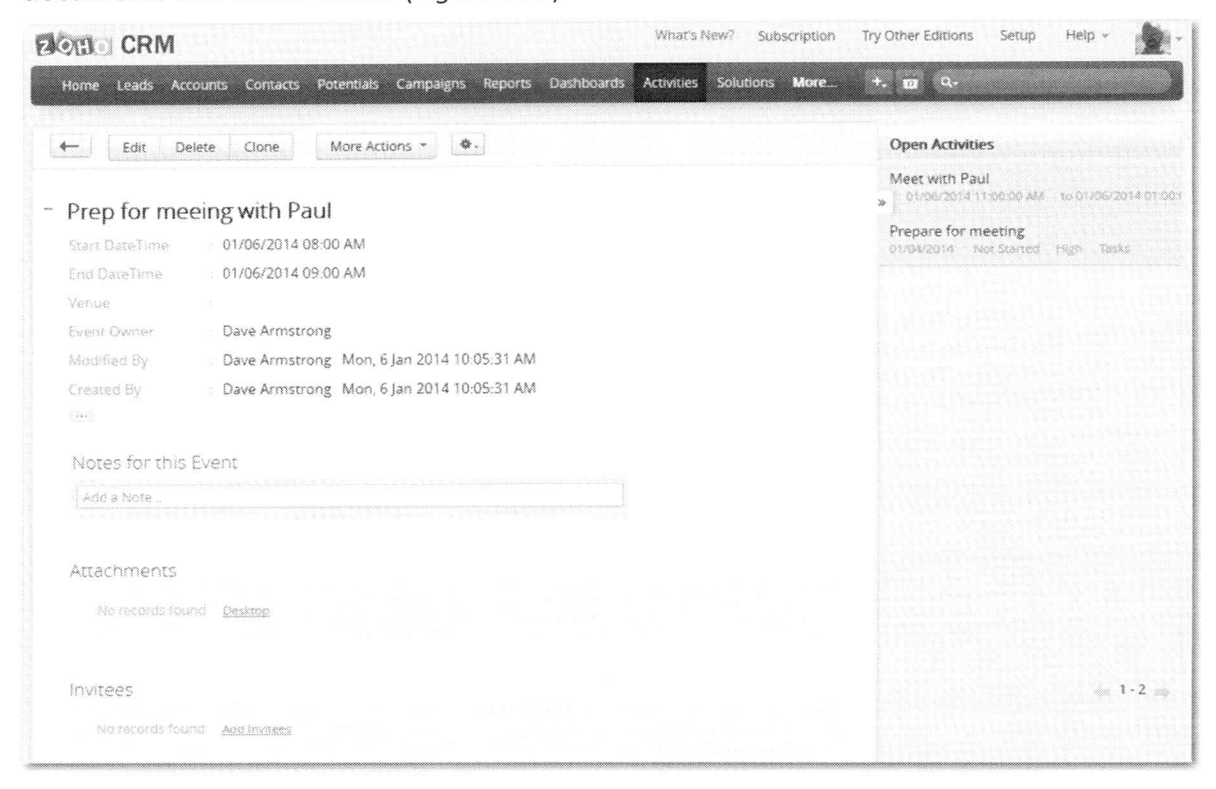

Figure 330: Viewing an event

While not as full featured as Google or Outlook Web App, for most people the core calendaring tools are there.

Setup Features on the Home Screen

If you click on the Setup link in the upper right, you can get to the setup features of Zoho CRM.

From here you can (*Figure 331*):

- Add new users and set their permissions. You might give an assistant limited access, for example.
- Change your organization's information.
- Add or remove modules such as leads, accounts or contacts.
- Create email templates that include merge fields that allow you to personalize emails (*Figure 332*).
- Create a data collection form that can be embedded in a website or social media app. The forms can collect leads information and insert it into either your leads or contacts or even a case opened up for an existing client.

Chapter 12: Using Zoho CRM

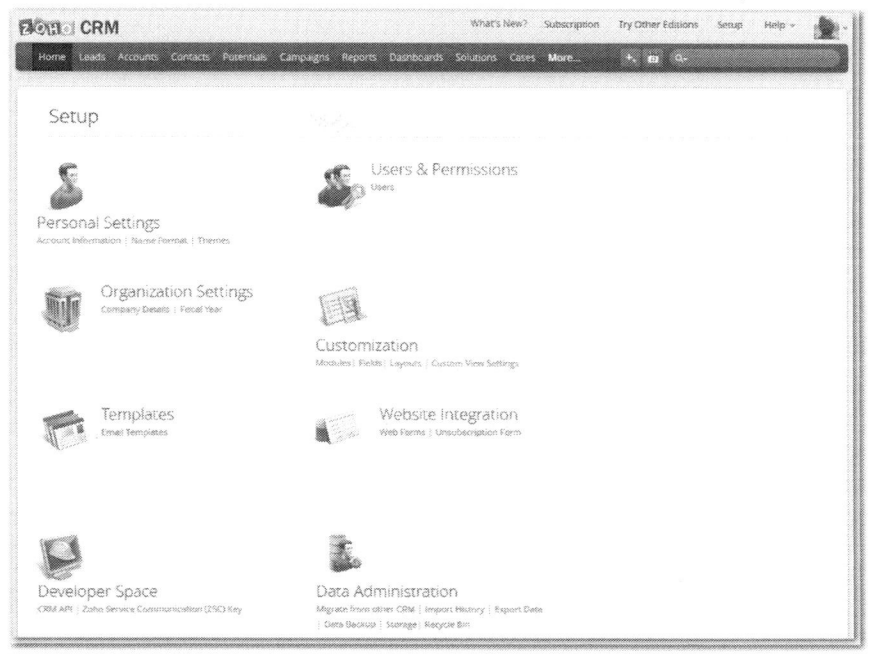

Figure 331: Setup features on the home screen

Using templates, allow you to dress up your email with HTML and images. You can categorize your email templates into folders.

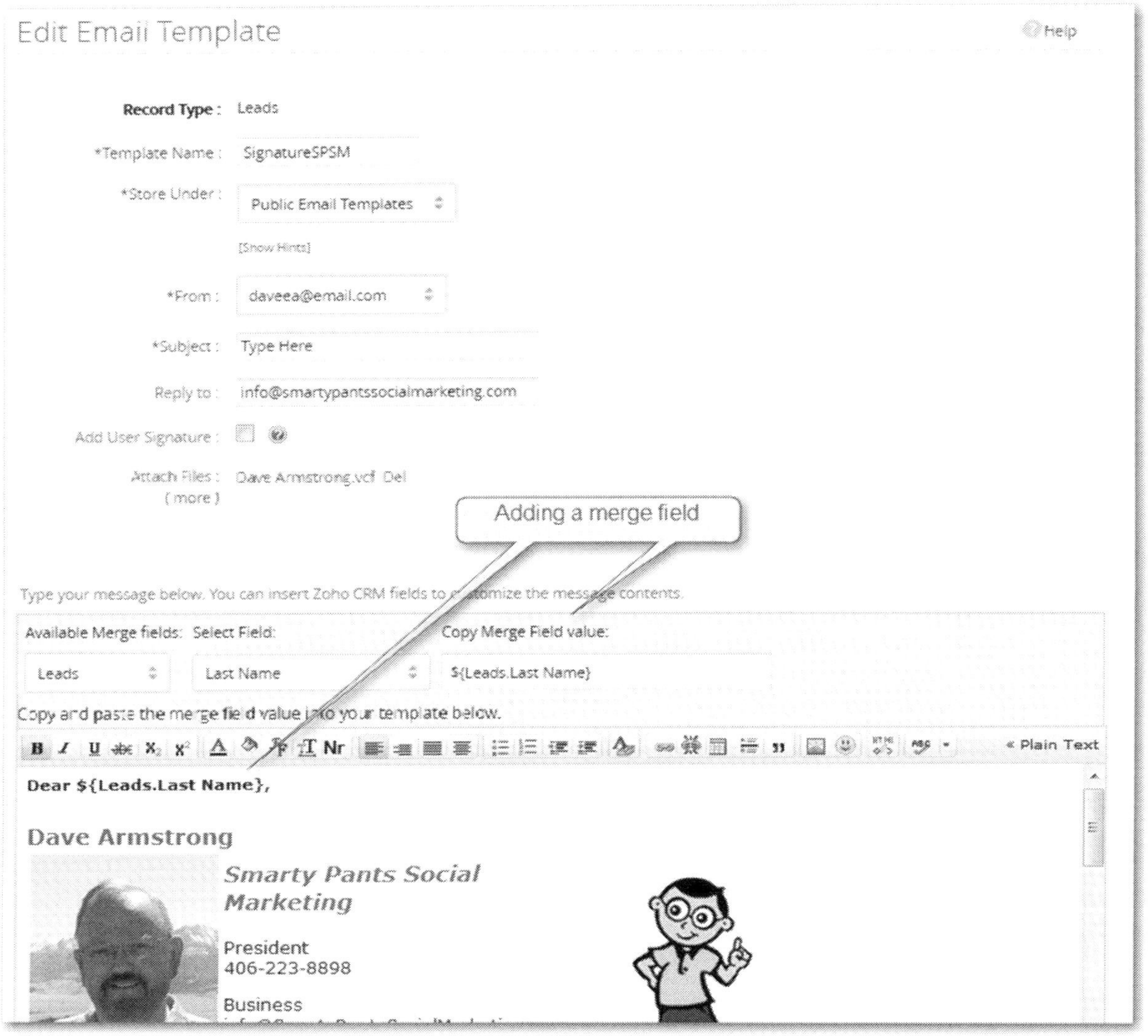

Chapter 12: Using Zoho CRM

Figure 332: Creating an email template

Chapter 13: Using Zoho Productivity Apps

What are Zoho Productivity Apps?

Like most of Zoho's products, they offer a free limited version. However, even the free is a generous 5 GB of space and use of their productivity apps.

As we mentioned earlier, the apps give you a word processing app similar to Google's Document or Microsoft's Word. They add to that a spreadsheet and presentation tool. The suite of office tools is very similar to the Google and Microsoft offers, discussed in other chapters.

If you want to evaluate, you can always start with the free suite and, if you commit to it, you can easily upgrade. The free 5 GB could store thousands of documents.

Chapter 13: Using Zoho Productivity Apps

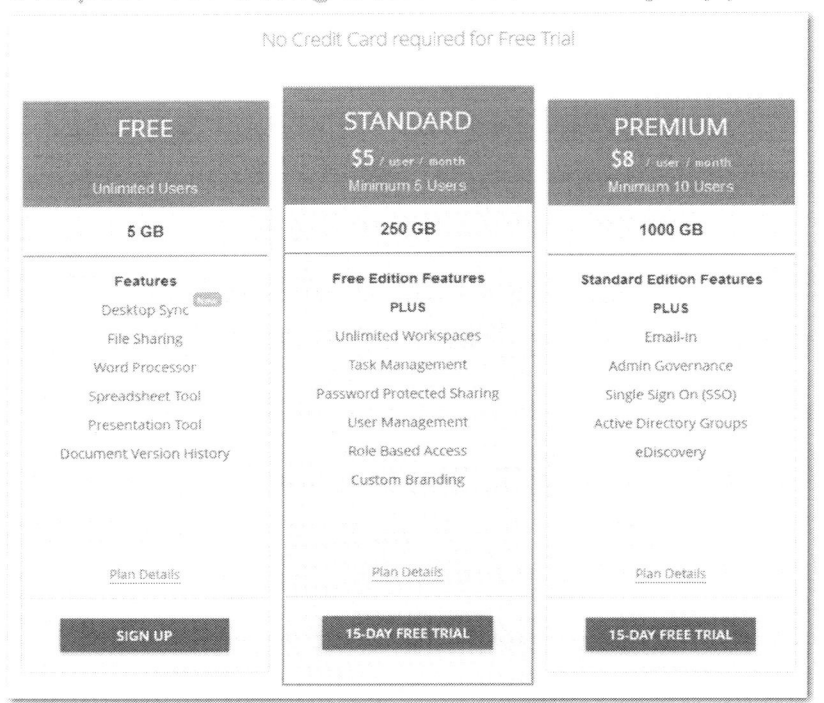

Figure 333: Zoho Docs pricing

The main screen of Zoho Docs initially invites you to set up your organization and add users. It allows you to start uploading your existing files from Microsoft apps on your local hard drive or from Google Drive. They are converted into Zoho Docs, but much of the original formatting is preserved. You can export any Zoho Docs file into its Microsoft equivalent, as well as, several other formats (*Figure 334*).

Chapter 13: Using Zoho Productivity Apps

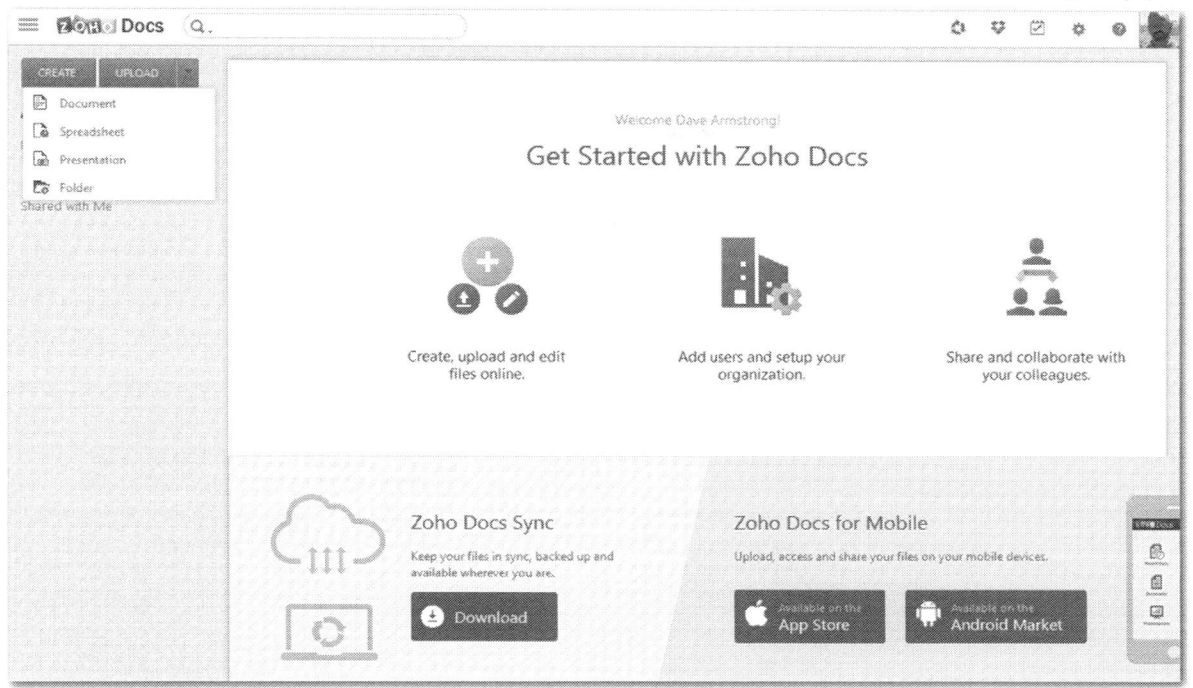

Figure 334: Zoho Docs main screen

Moving Between Zoho Apps

In the upper left, is a small icon that looks like three horizontal lines. When clicked, it opens a list of all of the Zoho apps. Clicking any of the icons opens another browser tab with that app loaded. You can quickly jump between apps.

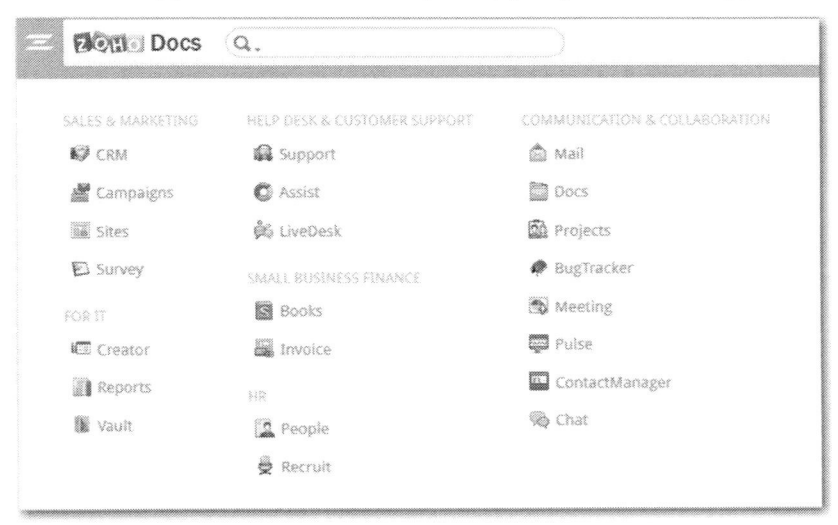

Zoho's Writer App

Chapter 13: Using Zoho Productivity Apps

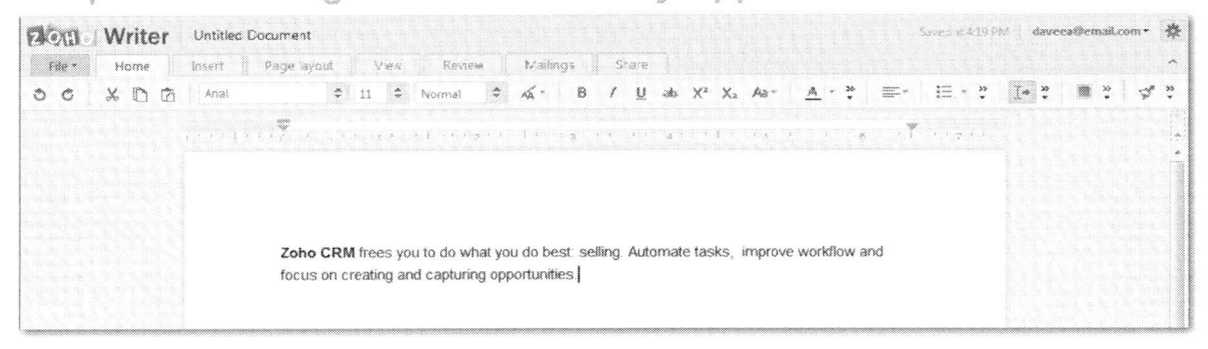

Figure 335: A Writer new document

Writer (*Figure 335*) is Zoho's word processing app. In many ways, it has more features than either Microsoft's Word or Google's Document. For one, you can mail merge which is missing in Google Document, without special scripting.,

It has a scaled down version of the Microsoft ribbon. This makes it a bit easier to use than Google Document. The ribbon clones Microsoft's.

Since word processing is generally understood by anyone who has worked in an office, I will not explore in depth. However, I will explore the spreadsheet. All of the apps, share most of the menu tabs you see in Sheet.

Zoho's Sheet App

All three web based spreadsheet applications share a common interface and similar functionality. They all emulate Excel. There are a series of tabs across the top and each tab shows grouped functions when clicked. There is also a file tab that is equivalent to Microsoft's backstage.

When you first open a new sheet, the **Home** tab is the default. This tab has all of the text formatting features, as well as, sorting and filtering functions (*Figure 336*).

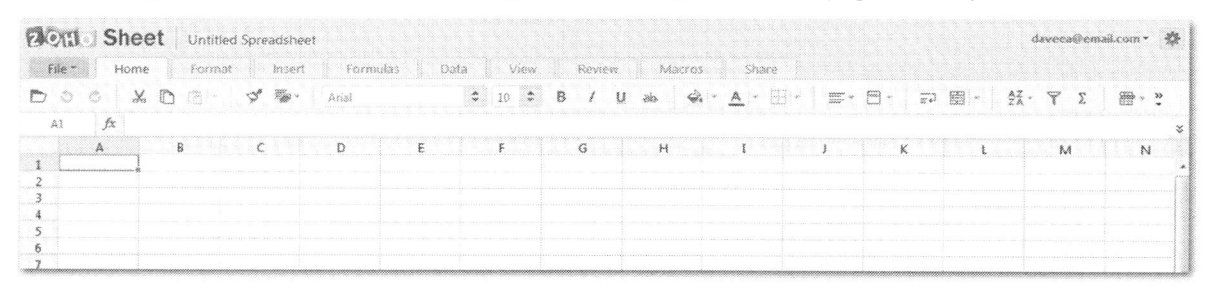

Figure 336: A new Sheet

Your first step is to give your document a meaningful name. Click on the **Untitled Spreadsheet** link at the top, and edit the name (*Figure 337*).

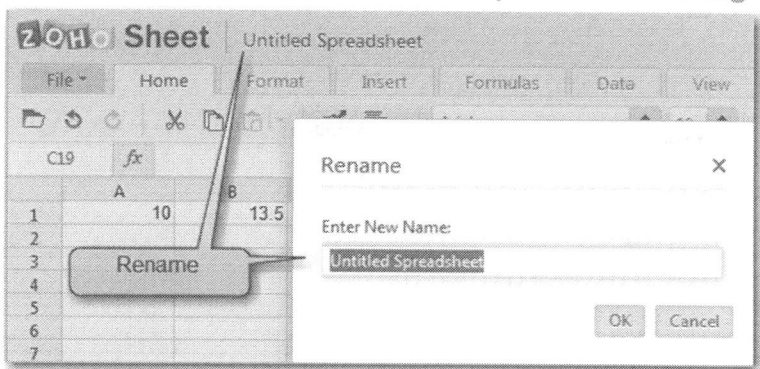

Figure 337: Changing the Sheet's name

This is not a tutorial on how to use spreadsheets, but like Excel and Google Spreadsheet you add static data and formulas that calculate that static data. In our example, we are multiplying the value in cell A1 by the value in cell B1. Like all of the other spreadsheets, a formula starts with the equal symbol (=) (*Figure 338*).

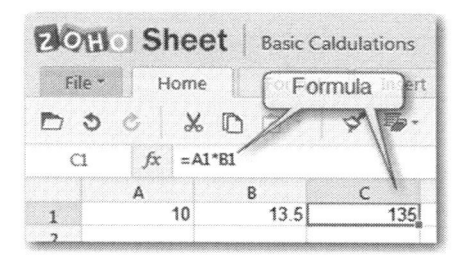

Figure 338: Adding static data and a formula

Let's Explore the Sheet Menu Tabs

The **File** menu works much like the File/Backstage view in Excel. You can create new, rename or open existing sheets. You can also import files from your hard drive or by typing a URL, you could import spreadsheets from remote locations on the web.

You can export the sheet into several formats, including the OpenDocument standard (*Figure 339*).

Chapter 13: Using Zoho Productivity Apps

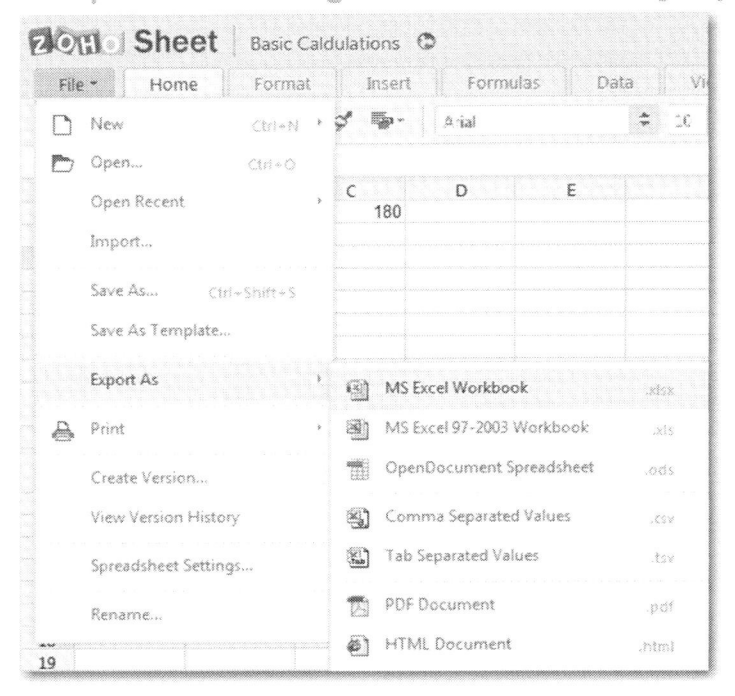

Figure 339: The file menu

Next, let's explore the different tabs that we use to navigate to a set of features or functions.

The Sheet Home Tab

This is almost a direct copy from SkyDrive's Excel (*Figure 340*).

We use it to:

- Cut, copy and paste.
- Format and colorize text and backgrounds of cells.
- Draw borders around cell(s).
- Align and span cells.
- Sort and/or filter the rows.
- Insert rows or columns.

The **Home** tab gives you quick access to some features buried within other tabs. This is convenient, as you will be in the **Home** tab most of the time.

Figure 340: The Home tab

The Sheet Format Tab

The **Format** tab allows us to format numbers and dates. You can also set up conditional formatting. You might want negative numbers to appear in parentheses and be in bold red (*Figure 341*).

Figure 341: The Format tab

Before you click the **Conditional Formatting** button, select the range you wish to format. The conditional Formatting dialog allows you to build conditional rules that, when true, change the formatting of the cells (*Figure 342*).

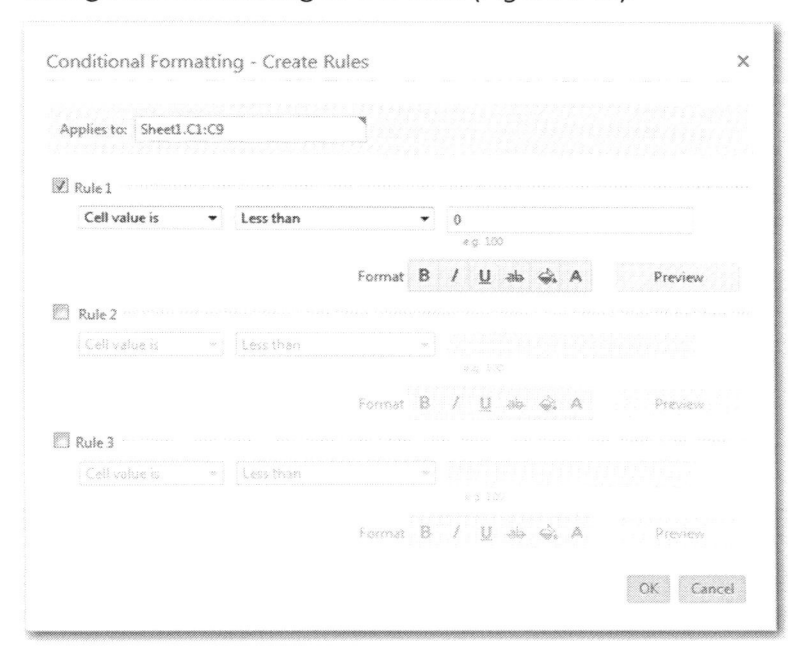

Figure 342: Adding conditional formatting

The Sheet Insert Tab

The Insert tab (*Figure 343*) allows us to:

- Insert a row or column.
- Insert a Chart or Image.
- Insert a Hyperlink.
- Insert a Button.
    - You can assign a macro to the button, as we will see later.

Chapter 13: Using Zoho Productivity Apps

Figure 343: The Insert tab

Adding a chart is almost identical to Excel (*Figure 344*):

- Select the data range you wish to chart.
- Pick a **Chart Type** and **Sub Type**.

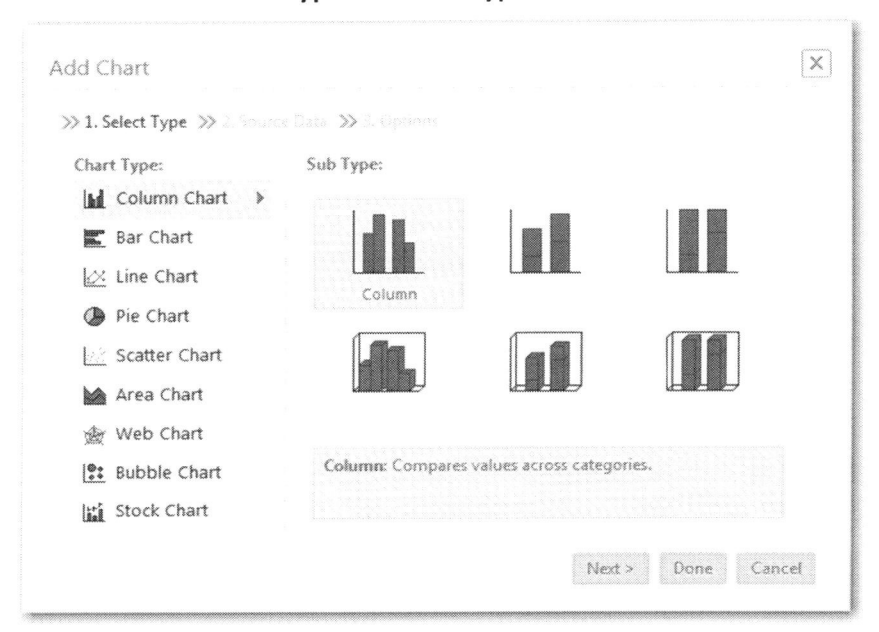

Figure 344: Inserting a chart

After selecting your range and chart type, choose **Next >** (*Figure 345*).

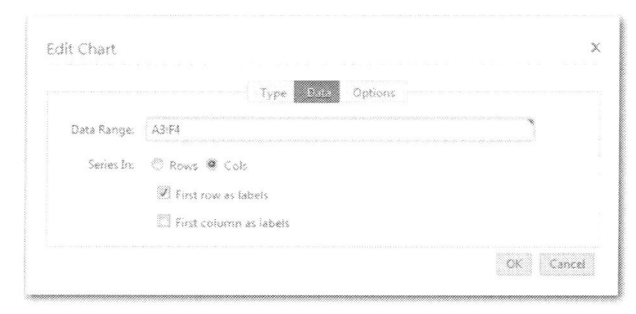

Figure 345: Checking/adding the range and identifying labels

Add a Chart Title, pick the **X-Axis** (across the bottom) and the **Y-Axis** (vertical) and choose **Show label**. Click OK to see the chart (*Figure 346*).

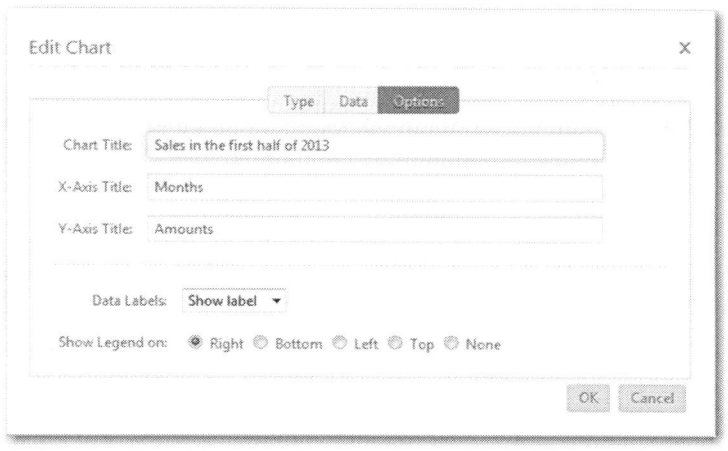

Figure 346: Adding the chart title and axis labels

You can drag the chart to the location on the sheet (*Figure 347*).

You can also:

- **Publish** - This creates embeddable code you can paste into one of your web pages. Note, that it is still live, in that, if you change the underlying data, the chart changes within your web page.
- **URL** - Once you have chosen **Publish**, you then have the option of linking to an image of the chart.
- **More->Save As Image** - Opens a file download window in your browser allowing you to save a PNG file to your hard drive.

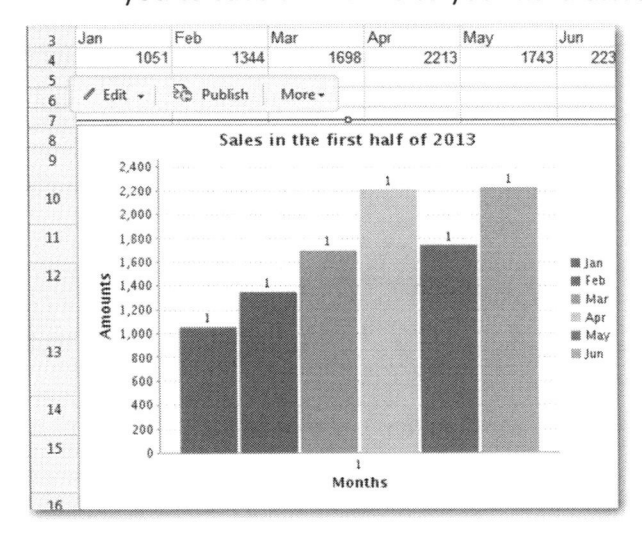

Figure 347: Created chart

Should you choose to embed a live chart or send a URL link to an image, you get the necessary HTML code to embed into the page or add a link within an email or web page.

Chapter 13: Using Zoho Productivity Apps

The Sheet Formulas Tab

The Formulas tab gives access to tools that help you write formulas (*Figure 348*). Once you become familiar with formulas, you will probably just type them in. For example, if I type =SUM a pop-up suggest a matching function. I would then follow the sum with open parentheses, two cell coordinates followed by closing parentheses (*Figure 349*).

Figure 348: The formulas tab

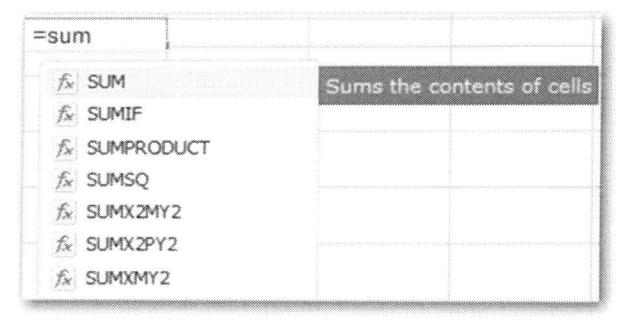

Figure 349: Formula auto completion

However, if you are new to formulas, where do you start? Click the **Insert Function** on the **Formulas** tab to open a list of the most common functions. You can filter for all of a common category with the dropdown (Figure *350*).

Chapter 13: Using Zoho Productivity Apps

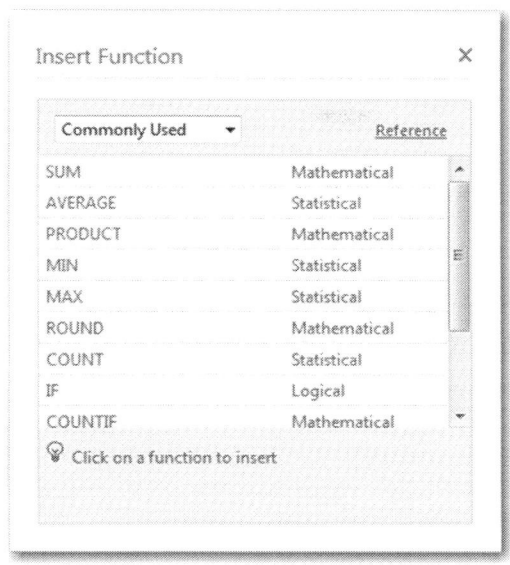

Figure 350: Picking a formula to insert

Complex, nested formulas are difficult to understand, even if you previously wrote them. You have the option to name a cell, or range of cells, which make the formulas more readable. In the example in (*Figure 351*), we start by naming A1, Months. We would then rename B1, EventsPerMonth.

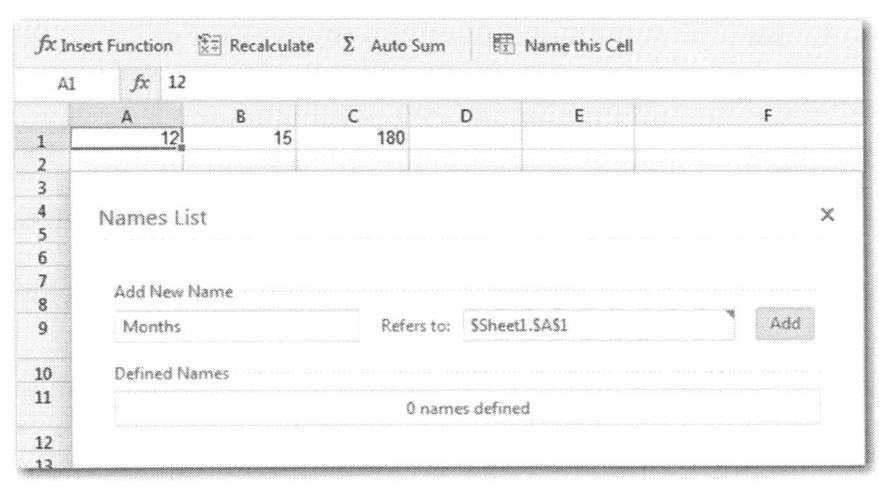

Figure 351: naming a field or range

We could then type out the formula as **=Months*EventsPerMonth** instead of **=A1*B1** (*Figure 352*).

How to Move Your Expensive Office to the Free Cloud
237

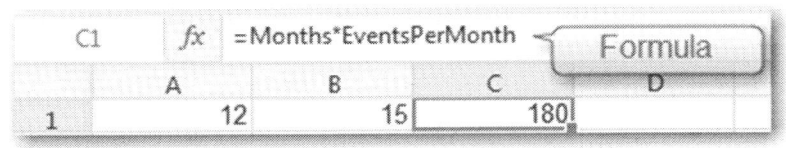

Figure 352: Formula using named ranges

The Sheet Data Tab

The Data tab allows us to manipulate the underlying data of the Sheet (*Figure 353*).

We can:

- **Sort** - Rearrange the data in an ascending or descending order.
- **Filter** - We can filter that data to see just the records that match a given condition. In an address list, you might just want to see the ones in your state.
- **Pivot** - You can create Pivot tables that allow you to see summaries of the data in different ways than just the two dimensions of a spreadsheet.
- **Goal Seek** - Goal Seek is used to find the exact input value which will generate the desired result of a formula. For example, let us say you have 2 input fields: Product Price and Units Sold. And there is a formula in the spreadsheet: Sales = Product Price x Units Sold. Assume the Product Price is constant. If you want to find out how many units to sell in order to achieve sales revenue of 1 million dollars, you can use the Goal Seek functionality.
- **Solver** - Choose a range of cells and Solver can find the Maximum, or Minimum in the range.

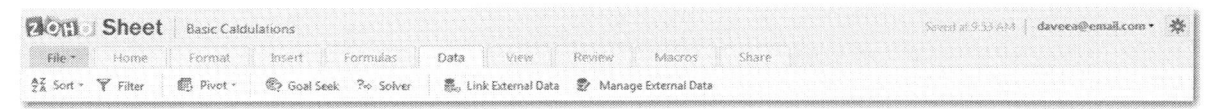

Figure 353: The Data tab

One of the more valuable features in the Data tab, is the ability to link to external data. Clicking the **Link External Data** button opens the **External Data Dialog** (*Figure 354*).

Where is the data coming from? The most reliable data would come from a CSV data file located on some web server. Perhaps, this is data you collect from your website. You need to provide a URL to that file. You can also load data from a RSS file or a HTML web page, although, this data may be less organized than CSV. After adding a URL, click next (*Figure 354*).

Chapter 13: Using Zoho Productivity Apps

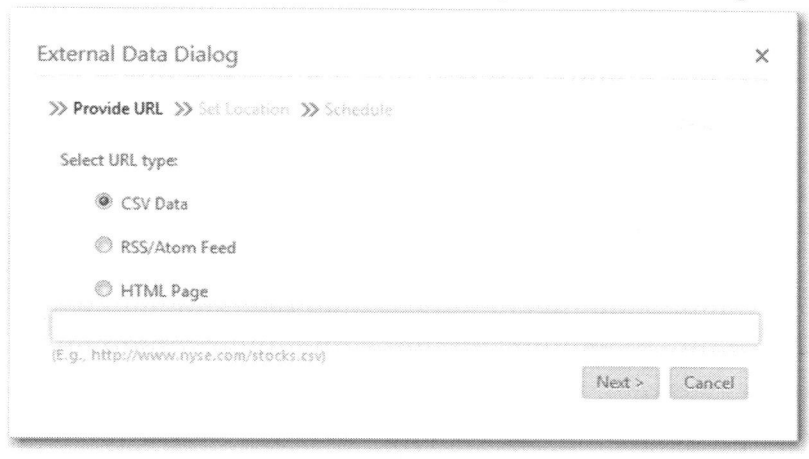

Figure 354: Connecting to external data via URL

Where do you want the data to go? Zoho's Sheet can have more than one sheet similar to Excel's workbooks. If you have more than one, pick the sheet. Next, decide where you want the external data to be inserted. This will be where the upper left corner of the data starts. (*Figure 355*).

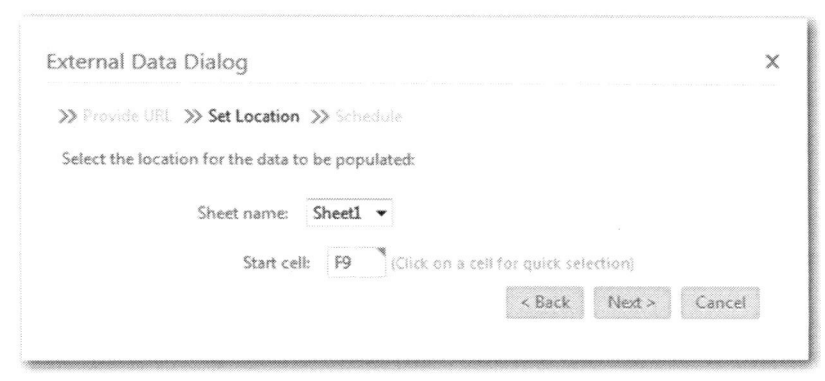

Figure 355: Placing the incoming data on the sheet

Do you want to do this only once or should you pull the data on a schedule (*Figure 356*)?

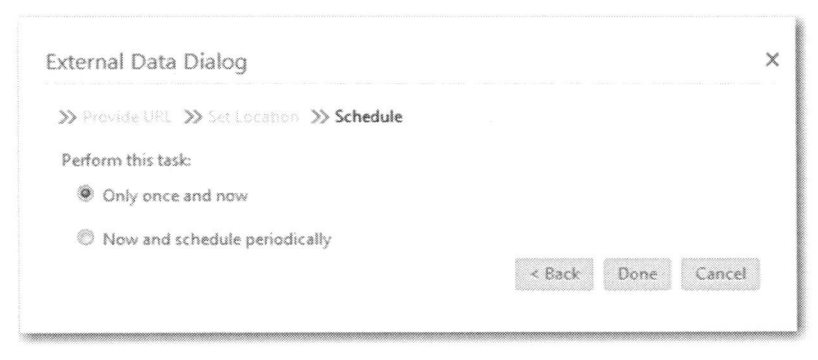

Figure 356: Scheduling the data import

Chapter 13: Using Zoho Productivity Apps

If you wish to schedule, you have choices such as every 60 minutes or Every Day (*Figure 357*). How often does the data change and how up-to-date need it be?

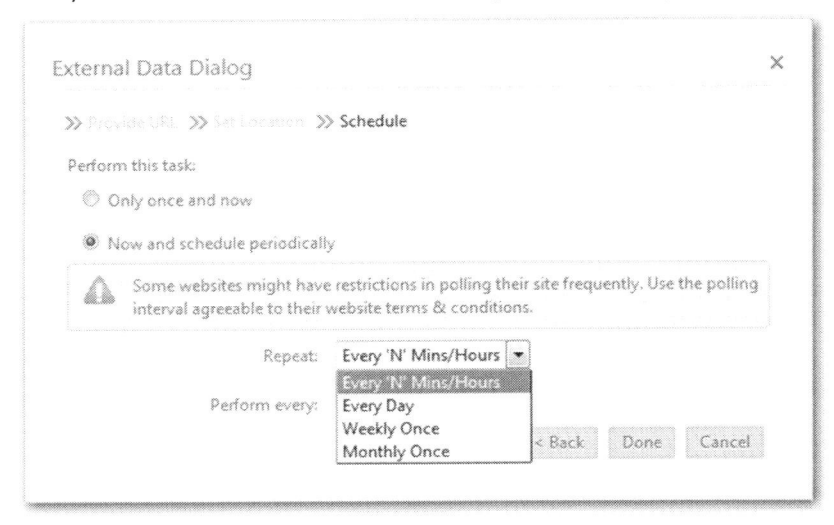

Figure 357: Creating a reoccurring schedule

I have blurred some of the imported data, as it is my live data. However, you can see the imported data.

Why would you need this? Raw data can be manipulated many ways in Sheet. You might have pivot tables created that feed off of the imported data. You might have statistical analysis in place.

Email Address	First Name	Last Name	Work Phone	Home Phone	Address Line 1
	Fred				
	Arlene				
	Sage				
	Ann				
	Joan				
	Brittany				
	Barbara & Michael				
	Billy				
	Riley				
	Barbara & Dean				
	Pat				
	Bruce & Angela				
	Buzz				
	Bruce				
	Andre				
	Chera				
	Chris				521 N. M Street

Figure 358: The imported data

How to Move Your Expensive Office to the Free Cloud

If you must have up to date data, you can manually refresh by clicking the **Manage External Data** link. This opens a list of all of your external links and allows you to **Edit**, **Refresh** or **Delete** the link (*Figure 359*).

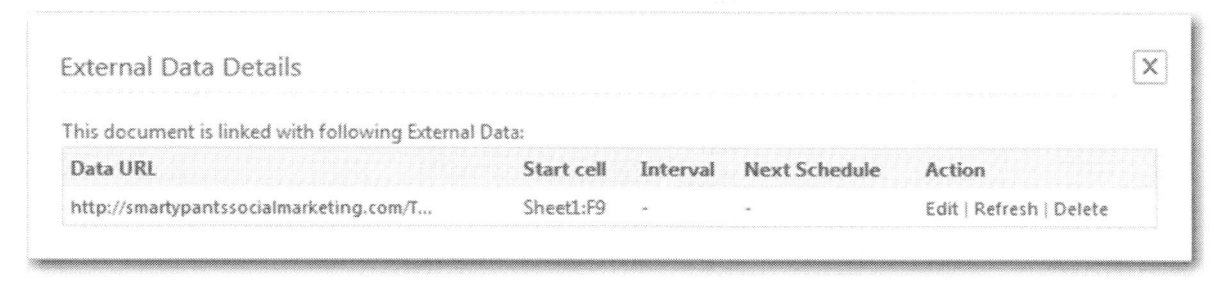

Figure 359: Manually refreshing the data

The Sheet View Tab

The View tab (*Figure 360*) allows us to freeze a row and column so that when we scroll the data, the labels do not move. You can go full screen to gain a little more screen real estate. The Go To icon allows you to jump to any cell coordinate or named range.

Figure 360: The View tab

The Sheet Review Tab

The **Review** tab (*Figure 361*) allows you to do a Find and Replace, you can **Add a Comment** to a cell or range of cells. You can **Create Version** with a friendly name, so you can go back to it later. **View Version History** and **Audit Trail** allow you to track changes and revert to an earlier version, if you wish.

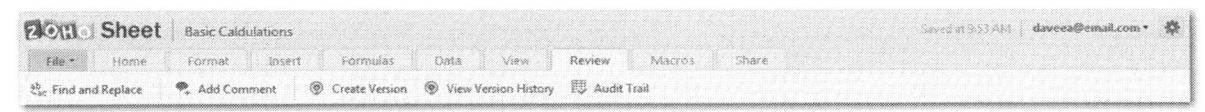

Figure 361: The review tab

Any change automatically creates a new version, but if you wish you can assign a friendly name that will help you find that particular state or version. It makes a named snapshot of the sheet at a certain stage of completion (*Figure 362*).

Chapter 13: Using Zoho Productivity Apps

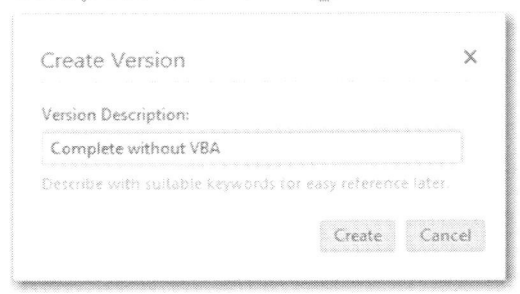

Figure 362: Creating a named version

Every change to the sheet creates a version. When the Version History list opens to the right of the sheet, you can see all changes and when they were made.

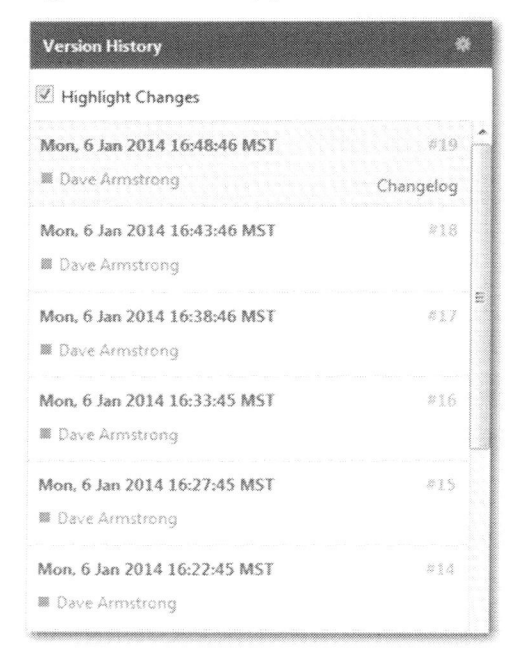

Figure 363: Checking version history

When you have selected a version, a **Changelog** link appears. Click it and you can see the changes made that generated that version (*Figure 364*).

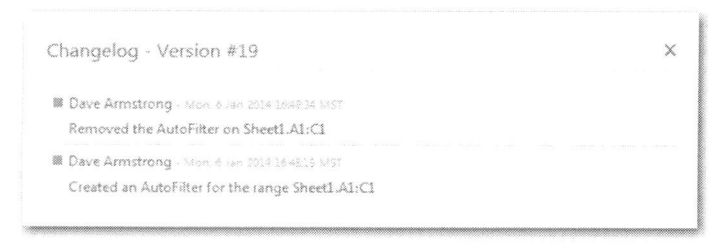

Figure 364: Changelog for last version change

You can revert to any of these versions, if you wish.

You have another way of seeing previous versions by clicking the **Audit Trail** icon. This opens a list of all of the changes and what the changes were (*Figure 365*).

You can filter list by:

- **User** - This is useful when you want to see just one person's edits in a collaborated Sheet.
- **Date** - If you think you know when the version was created, you can filter by a date range.
- **Sheet** - Remember that Sheet can be a workbook of several sheets. If you have more than sheet, you can pick a specific sheet.
- **Range** - In a large spreadsheet with many changes, you may wish to narrow the list down to just a portion of the sheet.

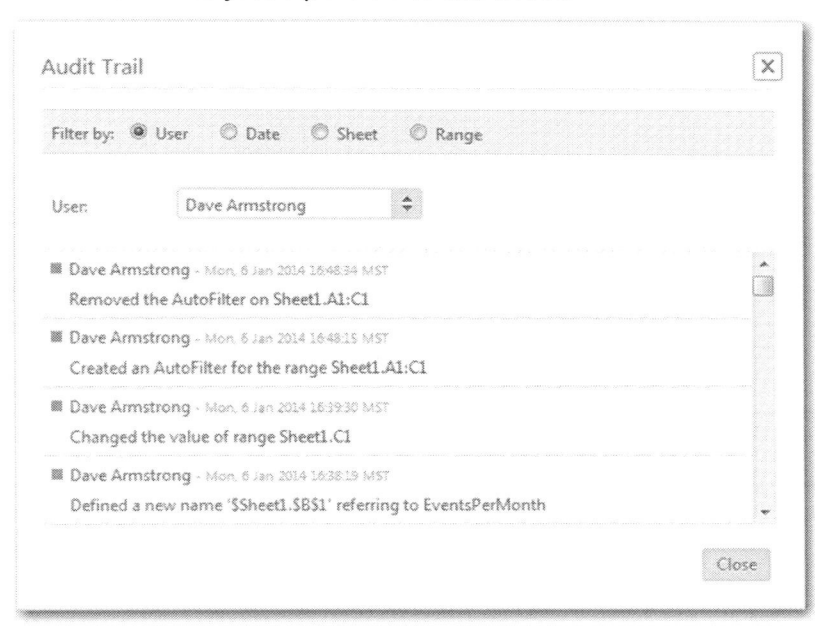

Figure 365: Audit Trail filtered by User, Date, Sheet or Range

The Sheet Macros Tab

Unlike the Microsoft web app version of Excel, Sheet has automation. Google Spreadsheet does have scripting automation which you can write in JavaScript, but Zoho's Sheet has the ability to record macros and then replay them as needed. Additionally, they can be edited and expanded using Microsoft's desktop Office app's language, **V**isual **B**asic for **A**pplications (VBA).

Chapter 13: Using Zoho Productivity Apps

If you find you are making the same keystrokes or taking the same steps to update a sheet, you need to learn about macros. As you can see, they can be as simple as recording a number of steps, or as complex as any programming environment.

The Macros tab allows you to record, run and edit macros (*Figure 366*).

The icons within the **Macros** tab are:

- **Create Macro** - Name and create macro from scratch.
- **Record Macro** - Give a name, start the macro recorder and make the changes you wish to record.
- **Run Macro** - Once recorded, this runs the macro. You might put a button on the sheet and link it to running a specific macro.
- **View Macros** - See a list of all macros where you can run, edit or delete any macro in the list.
- **VBA Editor** - In the editor, you can write code to automate almost any series of steps or changes.
- **Macros Help** - This icon takes you to Zoho's help files for using macros in Sheet.

Figure 366: The Macros tab

When you click the Record Macro icon, it opens the **Create Macro** dialog. Here you can name the micro and give a detailed description. The **Use Relative Reference** changes the method of recording the cell's position. Checking it means the macro might say, "Go left on cell and copy the contents". When unchecked, the macro might say, "Go to B1 and copy the contents." If you want to use the macro in different locations, you need to check this box (*Figure 367*).

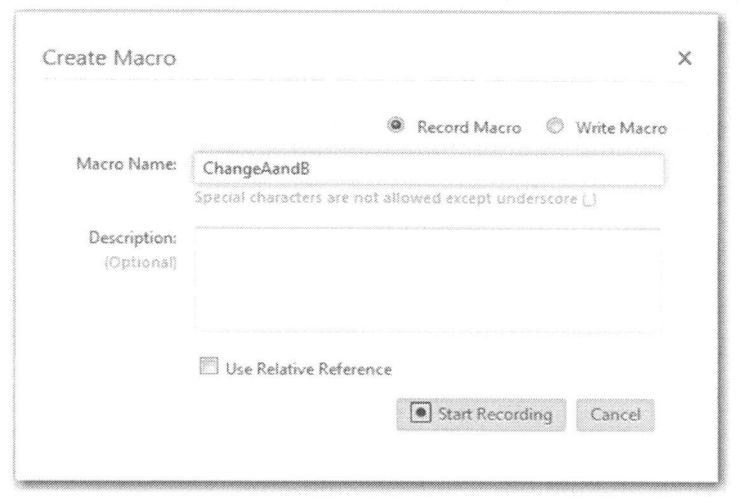

Figure 367: Naming and starting a macro

To run the macro, you need to click **View Macros** and click the link **Run**.

Figure 368: Running the macro from the macros list

Most of the time, recording a macro is all you need. When you record the macro, you are actual creating VBA code interactively. However, VBA is much more powerful than just creating macros, it is a full blown programming language based on Microsoft's powerful Visual Basic language. When you click on the VBA Editor, (*Figure 369*) it opens with all of your recorded macros, or other routines you have written, loaded in the editor.

Chapter 13: Using Zoho Productivity Apps

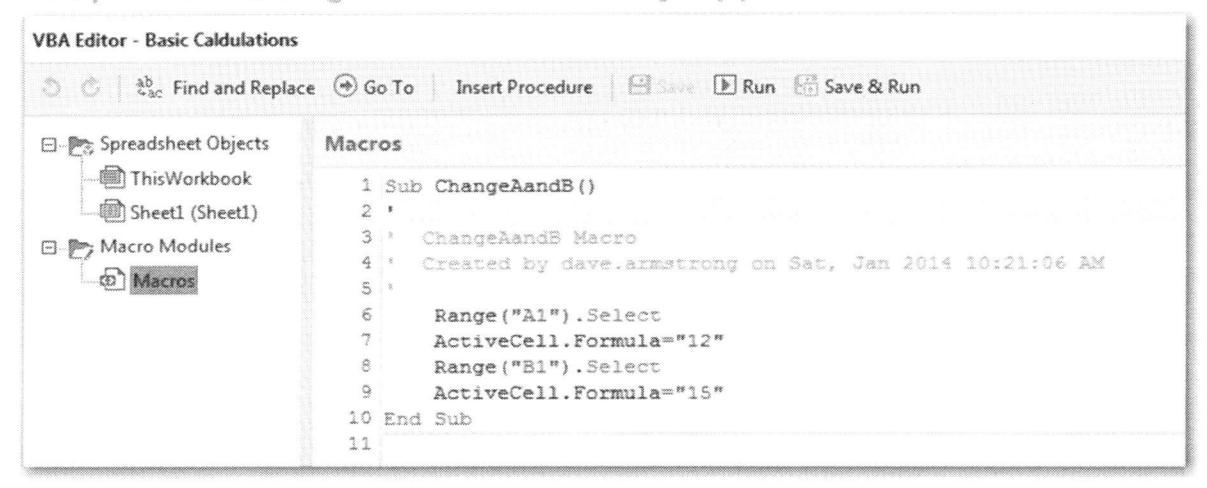

Figure 369: Under the hood, it is all VBA

The macro I named ChangeAandB is shown in VBA code. In simple terms, it says:

1. Go to cell A1 and select it.
2. Put 12 into the cell.
3. Go to cell B1 and select it.
4. Put 15 into the cell.

Not a very useful macro, but if you go to the help files at the Zoho website, you will get lots of ideas and free macros, that others have created and shared.

The Share Tab

The **Share** tab (*Figure 370*) allows you to share your work with others and, if you wish, allow them to collaborate with you in making changes.

Using the Share tab you can:

- **Share** - This opens a dialog (*Figure 371*) where you can add name, email address or a group name.
- **Collaborators** - This opens a text box where you can chat with your collaborators. If you gave Read/Write permissions, both of you can edit the same document.
- **Publish** - This will allow you to create a link to make the Sheet public. You can email or publish the link in allowing others to open and use the spreadsheet.
- **Embed** - This can only be used on one of your web pages, as email does not allow it. Anyone with access to the web page, can enter data and see calculations.

Figure 370: The Share tab

Chapter 13: Using Zoho Productivity Apps

In the **Share Settings** dialog you opened by clicking the share icon, you can add email addresses of those to which you wish to collaborate. You can give them permission to **Read/Write**, **Read Only** or be a **Co-Owner** that could modify or delete the Sheet.

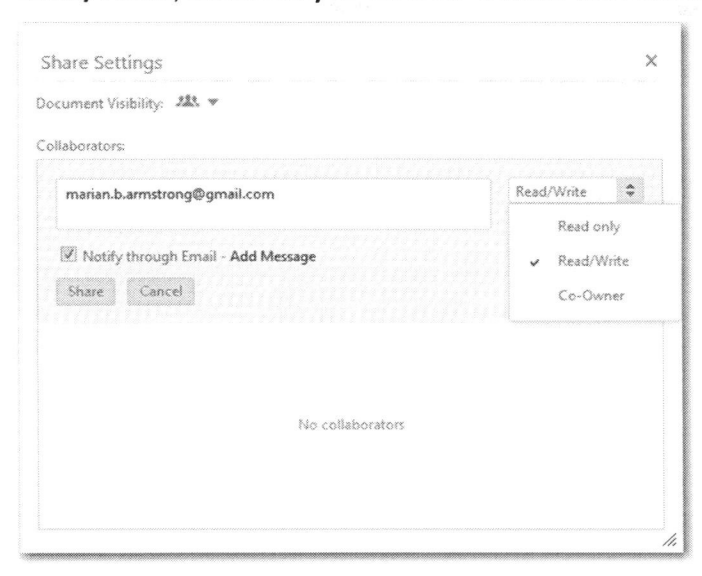

Figure 371: Adding collaborators

This is the email I sent to myself inviting myself to join me in editing the sheet (*Figure 372*). The changes I made were almost instantly visible to my other self.

Figure 372: Email invite received

The menu choice **Publish** helps me share the Sheet with other via a URL link. If I check **Allow to export**, they can download and save a copy in various formats. If I check the **Hide and lock formula cells**, they can change static data, but not the formulas (*Figure 373*).

Chapter 13: Using Zoho Productivity Apps

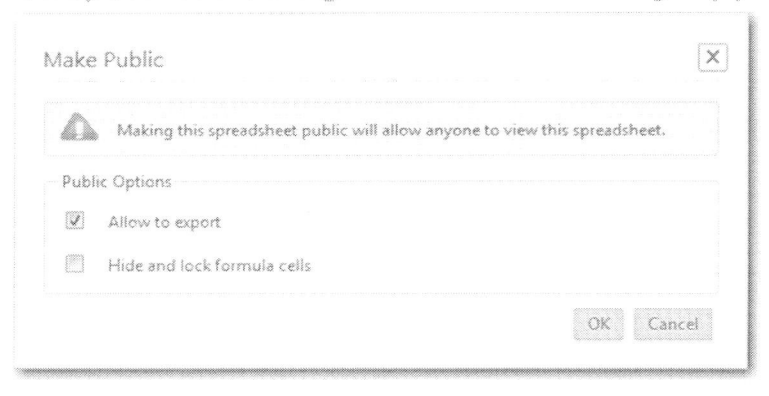

Figure 373: Making a public link to the Sheet

If you just want to show the sheet in an HTML page or a printable page, choose the appropriate tab at the bottom (*Figure 374*).

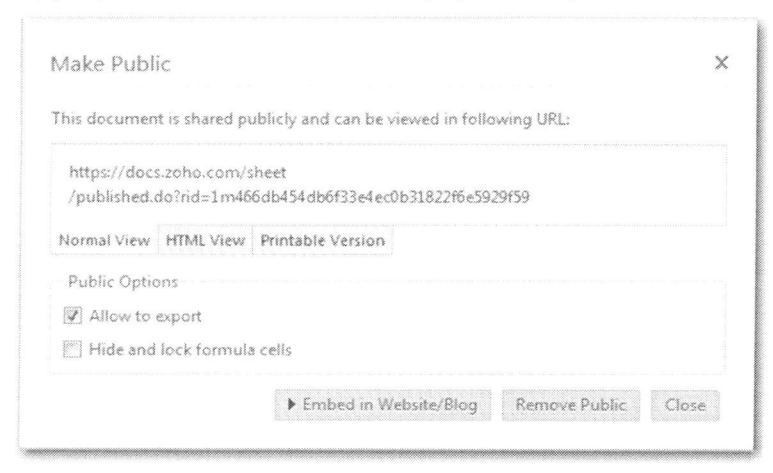

Figure 374: Cut and paste the resultant link

If you click the **Embed** link at the top of the page or click the **Embed in Website/Blog** button above, you get code that you can cut and paste into one of your webpages on your site. Most blog software allows you to embed HTML code.

Chapter 13: Using Zoho Productivity Apps

I have covered the spreadsheet application because it is the most complex and most of the other apps have similar menus, if not all of the functions, of the spreadsheet.

Compared to Google's Spreadsheet and Microsoft's Excel web app, the Zoho sheet is the most powerful.

Zoho's Show App

Show is Zoho's slide show or presentation application. It is very similar in use and features to Microsoft's Desktop PowerPoint. However, as a web app, it is not as full featured. In comparison, it is just as capable as the other web clones: Google's Present and Microsoft's PowerPoint web app.

We will not cover Show in as great of depth as Sheet and will only take a tour of the menus. Any basic book on PowerPoint 2010 or later, will teach techniques.

From the Zoho Docs main screen, click the **CREATE** button and select **Presentation**. This opens another browser tab with a new presentation showing. A popup window opens on top of the presentation and invites you to first pick a template with a layout and color scheme (*Figure 375*).

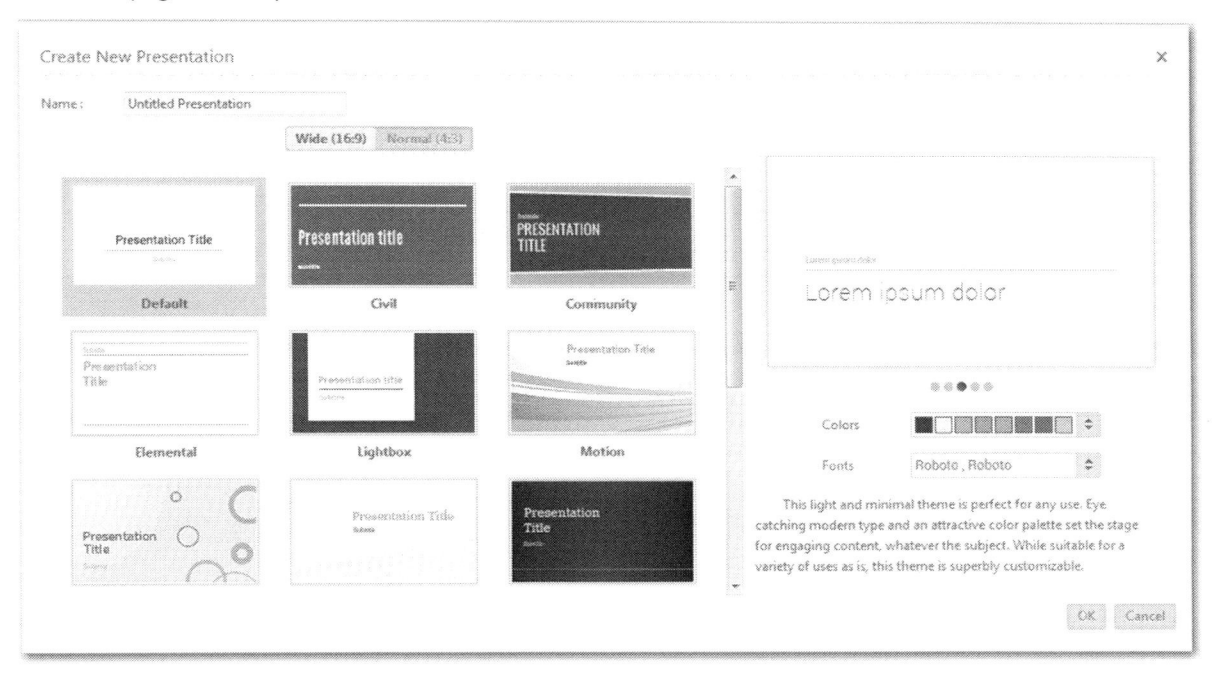

Figure 375: Picking a template

After selecting a template and clicking OK, the template is applied and the presentation is opened. The first thing is to change the name of the document from **Untitled Presentation** to something specific. Slides usually have one or more text boxes: a larger one for the main topic and smaller ones of lists and other text (*Figure 376*).

Chapter 13: Using Zoho Productivity Apps

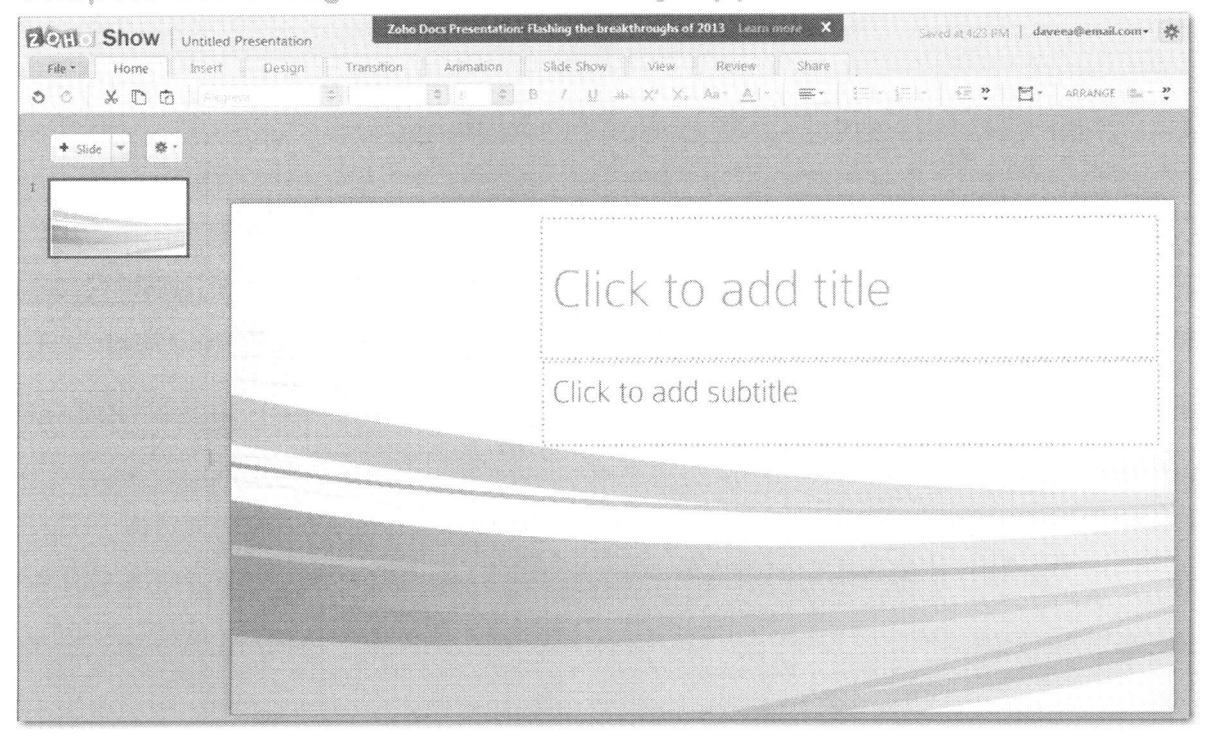

Figure 376: Adding and editing slides

Let's Explore Show's Menu Tabs

As mentioned before, Zoho Doc's menus are similar in concept to Microsoft's ribbon. All of the apps share a common set of tabs used for formatting, reviewing, etc.

While we will not go too deep in the menu's details, we will review in such a way as to help you learn where everything is and aid in your evaluation.

The Show Home Tab

As with the other **Home** menus, we have groups that allow you to do and undo, copy, paste and cut, format text, create list, set text alignment, arrange the layering of objects and to rotate objects. Some of these features appear elsewhere, but were put on this tab for your convenience (*Figure 377*).

Figure 377 The Home tab

The Show Insert Tab

The **Insert** tab allows you to insert images from various sources, shapes, text boxes, footers, page numbers, dates, hyperlinks and video. You can, also, insert a twitter feed

Chapter 13: Using Zoho Productivity Apps

and gadgets that can show video and sound from sites such as YouTube or Soundcloud (*Figure 378*).

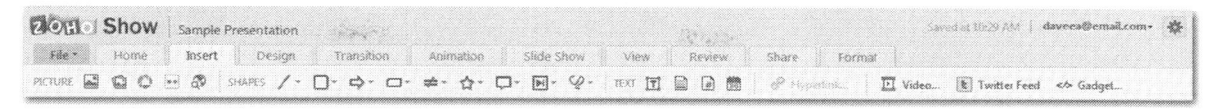

Figure 378: The Insert tab

The Show Design Tab

The **Design** tab allows you to change the theme, the default fonts and colors, the styles and orientation. You can change the slide widths, height and orientation (*Figure 379*).

Figure 379: The Design tab

The Show Transition Tab

The **Transition** tab allows you to create transitions between the slides and even automate the passage of slides with a *N* number of seconds between. This is great for a continually running, kiosk type display (*Figure 380*).

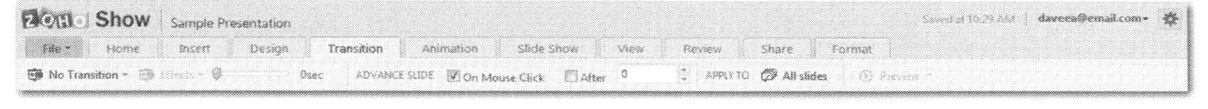

Figure 380: The Transition tab

The Show Animation Tab

The **Animation** tab allows you to animate items as they move on the slide. You could, for example, have an image spin as it came in from the right (*Figure 381*).

Figure 381: The Animation tab

The Show Slide Show Tab

The **Slide Show** tab controls the playing of the slides. You can start the slides from the beginning, first slide or from the current slide. You can create a custom slide show and play the slides in another order. You can even temporarily hide a slide you do not want shown (*Figure 382*).

Chapter 13: Using Zoho Productivity Apps

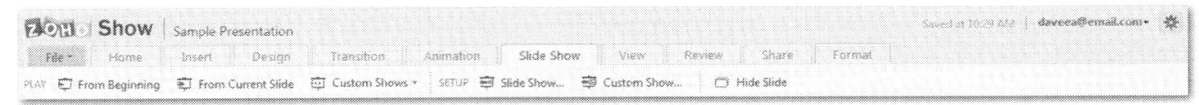

Figure 382: The Slideshow tab

The Show View Tab

The **View** tab gives you tools to sort or arrange your slides as if they were physical slides on a light box. You can change the size of the slides in design view using **ZOOM**. To properly align the object on the slides, you can turn on **Guides** and **Grids**. All objects then show you alignment clues (*Figure 383*).

Figure 383: The View tab

The Show Review Tab

The **Review** tab allows you to **Find and Replace….**, if you want to change a term throughout the slides. You can name a version and easily return to any version you have created (*Figure 384*).

Figure 384: The Review tab

The Show Share Tab

The **Share** tab allows you to share with others in collaboration. You can, **Publish** a link to the slides and **Embed** them into a web page. You can **Broadcast** your presentation to a remote audience. You can invite up to 10 people via email and send them the broadcast URL (*Figure 385*).

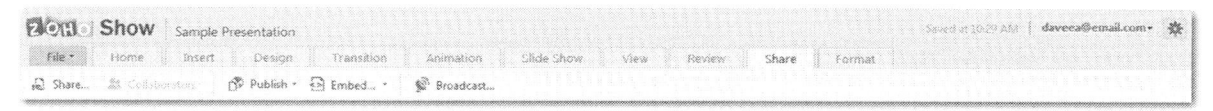

Figure 385: The Share tab

The Show Format Tab

The **Format** menu appears if you have an object selected. You have Preset shapes that can be used for text, fill, color and images formatting controls. You can apply shadows and apply line types and weights (*Figure 386*).

Figure 386: The Format tab

If you know Microsoft's PowerPoint, you will feel very comfortable with the menus. I find that all three office type web apps are similar. Perhaps they all copy each other and since Microsoft was first, their features are the standard. It could also be parallel evolution, in that, they all try to solve the same problems and are, therefore, similar.

Creating Folders

You could end up with hundreds or even thousands of documents, in time. Like storing files on your hard drive, you need some way to keep them organized. We do that, of course, with folders.

Using the same **CREATE** menu we used to create apps, one of the choices is folder. From the **Create Folder** dialog, type a name and click the **Add Folder** button.

Remember, to click on the position where you want to add the folder first. For example, I might create a top level folder and then open it up before adding a second level folder (*Figure 387*).

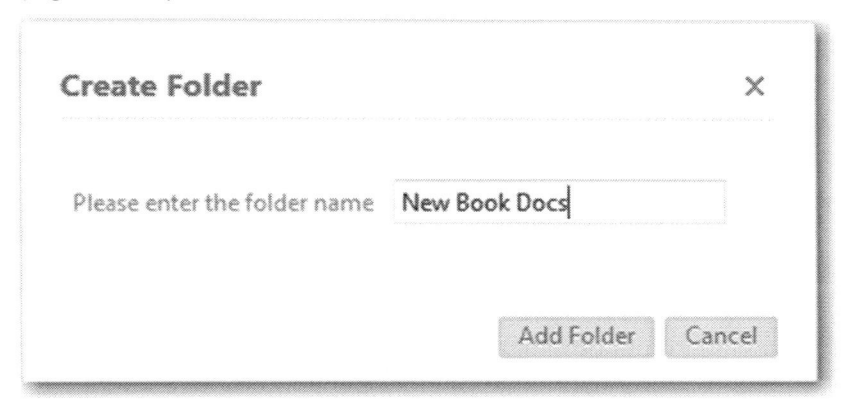

Figure 387: Creating folders to organize documents

You can see and navigate the folders in the left column of your Zoho Docs main screen. You can right-click the folder, if you want to rename or delete. You can drag and drop to rearrange the hierarchy of the folders (*Figure 388*).

Chapter 13: Using Zoho Productivity Apps

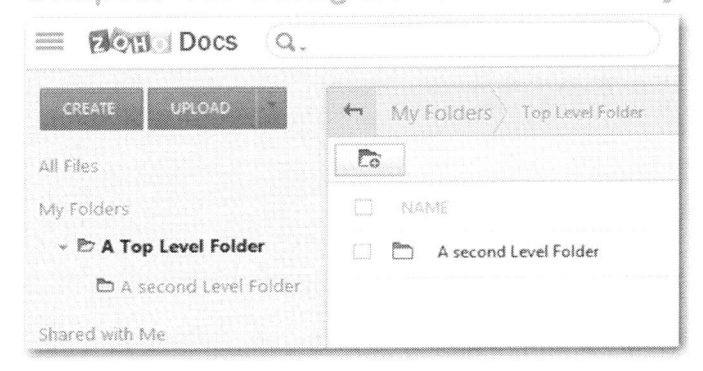

Figure 388: New folders in your list

Zoho Docs for Desktop

Like Google's Drive or Microsoft's SkyDrive, Zoho gives you storage space for both files you upload and documents you create with Zoho Docs. They provide a download that will sync all of the files in the Zoho cloud with your desktop. Want to upload a group of files? Just drag and drop them on the Zoho Docs folder installed by the Zoho Docs for Desktop app that you downloaded and installed (*Figure 389*).

You can download the app from here: https://www.zoho.com/docs/file-sync.html.

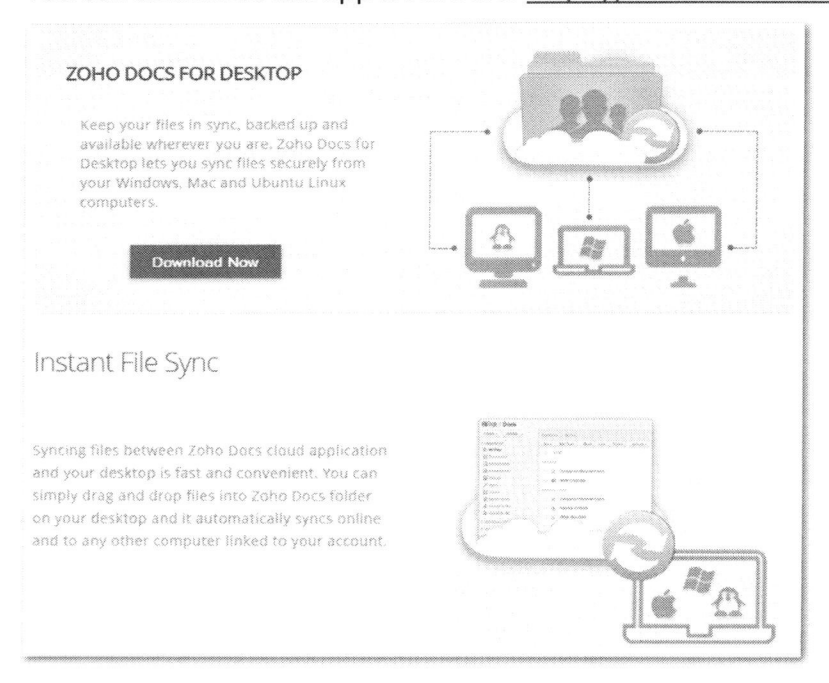

Figure 389: Download the desktop app

I will assume you know how to download and install a file. Remember, where you saved it and double-click to start the installation program. Follow the Wizard that installs the

Chapter 13: Using Zoho Productivity Apps

software. When you start the first time, the software asks for your Zoho **Username** and **Password** (*Figure 390*).

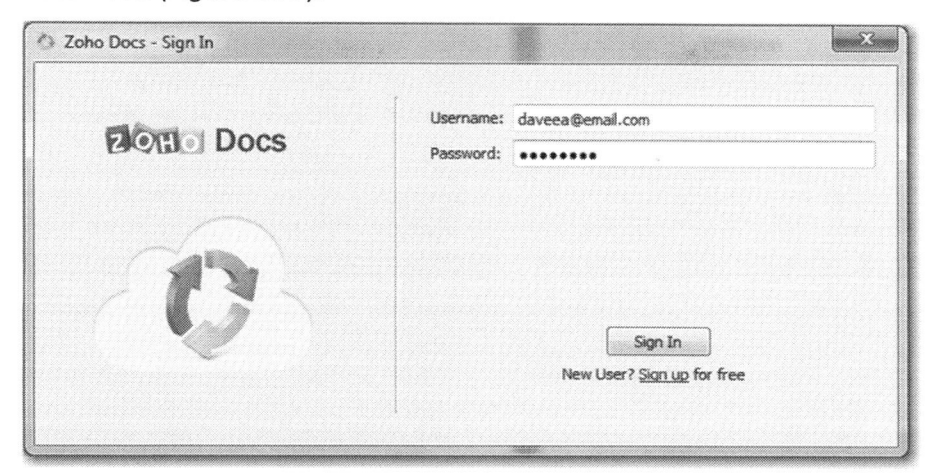

Figure 390: First sign in to Zoho Docs

Next, you will be offered a location to place the local copy of the synced files. Accept the default. If you do not want all of the files and folders synced, you can **Choose Folders** and deselect the ones you do not want. Unless you have a lot of files, keep the default, sync all folders (*Figure 391*).

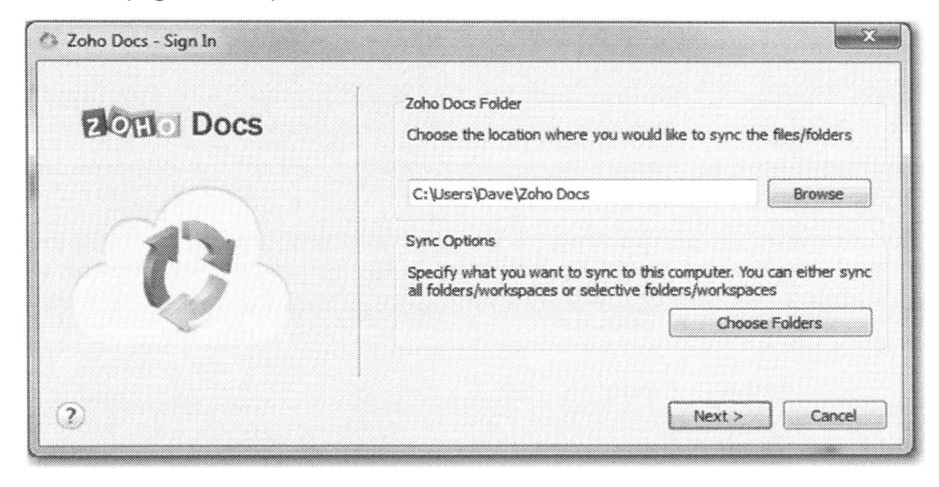

Figure 391: Creating a local folder to sync

Once installed and after a short wait, you will see a new folder under your **Favorites** in Windows Explorer. The folder is called Zoho Docs and it contains and links to all of the folders, files and documents you have created.

Chapter 13: Using Zoho Productivity Apps

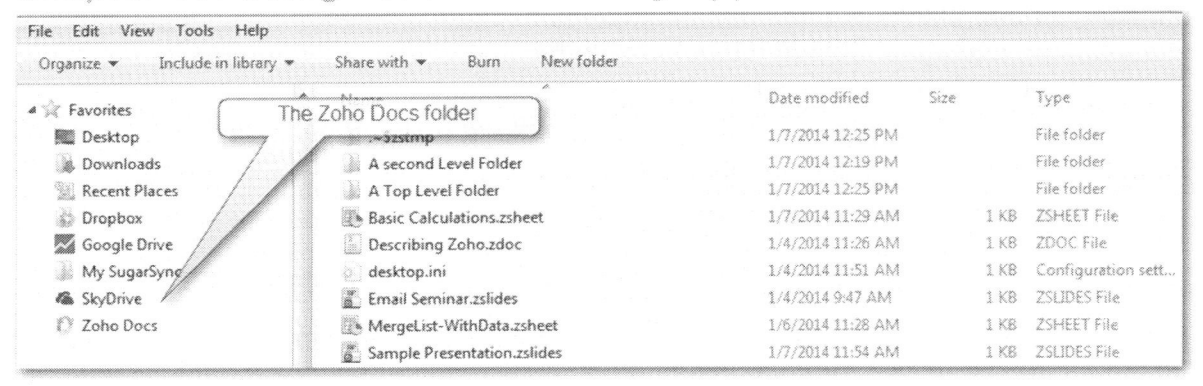

Figure 392: Windows Explorer view of Zoho Docs

Integration with Google and Microsoft

In spite of the slight superiority of Zoho Docs over Google Drive and SkyDrive, you may already be wedded to one or the other. If so, Zoho CRM is now integrated with Google Drive apps, if you would rather use them.

A third party, Zapier https://zapier.com/zapbook/skydrive/zoho-crm/ has tools that somewhat integrate Zoho and SkyDrive.

If you are just now moving to cloud storage and office web apps, Zoho offers a serious suite of products.

There is a lot more to Zoho, but that is another book.

Chapter 14: Using Skype

One of the challenges of having a distributed virtual office, is communication. In a workplace, you can leave your desk, walk over to your fellow workers and discuss a work related issue. This has been the way people collaborate, face to face, for thousands of years. In a virtual office, you are at different locations, sometimes thousands of miles away.

Let's rethink this. Is a face to face meeting really that efficient? You lose time on that walk to and from your colleague's desk. Additionally, many business interactions denigrate into personal, and from a business point of view, mostly nonproductive conversations. While you might argue that these personal interactions build cohesive teams, too much water cooler time can hurt productivity, especially, for those that work on computers much of their time and need to be at their desk.

Many large companies, with hundreds of employees in the same location, are adopting what we will discuss in this chapter, virtual communication. IM (instant messaging) is very efficient. A quick, nonintrusive text message may suffice and may take only seconds. Typing text keeps conversations short and to the point. Need more nuance and details? A quick phone call can give more depth to planning and collaboration.

What is better than a phone call? Video simulates much of what we get in face to face interactions. Some behavioral scientists suggest that as much as 50% of our communication is nonverbal. Is the person at the other end of our conversation bored, angry or excited about our topic? This may be difficult to pick up over an audio/phone exchange and, even worse, in text messaging. There is no sarcastic font.

Chapter 14: Using Skype

Whether you totally adopt a virtual office, or just want the benefits, this chapter will evaluate Skype. Skype solves many interoffice problems and is free or nearly so.

Skype

I love Skype and consider it the best value for interoffice communication. To start with, it is free for person to person text messaging, voice conversations and video, if you do it computer to computer.

If you want to hold video meetings, you need only purchase a Premium account for $9.99 a month. That person can set up group video conferencing, while the other staff only need the free version to participate. The $9.99 a month includes unlimited calling in the US and Canada.

Be aware that Microsoft continuously updates and improves Skype. This means that some of the screens you see in the chapter will become obsolete in time. The changes are usually evolutionary and you should be able to figure the changes out.

Downloading Skype

Skype is a desktop client, but you often have to go to the website to make purchases and other changes to your account. You use the same username and password for both the client and website.

Go to www.Skype.com and click the **Join us** link at the top (*Figure 393*). While you could do this later when you download and install the desktop, setting up your account is a little quicker and easier in the website.

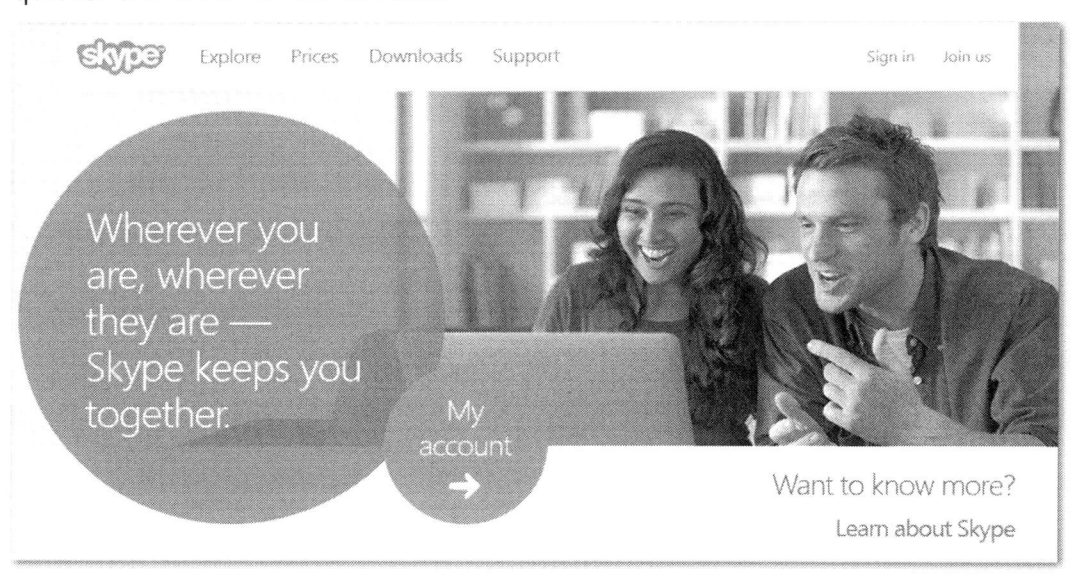

Figure 393: Skype's home screen

Chapter 14: Using Skype

After clicking the download link, you need to choose what kind of device you will use to make calls. We will cover the computer version (*Figure 394*). If you have downloaded and installed software before, you know the drill.

1. Click the Computer square in the web page.
2. In a few seconds, a pop up window will ask if you want to save the file. Answer, yes, and remember where you saved it. The default is your Download folder under favorites.
3. Open Windows Explorer, find and double-click the file. Follow the prompts.
4. At some point, you will be asked to either sign in or join Skype. If you have already joined at the website, enter the user name and password you chose.

Figure 394: Download the computer software

Since Skype and its website are constantly changing, you might want to go to the website and find the help section under support and bookmark it. As changes show up, you can go there to help you catch up on new releases. The help screens are well designed and include search (*Figure 395*).

Chapter 14: Using Skype

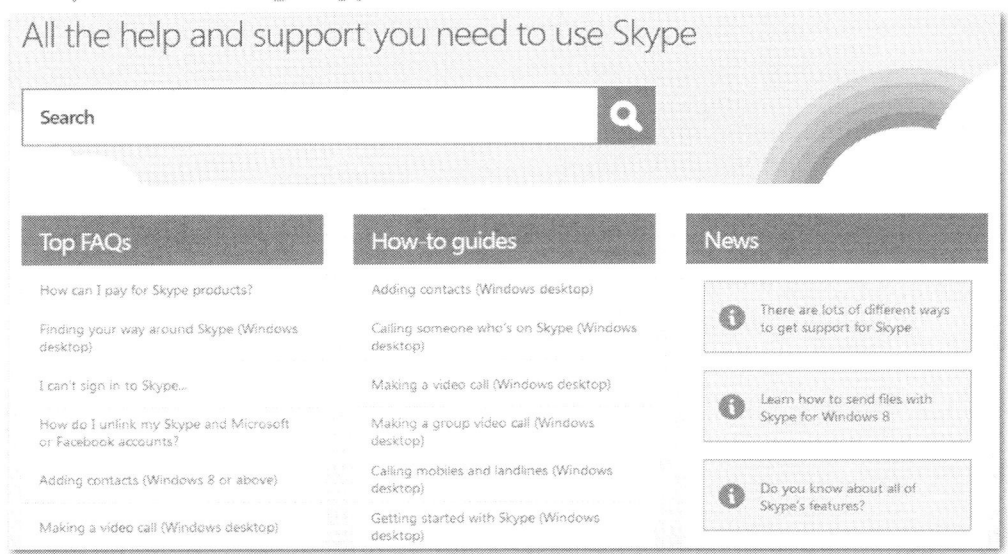

Figure 395: Skype's up-to-date help and how to guides

Skype's Main Screen

You can adjust Skype to open every time you start windows. In an office environment, where you constantly use Skype, this is a good idea, as we will discuss later.

Regardless of how you start Skype, the basic screen gives you quick access to most of the features you need with a single click or two. There is also a rich set of menus for changing settings. The menus show keyboard shortcuts for the most common features. Learn these, as they can greatly speed up the use of Skype.

Let's take a tour of the main screen (*Figure 396*):

1. Click the phone icon to call mobiles and landlines.
2. Click the group icon to start a new chat, create a group, and send new messages or files. This is computer to computer unless you send SMS (text to mobile phones).
3. Click the contact plus icon to add a contact. Search for people you know using their name, Skype name or email.
4. These are your current contacts. Those with the small green icon are connected by computer.
5. Those with the phone icon are mobile or landline phones.
6. The menus are across the top. We will discuss later.
7. You cannot see it here, but once you have selected a recipient, you will see their information here.
8. This shows your name and picture and any custom messages you have created when you created your profile.

Chapter 14: Using Skype

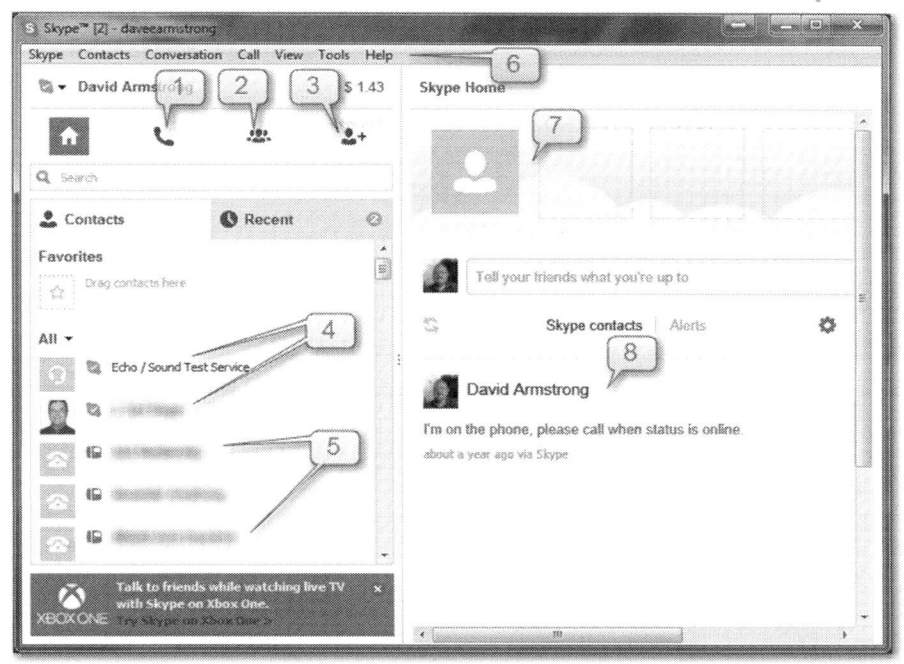

Figure 396: The Skype home screen

Searching for, Adding and importing Contacts

Having clicked the contact plus icon, I get the search (*Figure 397*). I can type just a first and last name, an email address or, if I know it, a Skype name. As you see, I got a list of possible candidates, most in Australia. I happen to know my friend lives in Elmhurst and that is his picture.

Figure 397: Finding other Skype users

How to Move Your Expensive Office to the Free Cloud

Chapter 14: Using Skype

Once I click on his name in the search results, I can see, for sure, it is him (*Figure 398*). However, before I can talk with him, he needs to approve my request to add him to my contacts. I click the **Add to Contacts** button.

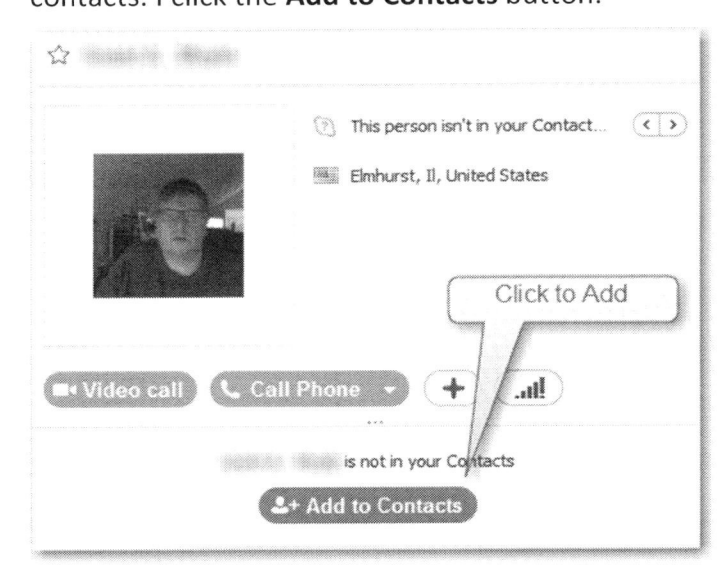

Figure 398: Adding a contact to your list

I can add a short note. I may need to remind him of where we met, if he is not a close friend. Click the Send button after your message is customized (*Figure 399*).

Be aware that there are many trolls that will ask to connect to you. They are selling something and it usually is a sham, or at least unsavory. Unless you really want to talk to Russian women or a Nigerian prince, you should ignore those requests.

Figure 399: Asking permission from a new contact

Sending Instant Messages

Chapter 14: Using Skype

If Skype only did instant messaging, it would still be a great product. Understand that IM is done computer to computer and the other person needs only have a Skype account and be on Skype. Using this for your staff's interoffice communication, is a great choice.

As you can see in (*Figure 400*), you only need to:

1. Click the group icon.
2. Drag one or more of your contacts over to the top left area (we will discuss later).
3. Go to the bottom of the panel and start typing.
4. You and your contact(s) can see the discussion. The other person's conversation is below their name in blue.

IM has many advantages over a phone call, for example:

- It is much less intrusive. I do not have to answer a phone before it stops ringing.
- Since you type your messages, it forces you to be brief and concise.
- If gives you an audit trail of any IM conversation. Not sure later what was said? Review the message.

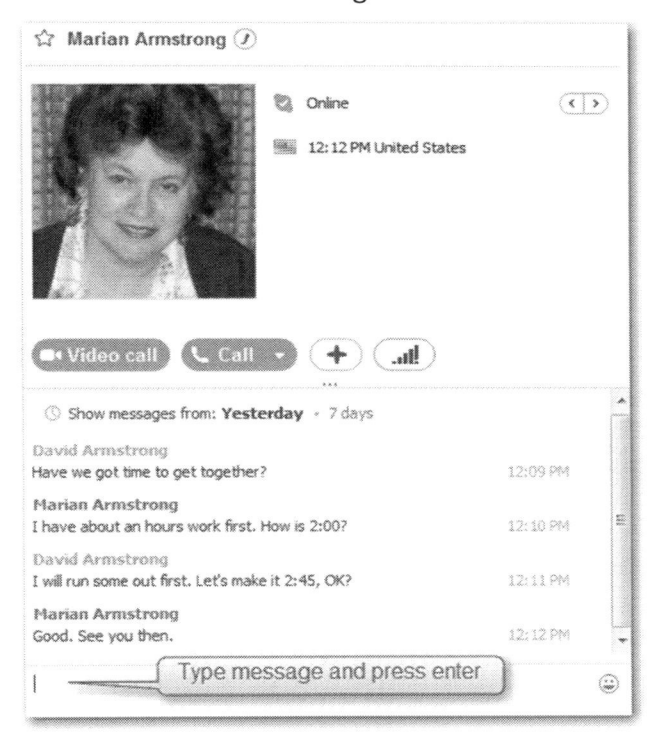

Figure 400: Instant messaging with a contact

You configure Skype by making the menu choices **Tools->Options...**. You have a lot of settings you can set or adjust to get Skype to work a certain way (*Figure 401*). Let's look at some of the IM settings:

- If you are using this for interoffice communication, you probably want to allow only staff in your contact list. All of your staff should have each other in their contact list. Allow just anyone and the trolls will find you.
- **Keep history forever** is probably right, as you may need the messages and, depending on your industry, it may be mandatory.
- Check **Open a new window when I receive a new message in Compact view**.
- **Pressing Ctrl+V will...**, your choice.
- **Pressing Enter will...** Like to break the message up into paragraphs? If so, check **insert line break**. You will need to click a button to send a message.
- Check **Show when I am typing** so they know you're still composing your message.
- **When I receive a file...,** your choice, although, having a predetermined folder might make finding files you have received easier.

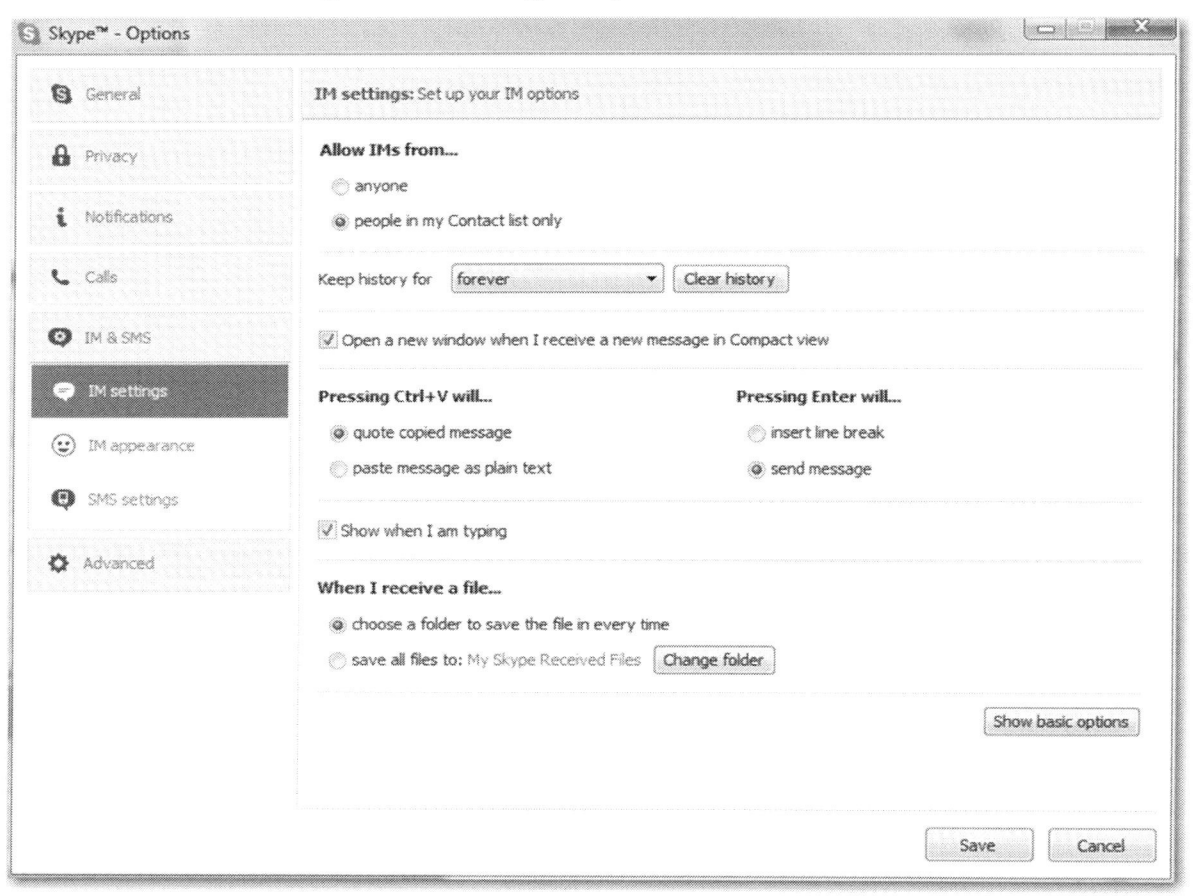

Figure 401: Changing your IM and SMS settings

Sending SMS Messages to Mobile Phones

Chapter 14: Using Skype

SMS stands for **Small Messaging Service** and we use it to text between mobile phones. First, be aware that, unlike most mobile carriers, Skype does not offer free, unlimited SMS messaging, regardless, of what plan you opt for. You will have to purchase Skype credit and use it to pay for each message. SMS messages overseas can be quite expensive. They do tell you how much a message will cost before you send it and will track and show your Skype credit balance.

Here are the SMS settings and some suggestions (*Figure 402*):

- Skype can send, but not receive SMS. If you want a reply on your mobile phone, you need to check the **My mobile phone number**.
    - If you have not added a mobile phone number in your profile, you will need to use the click the **Verify a different mobile phone number** link (may have slightly different text if you have none in profile). Skype will send a code to the phone and you will then need to enter the code back into this window.
- The link **SMS destinations and rates** does not show SMS rates, only phone plans.

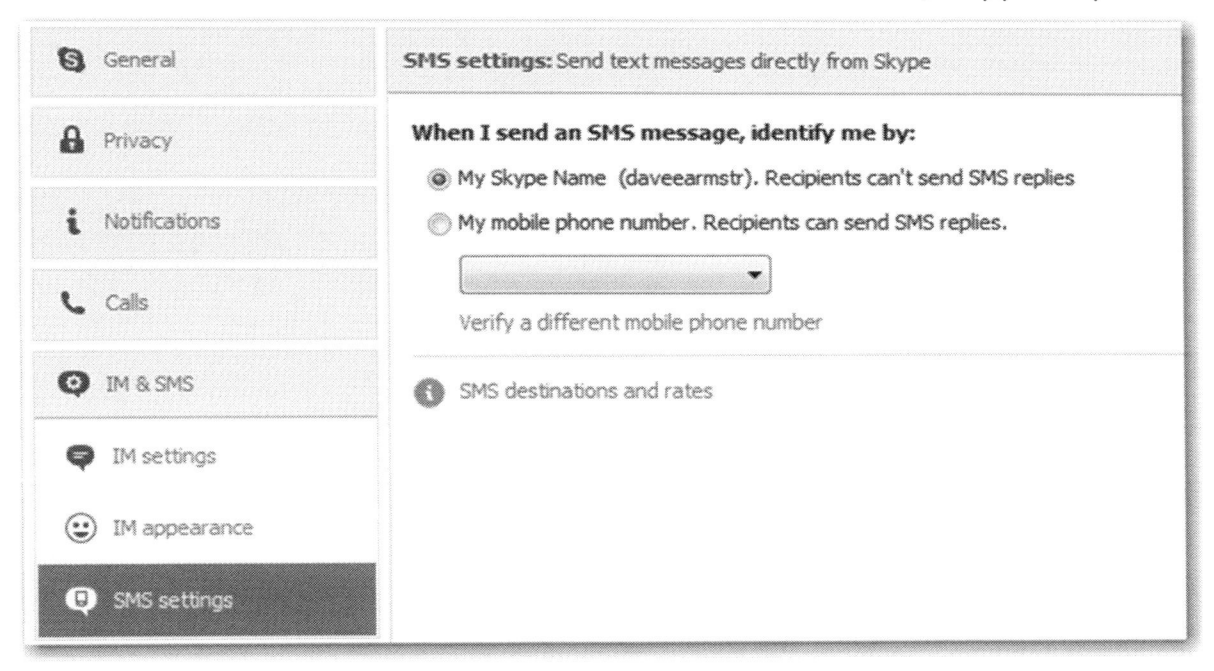

Figure 402: SMS settings

Anytime you type a message at the bottom of the panel, you can change the way it is sent from IM to SMS. Click the via **Skype** link and choose **SMS (mobile number)** (*Figure 403*).

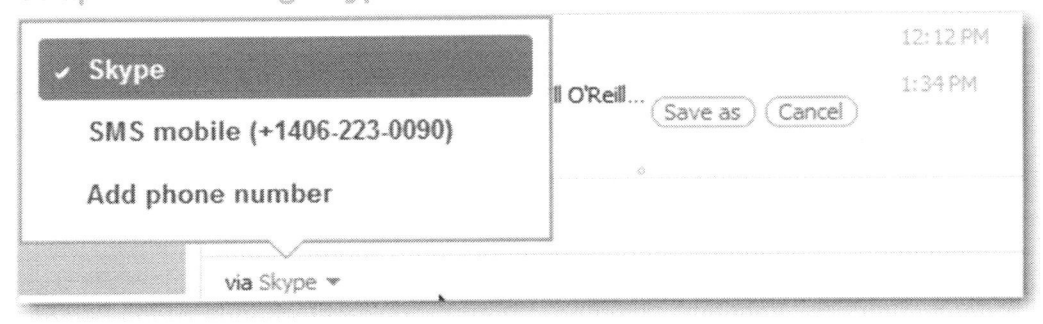

Figure 403: Sending an SMS message to a phone

Before you send, look for the cost of the message in the lower right (*Figure 404*). This message will cost 11.2 cents.

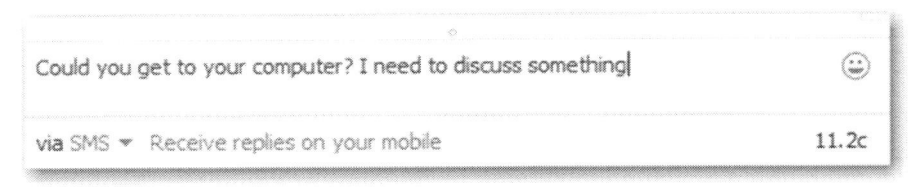

Figure 404: Note cost from Skype Credits

Sending Files

To the right of the **Video call** and **Call** buttons, is a plus button (*Figure 405*). You can send files while using IM, video calls and Skype computer to computer calls. While off this topic, you can also record a short video message and send to the contact.

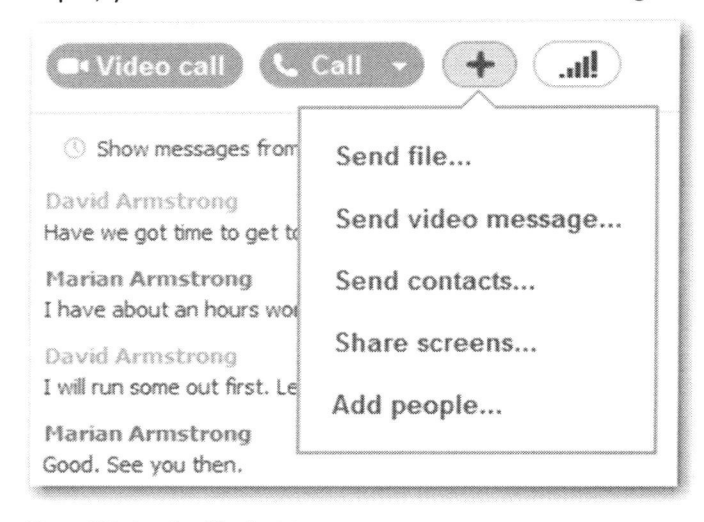

Figure 405: Sending files by IM

A similar plus menu is available while on a call or video call. As you can see, you can send a file in any of the computer to computer communications (*Figure 406*).

Chapter 14: Using Skype

Figure 406: Sending a file while in a phone or video call

To Send a File Using Skype

Using the usual Windows file open screen, you locate and select the file and click the **Open** button. Both of you can watch the uploading/downloading process. Once the download is complete, you click the **Save as** button (*Figure 407*).

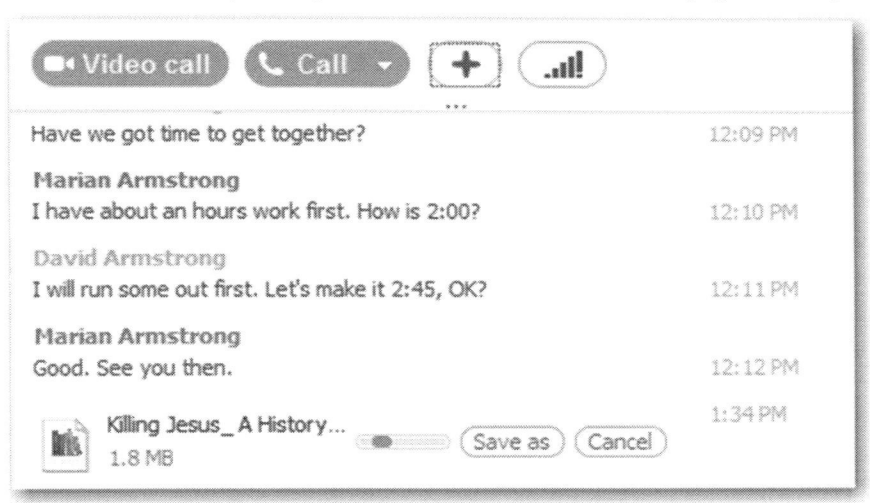

Figure 407: Receiving a File via IM

Unless you turn the warning off, you may see the dialog warning in (*Figure 408*) about viruses. If you do get a file from an untrusted contact, you might have your virus software check it before you open or start the file if it is an executable (.exe) file.

Chapter 14: Using Skype

Figure 408: Warning when saving the file

After you click the **OK** button in the warning dialog, you will be asked where you want to save it (*Figure 409*). As we mentioned earlier, you can set up an "always use" folder that will bypass this save window.

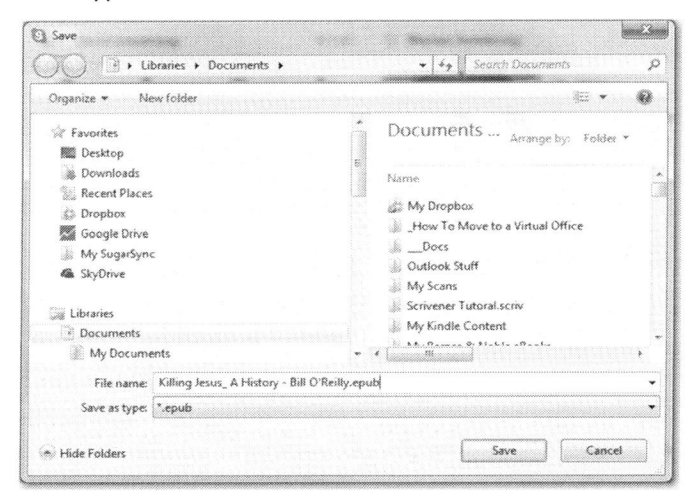

Figure 409: Picking a locations and/or name

You will need to click the down arrow to the right of the file icon to see the progress of the files, if you are downloading more than one. The **Save all** button will save all of the files as we saw above (*Figure 410*).

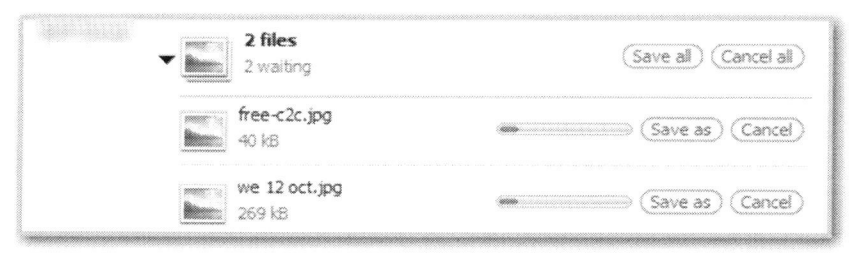

Figure 410: Saving multiple files

Quick Trouble Shooting Your Speakers, Microphone and Webcam

Chapter 14: Using Skype

At any time, you can check Skype setup to see if your microphones, speakers, computers speed and Internet connection are working. This bar type icon, to the left of your other buttons, is a window showing the settings. You can click it anytime for a quick tweak, if something does not seem to be working (*Figure 411*).

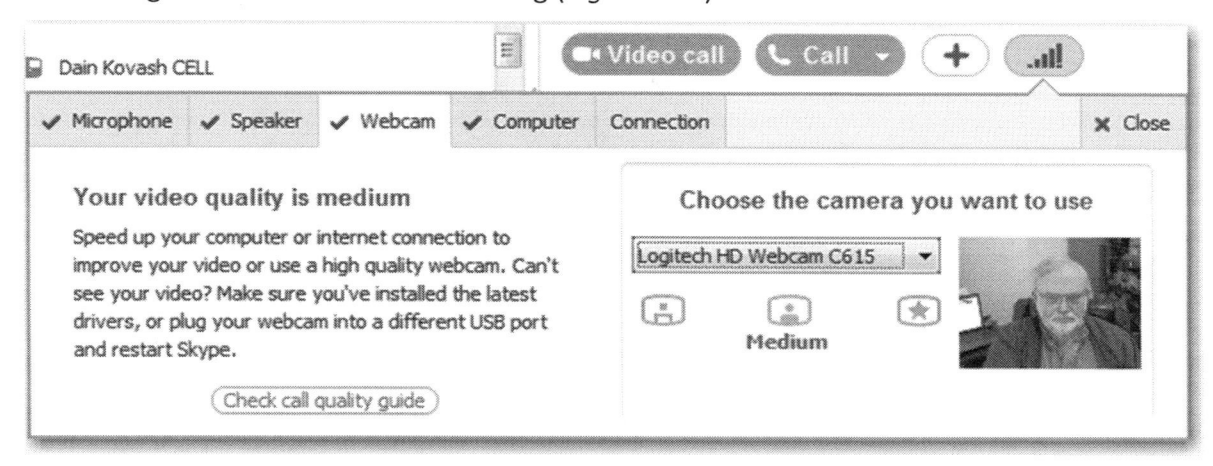

Figure 411: Checking and adjusting your equipment and connection

Making Skype Calls

Once you have selected one or more contacts, you can click the **Call** button, if they are on Skype. If they only have a phone number, clicking the **Call** button will dial their phone. Calling a contact that has both a Skype account and a phone number may require you to tell Skype which to use (*Figure 412*).

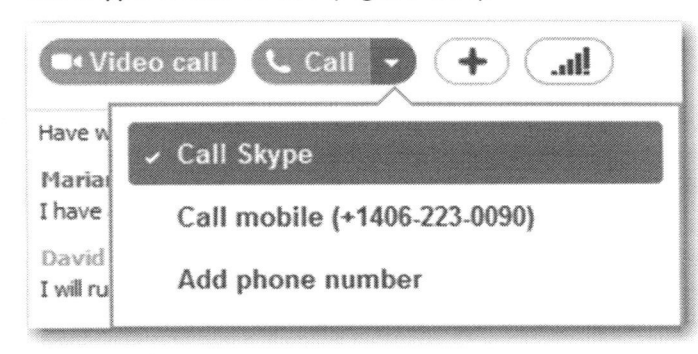

Figure 412: Calling via Skype or phone

As Skype tries to make the call, you will see the screen in (*Figure 413*) and will hear the phone ringing.

Chapter 14: Using Skype

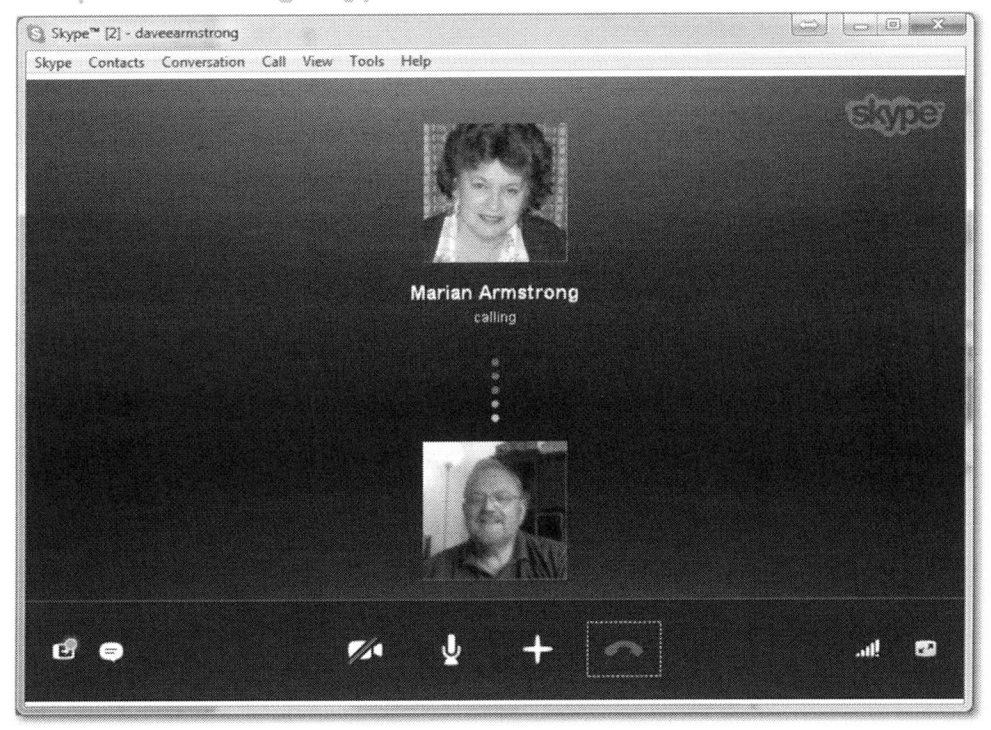

Figure 413: Waiting for an answer

Once connected, you can bring up a menu at the bottom by moving your mouse over the bottom of the screen. The menu icons fade in or out depending on whether your mouse is near them.

Here are the icon menu choices (*Figure 414*):

1. Show contacts in a slide from the left view of your contact panel. You can drag new people into the call.
2. Show IM. This opens a text messaging area that slides up from the bottom. Great, if you want to share notes of the phone discussion.
3. Turns on the video, if both have a webcam.
4. Mutes, unmutes the microphone.
5. Opens a menu offering the ability to:
    a. **Send files...** as we discussed.
    b. **Send Contacts...** information. This opens a pick list of contacts.
    c. **Share screens...** we will discuss this shortly.
    d. **Add people to this call...** brings up another list of contacts overlaying this screen.
    e. **Show dial pad** opens a typical dial pad. Useful for adding someone not in your contacts.
6. **Hang Up.**

Chapter 14: Using Skype

7. Adjust and trouble shoot settings.
8. Click to go full screen. You may need to do this on group video calls.

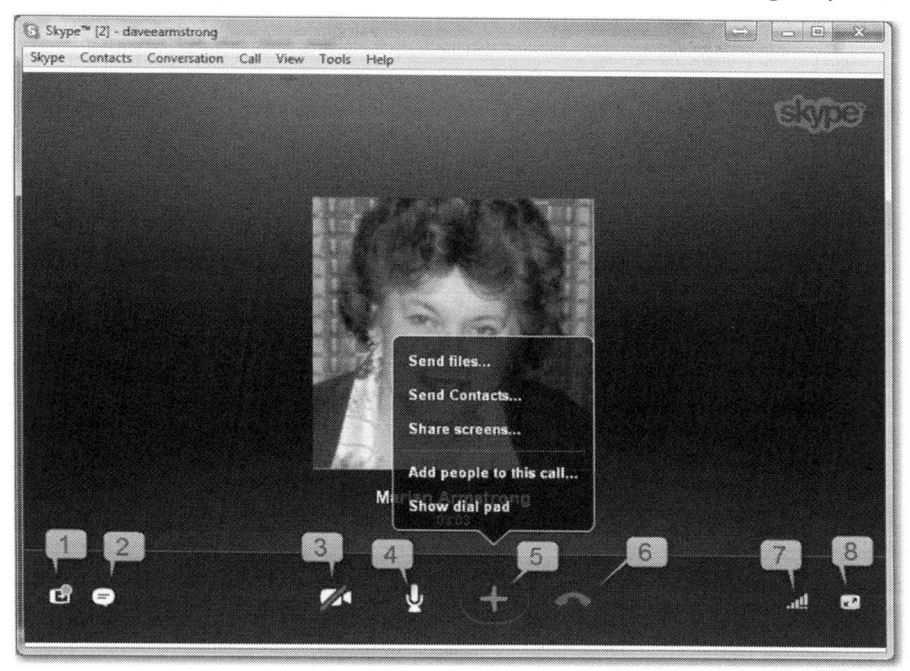

Figure 414: Connected phone call screen

Sharing Screens

One of the great features of Skype computer to computer calls is you can share a screen with a contact, as they can with you. Click the plus icon and then **Share screens....** (*Figure 415*).

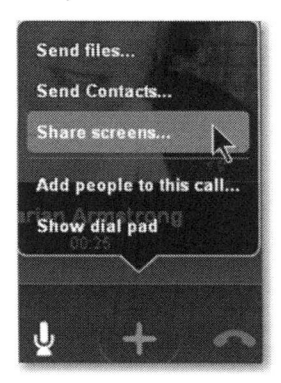

Figure 415: Sharing your screen

If you have two monitors as I have, you will first need to pick one of your screens. The down arrow in the lower left of *(Figure 416)* will open a choice of the whole screen or an applications screen. Choose **Share desktop** to share the entire monitor or **Share window** to share just a single running application on that monitor.

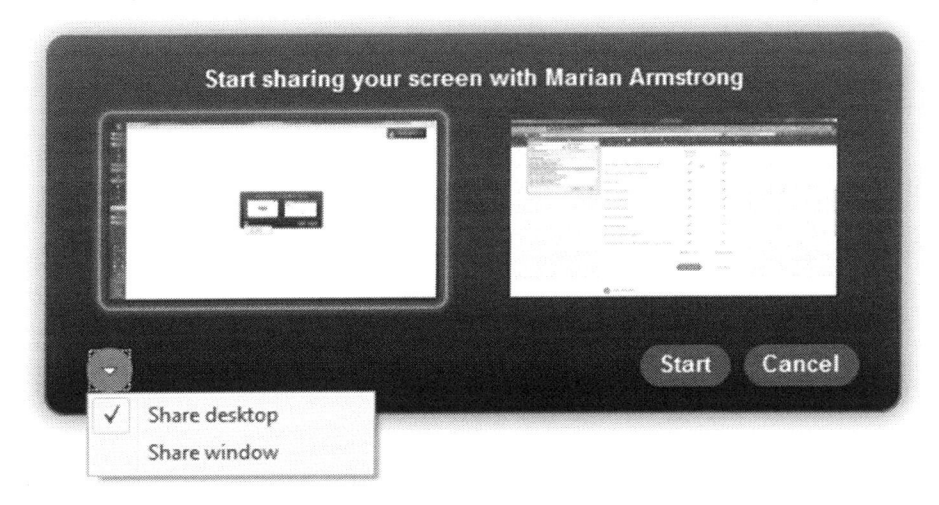

Figure 416: Pick your screen if you have more than one

In (*Figure 417*), you see all open apps. Pick the one to share and then click **Start**.

You may not want to share your entire desktop and show all of your screen's running apps. This is especially true, if you are making a presentation.

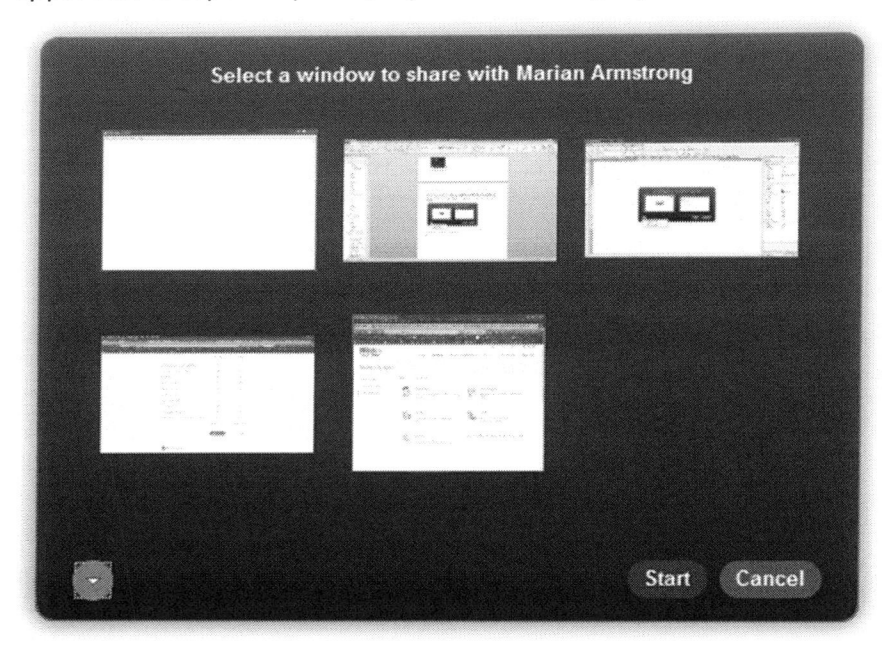

Figure 417: Pick the windows application to share

The screen you are sharing shows in the lower left. They see your screen in a window on their computer. This is great for walking someone through a software app or web site (*Figure 418*).

This is a great tool for giving webinars or seminars over the web. Most of these are created out of a mix of presentation software: like PowerPoint, Google's Present or Zoho's Show and live software or websites.

Figure 418: Your screen shared

Group Video Conferencing

One of the downsides to a totally virtual office, is people miss the contact that they would normally get in a workplace office setting. Video calling and conferencing can make up for much of that loss. We need to see faces and, although, IM and voice calling are efficient, they do not satisfy the urge to visually make contact as well as video.

I have worked with large companies that live on meetings. They were a real pain to schedule, as members moved around their schedules. Often, I had to leave building A and take a taxi to building B. Plus, if something more pressing than the meeting came up, I had to leave the room, the building, etc. Now, imagine the attendees live in another city.

Video conferencing solves many of these issues. Since the meeting occurs with everyone at their desk, a need for a five minute meeting does not require a half hour or more. Should an important phone call come in, I can mute my meeting screen, answer the call and jump back in. Using a Skype $19.95 add on called Evaer, http://www.evaer.com/, you can record up to a 10 way group video call. Great for someone who just could not attend, but needs to keep in the loop.

Start by clicking the group button (*Figure 419*).

Chapter 14: Using Skype

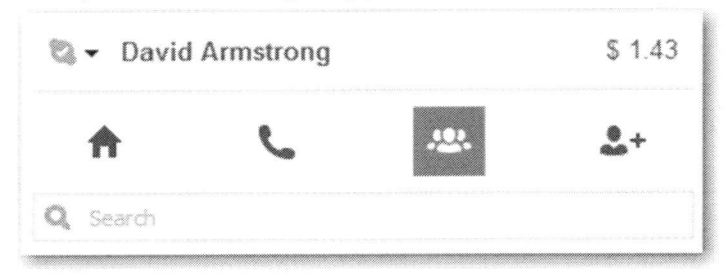

Figure 419: Starting a group video

Start a meeting by dragging contacts you wish to attend into the empty group area on the upper right (*Figure 420*).

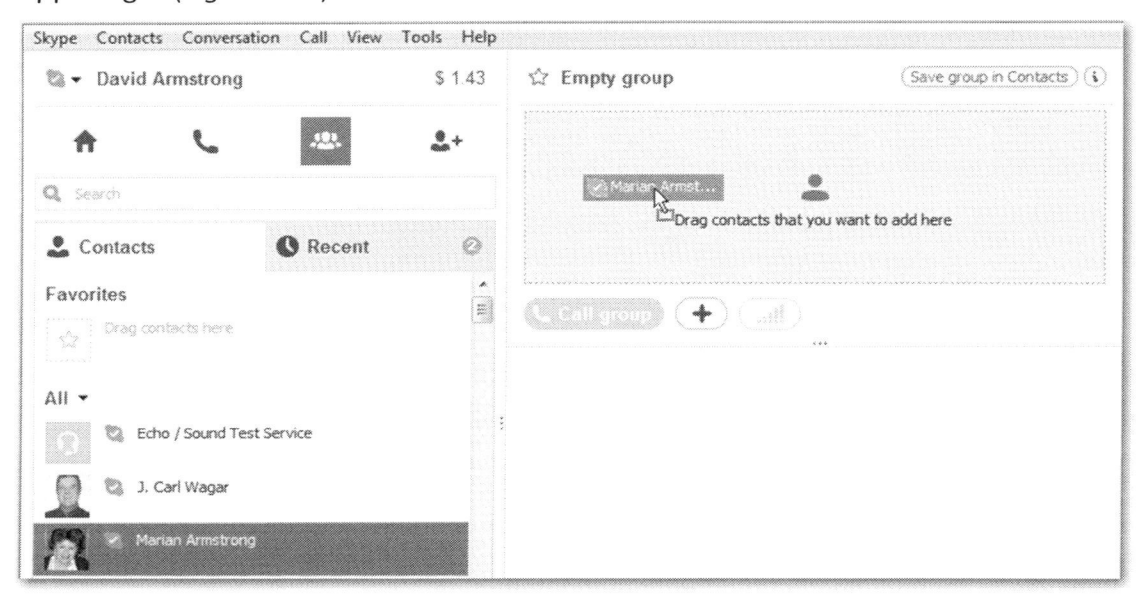

Figure 420: Dragging contacts into the group

Alternately, click the plus icon to open the pick list (*Figure 421*). Drag the contacts from the left column to the right.

Notice, you can include non-contacts via telephone at the bottom left. Once you have your group in place, click **Add** and then **Call group** to start the conferencing. If you have any phone calls in the group, you will need to greet and tell them they are in the meeting.

Chapter 14: Using Skype

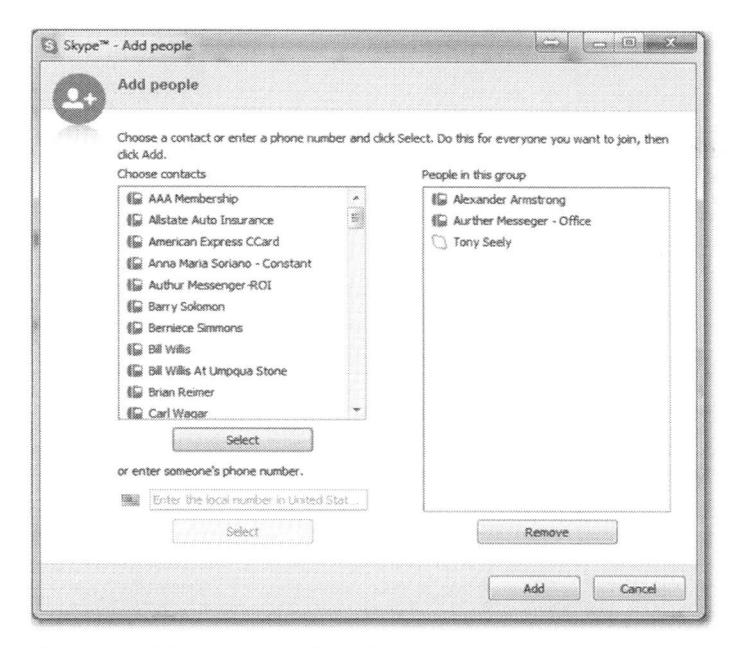

Figure 421: Adding contacts with a pick screen

If successful, you should see something like you see in (*Figure 422*). Be aware the more people you have in the meeting, the more bandwidth you may need. When you set up your staff's offices computers, buy as much bandwidth as you can afford, if you are going to use video conferencing.

Figure 422: Group meeting in progress

Chapter 14: Using Skype

Calling Landlines and Mobiles

As we will see later when we discuss pricing, you can call anywhere in the US and Canada for as little as $2.99 a month. Start by clicking the phone icon and then typing the phone number into the text box to the upper right (*Figure 423*). Spaces and dashes are optional.

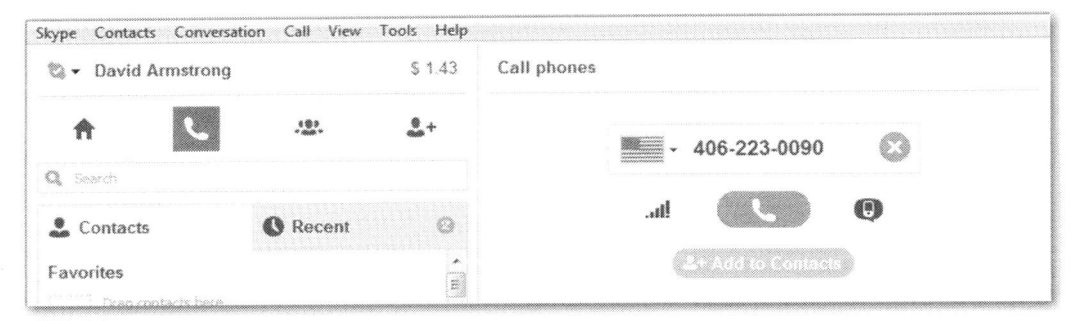

Figure 423: Dialing a phone line

Since you are calling from a US phone number, Skype assumes most calls you make will be in the US. If calling outside the US and Canada, you may need to tell Skype which country code to use.

You do not have to know the international calling prefix. Just pick your country and Skype adds the correct prefix. If you look carefully at the list, you will see the correct prefix. For example, to call the UK you would prefix the phone number with +44 (*Figure 424*). If you call the number often, you might want to add the prefix to the number you store. If you do so, Skype will recognize the number as being a UK number.

Figure 424: Calling out of the country

Skype Menus

Chapter 14: Using Skype

Like any well designed app, Skype's day to day use rarely requires using the menus. However, let's tour so when you do need them, you know where to look (*Figure 425* through *Figure 432*).

Figure 425: Skype menu

The most import use of the Skype menu is to change your online status. If I change my status to **Away** and a call comes in, it goes to my voice mail. They can see my status is **Away** before they call.

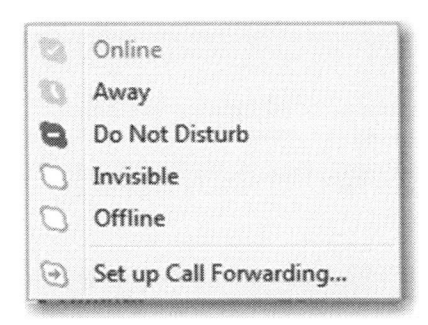

Figure 426: Changing my online status

Profile and **Privacy...** open the options screen. **Account...** takes me to a Skype page where I can purchase and control my account details.

Figure 427: Contacts menu

The Contacts menu allows us to:

- **Add Contact** opens a submenu where you can add from Skype or a phone number.
- **Import Contacts...** opens a screen where I can choose to import contacts from Facebook, Outlook, and 13 other online email apps.
- **Create New Group** opens the drag contacts to the panel we saw earlier.
- **Contact List** gives a menu of all groups created earlier.
- **Show Outlook Contacts** adds all of your desktop Outlook contacts. This works only if Skype and Outlook are on the same machine. Clicking **Contact Lists->Microsoft Office Outlook** filters to just the Outlook contacts.
- The last three menu items sort and filter your list.

How to Move Your Expensive Office to the Free Cloud

277

Chapter 14: Using Skype

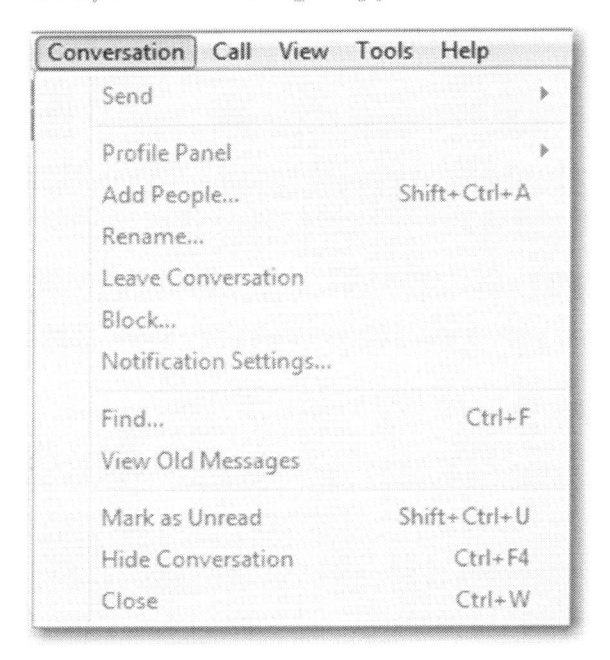

Figure 428: Conversation menu

As expected, you can use the Conversation menu to:

- **Send** IM or SMS after a contact is selected.
- **Profile Panel** allows you to resize the area showing contact info.
- **Add People...** opens the pick dialog.
- **Rename...** allows you to rename a selected contact.
- **Leave Conversation** allows you to leave an ongoing call or conference.
- **Block...** allows you to block the selected contact.
- **Notification Settings** controls a taskbar icon that will blink when an IM conversation is updated.
- **Find...** Text search messages.
- **View** Old Messages filter on date spans.

The last three choices are rarely used.

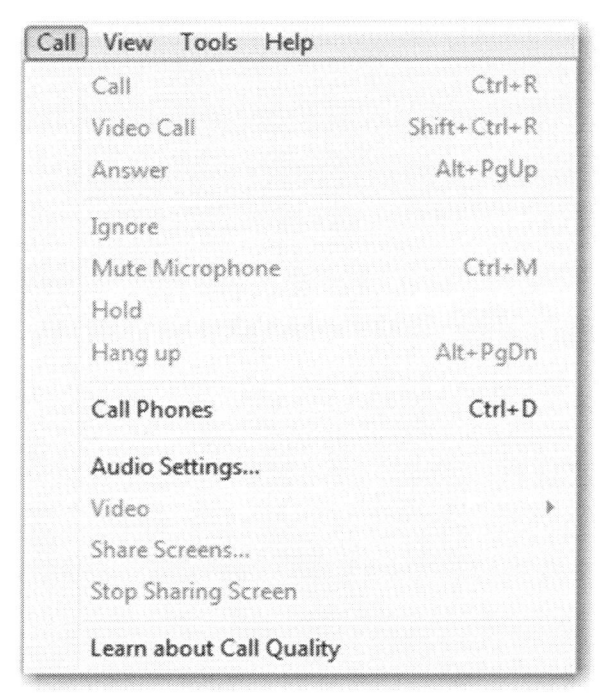

Figure 429: Call Menu

The Call menu echoes some of the call features we discussed earlier. Its greatest value, to me, is showing me the keyboard shortcuts available.

Chapter 14: Using Skype

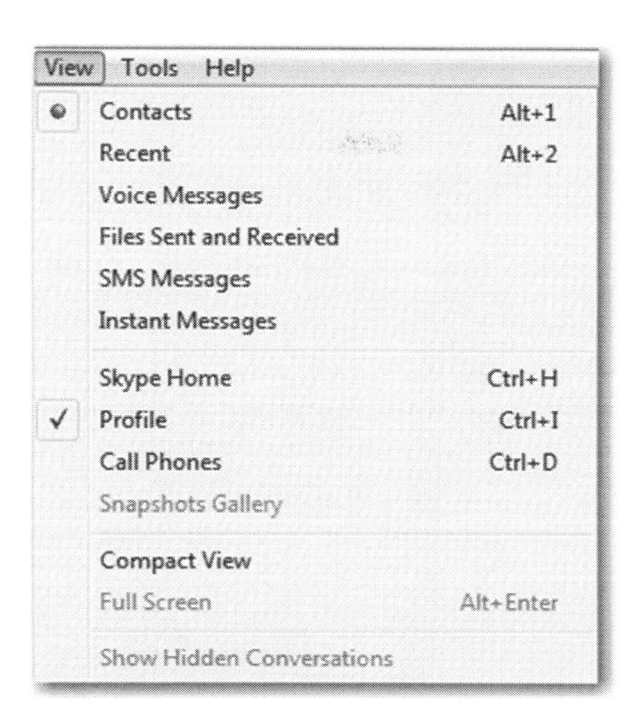

Figure 430: The View menu

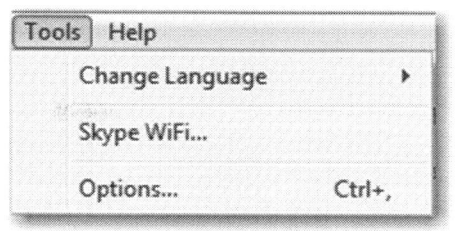

Figure 431: The Tools menu

You can use the **View** menu to see different panels and records of past calls, IM and SMS:

- **Contacts** show all contacts in your current group.
- **Recent** filters that list to just those you have communicated with recently.
- **Voice Messages** shows calls you have missed.
- **Files Sent and Received** shows a history of files exchanged.
- **SMS and Instant Messages** show a history of their use.
- **Skype Home Profile** and **Call Phones** show different views of Skype.
- **Compact View** splits the LR panels.

The Tools menu allows you to:

- **Change Language** to one of the 38 supported by Skype.
- **Skype WiFi...** Guides you through connecting to your Wi-Fi access point. Works well at Starbucks!
- **Options...** opens a second screen where you can manage all of the preferences you have for Skype.

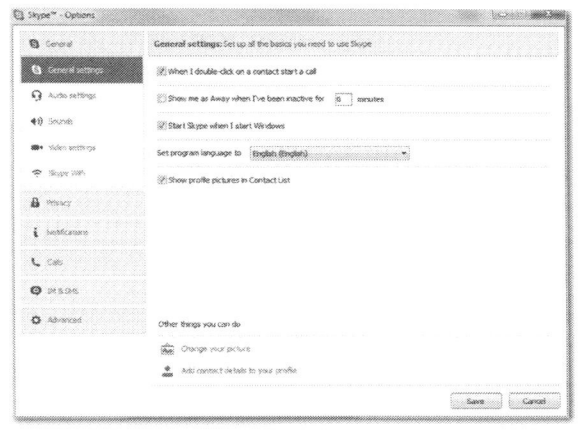

From here you change your audio and video setup, change notification sounds and enable Wi-Fi. We were here earlier configuring IM and SMS.

Most settings are self-explanatory and we will not cover them any deeper.

Chapter 14: Using Skype

Figure 432: The Help menu

Several times we have mentioned how quickly Skype changes. New features are added and changed.

The good news is they also update the Help features at the same time.

- **Learn about Skype for Windows** provides a simple, high level view of Skype on your version of Windows.
- **Go to Support** opens a page with FAQs and Hot-to guides.
- **Ask the Skype Community** opens forums where you can share knowledge with other users.
- **Heartbeat** opens a web page that shows how your app and account are working.
- **Check Quality Guide** opens a web page with advice on getting quality calls.
- **Check for Updates** will assure you always have the latest release. Most upgrades are automatic with your permission.
- **Give feedback** to report bugs and suggest improvements.

Skype Pricing

Here is the pricing of Skype products and services:

1. **Computer to computer** - When using Skype computer to computer, it is free. This includes texting, voice and video between two individuals. To connect your staff to each other, this may be all you need.
2. **Land and Mobile Phones** - If you want to call land lines and mobile phones, Skype allows you to purchase credits, which you use to pay the 2.3 cents a minute for US and Canadian calls. A better way to use Skype, is to purchase a subscription. Here are the monthly charges:
    a. Unlimited US and Canada $2.99
    b. Unlimited North America $7.99

Chapter 14: Using Skype

    c. **Unlimited World** $13.99 (*Figure 433*).

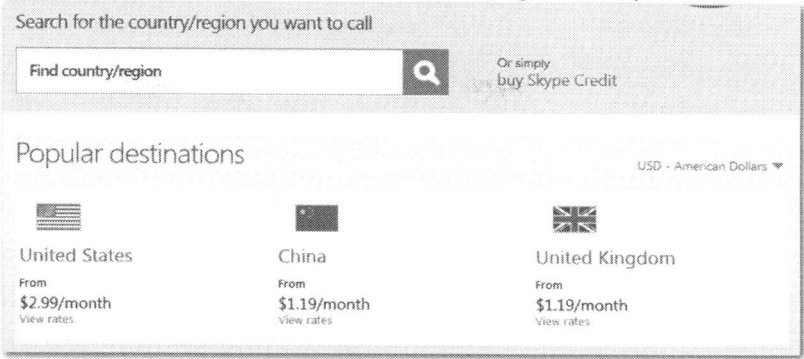

Figure 433: International calling pricing

3. **Premium Account** - gives you group video, group screen sharing and cuts out the advertising. You only need one premium account to originate a group video meeting (*Figure 434*).

Figure 434: Skype Pricing

4. **Skype Number** - gives you an inbound number. It will be in your calling area. It cost $60 a year or $18 for three months. If you do international business, having an in country phone would be a great investment.
5. **Skype Store** - Skype sells headsets, webcams, and several desktop phones including a video phone that needs no computer. Additionally, you can have Skype on your tablets, smart phones and even your TV with the purchase of their TV cams.

Chapter 14: Using Skype

Skype is particularly useful when combined with the contacts you store in web Outlook, OWA. You can dial the number without leaving the Outlook web app.

Figure 435: Using Skype from within Outlook

If you would rather not use OWA, you can download and install the **Click to Call** browser add-on. While it only works on Windows browsers, it makes calling any phone number listed on a web page easy. Any phone number on the web page is just a single click to call. You may have to allow the browser add-on permission to install, depending on the browser. You can download from:

http://www.skype.com/en/download-skype/click-to-call/downloading/

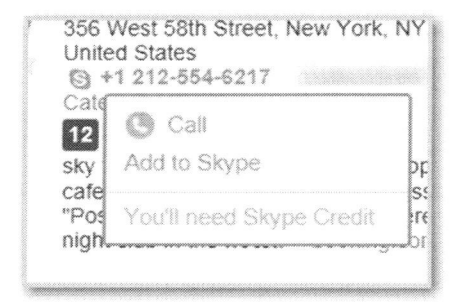

Figure 436: Calling from any web page

Chapter 15: Conferencing and Screen Sharing

While I love Skype and consider it a great value, as it is free to cheap, there are other products that compete and even offer free versions. One of the products you may want is remote control software, as your office computers may not be in one place with a virtual office. You will want to do computer maintenance and install new software. At the end of the chapter, we will look at TeamViewer which does that very well.

This chapter does not teach detailed step-by-step guidance, such as we saw in the previous chapter on Skype. However, the apps are discussed in enough depth that you can compare the different products.

There is a great article on Infoworld's website that compares three services. Go to http://goo.gl/USVp2z.

Here is a graphic of their evaluation of the three products.

Test Center Scorecard	Features	AV quality	Ease of use	Administration	Interoperability	Value	Overall Score
	25%	25%	20%	10%	10%	10%	
Cisco WebEx Meetings	9	9	9	8	9	8	8.8 VERY GOOD
	25%	25%	20%	10%	10%	10%	
Citrix GoToMeeting	8	9	9	9	8	8	8.6 VERY GOOD
	25%	25%	20%	10%	10%	10%	
MyTrueCloud My Web Conferences	9	9	7	7	8	9	8.3 VERY GOOD

GoToMeeting

http://gotomeeting.com

This is a very popular program that was created and marketed by Citrix Systems. They give a free 30 day trial so you can safely try it out. The default plan gives you one organizer seat, although, you can buy more. The organizer is the person that starts and manages the meeting. As the non-organizers join the meeting, they are required to download a small app that interacts with the browser to allow them to attend the meeting. They only have to do this when they attend their first meeting.

The prices are:

- Monthly - $49.00 per organizer seat.
- Annually - $468.00 per organizer seat.
- GoToMeeting provides VoIP (computer-to-computer) voice, but charges for those attending by phone.

The subscription includes:

- Unlimited meetings with up to 25 attendees.
- Integrated conference calling service, including VoIP capability.
- Industry-leading security.
- Unlimited software and service upgrades.

Here are some of the long lists of features:

- Share keyboard and mouse control. This can be handed off to attendees.
- Mobile apps for iPad, iPhone and Android devices.
- Email and instant messaging integration. Start scheduled or spontaneous meetings from Outlook.
- End-to-end encryption and authentication security provided by a Secure Sockets Layer (SSL) Web site with end-to-end 128-bit Advanced Encryption Standard (AES) encryption and optional passwords.
- Specific application sharing for showing only selected programs with attendees.
- Multi-monitor support for a client PC.
- Meeting recording and playback for recording and saving meetings to a user desktop for later review.
- Total audio package provides toll based phone or conferencing via VoIP.
- High definition Video.

Chapter 15: Conferencing and Screen Sharing

- Desktop recording/meeting playback. You can later offer the meeting to those that could not attend.

My Take on GoToMeeting

I have both organized a GoToMeeting session, and have attended many GoToMeeting sessions and webinars (web based seminars).

The software works well if you have the bandwidth. While you can have up to 10 video attendees at a time, there is a noticeable slowdown as you reach that number.

The one feature I do like is the flyaway dashboard that controls the meeting. It moves out of the way when not needed.

From a cost perspective, they charge for each phone-in attendee. This could be expensive if you use it with audio over the phone lines. A headset and VoIP (voice over internet protocol) is the way to go.

Figure 437: GoToMeeting dashboard

WebEx

http://www.webex.com

WebEx, also owned by Citrix Systems, has all the features of GoToMeeting, but has some features that are great for streaming video. They use their servers to stream video to the users. This means that you can host many more attendees. Many webinars are hosted on WebEx, some with hundreds of attendees.

They, also, have what they call a meeting space where you can plan, prepare and organize all of your documents, manage scheduling and emails.

They offer a 14 day free trial so you can evaluate.

Here is their pricing and plans:

- Basic - is free for up to 3 people. You get:
    - Up to 3 people per meeting.
    - 1 host license that starts and controls the meeting.
    - Standard quality video.
    - VoIP only, no phone in.
    - 250MB storage.
- Premium 8 - $24.00 per host, per month, or $19.00, if paid annually. You Get:
    - Up to 8 people per meeting.
    - 1 host license.
    - High-definition video.
    - VoIP and phone in. Toll-free call in is optional.
    - 1 GB storage.
- Premium 25 - $49.00 per host, per month, or $39.00, if paid annually. You Get:
    - Up to 25 people per meeting.
    - Up to 9 host licenses. You will pay for each one.
    - High-definition video.
    - VoIP and phone in. Toll-free call in is optional.
    - 1 GB storage.
- Premium 100 - $89.00 per host, per month, or $69.00, if paid annually. You Get:
    - Up to 100 people per meeting.
    - Up to 9 host licenses.
    - High-definition video.
    - VoIP and phone in. Toll-free call in is optional.
    - 1 GB storage.

Chapter 15: Conferencing and Screen Sharing

As you can see, you can video conference or train while showing a presentation (*Figure 438*).

Figure 438: Presenting and discussing slides in WebEx

My Take on WebEx

I have both attended and hosted meetings on WebEx. There are a lot of similarities between GoToMeeting and WebEx. My feeling is WebEx is a broader product with some great organizational features. It also performs better when you have a larger amount of attendees, especially if they use video.

My TrueCloud

http://www.mytruecloud.com

While a newer company with nowhere the clout of Citrix Systems, My TrueCloud may give you a good alternative and may give them a run for their money.

My True Cloud has a whole suite of integrated products, including CRM. They seem to call their web based collaboration product My Web Conferences. However, they advertise it just as My TrueCloud, so I will use that name.

One of the things I like is, unlike GoToMeeting and WebEx, My TrueCloud users do not have to download any browser plugins. They do require the browser have Flash installed and JavaScript enabled. Most Windows PC browsers do allow flash, but Apple products, especially iPads, iTouch and iPhone do not.

One feature you may like, if you have dial in attendees, is that most of the My TrueCloud plans offer free toll-free phone minutes. Since phone charges can add up quickly, this may be an advantage. Since I am evaluating tools for interoffice communication from computer to computer, you may not need phone minutes.

There are six plans depending on how many attendees you invite. I will only list the lower priced three.

Here is their pricing:

- My 10 - $19.00 per month:
    - Up to 10 people per meeting.
    - Number of concurrent meetings, 1.
    - Number of free telephone minutes, 0.
    - 5 GB of Storage.
- My 25 - $32 per month:
    - Up to 25 people per meeting.
    - Number of concurrent meetings, 1.
    - Number of free telephone minutes, 200.
    - 5 GB of Storage.
- My 50 - $69.00 per month:
    - Up to 50 people per meeting.
    - Number of concurrent meetings, 2.
    - Number of free telephone minutes, 500.
    - 2 GB of storage.

They do give a 30 day free trial so you can evaluate yourself.

My take on My TrueCloud

While the price is attractive, My TrueCloud is not as mature as either GoToMeeting or WebEx. If Price is a serious consideration, I would try Skype first. For small businesses, you get the core features for only $9.99 a month. If you find it lacking, use the free trials to evaluate these products.

Chapter 15: Conferencing and Screen Sharing

TeamViewer

http://www.teamviewer.com

TeamViewer software has several functions, all of which are very useful in the virtual office. One of its best advantages is, you do not have to install the software on a computer to use it.

You download a small exe file and save it to your drive. When you double click the file, it does not install, but instead simply runs the connection software. On machines that are locked down, this is a real blessing and eliminates the many issues that can occur with installing software.

You can get the entire set of TeamViewer user manuals in PDF form from here: http://www.teamviewer.com/en/help/firststeps.aspx.

The software has two main features:

1. It is a screen sharing application that just happens to have excellent audio and video features.
2. It is an online meeting and presentation tool.

Copying from their website, the remote support and access give you:

- **Remote Support** - *no need for any installation on the client side.*
- **Remote Administration** - *24/7 access to remote computers and servers.*
- **Remote Access** - *access your data and applications – anytime, anywhere.*
- **Home Office** - *access your office computer from home.*

The online meeting and online presentations give you:

- **Online Meetings** - *have up to 25 participants.*
- **Online Presentation** - *boost your sales potential.*
- **Training Session** - *cut costs by conducting training online.*
- **Online Teamwork** - *collaborate online on documents in real-time.*

This software runs on Windows, Mac, Linus and Apple's iOS and Android. You can remote control, do a meeting and transfer files; all from your PC, smart phone or tablet.

TeamViewer makes most of their software free for personal use and it is on the honor system, as it is the same software, regardless, of your use. Use it commercially and you will pay a onetime purchase cost (*Figure 439*):

Chapter 15: Conferencing and Screen Sharing

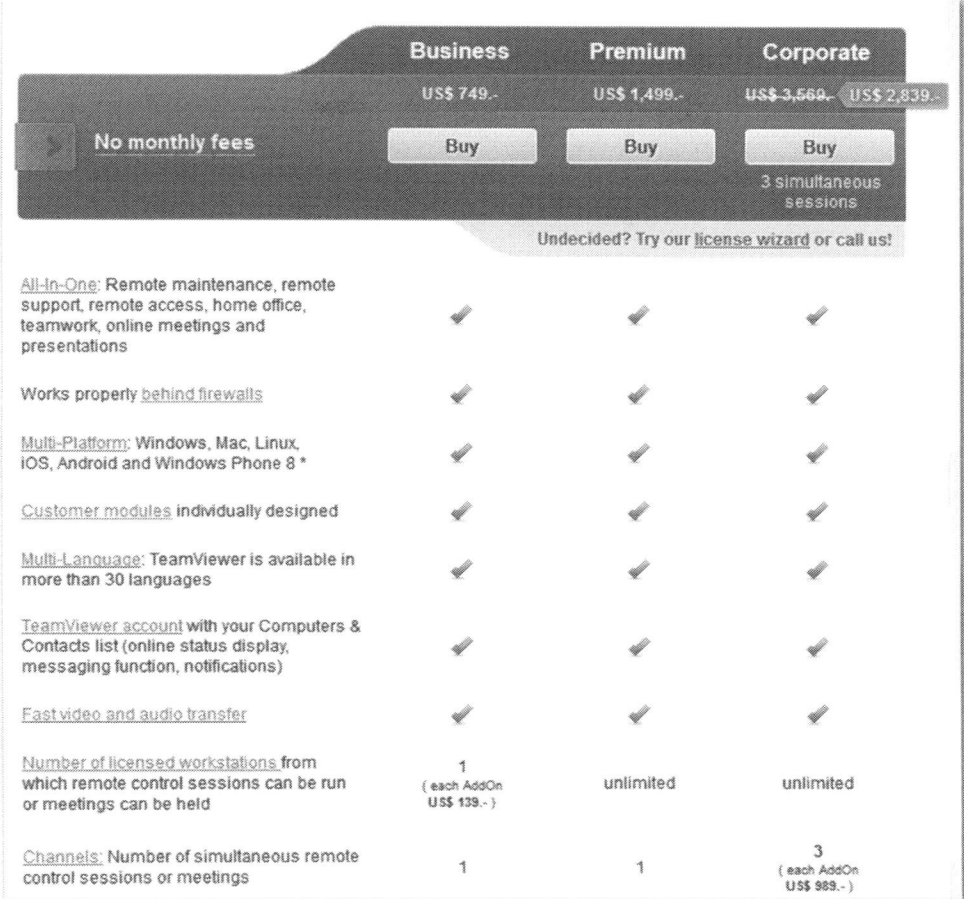

	Business	Premium	Corporate
	US$ 749.-	US$ 1,499.-	~~US$ 3,569.-~~ US$ 2,839.-
No monthly fees	Buy	Buy	Buy
			3 simultaneous sessions
All-In-One: Remote maintenance, remote support, remote access, home office, teamwork, online meetings and presentations	✓	✓	✓
Works properly behind firewalls	✓	✓	✓
Multi-Platform: Windows, Mac, Linux, iOS, Android and Windows Phone 8 *	✓	✓	✓
Customer modules individually designed	✓	✓	✓
Multi-Language: TeamViewer is available in more than 30 languages	✓	✓	✓
TeamViewer account with your Computers & Contacts list (online status display, messaging function, notifications)	✓	✓	✓
Fast video and audio transfer	✓	✓	✓
Number of licensed workstations from which remote control sessions can be run or meetings can be held	1 (each AddOn US$ 139.-)	unlimited	unlimited
Channels: Number of simultaneous remote control sessions or meetings	1	1	3 (each AddOn US$ 989.-)

Undecided? Try our license wizard or call us!

Figure 439: TeamViewer pricing

TeamViewer Full Version

The TeamViewer Full Version will allow you to control another computer, host a meeting and allow others to control your computer should you choose.

When you install, you have several options from which to choose.

You have these options (*Figure 440*):

- **Install** - This install, like most other Windows apps, will put an icon on your desktop and an entry in your start menu.
- **Install to control the computer later from remote** - This installs the TeamViewer Host program we review below. The computer will not be able to start a meeting and/or connect to another computer, it receives a connection only. This gives a licensed workstation access to this computer. Put this on your staff's computers and keep the full program on your computer.

Chapter 15: Conferencing and Screen Sharing

- **Run only** - This loads the full version, but does not install. If your computer does not allow installations, this may be your only way to run. It acts as if you are installing each time you run and it will be a little slower to start.

How do you want to use TeamViewer? You have these options:

- Company / commercial use - You will need to purchase a license. While $749 may seem a bit steep, it is a onetime purchase.
- Personal / non-commercial use - Start here and if you find TeamViewer useful, purchase the commercial license.
- Both of the above - I am not sure why we need both.

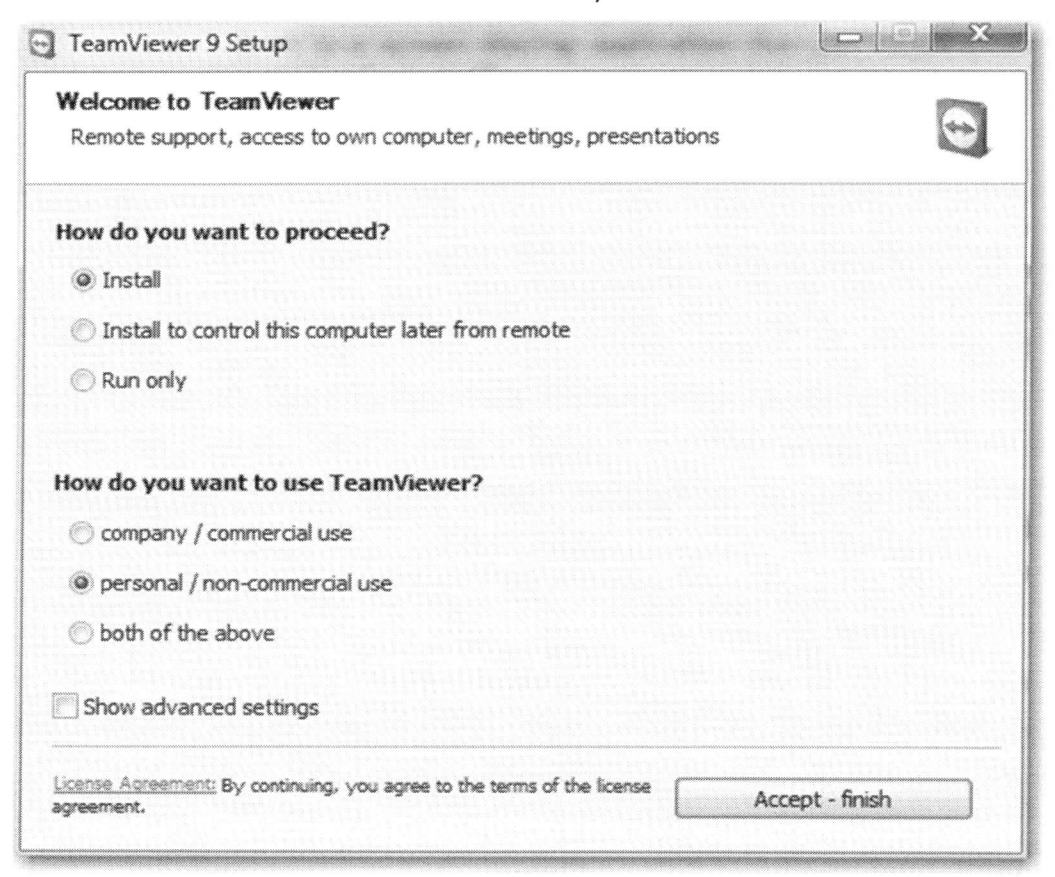

Figure 440: Installation options

Clicking the **Show advanced settings** box opens a new screen (*Figure 441*). From it, you can also install remote print, configure VPN (virtual private network) and install an add-in for Outlook. The remote print might be useful, although, we discuss using Google Cloud Print in another section.

Creating a VPN is beyond the scope of this book, but if you handle sensitive data, a VPN keeps others from accessing your data stream.

The add-in for Outlook allows you to schedule and send email about a meeting.

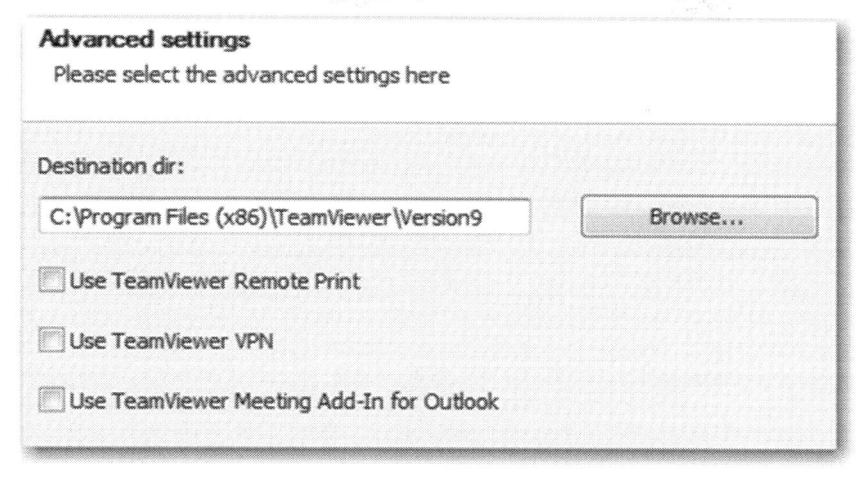

Figure 441: Advanced installation settings

This is the TeamViewer full version (*Figure 442*).

Let's explore the screen:

1. **Your ID** and **Password** is generated by TeamViewer. You would give those to anyone that you want to allow to connect to your computer.
2. You can provide your own personal password, should you want to access your computer from other locations. Keep TeamViewer full (shown) or TeamViewer host (discussed later) running on your computer, if you want remote access.
3. If you want to connect to some other computer, you need their ID and password. You will need the password as you log on to the other computer.
4. Once you have typed the **Partner Id**, click the **Connect to partner** button. A pop-up window will ask for the password (not shown).
5. The panel to the right can be shown or hidden by clicking the chevron button (>>).
6. After you have connected to other computers, you can add them to your computer list on the right. Later, you can connect to them without an ID or password by double clicking their computer name in the list. You can see if their computer is online and have TeamViewer running.
7. Clicking the Add remote computer link, opens a screen similar to what we discussed in 3 and 4 above.

Chapter 15: Conferencing and Screen Sharing

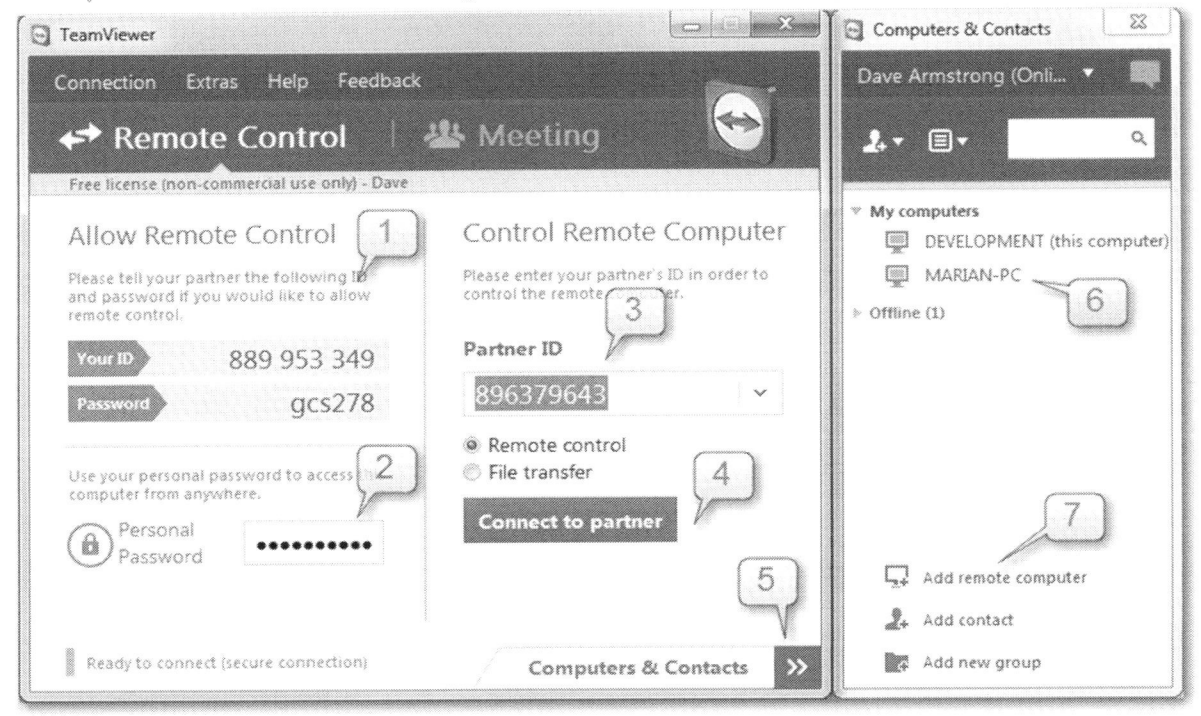

Figure 442: TeamViewer full version opening screen

Once connected, you can see the other computers screen (*Figure 443*). You will also see what the other person is doing with their typing and mouse movements. You both share control of the screen. You can use your mouse and you can type text from your keyboard.

Think how you might use this:

- You could troubleshoot one of your staff's computers from your own desk.
- You could train someone on how to use Windows or a software app.
- As you will see shortly, you can pass files between the two computers. You might retrieve todays call records from a remote machine after hours.
- You could log in with an admin account to install or remove software.

Chapter 15: Conferencing and Screen Sharing

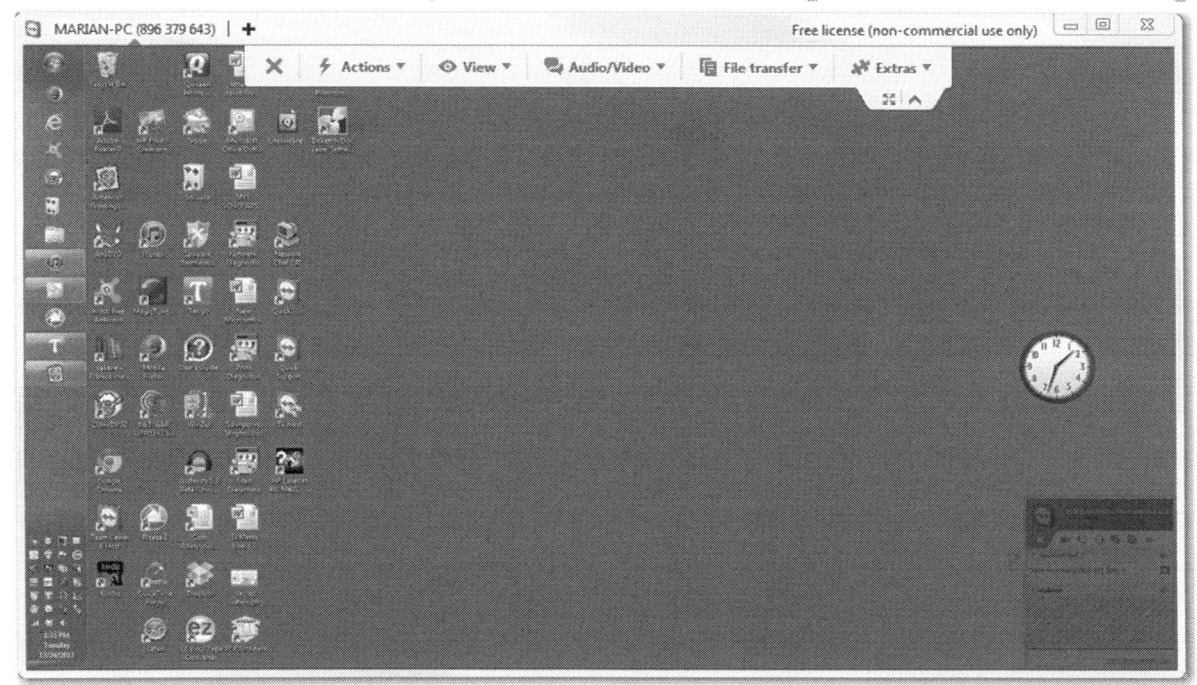

Figure 443: Controlling the remote computer

Notice, the small window in the lower right? You have one, also, outside of the windows showing the other screen. This dialog allows you to control communications with the person at the other end (*Figure 444*).

From left to right, the icons are:

Video - Turn video on or off.

Conference call - As we will see later, others can use their TeamViewer to join once you start the conference. They will need an ID and password to join.

Voice over IP - You need this to be able to discuss what is happening on the screen.

Chat - If the other computer does not have a webcam or microphone, you can always fall back to chat.

File box - This opens up an area at the bottom of the screen where you can drag files that will upload to the attendees.

You can go full screen and minimize the panel. Note, that you have access to the video windows on the other computer. You can control their video, sound, etc. You may need to turn the sound level down on both computers to prevent feedback. A headset eliminates the feedback loop issue and I recommend purchasing one.

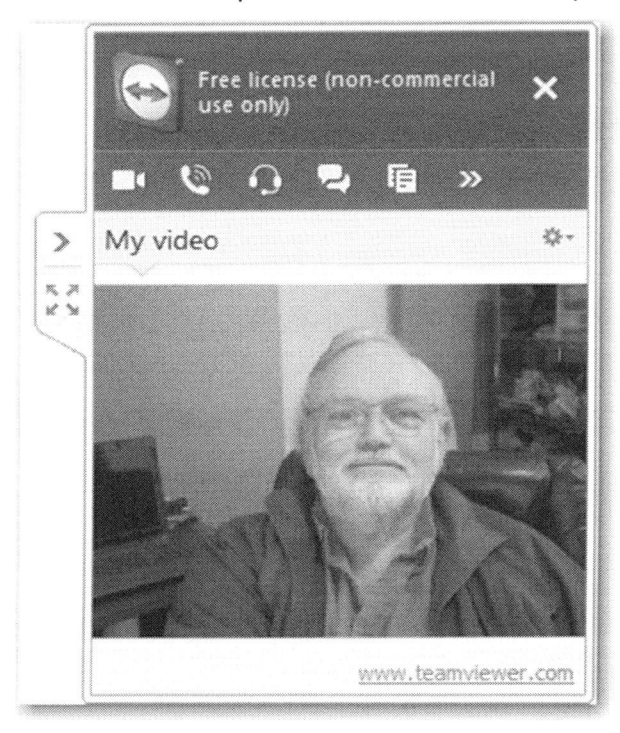

Figure 444: Managing your chat, audio and video

There is a series of menus at the top of the view of the remote computer.

Let's explore them (*Figure 445* to *Figure 450*).

Chapter 15: Conferencing and Screen Sharing

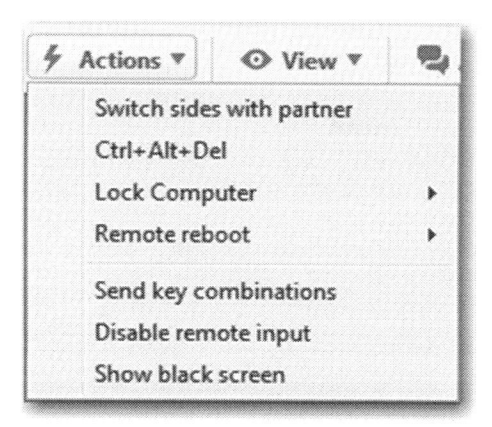

Figure 445: Actions menu

You can extend your control over the remote computer with the **Actions** menu.

- **Switch sides with partner** - When you first connect, you control the process. You can reverse the roles.
- **Ctrl+Alt+Del** - Sends the CTRL + ALT + DEL key combination to the remote computer.
- **Lock computer** - After locking, you then can log in with a different account such as the admin account.
- **Remote reboot** - Allows you to remotely log off, reboot or reboot in safe mode.
- **Send key combinations** - Transmits key combinations (such as ALT+TAB) directly to the remote computer and does not execute the command locally.
- **Disable remote input** - Shuts down the remote keyboard and mouse.
- **Show black screen** - Switches the monitor of the remote computer to a black screen. Hides your activity on the remote screen.

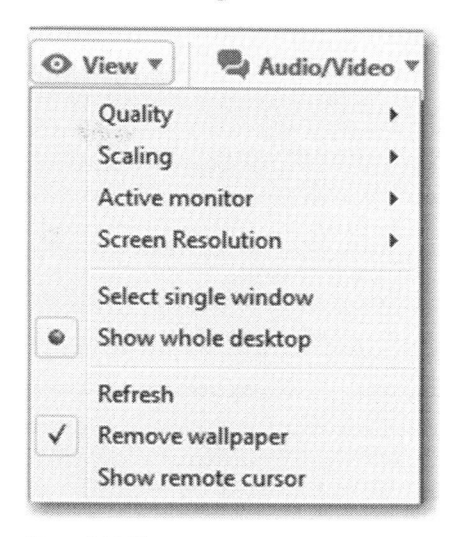

Figure 446: View menu

The **View** menu allows you to fine tune the size and quality of the computers' monitors.

- **Quality** - Use this to control the screen quality vs. speed.
- **Scaling** - Unless both monitors are the same size/resolution, you may need to adjust the remote screen's display.
- **Active monitor** - If the remote computer has more than one monitor, you can choose which or both.
- **Select single window** - If you want to work with just one app, you can chose just a single app's window.
- **Show whole desktop** - Toggles between the single windows and full desktop.
- **Refresh** - If auto refresh fails, you can do a refresh.
- **Remove wallpaper** - Hides the wallpaper on the remote computer. Might improve connections speed.

Chapter 15: Conferencing and Screen Sharing

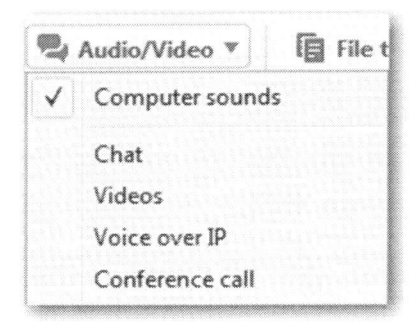

Figure 447: Audio/Video menu

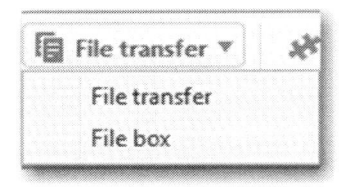

Figure 448: File transfer menu

The Audio/Video menu controls how you connect for communication between you and the person at the remote computer.

- **Computer sounds** - If activated, you will hear sounds created by the remote computer.
- **Chat** - This opens a widget for text based communication.
- **Videos** - This opens a video widget for using webcams, as discussed in (*Figure 444*).
- **Voice over IP** - Opens a widget for voice communications.
- **Conference call** - Opens a widget for starting or taking part in a conference meeting.

The File transfer menu allows you to open a drag and drop type interface for moving files between your two computers.

- **File transfer** - This opens the screen you see in (*Figure 449*). You can drag files to or from each computer. Once the transfer is started, you see a progress window.
- **File box** - Opens a simple widget that allows you to share files with your partner in a remote control session.

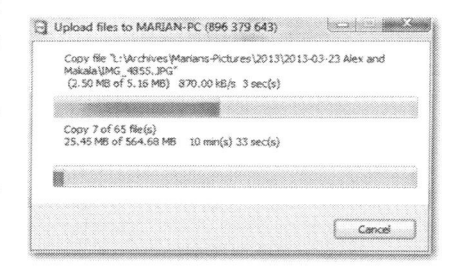

Chapter 15: Conferencing and Screen Sharing

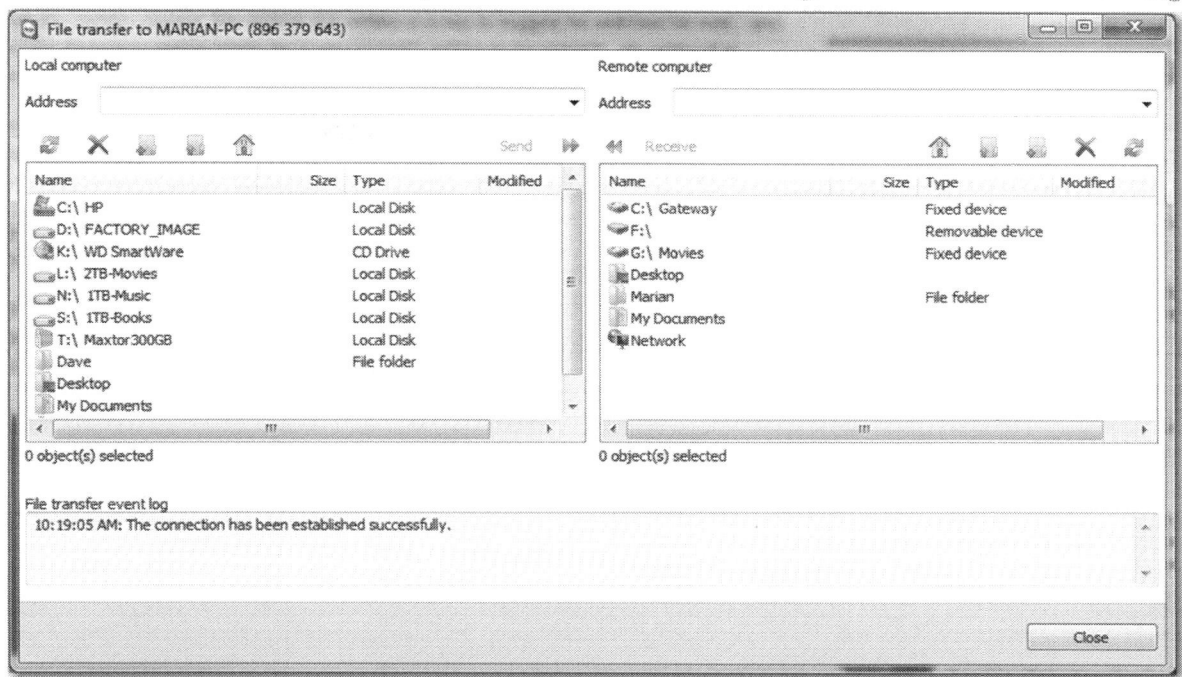

Figure 449: File transfer window

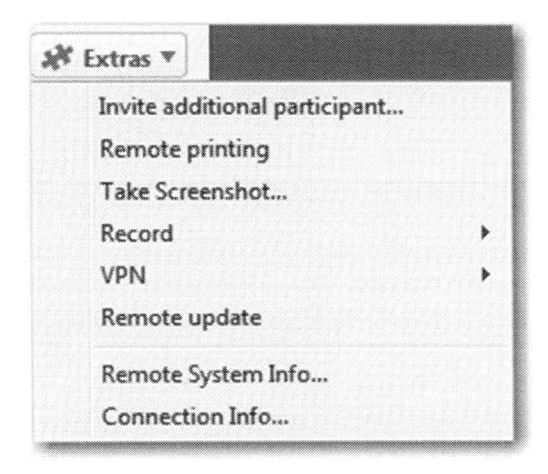

Figure 450: Extras menu

The Extras menu is a catch-all menu for items not categorized in the other menus.

- **Invite additional participant...** - opens a dialog to invite others.

- **Remote printing** - enables printing from the remote computer on a local computer.
- **Take screenshot...** - takes a screenshot of the remote screen.
- **Record** - Records the current session as a video.
- **VPN** - Starts, stops and configures a VPN session for security.
- **Remote update** - Starts checking for a more recent version of TeamViewer on the remote computer and installs an update if necessary.
- **Remote System Info...** - Opens system information on the remote computer.

TeamViewer QuickSupport

Chapter 15: Conferencing and Screen Sharing

Most of your staff will not need the TeamViewer full version we just discussed. If you just want to be able to connect on demand, they can download TeamViewer QuickSupport.

When you double-click the downloaded file, it does not install like most programs. It just runs. When the window in (*Figure 451*) opens, click **Run**.

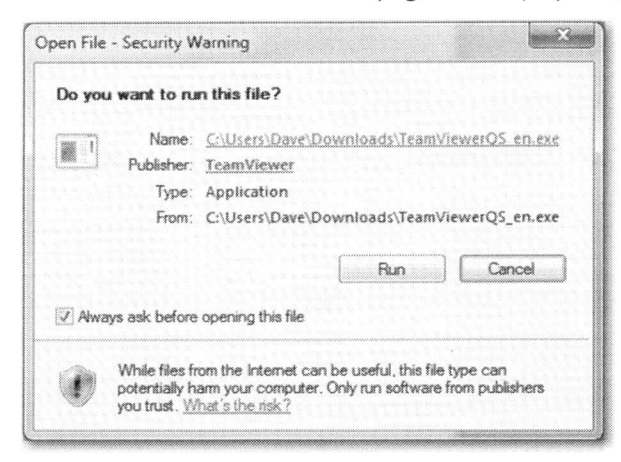

Figure 451: Running TeamViewer QuickSupport

QuickSupport opens and they need only to email or somehow tell you the ID and password (*Figure 452*). You can then connect.

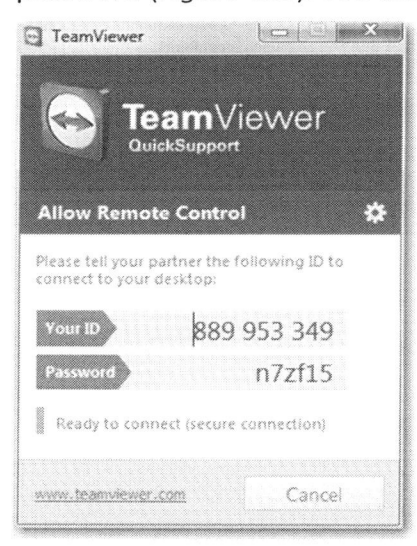

Figure 452: The TeamViewer QuickSupport screen

Since you may not allow your staff to install software, the run-but-not-install strategy will solve that problem.

TeamViewer Host

An even better long term solution, is to download TeamViewer Host and install it on the remote computers. This starts when Windows starts and is always running. You can connect anytime. After installation, you will, as usual, need the ID and password to connect (*Figure 453*).

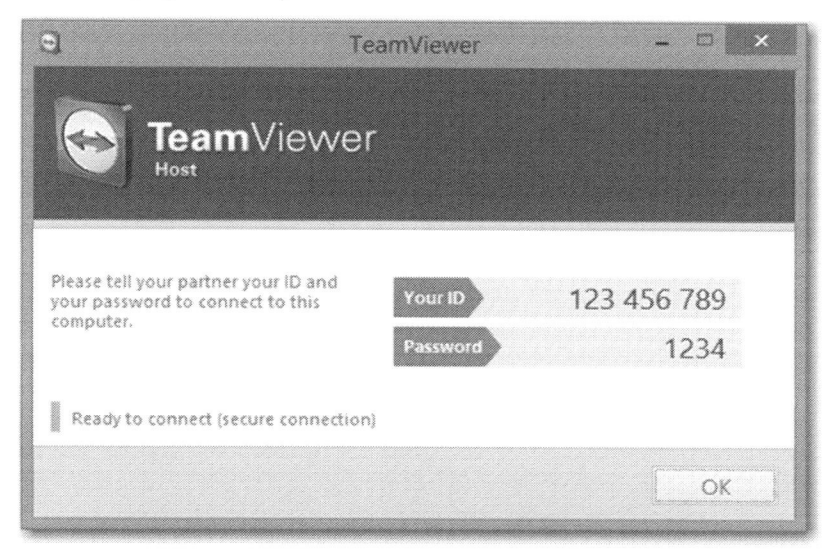

Figure 453: The TeamViewer Host screen

TeamViewer QuickJoin for Conferencing

If you want to invite others to a conference call, and they do not have TeamViewer Full, they will need to download and run TeamViewer QuickJoin.

Again, like QuickSupport, they do not need install, just download and run. Once they have it running, they will need to type in the Meeting ID you provided and their name. Before you ask them to join, you will need to start the meeting.

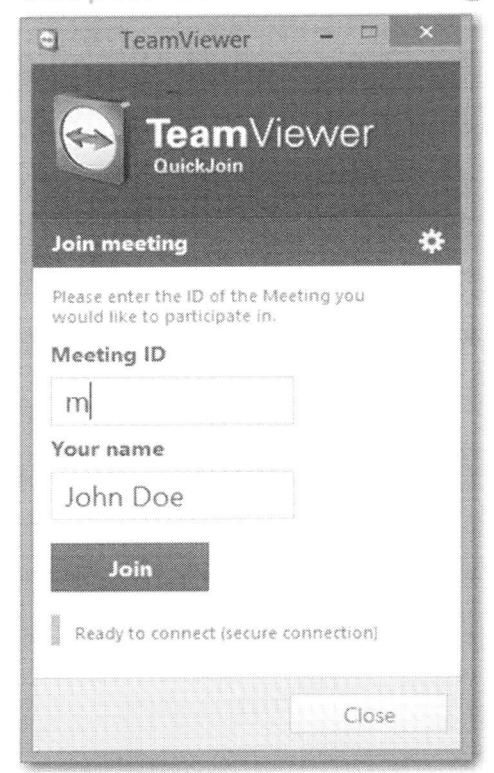

Figure 454: The TeamViewer QuickJoin screen

TeamViewer provides some great tools for both remote control and video/voice conferencing. The best bet is to probably install TeamViewer Full on your computer and TeamViewer host on the remote computers so you can always remotely connect and then run QuickJoin when you schedule meetings.

Chapter 16: Managing Incoming and Interoffice Calls

In the last two chapters, we looked at tools you could use for interoffice communications. Instead of walking over to your desk or office, we can use these tools to chat, communicate by voice or use video for a quick conversation or meeting.

These same tools can be used for group meetings and most of them integrate with Outlook so that you can plan and notify attendees. They can confirm or request another date, all from Outlook.

This chapter is about incoming calls. First, we again look at Skype, an inexpensive solution, if you have a very small office or you do not mind each of your staff having a direct number. Next, we look at the main two competitors in virtual phone systems, Grasshopper and RingCentral. There are many others and I am not recommending these two over their competitors. However, they do offer a full set of features and are good examples of what you can get.

Ideally, a virtual phone system should offer:

1. Automated, menu driven call routing. Dial 100 for Jim, 110 for Jane, etc.
2. For an extra fee, for certain times a day, a real live person (optional).
3. Voice mail for each person on staff that talks to or supports customers.
4. A local, and or, toll free incoming number.
5. The ability to customize your greeting and assign extensions.
6. A name directory for those that do not know an extension.

Not essential, but nice to have:

1. Conference calling.
2. Call forwarding.
3. Voice mail to email translations.

4. Music on hold.
5. Screen call via caller ID.

Let's look at three of the most popular candidates.

Skype

We covered Skype in another chapter, so we will just discuss it here as an incoming phone system.

For $5 a month for each person, you can have an incoming line. For another $2.95 a month, you can make unlimited calls to anyone in the US and Canada. If you are a one person business, this is all you need. However, there is no ability to transfer calls once a call is received. If you want to have video conferencing, the meeting organizer needs a premium account for $9.99 a month. However, having individual phone numbers for the same business, may be a problem.

CON - When people want support and they call sales, they are not going to be happy when you tell them they have to call another number.

PRO - If these are sales reps with assigned customers, bypassing the switchboard with a direct number might be a plus.

If you are a business with several employees, you will probably need more than just Skype. However, as we will see, the ideal and least expensive plan might be to use Skype for outgoing calls and as extension numbers and one of the following services for incoming.

Grasshopper

http://grasshopper.com/

Grasshopper has a simple to use interface and is typical of current virtual phone systems. We will look in detail at Grasshopper, but first, here is a link to a NextAdvisor review of the top six systems: http://www.nextadvisor.com/virtual_phone/compare.php.

Grasshopper Cost

They have four tiered plans (*Figure 455*). These are the sum of both incoming and outbound minutes, if you option to call out. As Grasshopper suggest, combine Skype for calling and a receiving phone number with their incoming service. They can then forward incoming calls to the individual Skype numbers. Grasshopper gives a 30 day free trial so you can try before you buy.

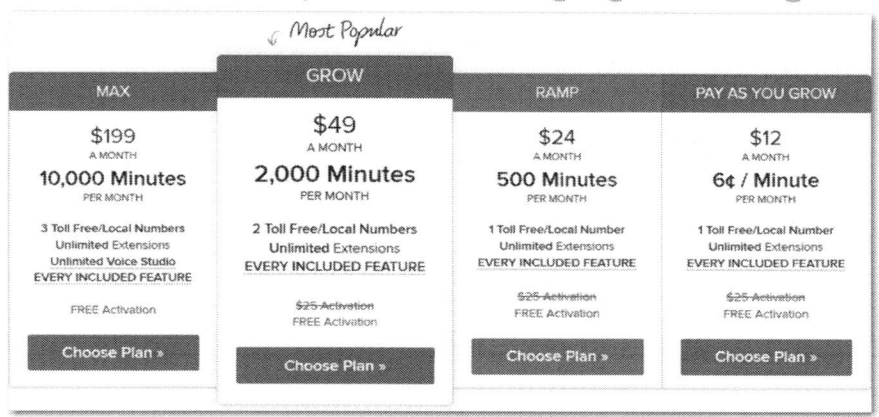

Figure 455: Grasshopper pricing tiers

Here are the main features of Grasshopper:

- No hardware to purchase or install. It is all managed through their web interface.
- Set up unlimited extensions and rout them to existing phone numbers.
- Customize your greeting message and menu structure.
- You can get one or more toll free or local numbers for incoming calls.
- Set up call forwarding to your mobile number. They have an app for calling out with your mobile that shows your business number. No one needs to know you are calling from a mobile phone.
- Screen calls from the caller ID. Accept or send to voicemail.
- Transcribed voice mails (extra charge) as well as incoming faxes are sent to a selected email box.
- Use their Voice Studio to hire a professionally recorded greeting.
- Have music for on hold time.
- You may be able to keep your existing number.

Signing UP for Grasshopper

Once you have selected a plan, your next step is to pick a number. It can be an 800 number with or without an easy to remember name (1-800-CALLPAUL). To get a local number, select your state and then closest city. This is what you see after picking the number (*Figure 456*).

Figure 456: Pick your phone number

After picking your number, you must add your business information and a credit card. You will be billed, but you have 30 days to cancel for a full refund. Lastly, you see a summary of your order. Note, that they include taxes and surcharges. I assume that since a real phone line is being used, they must pass through the taxes like other phone companies (*Figure 457*).

Figure 457: Your order summary

Grasshopper will send you an email telling how you need to finish setup and a login link (*Figure 458*). Login in and the first thing you are asked is to create a password.

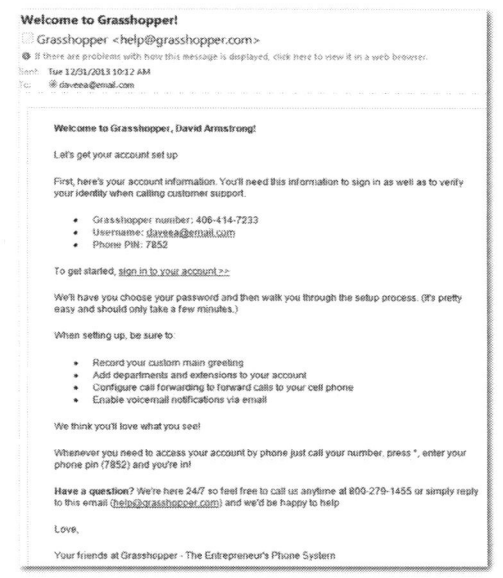

Figure 458: Grasshopper's confirmation email

Configuring Grasshopper

Since you are a new account, Grasshopper starts a wizard series of web pages that allow you to pick a greeting type, route your extensions to the person's actual phone number and record a greeting with a spoken menu.

First, you need to pick a Greeting template. The simple greeting is great if you have several people ready to answer incoming calls. Dialing 0 makes all on-hook phones to simultaneously ring. The department greeting template has multiple choices and a name directory. This example will use the department template (*Figure 459*).

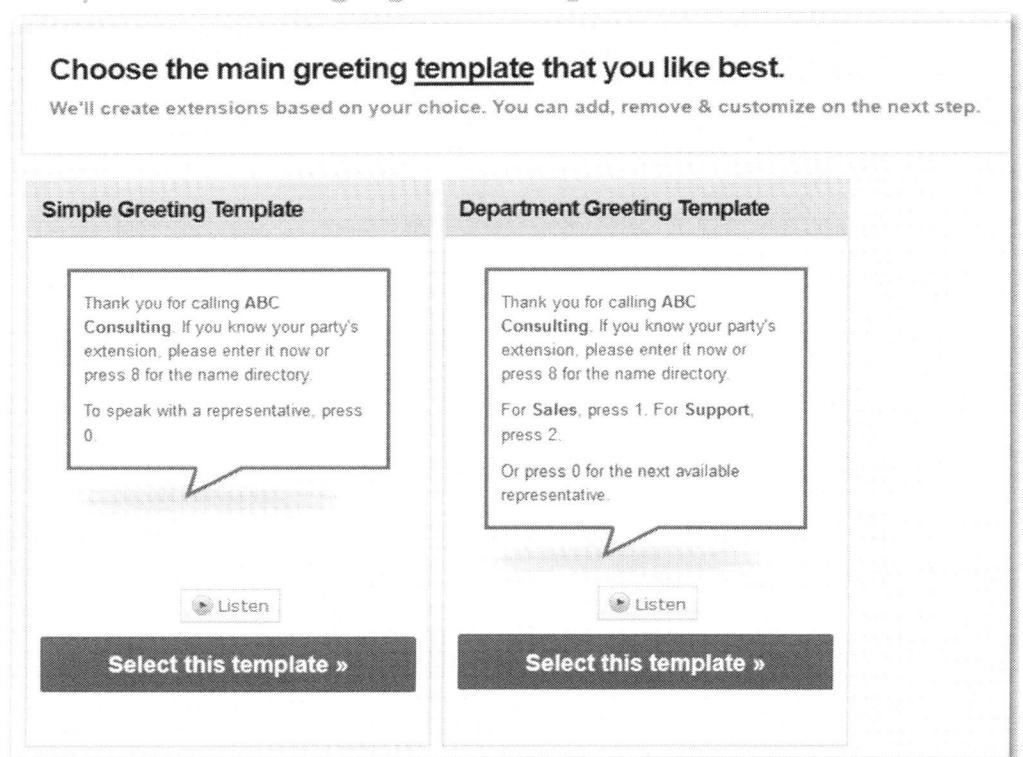

Figure 459: Picking a greeting template

You can click the **Listen** button to hear a sample of what the greeting might sound like without a company name.

Call Forwarding Setup

Notice, that the tabs at the top tell you, that you are in the second tab, **Extensions**. Don't worry if you do not get it right in this setup wizard, as you can always come back later and fine tune or add new numbers.

If you read the suggested script and look at the three extensions, you can see that the extension number is the number the caller keys into the phone's keypad. The names associated with that extension number is just an identifier so you can keep them straight. For example, Representative could be changed to Operator and it would configure it to ring through to your assigned receptionist (*Figure 460*).

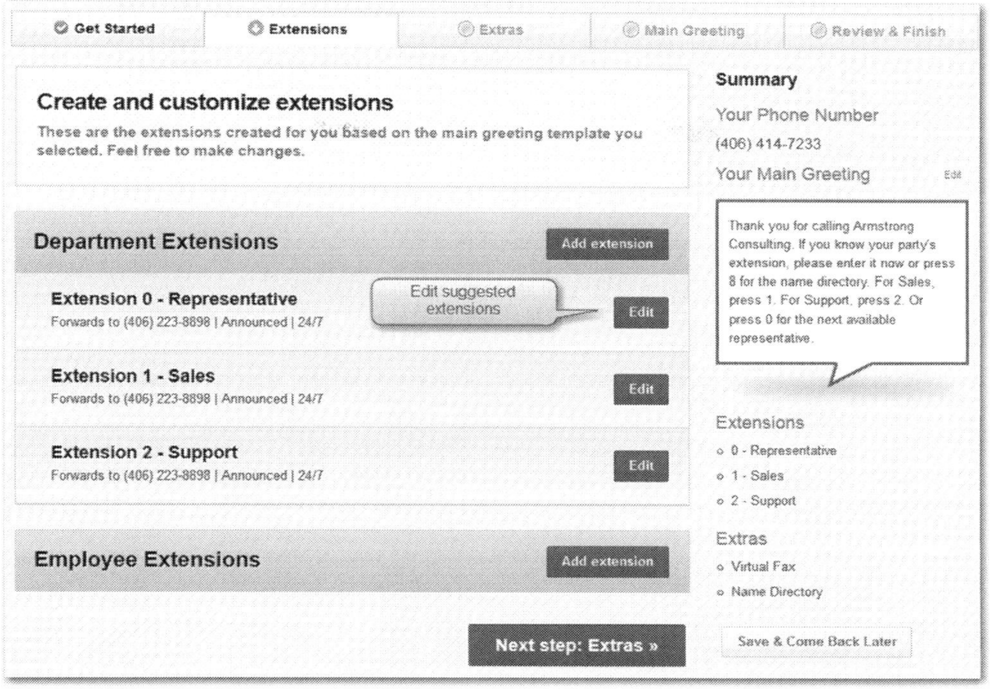

Chapter 16: Managing Incoming and Interoffice Calls

Figure 460: Customizing your extensions

When you click the **Edit** button, you open up the edit screen for that extension (*Figure 461*).

Let's explore the options:

1. You can change the **Extension #** and the **Extension name**. This will be the number the caller pushes to go to this extension and the name used on screens and reports.
2. Pick a **Phone PIN** that you can remember. When you set up your individual greeting and availability, you will need this number to identify yourself.
3. Select your correct **Time Zone**. This is especially important if some of your staff work outside of your main time zone. You want accurate timestamps on calls.
4. The **User Access** link opens to allow you to add an email address to the receiver of this extension and an Invite link to send an email giving them the details of how to use and receive calls.
5. We will see how to **Edit** the phone number, availability and how the message is received. We will learn that next.
6. You can have the incoming message routed to more than one call by clicking the **Add a forwarding number** link.
7. Missed calls can be sent as MP3 sound files, if you provide an email link. In most cases, you just click the email's attached file and you can listen on your smart phone or on other computers that allow you to access your email.

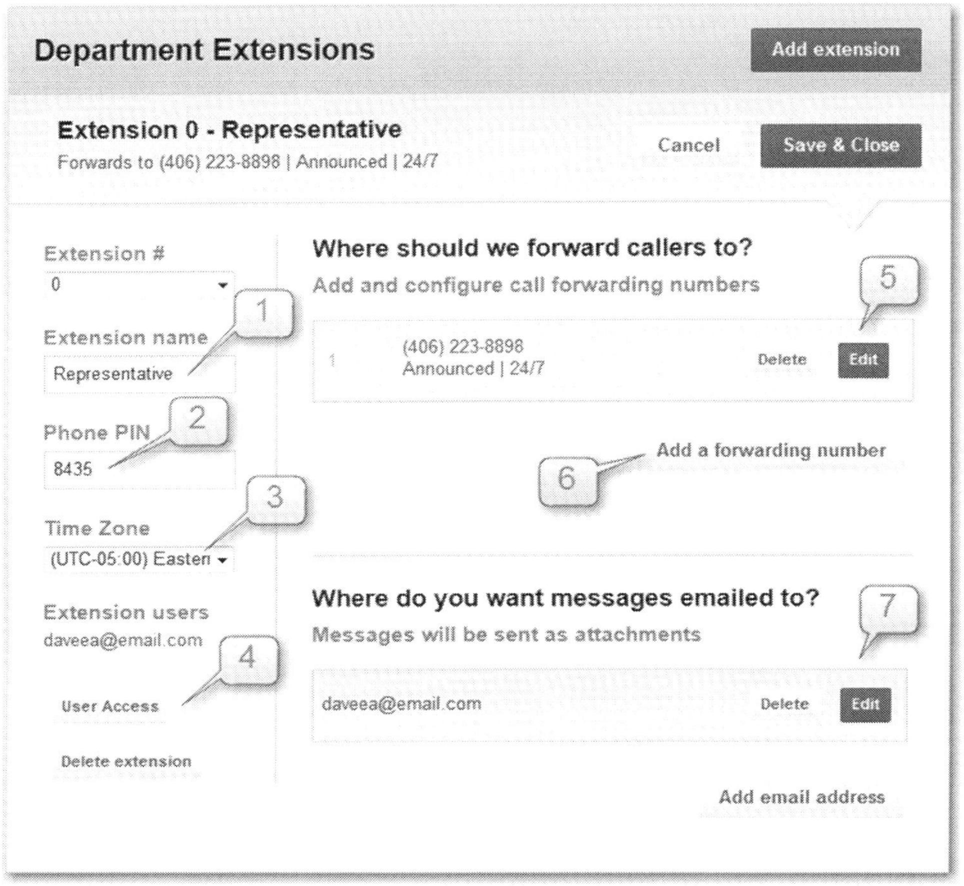

Chapter 16: Managing Incoming and Interoffice Calls

Figure 461: Editing the extension information

Clicking the **Edit** button, opens that extension's settings in the main area (*Figure 462*).

Here you can:

- Change the forwarding number.
- Change the amount of ring time in seconds.
- Adjust the schedule of when the incoming call is forwarded. For example, after work hours, you may want the call to go to voice mail.
- You can adjust how you receive the call:
    - **Calls will be announced when you pick up** - When you pick up the phone, you will first hear the caller ID if available.
    - **Calls will connect to you as soon as you pick up** - More typical call routing.
    - **Callers will be asked for their name, then announced to you** - This sounds great, but may irritate some callers.

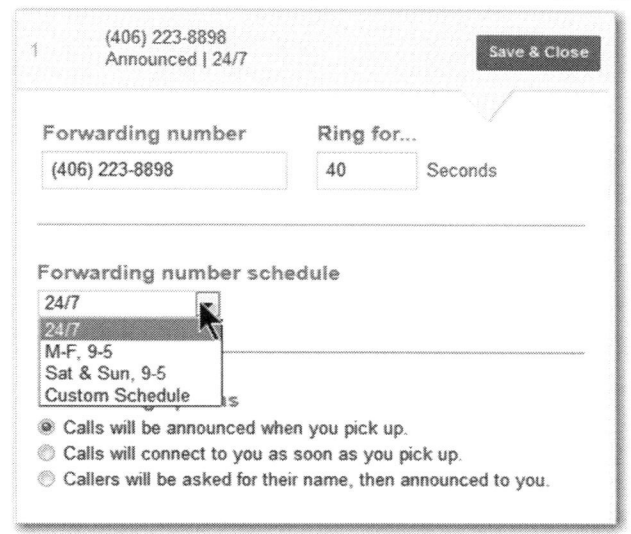

Figure 462: Editing extension parameters

If you scroll down in this edit screen, you will see where you can create your individual greeting. For example, "*Hello, this is Dave Armstrong and I am away from my desk or talking on the phone...*". We will learn how to record greetings, a little later, when we create our main one. You can always return later to personalize your individual greeting (*Figure 463*).

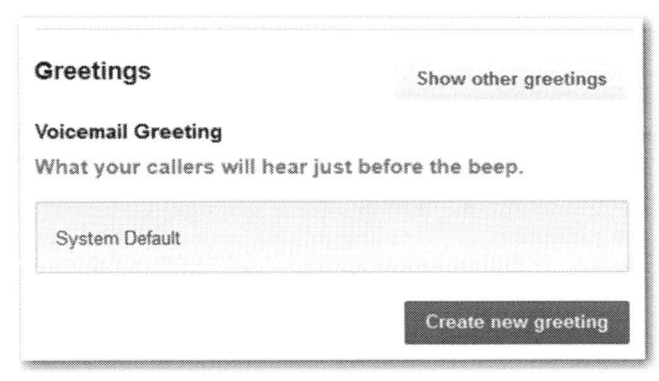

Figure 463: Creating an extension's greeting

Recording Your Voice Greeting

After you have your extensions setup, you can now move to the next step and record your default, main greeting callers hear. You need to have the names and associated numbers in place, as they will be in your message.

You have four ways to create your greeting. For a $75 fee, depending on your plan, you can have a professional create your greeting. You could use a free audio tool, such as Audacity. http://audacity.sourceforge.net/. Add a good USB microphone and you can make a quality recording and then upload it. If you want to make your own, click the **Record Myself** link (*Figure 464*).

Record Main Greeting

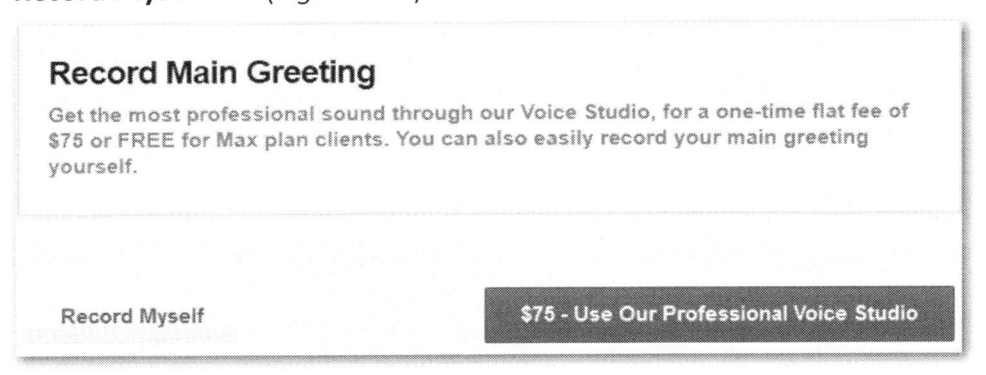

Get the most professional sound through our Voice Studio, for a one-time flat fee of $75 or FREE for Max plan clients. You can also easily record your main greeting yourself.

Record Myself $75 - Use Our Professional Voice Studio

Figure 464: Pick self or professional recording

Based on the choices you made when you edited your extension data, Grasshopper gives you a suggested script (*Figure 465*).

Your choices are:

- Record by phone - This is not the best quality, but it is easy and the only choice if you have no microphone.
- Record using my computer's microphone - A good USB type microphone is best and you may have to adjust your sound levels, etc.
- Upload existing MP3 file - This choice allows you to edit the file using a sound editor, such Audacity. You might put a low level music background tract, record in stereo, etc.

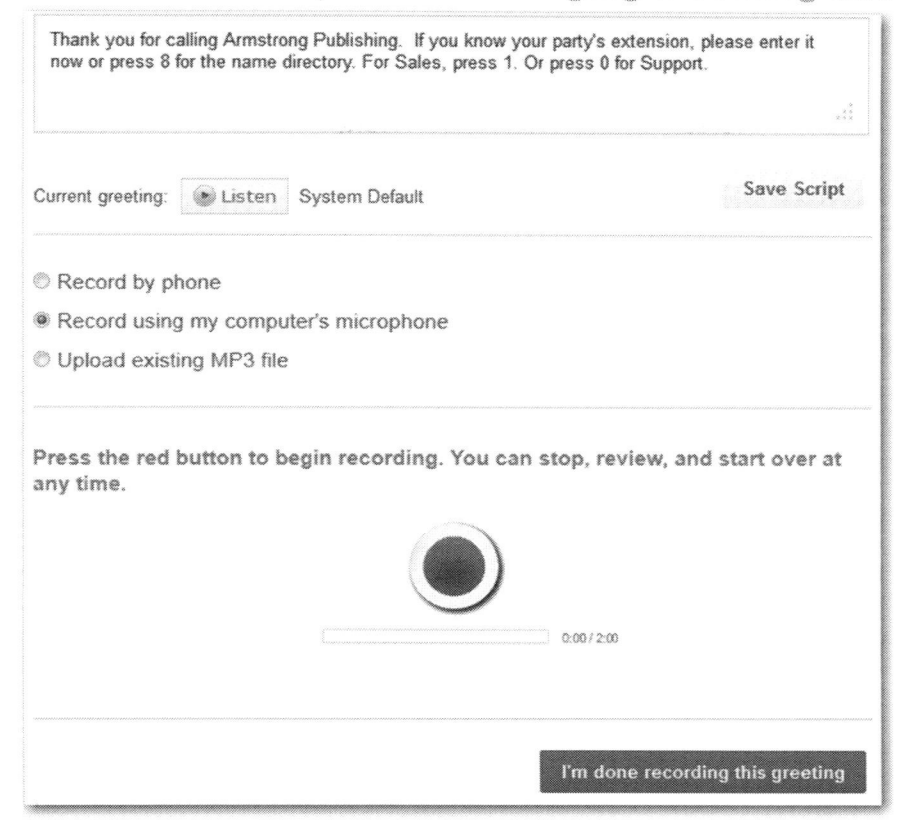

Figure 465: Ready to record your greeting

The next step in your wizard, shows you what you have as account features and gives you the opportunity to purchase more features (*Figure 466*).

Let's look at the extras and what they cost:

- **Virtual Fax** - Incoming faxes are converted into a PDF, attached to an email and sent to a selected email account. I think it is free with all plans.
- **Name Directory** - As we saw above, you can have a name directory. Callers can search that directory with their keypads by spelling out part of their names. Also, free.
- **Call Blasting** - Will ring multiple phones at the same time. This might be great for a pool of support or sales staff.
- **Read Your Voicemail** - This transcribes your messages into text and emails that text, along with an attached MP3 file to you.

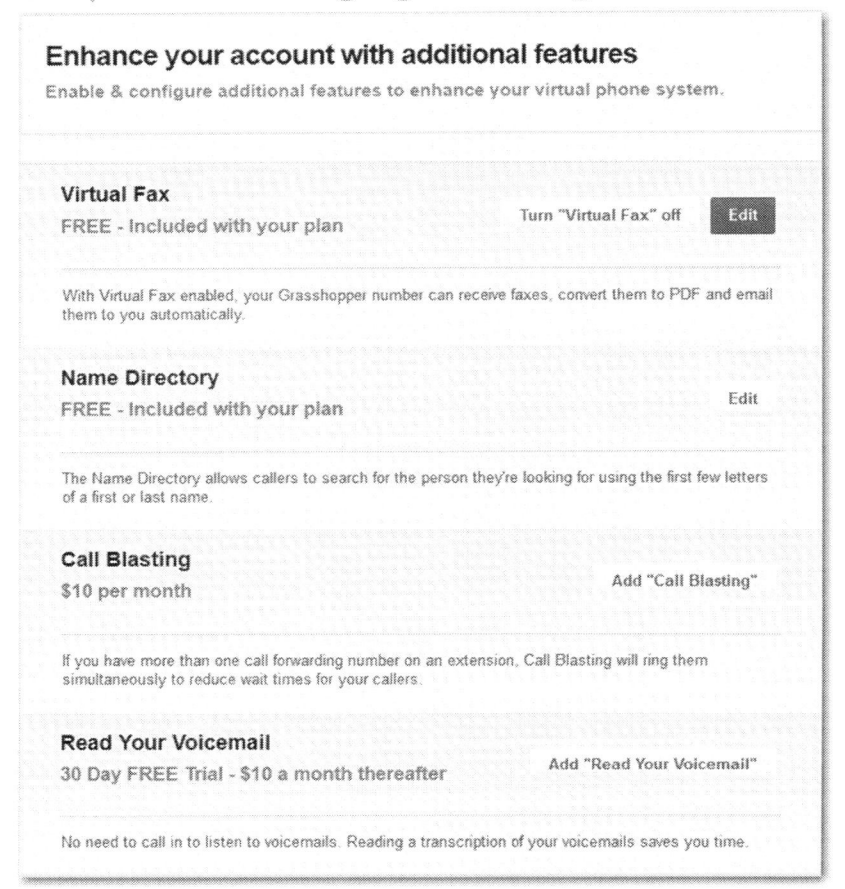

Figure 466: Adding extra features

Our next section, discusses the day-to-day use of Grasshopper.

How to Use Grasshopper

There are three dashboards or web pages, each having tabs that allow you to get to the functions needed to use Grasshopper (*Figure 467*).

The three dashboards are:

1. **Messages & Calls** - Use to see **All Messages** including **Voicemails**, **Faxes**, **Deleted**, **All Calls** and **Missed Calls**.
2. **Extensions** - This gives access to extension editing, as you saw in the setup wizard.
3. **Settings** - Gets you to your main greeting, user permissions and your billing info.

Message & Calls allow you to see all of the call activity. You can narrow the view to just Faxes or Missed Calls (*Figure 467*).

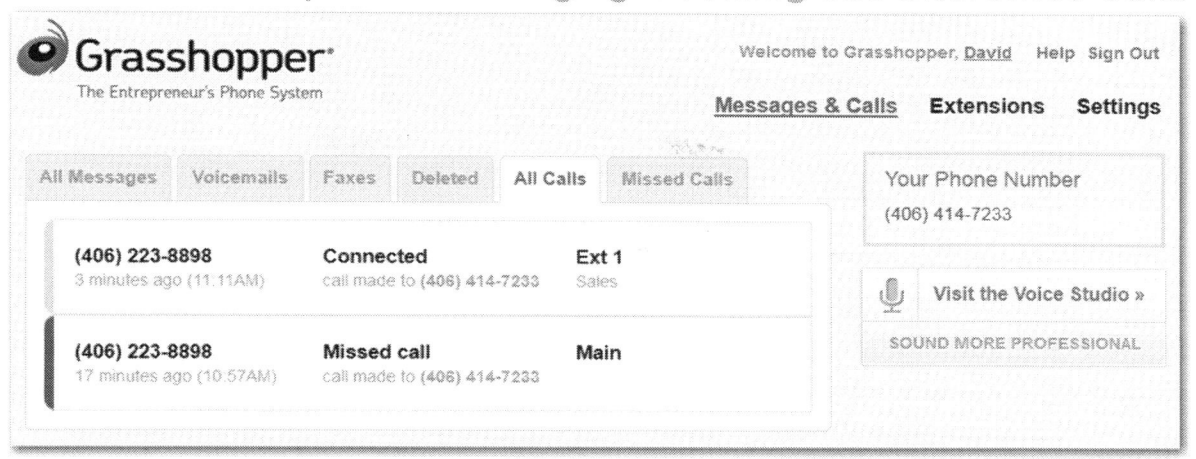

Chapter 16: Managing Incoming and Interoffice Calls

Figure 467: The messaging dashboard

Double click any entry to open and view details. If the call was a voicemail, the recording starts playing (*Figure 468*).

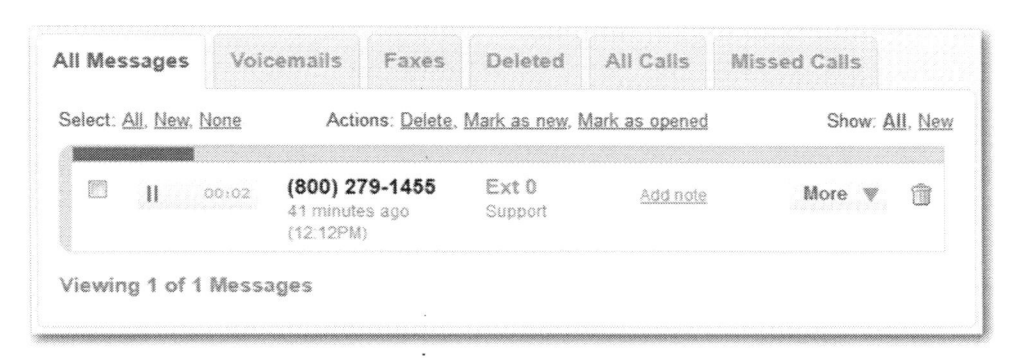

Figure 468: Listening to a missed call

Grasshopper will send an email anytime a voicemail is created with a MP3 sound file attached. Depending on your computer setup, you should be able to just double click the attached file to hear the message.

If you have paid for the extra text translation, you will also be able to read the message. Here is what a voicemail email looks like in Outlook (*Figure 469*).

Chapter 16: Managing Incoming and Interoffice Calls

*Voicemail from 800-279-1455

Grasshopper <notifications@grasshopper.com>
Sent: Tue 12/31/2013 10:12 AM
To: daveea@email.com

Message grasshopper_800-279-1455_12_31_2013_121293248.mp3 (156 KB)

New Grasshopper Voicemail

Caller: 800-279-1455
Extension: 0 - Default Extension
Grasshopper #: 1-406-414-7233
Timestamp: 12/31/2013 12:12:12 PM (UTC-05:00) Eastern Time (US & Canada)

Read Your Voicemail *(human transcribed)*

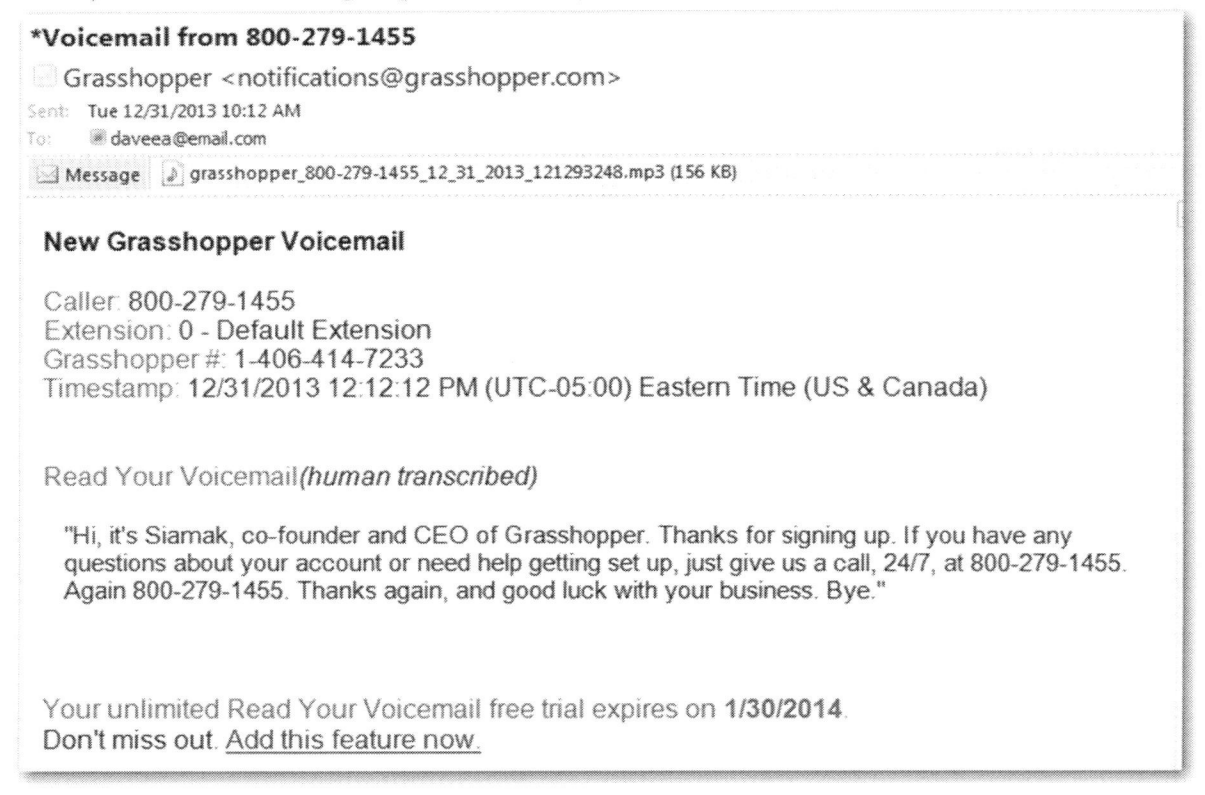

"Hi, it's Siamak, co-founder and CEO of Grasshopper. Thanks for signing up. If you have any questions about your account or need help getting set up, just give us a call, 24/7, at 800-279-1455. Again 800-279-1455. Thanks again, and good luck with your business. Bye."

Your unlimited Read Your Voicemail free trial expires on **1/30/2014**.
Don't miss out. Add this feature now.

Figure 469: An email with the voice message attached

The Extensions dashboard gives you access to your call forwarding to the different extensions. You can add, delete and configure as you saw earlier in the setup section of this chapter (*Figure 470*).

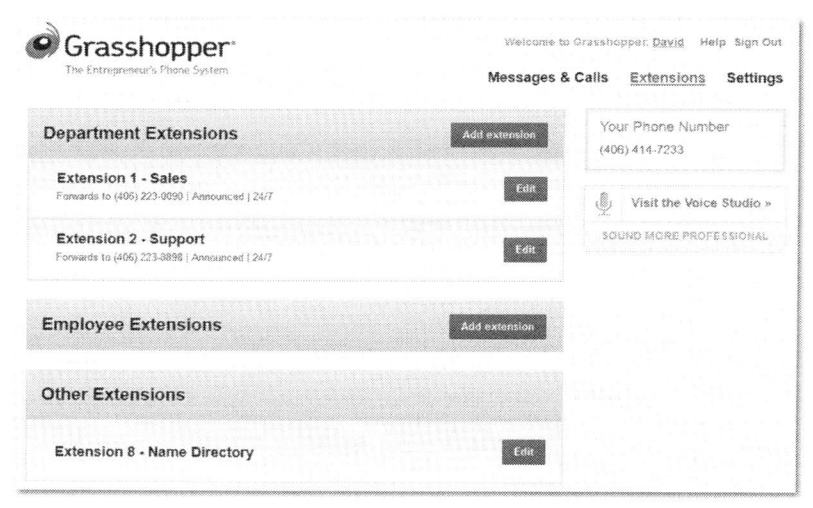

Figure 470: The extension dashboard

Chapter 16: Managing Incoming and Interoffice Calls

One of the **Other Extensions** is the **Name Directory**. Click the **Edit** button and you can map an individual's name to a numbered extension. When a caller knows the name of an individual, they can use the phone's keypad to spell out up to 5 characters of a name. Upon a successful match, they are routed to that extension (*Figure 471*).

Figure 471: Adding names into a name directory

The last dashboard, **Settings**, give you access to **Your Account** (admin profile showing your current plan), your **Extras**, **Your Numbers** (you can have more than one incoming number), your **Main Greeting** and **Users** (*Figure 472*).

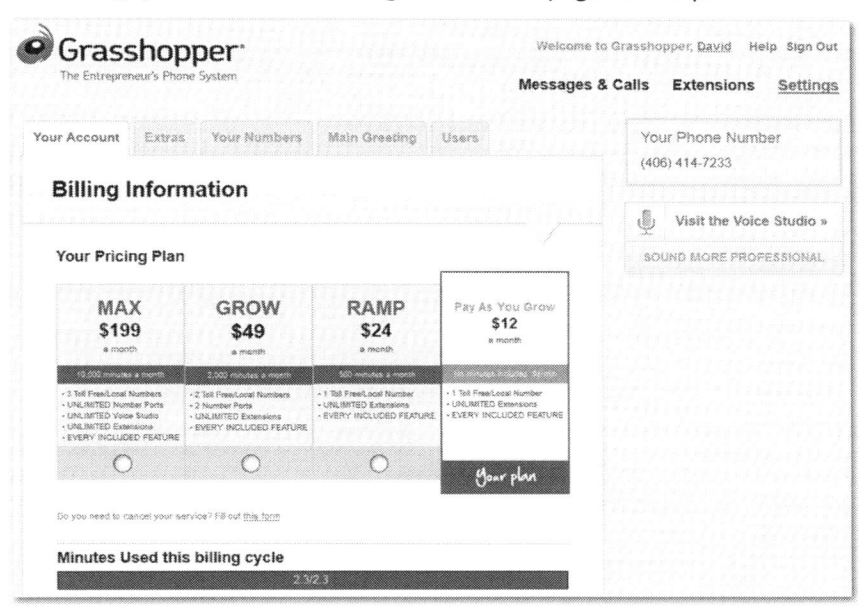

Figure 472: The settings dashboard

Chapter 16: Managing Incoming and Interoffice Calls

You can upgrade or downgrade your plan at any time when in the **Your Account** tab.

The User tab opens the **User Management** window, where you can give permission to each of the extensions, so that they may manage their own greetings. If you give them Administrator privileges, they can do more, such as changing their hours, etc.

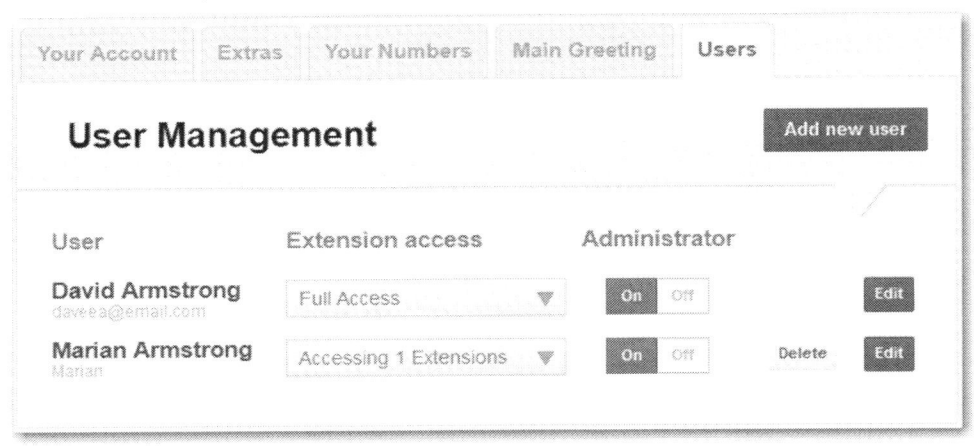

Figure 473: Setting extension access

Going Mobile with Grasshopper

Grasshopper has an Android and iPhone app that allows you to:

- Make calls from your Grasshopper number.
- Check voicemails.
- Return missed calls.
- Change call forwarding settings.

Go to Google's app store, Google Play and download. http://goo.gl/OdVQAs. Below are some screen captures from an Android phone (*Figure 474 through Figure 481*).

Chapter 16: Managing Incoming and Interoffice Calls

Figure 474: Dialing using call out feature

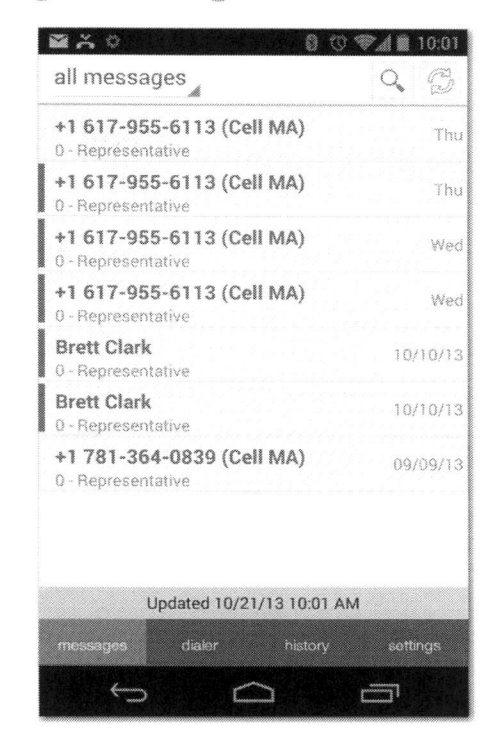

Figure 475: Checking Messages

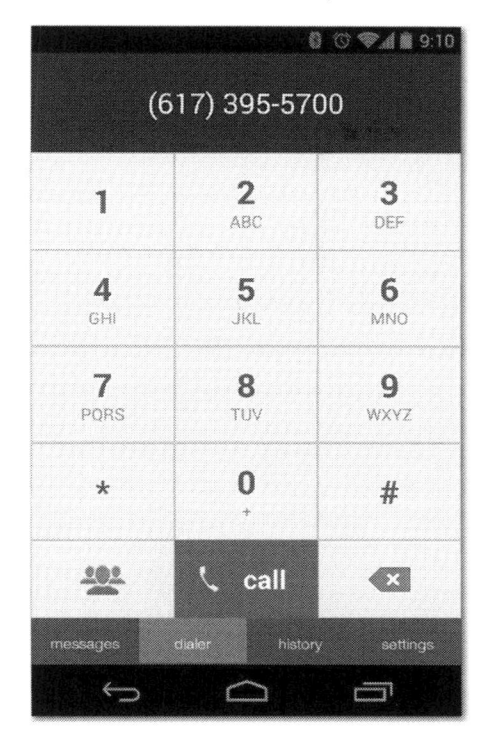

You can call out and the person called only sees your business number. However, depending on how you configure the phone app and settings in your Grasshopper account, you may incur charges if you pay as you go, or the minutes may count against your plan's minutes.

These are the incoming calls that you missed and they left messages. Tap a call to view the details and to listen to the message.

The main screen is both the dialer and has buttons at the bottom that lead to the other screens where you can: check messages, see a history of your calls and change your settings (*Figure 474*).

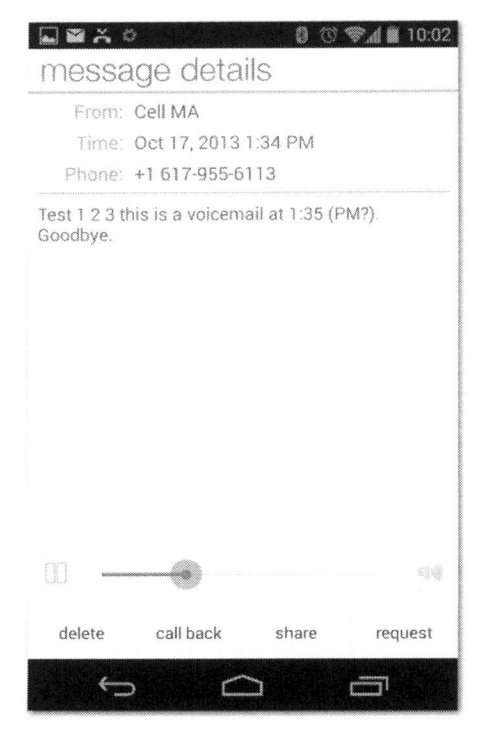

Chapter 16: Managing Incoming and Interoffice Calls

Figure 476: Listening to a message

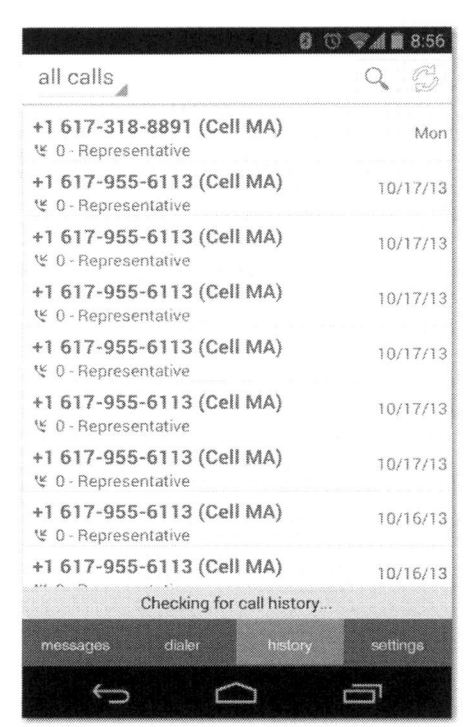

Figure 477: Checking the call history

You can listen to the message and if you have added it to your plan, you can read a text translation.

Note, that you can call back, share with another extension or email to another.

You can see a call history of all calls or a filtered list based on categories such as missed, message, etc.

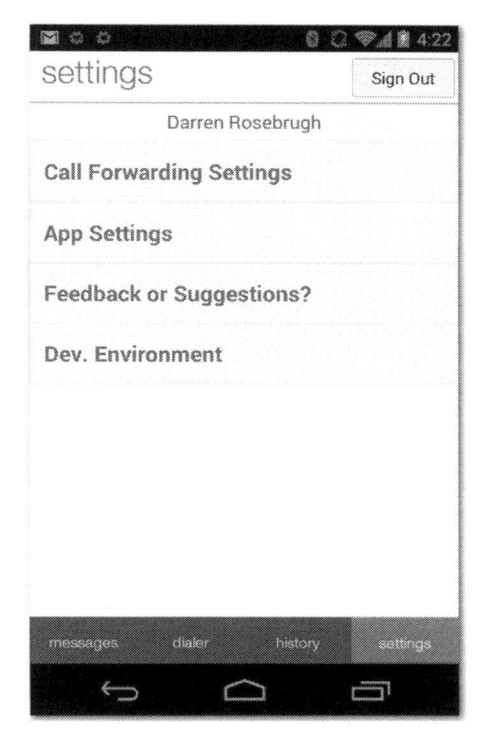

Chapter 16: Managing Incoming and Interoffice Calls

Figure 478: The main setting screen

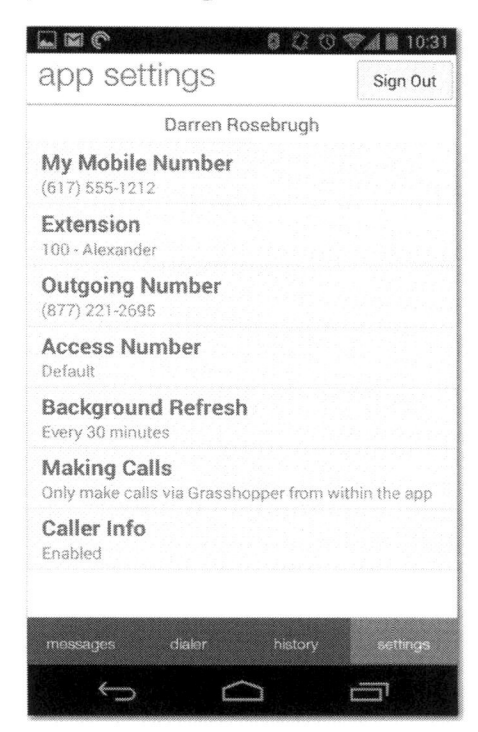

Figure 479: Viewing/changing the app settings

From your settings screen, you can change your call forwarding settings. For example, you might arrive home and want to forward calls to your home phone.

You can also change the general app settings as you see on the right.

Use the setting to map your phone to a particular extension, change the outgoing number and decide if you want to dial out through Grasshopper or your mobile phone service. Regardless, the **Outgoing Number** is shown to the recipient of the call.

The settings screens give you control over what the recipient of the call sees as a caller ID. If the **Caller Info** is **Enabled**, they see the value in the **Outgoing Number**. This should probably be your Grasshopper number, if it is a business call.

You may occasionally want to handle the calls from another extension. Change the **Extension** value to have that extension forwarded to you.

If you want to avoid using Grasshopper to call out and still want to show your Grasshopper business number, you can change the **Making Calls** value to not use Grasshopper. Those calls will then count against your mobile usage rather than Grasshopper.

Chapter 16: Managing Incoming and Interoffice Calls

Figure 480: Changing call forwarding

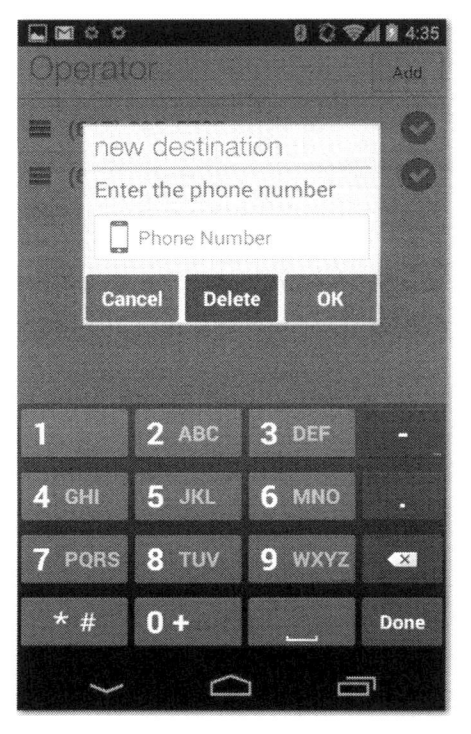

Figure 481: Entering the new forwarding number

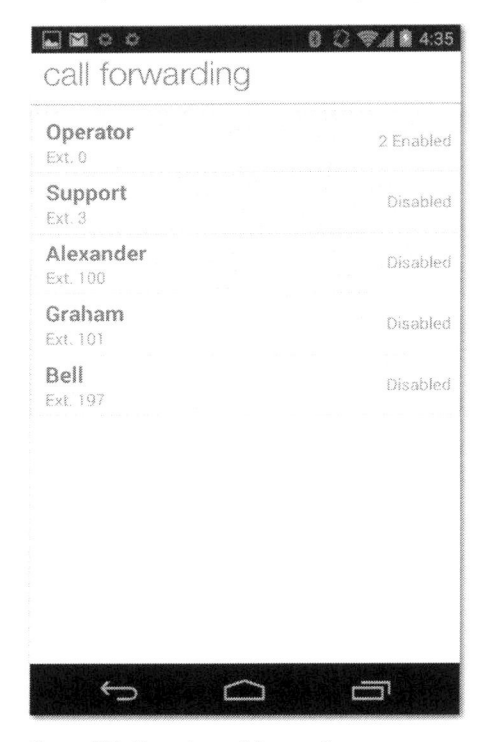

Through this phone app, you can control your forwarding features. You can enable or disable any extension. You can also change what number the extension rings to. For security reasons, you will need your admin pin number to change.

Tap any of the extensions and you can route to a new number.

You have many of the admin features you have in your dashboard on your phone. You have an admin pin number that you will need to reroute extensions.

As you can see, Grasshopper is a well-developed product. It is easy to use and understand and when you combine it with Skype for calling out, it is a bargain compared to traditional PBX systems.

Chapter 16: Managing Incoming and Interoffice Calls

RingCentral

I am not going to cover RingCentral with the detail we did with Grasshopper. As a Grasshopper user, I know it well and am happy with my choice. However, I know RingCentral customers that love their service.

There are some differences in how they price. For example, they charge by the user, whereas, Grasshopper has a single price and gives you unlimited extensions. Depending on your number of staff, this could get expensive.

Here is their pricing as of January, 2014 (*Figure 482*):

Select an Edition that fits your needs	Standard $24.99[1] /mo per user	MOST POPULAR Premium $34.99[2] /mo per user	Enterprise $49.99[3] /mo per user
	30-Day Free Trial[4]	30-Day Free Trial[4]	30-Day Free Trial[4]
Call Management and phone system administration	✓	✓	✓
Mobile Apps for iPhone, iPad, Android and BlackBerry	✓	✓	✓
Unlimited calling[5]	✓	✓	✓
Toll-free minutes[6]	1000 mins	2500 mins	Unlimited
Phone Rental Option: Desk and conference phones[7]	✓	✓	✓
Unlimited Internet Fax[5]	✓	✓	✓
Unlimited Business SMS	✓	✓	✓
Unlimited Conferencing	✓	✓	✓
Integrations with Microsoft® Office & Outlook®, Google, Box, and Dropbox	✓	✓	✓
Salesforce CRM integration		✓	✓
Automatic Call Recording		✓	✓
Premium Support[8]		✓	✓

Need help deciding? Call us today: 1-877-682-8209

Figure 482: RingCentral pricing plans

The good news is they give a free 30 day trial, so you can decide for yourself.

Chapter 16: Managing Incoming and Interoffice Calls

They also offer a full set of VoIP phones for those that are headset adverse. These seem to be customized, so you can transfer calls via the keypad (*Figure 483*).

Polycom VVX-500 / Color Touchscreen Desk Phone

A revolutionary color touchscreen IP phone with speakerphone, presence, Gigabit ethernet, and more. Includes power adapter.

- 12 touch keys can display the presence status for up to 10 users on the phone display
- Intelligent context-based softkeys
- Future expansion via USB flash drive, camera, and other options
- Large backlit capacitive multi-touch display
- Polycom HD (high-definition) voice technology
- Share a single network connection with your phone and PC using the integrated 2-port Gigabit Ethernet switch
- Dedicated RJ-9 headset port
- Integrated Power over Ethernet (PoE) support (Class 2)

$299.00
List Price $339.00
or $20.00/month

Download Datasheet »   + Compare

save $40

Figure 483: A VoIP phone form RingCentral

Personally, I prefer a USB headset and a webcam for video. Many headsets have noise canceling so the person at the other end of the call does not hear the sound of your computer or fan. The headset frees the hands for typing, important if you are presenting or typing in orders, support tickets, etc.

Skype sells several headsets and webcams as well as wireless portable and desk phones. http://shop.skype.com/accessory.html/?opt=variation1

RingCentral is similar to Grasshopper, in that, you can change answering rules, hours of operation and record greetings and record calls, if needed. They offer mobile and tablet apps and include business SMS to those mobile apps. It is included in their plans, whereas, Skype charges for each message.

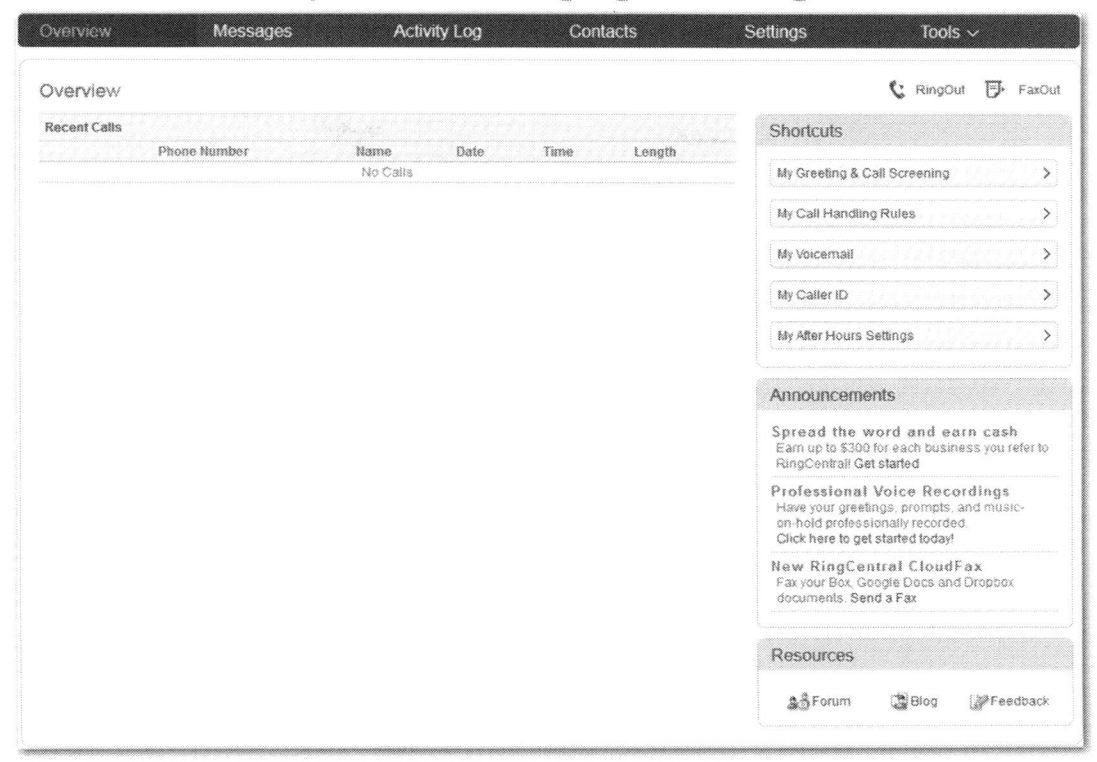

Chapter 16: Managing Incoming and Interoffice Calls

Figure 484: The user's dashboard overview tab

The Overview page is your account home page. It shows your recent voicemail and faxes, recent inbound and outbound calls, your account status and announcements. Let's take a look at the navigation bar across the top of this page and see how to use it. Some features are described in more detail later in this document (*Figure 484*).

Figure 485: The message view

Chapter 16: Managing Incoming and Interoffice Calls

Your voicemail and fax messages are stored here (*Figure 485*).

Under Messages, you can:

- Review inbound and outbound callers.
- Listen to voicemail.
- View faxes.
- Save voicemail and received faxes to your computer.
- Forward messages and faxes by email.
- Click on a caller's number to call them back.
- Delete and undelete items.
- Block callers.

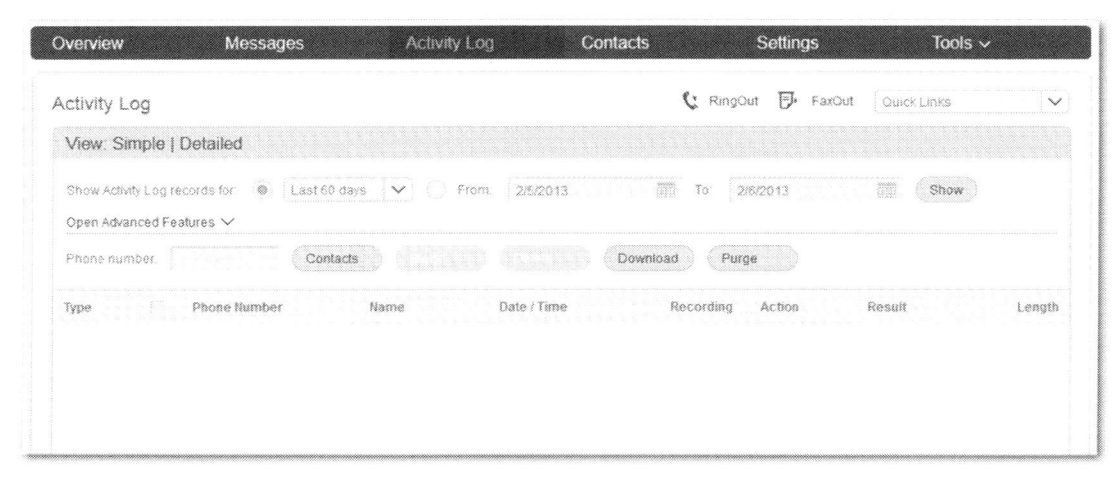

Figure 486: The Activity Log view

The **Activity Log** provides customized reports on inbound and outbound calls and faxes for the company number and specified extensions. Select the time period, type of call (inbound or outbound), blocked calls, or recorded calls.

Save reports for analysis or you can have the activity log delivered to an email address daily, weekly, or monthly on specified days (*Figure 486*).

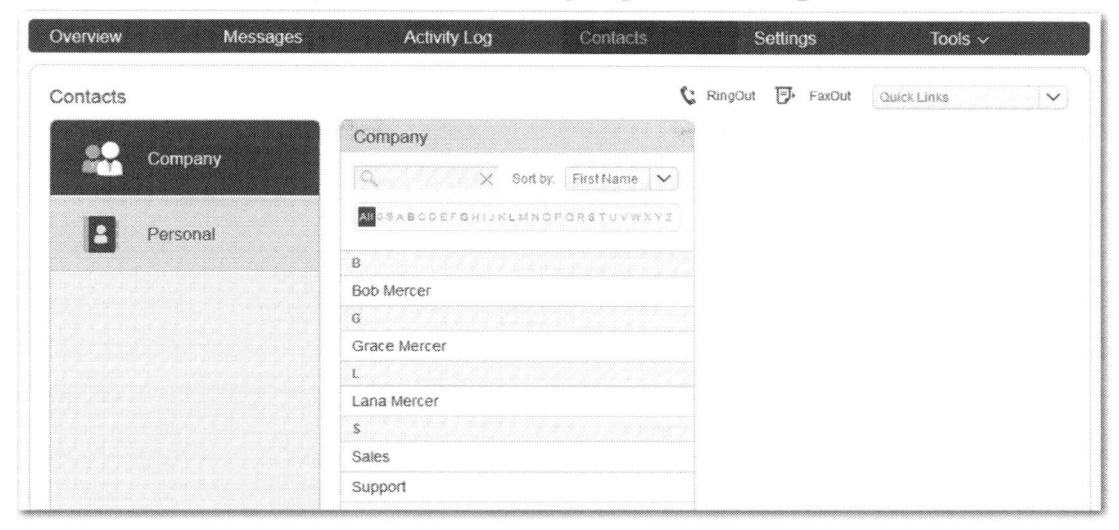

Chapter 16: Managing Incoming and Interoffice Calls

Figure 487: The Contacts view

Contacts include **Company** contacts which are all the users of your RingCentral system. It includes your **Personal** contacts, which you can add manually, or import from a comma-separated variable (CSV) text data file, or from Microsoft Outlook (*Figure 487*).

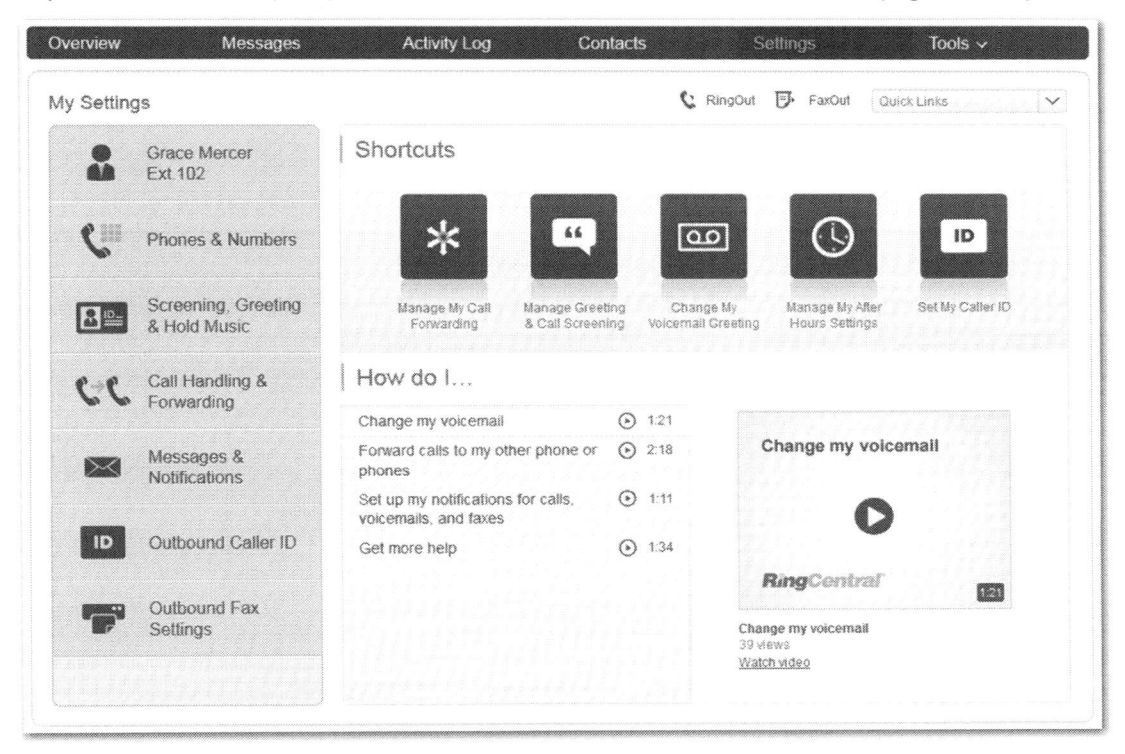

Figure 488: The Settings view

Use **My Settings** to make changes to your personal settings (*Figure 488*).

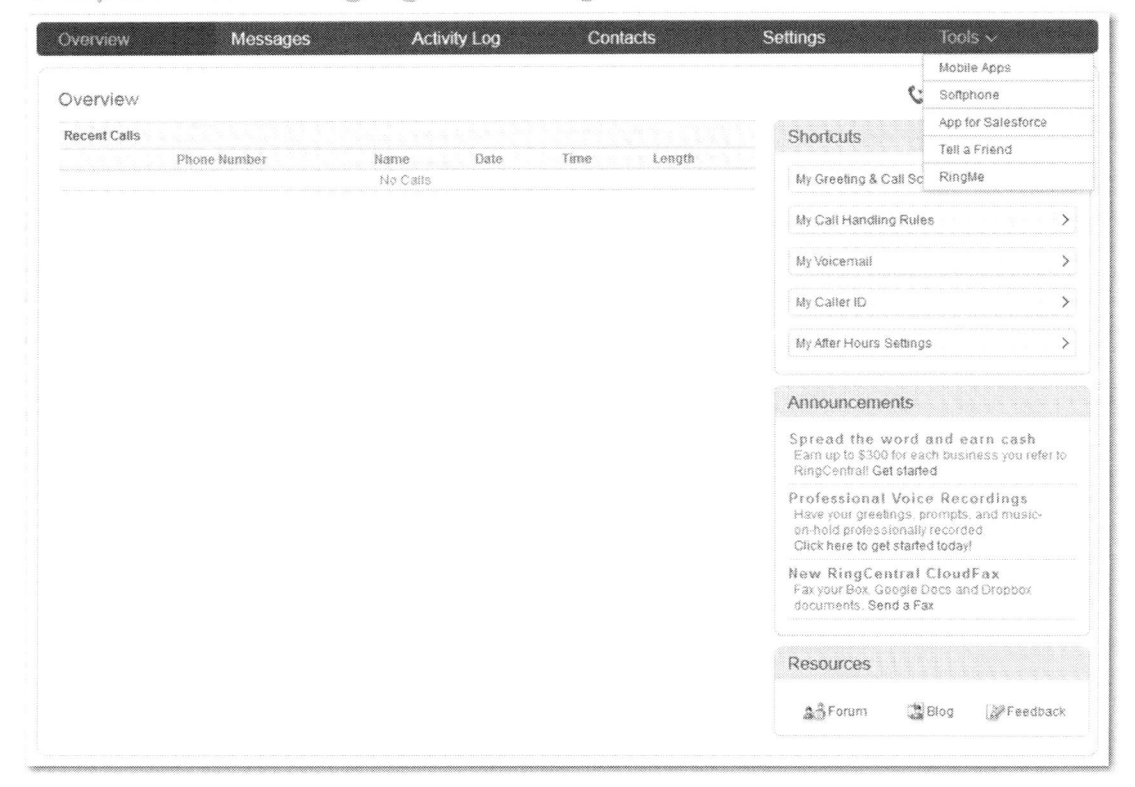

Chapter 16: Managing Incoming and Interoffice Calls

Figure 489: Accessing Tools

The Tools menu allows you to obtain the latest tools to enhance your productivity and customize your service to suit the way you work (*Figure 489*).

Mobile Apps

Download the iPhone app or the Android app to take your RingCentral service on the go.

Softphone

Use the Softphone application to control your calls from your PC. Answer or screen incoming calls, send to voice mail, transfer, disconnect, or monitor voice messages as they are being left and pick up the ones you want to talk to.

App for Salesforce

Use this link to access a download for the RingCentral App for Salesforce. For more information, see Features - Salesforce Integration.

Tell a Friend

Refer a friend to RingCentral using this simple form and receive referral rewards.

RingMe

Chapter 16: Managing Incoming and Interoffice Calls

The RingMe button gives your customers the ability to call you by clicking on the button on your web site or email signature. They give you HTML code you can embed in any of your web pages.

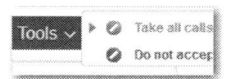

Figure 490: Changing call availability

Do Not Disturb (DND)

On the upper right of every page of your online account, is a small button labeled **DND**, or Do Not Disturb. Click **DND** to toggle to other settings:

DND Off . Green means that you will take all incoming calls.

DND On. Red is set to, "Do not accept any calls", and all callers are sent to voicemail.

Figure 491: Calling, or faxing out

RingOut

RingOut enables one-touch calling from any phone or Internet-enabled computer, allowing you to make calls using your business caller ID from any location, such as a hotel room. The RingOut icon appears near the top of every online account page (*Figure 491*).

1. Click on the **RingOut** icon on any account page to bring up this menu pop-up.

2. In the **Call to** box, enter or select the number you wish to call. You can also choose from among recent calls, or from your contact list.
3. **Current Location** should list your RingCentral number; or you can choose Custom phone number and enter another phone number you'd like to use for this call instead.
4. **Prompt me to press 1 before connecting the call** is pre-checked. When the system calls, you will hear, "Please press 1 to connect." This protects you, in case you mistyped your own number, or if your voicemail picks up too quickly.
5. Now click **Call**. The system first calls you. When you answer (and press 1 as instructed), it then calls the other number and connects you.

Virtual Phone System Wrap-up

In this chapter, we have reviewed two different type plans. Grasshopper is not considered a full PBX plan and does not make the list in (*Figure 492*). However, it is less expensive if you have a number of employees.

RingCentral offers some additional features, including Faxing in the Cloud and traditional desktop and conferencing phones.

You can see the web comparison by clicking the link below.

http://virtualphonesystemreviews.com/compare-business-voip-systems/

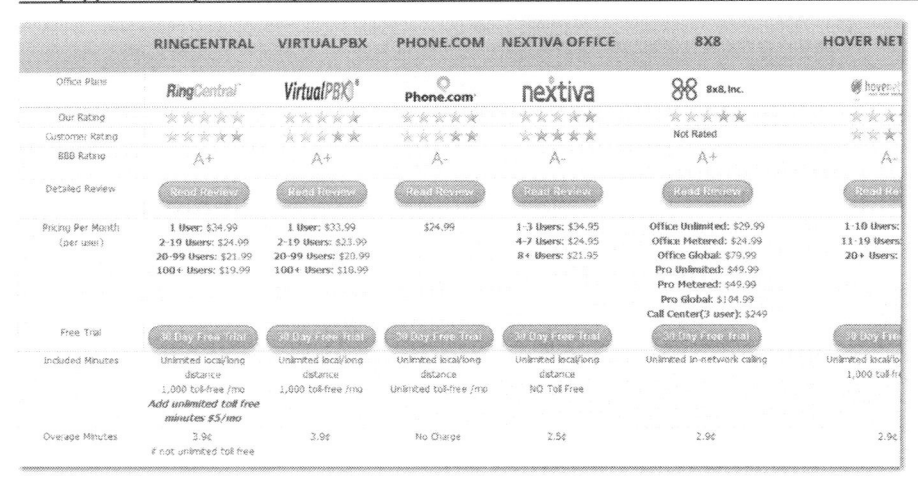

Figure 492: Comparing virtual PBX plans

Chapter 17: Collaborating With Google Sites

Whether you are completely virtual in individual home offices are just looking for better communication between your staff, the collaboration tools we discuss here can work wonders for businesses.

There are many competing cloud applications that are designed to help you plan and track projects. If you are a software development company or an engineering firm, these may be justified in both cost and effort. However, for many nontechnical companies, they are massive overkill.

We are going to be learning about Google's free websites. They are easy to create, no programming skills needed, and they have templates for many different types of websites. We are going to study two that every company needs. The first is for project planning and the second is a company intranet site where anyone can post company information. An intranet is a private internet site that is used only within the company.

Using Google Sites to Collaborate

Since you have a Google email and password, you need to only go to http://sites.google.com. When I get there, I see that I have previously created three sites (*Figure 493*).

Chapter 17: Collaborating with Google Sites

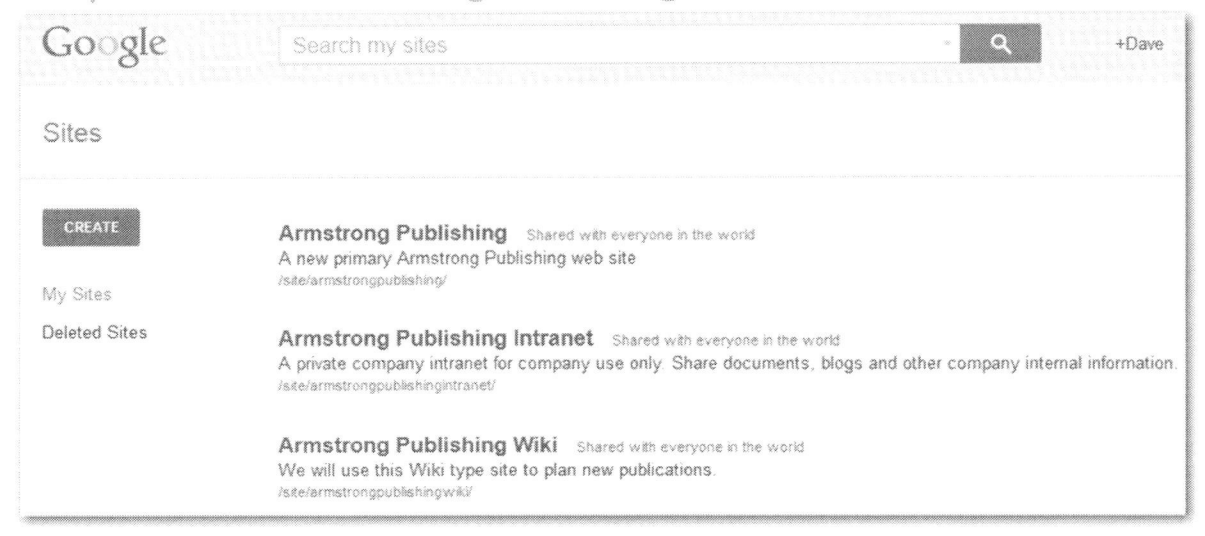

Figure 493: My Google sites

Adding a New Project Management Site

I would like to add a new site that I can use for project tracking. I start by clicking the CREATE button on my Sites page. This opens a creation page with several types of sites listed. Since I do not see my type of site, I click **the Browse the gallery for more** templates (*Figure 494*).

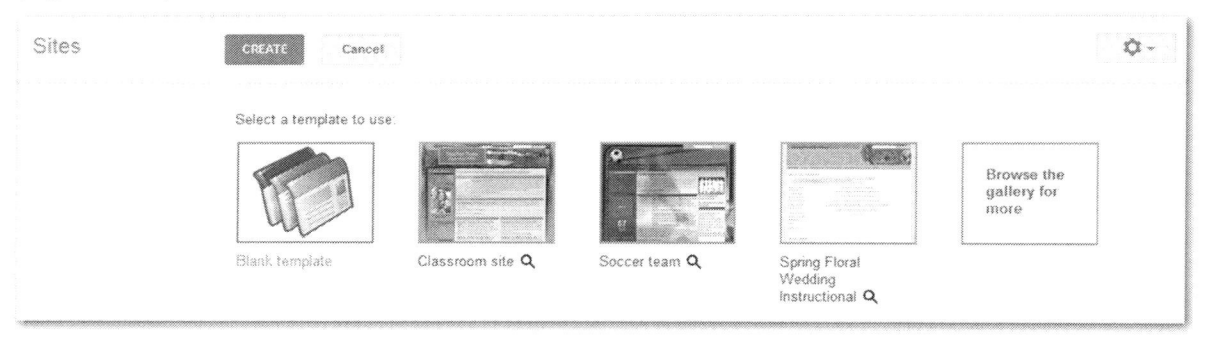

Figure 494: Picking a template

This gives me access to all of the templates. Notice, that they are categorized and the category I am interested in is **Business Collaboration** (*Figure 495*). The fifth one down is called Project work site which seems like what I am looking for.

Chapter 17: Collaborating with Google Sites

Figure 495: More Templates

When I click on that image, I get a larger image and description. If I click on the Gadget from template directory link, I can see a demo of the site. Click the **Select** button at the bottom of the page to select it.

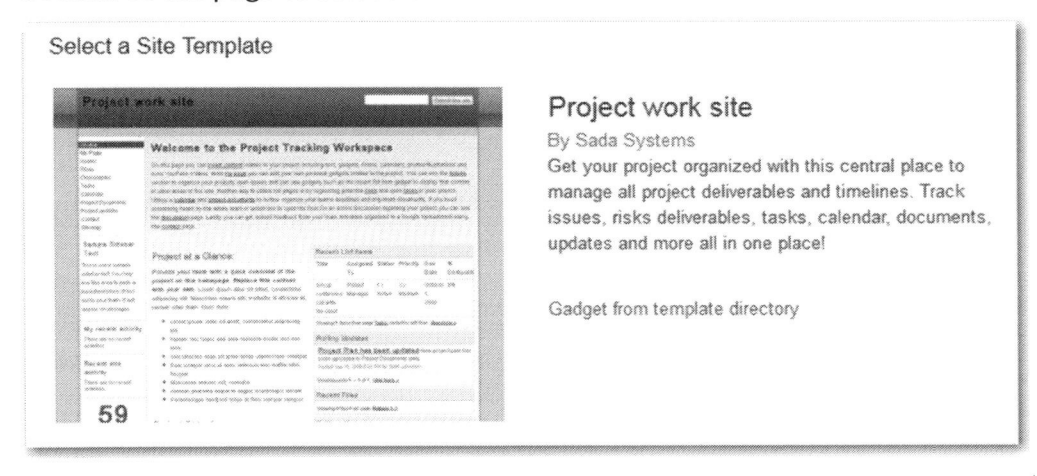

Figure 496: A project planning site

Chapter 17: Collaborating with Google Sites

This tells Google what kind of site I want and this decision determines the number and type of pages I will have. I can always edit the layout, page types, etc. I need to click the **Select a theme** link to open the themes.

I need to name my site and pick a theme. Themes determine the colors, image placeholders and fonts of my site (*Figure 497*).

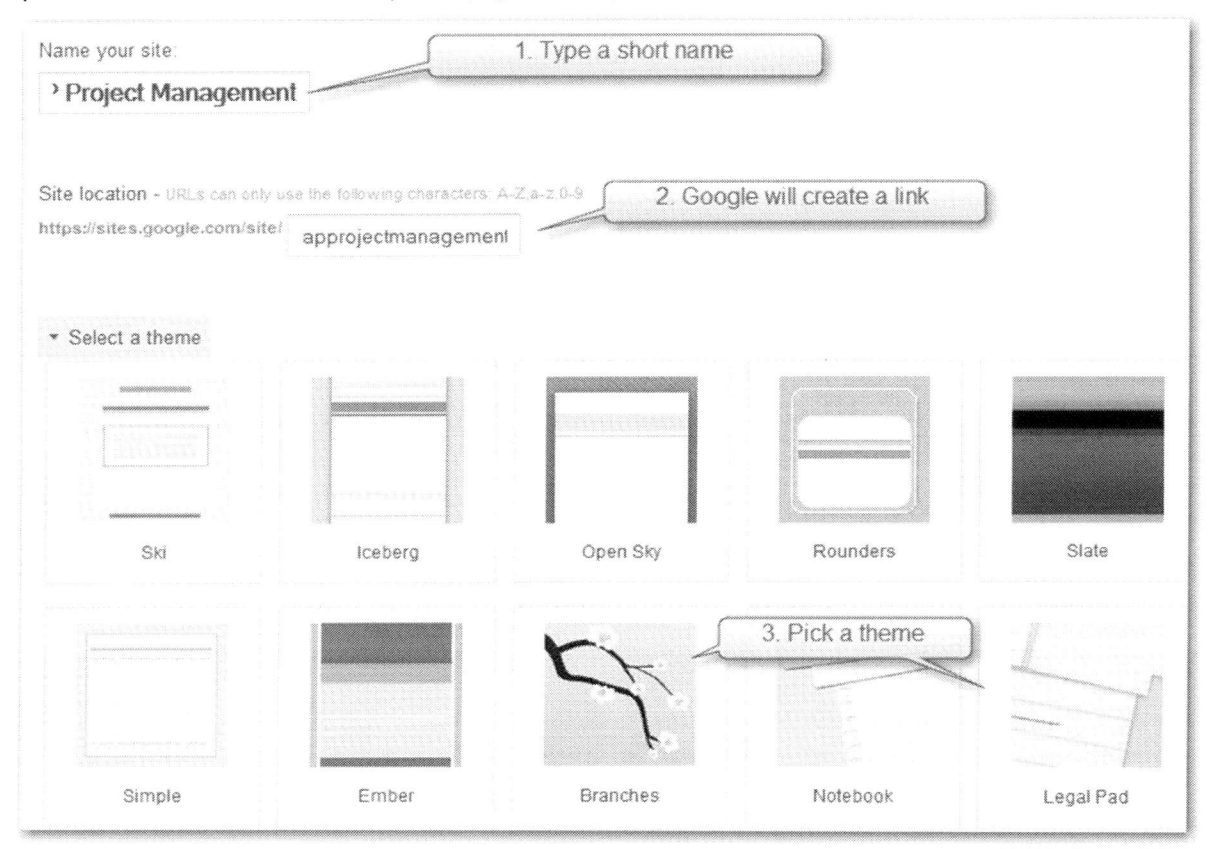

Figure 497: Naming and picking a theme

When I have a theme selected, I need to scroll down and add an optional site description. If this site is only for adults, click the check box. Lastly, type the scrambled text to assure Google you are not some kind of robot trying to mess up their servers (*Figure 498*).

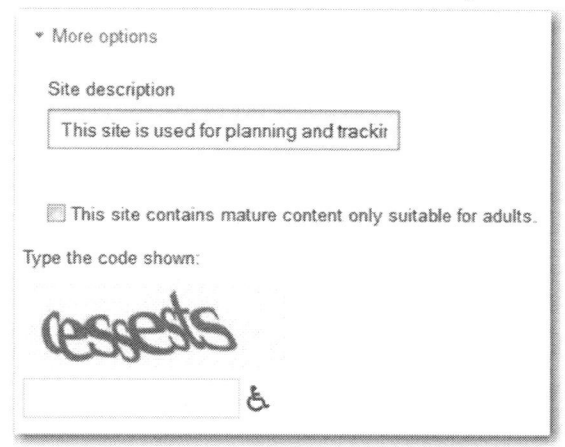

Figure 498: Describing the site

Exploring the New Project Management Site

Here is my new project planning and tracking web page (*Figure 499*). This is a long page and I have captured the bottom half in (*Figure 500*). The navigation is in the left column, although, some of the links page's functionality is on this home page, such as the calendar.

Here are the navigation links:

- **My Page** - This is a private page for you to add your notes. Only you will see it.
- **Issues** - You can:
    - Describe the issues via a title.
    - Assign it to yourself or others.
    - Give them a status of active, on-hold or closed.
    - Give them a priority of low, medium, high or critical.
    - Assign a due date.
    - Upload any files you need to document the issue.
- **Risk** - You can:
    - Describe the risk via a title.
    - Assign it to yourself or others.
    - Give them a status of active, on-hold or closed.
    - Give a category of low, medium or high risk.
    - Assign a due date.
    - Upload any files you need to document the risk.
- **Deliverables** - This is a calendar where you can view the promised deliverables.
- **Tasks** - You can:
    - Describe the task via a title.
    - Assign it to yourself or others.
    - Give them a status of active, on-hold or closed.

- o Give them a priority of low, medium, high or critical.
- o Assign a due date.
- o Guestimate the percentage of completion.
- o Upload any files you need to document the risk.
- **Calendar** - A general calendar for planning any important dates for your projects.
- **Project Documents** - This allows you to upload any project document related to the projects. This makes these documents available to all those involved.
- **Project updates** - This is a blog that anyone can post updates to. As milestones are completed, the person can post their notes.
- **Contact** - This is a form allowing anyone to post feedback to the admin. It is based on Google forms and will accumulate in a spreadsheet. This can be as sophisticated as a survey, as we discussed in the Google Docs chapter.
- **Sitemap** - This gives a hierarchical view of the pages.

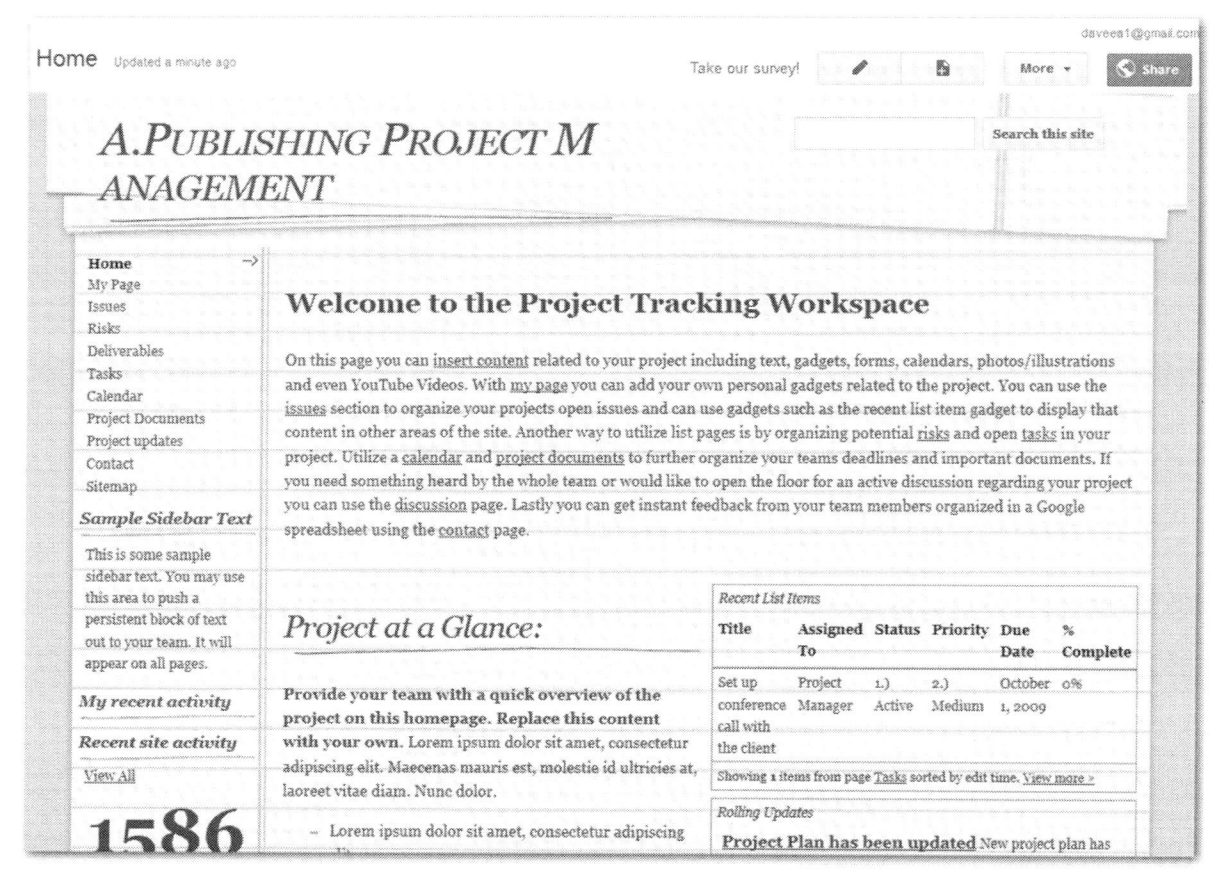

Figure 499: The completed site

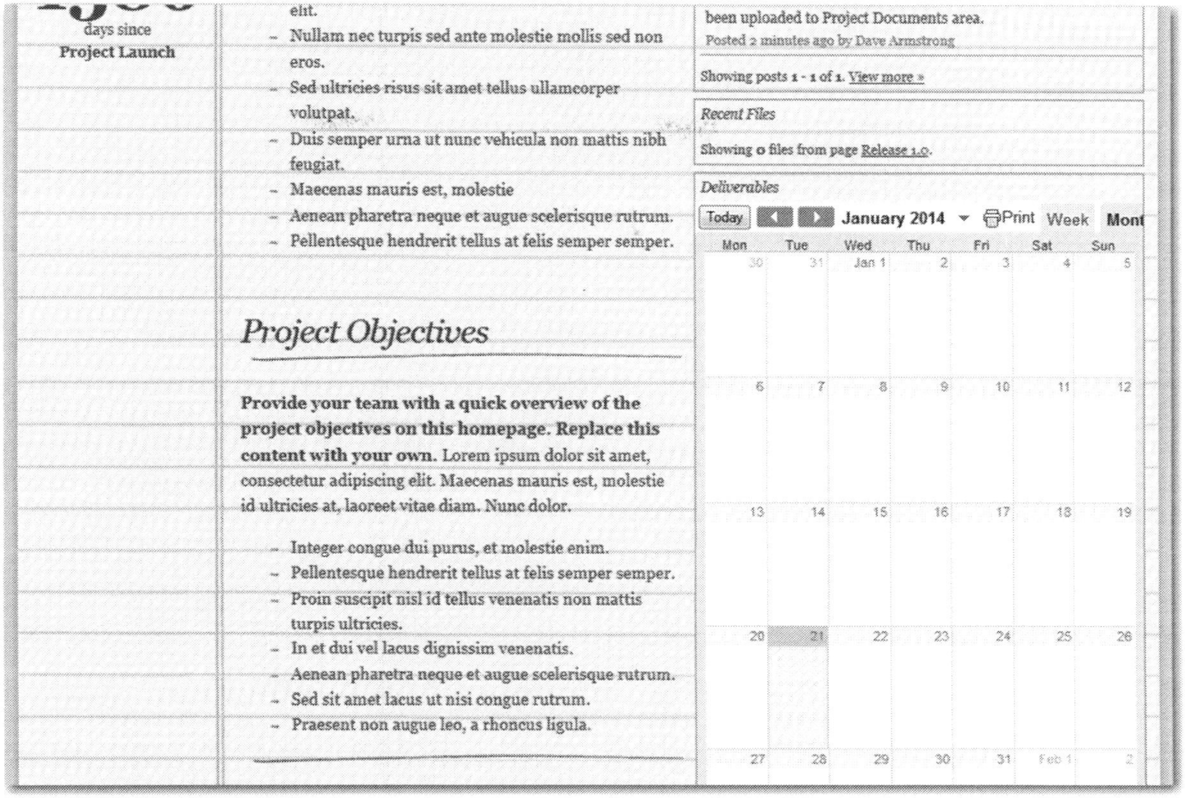

Figure 500: The completed site (continued)

Editing the Project Management Site's Pages

Editing a page is much like working in a word processing app. You can: overtype the place mark text, add links (*Figure 502*) and add images (*Figure 503*).

Chapter 17: Collaborating with Google Sites

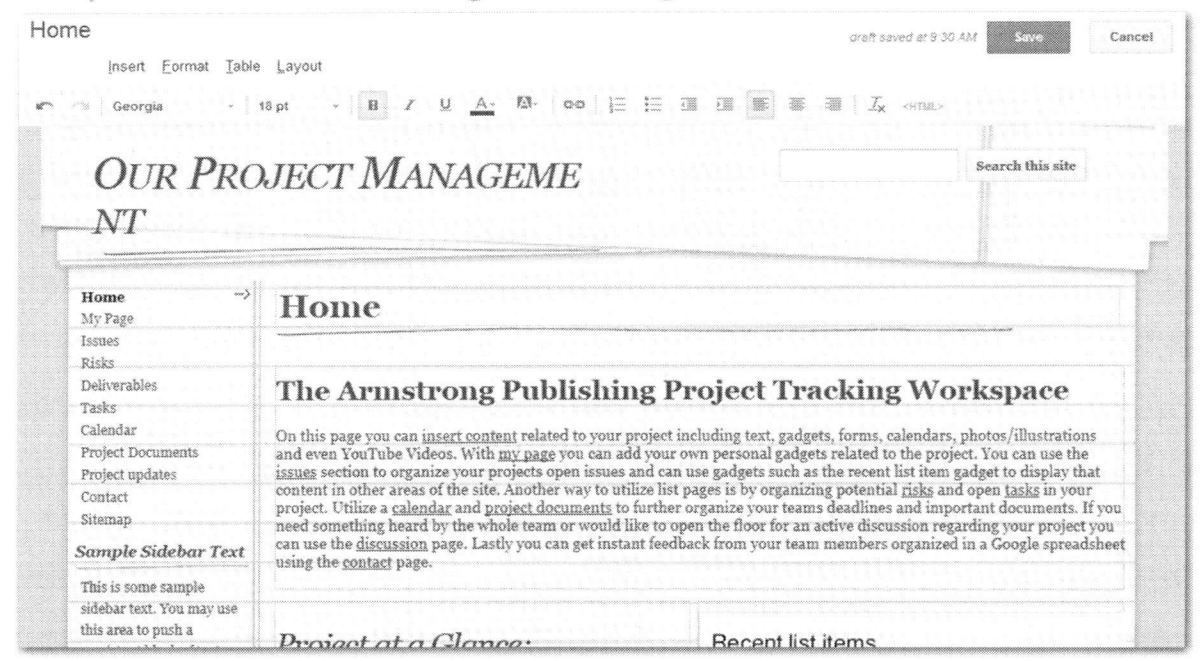

Figure 501: Editing your pages

Figure 502: Adding a link

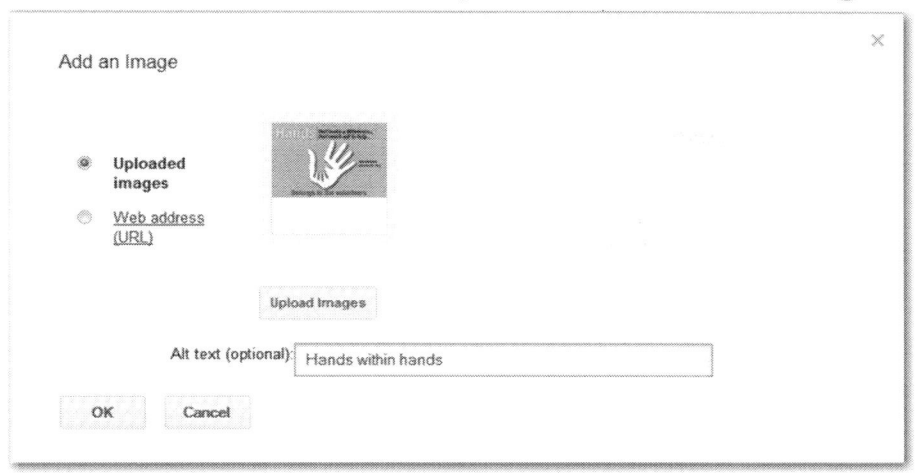

Figure 503: Adding an image

After inserting an image, you can justify it left, center or right. You can also resize it and change whether the image is inline or boxed.

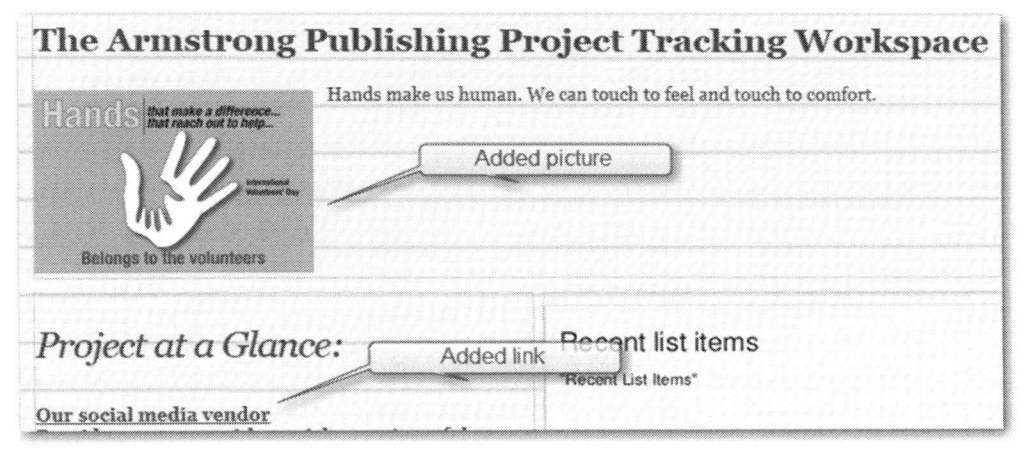

Figure 504: Added an image and link

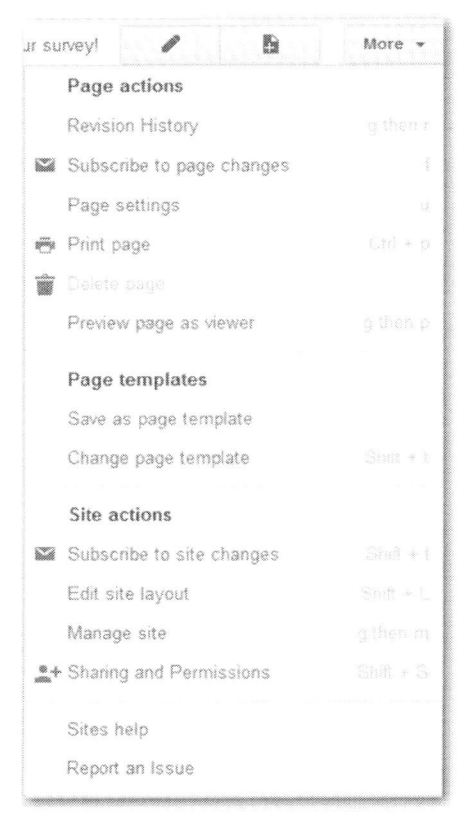

While these prefab sites save a lot of time, they can be extended and changed. Without knowing a bit of knowledge of HTML, the language of the web, you can rearrange, add or remove pages, change background colors and link the pages together in any way you wish.

General changes come from the menus **Edit Icon (pencil)->Manage site** (*Figure 505*).

Figure 505: Managing the site

Managing the Project Management Site's Structure

This **Manage Site** dialog allows you to make sweeping changes to the site. For example, you can rename the site with a better, more descriptive name. You can also add a **Site description** and change the initial landing page, although, **Home** is generally used (*Figure 506*).

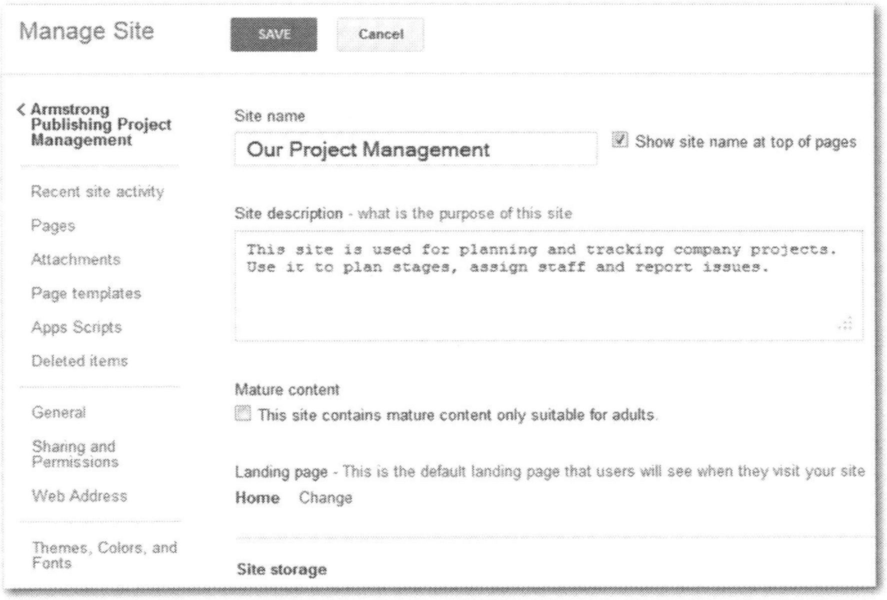

Figure 506: Adding a description

The link they provide is very long. While there is nothing wrong with a link like this for internal consumption:

https://sites.google.com/site/apublishingprojectmanagement/home.

It is possible to have an actual domain name assigned such as www.mybusiness.com. However, this is for your internal business use and you probably do not want anyone outside of your business to visit it. The best bet is to use the long name, bookmark it so all staff can visit with a favorites or bookmark click (*Figure 507*).

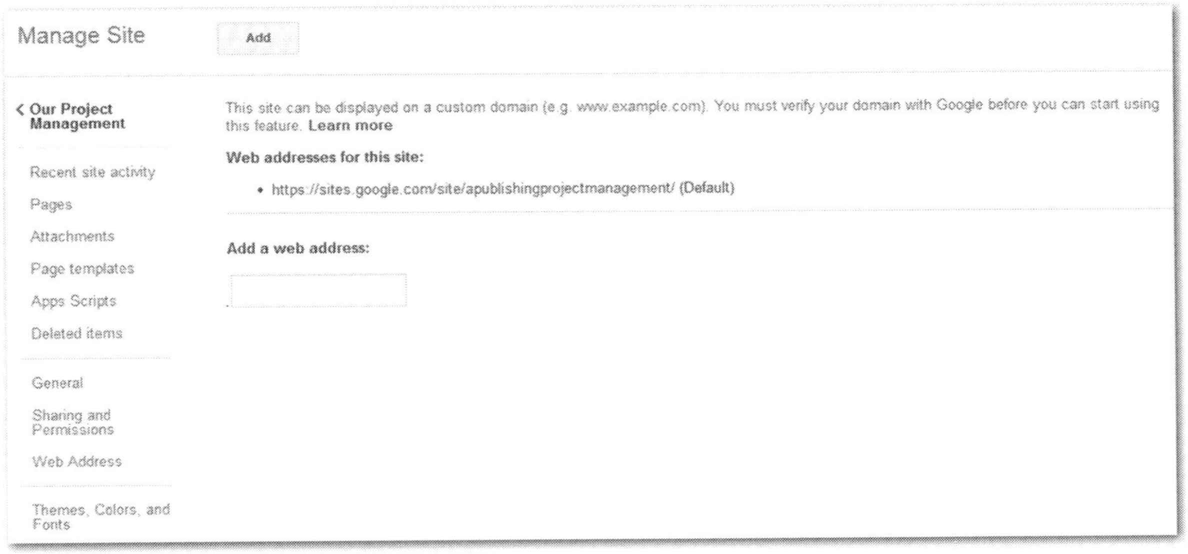

Figure 507: Customizing the domain name

Chapter 17: Collaborating with Google Sites

The Themes, Colors and Fonts section allow you to make sweeping changes in the color scheme of the website (*Figure 508*). Each section of the page is listed, starting with the **Entire page**, followed with the **Site header**, **Content area**, etc.

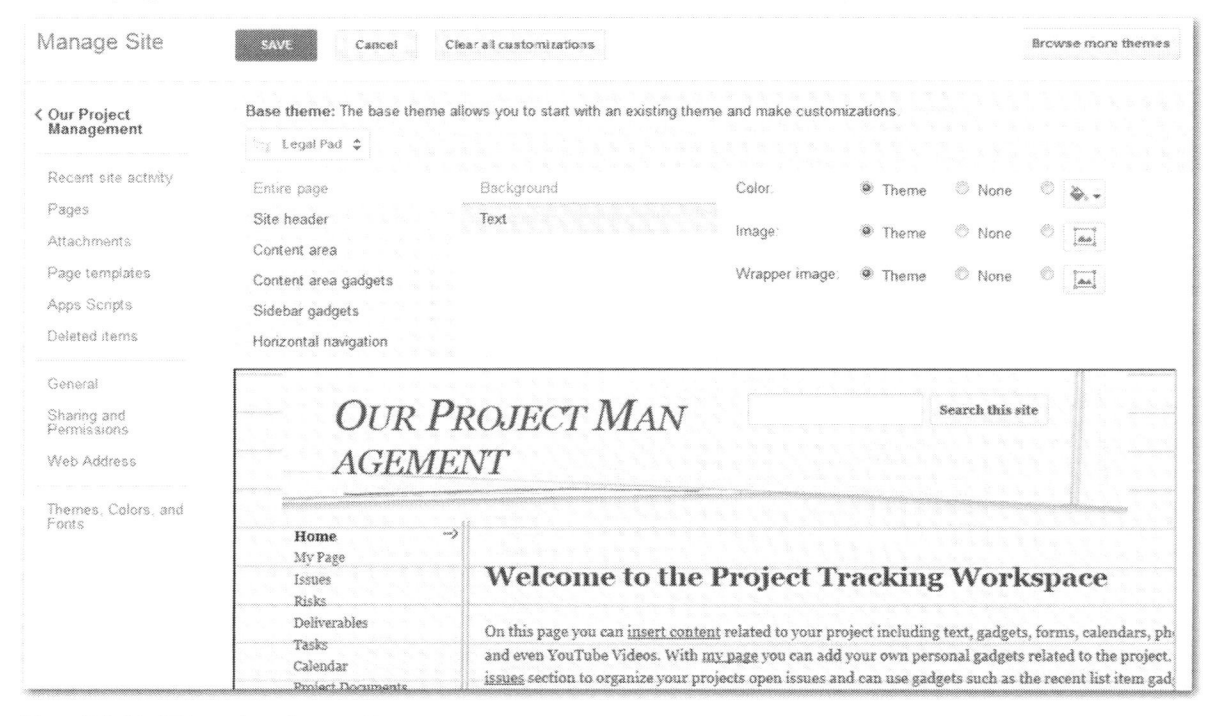

Figure 508: Modifying colors, fonts and images

If you return to your list of sites, you will see the new entry for the project management site (*Figure 509*).

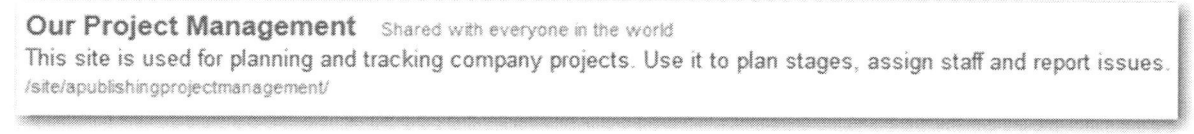

Figure 509: New listing in your sites

Using Google Sites as an Intranet

While there are many different types of websites at Google Sites, we are discussing only the ones that help a business collaborate internally. This second site is your company intranet. The Internet is available to anyone with a browser. An intranet uses the same web based technology, but is for internal use. Using the same techniques and wizards we saw earlier, I have created an intranet site (*Figure 510*).

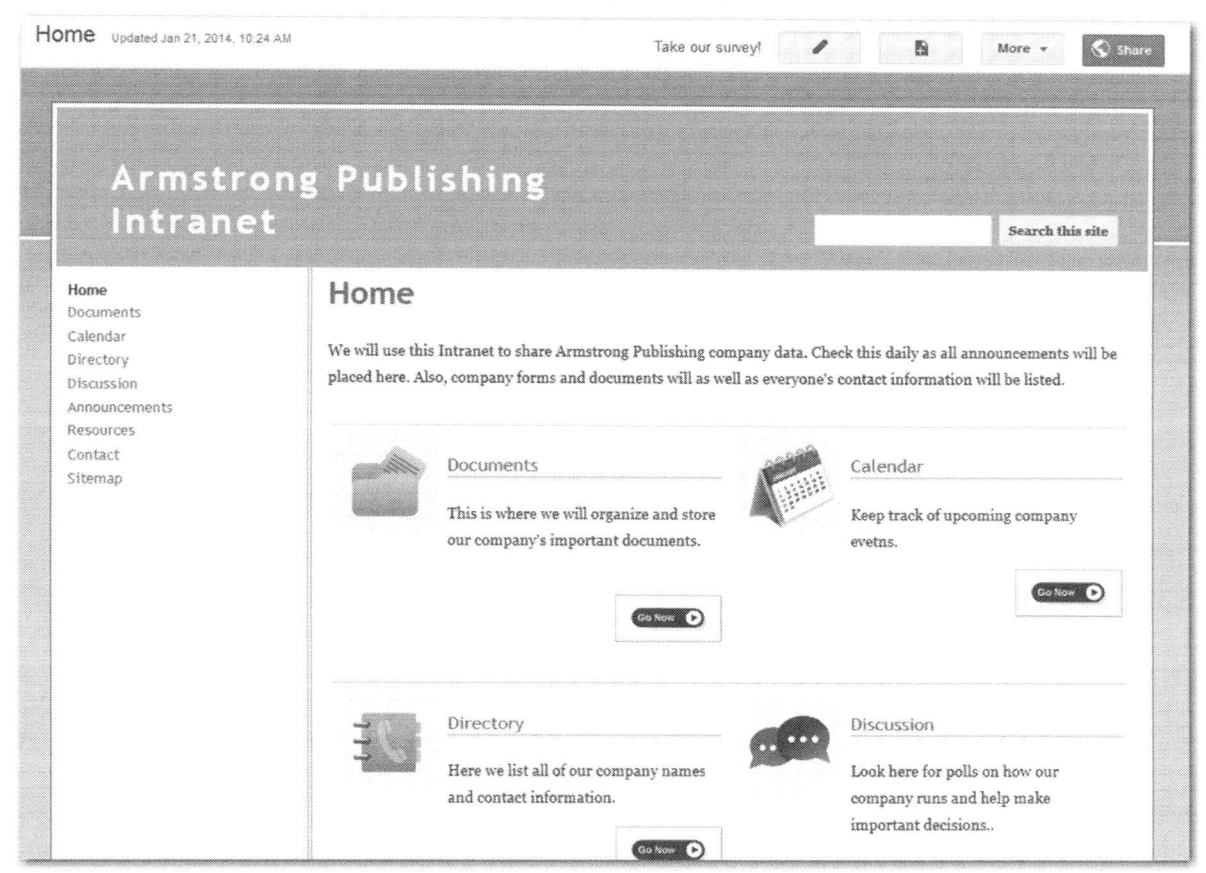

Figure 510: The Intranet home page

Intranet Documents Links

The Documents link opens the Documents page. Use this to store documents of forms that the company needs to make available to staff. There is some overlap with the menu choice **Resources**, as we will see later (*Figure 511*).

Using the menu items above the list, you can:

- **Add file** - This opens a "file find" Windows dialog to locate the file you wish to upload.

Chapter 17: Collaborating with Google Sites

- **Add link** - This opens a dialog where you can add both the URL and the text you wish to see in the list.
- **Add from Drive** - This opens your Google Drive dashboard where you can pick the file you wish to add to the list.
- **Move to** - This allows you to create new folders to organize your documents.
- **Delete** - After selecting the files you wish to delete by checking the boxes to the file's left, you can click the **Delete** button.
- **Subscribe to changes** - If you use an RSS reader (Outlook is one of many), you can subscribe to this list. Any changes are pushed to your reader. The changes come to you and you do not have to visit just to see what is new.

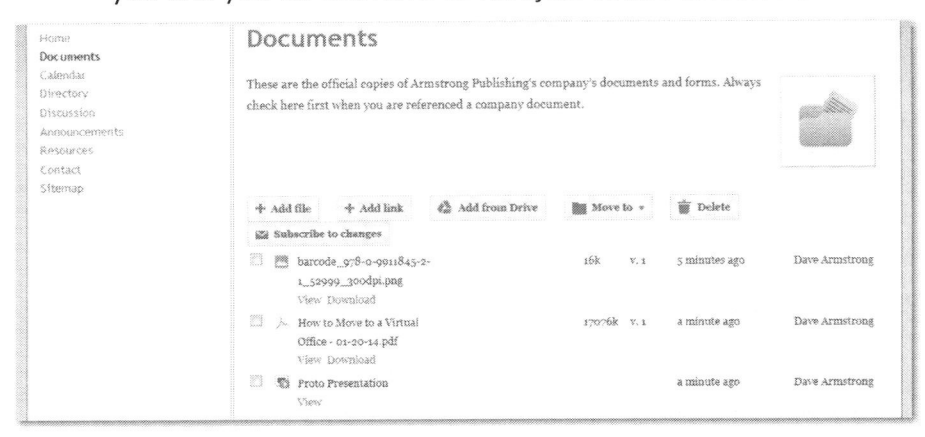

Figure 511: The Documents page

Intranet Calendar Link

(*Figure 512*) The calendar is a standard Google calendar and, as such, you can click the **+ Google Calendar** button at the bottom. This opens the calendar and asks you if you want to add this calendar. Answer, yes, if you would rather view in your Gmail/Calendar app.

Figure 512: The Calendar Page

344

Intranet Directory Link

The directory is a great place to list all of your staff. There is a place for their **Name** (last, first if you are going to sort), **Position**, **Phone**, **Cell** and **Email**. The sort order and field position can be customized. You can also add new and remove fields (*Figure 513*).

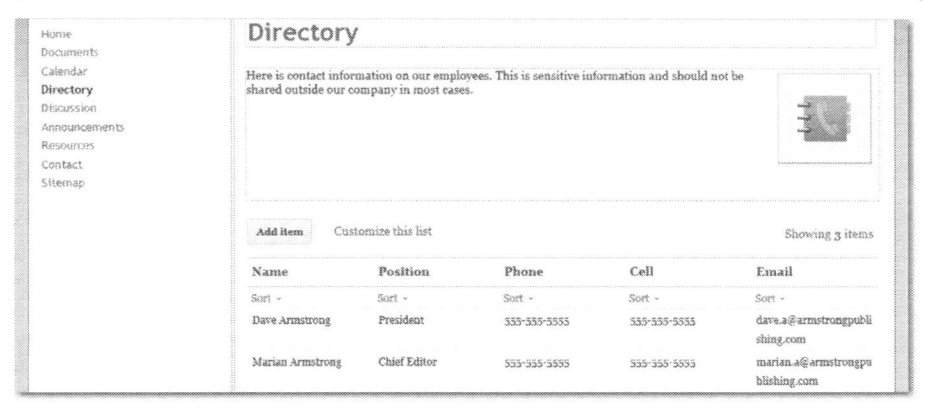

Figure 513: The Directory page

Intranet Discussion Link

The Discussion page is a shared blog. Anyone can add a post and others can add to the thread. This is a great way for you, as manager, to see what the employees are actually thinking and saying. Like the Documents and other pages, you can subscribe to start the post flowing to your RSS reader.

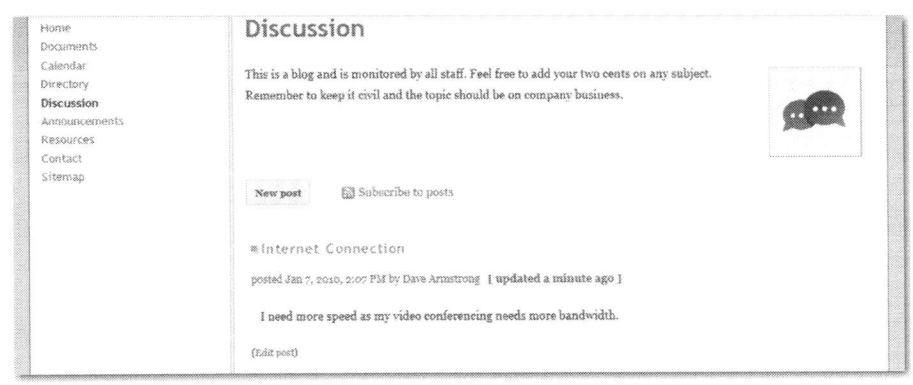

Figure 514: The discussion page

Intranet Announcements Link

Adding the latest company Announcements, is a great way to get the word out. Suggest that the staff subscribe, so they do not miss an important announcement.

Chapter 17: Collaborating with Google Sites

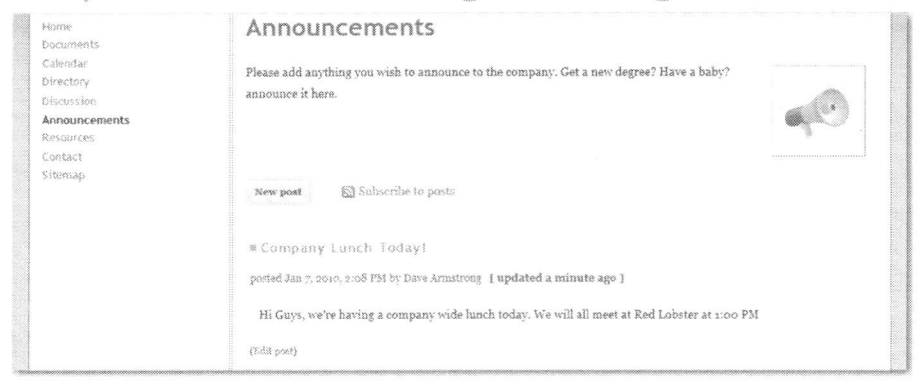

Figure 515: The Announcements page

Intranet Resources Link

The Resources page somewhat duplicates the Documents page. Regardless, they are a great way to give easy access to files the staff needs on a frequent basis (*Figure 516*).

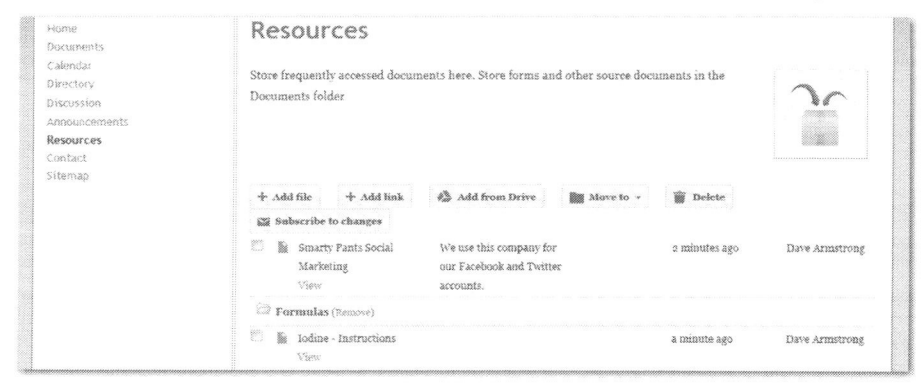

Figure 516: The Resources page

Chapter 18: Wrapping it All Up
Microsoft, Google or Zoho

We have reviewed three different suites of office productivity tools. All are free for modest businesses with paid versions, if you need more. How do you choose?

Choose Microsoft

If you are a Microsoft Office fan, SkyDrive is closest to using the desktop version. If all you ever use is Word, PowerPoint and Excel, you are set as long as you do not need the extra features that desktop Office provides.

Choose Google

If you are already wedded to Google though Gmail, Calendar or are using Hangouts for your calling, Google would be great for you. If you use an Android smart phone, you are deep into using Google and they would be a natural choice.

Choose Zoho

How do you track your prospects and customers? Those businesses that effectively use CRM, or customer relationship management software, grow faster and are more successful.

Would it be useful to have an excellent, low cost CRM system that integrates all email, phone calls and snail mail? The Zoho apps are as good as Google or Microsoft and in some respects better. They have built integration into both Google and Microsoft Web apps. If you track prospects and customers, Zoho has a lot to offer.

Chapter 18: Wrapping it All Up

Here is a table of comparison:

Microsoft	Google	Zoho CRM and Docs
7GB Storage	15GB Storage	5GB Storage
Word	Document	Write
PowerPoint	Present	Show
Excel	Spreadsheet	Sheet
Outlook	Gmail	MailMagnet
Excel Survey	Form	Zoho Creator
OneNote	N/A	N/A
Remote PC Connection	N/A	N/A
People	Contacts	Full CRM

Pick the one closest to your current situation. If you are new to all, any would make a great choice with Google being the best choice by a hair.

Compare Your Cost

As the title of this book suggest, we can build a virtual office for free and if you are a small business you almost can. However, adding Skype and perhaps Grasshopper to the mix is very affordable with Skype costing only $9.99 for video conferencing and $2.99 a month plus $5.00 for each phone number. Here is an example of the monthly cost for a small office of three:

Service	Monthly Cost
Microsoft, Google or Zoho apps	**Free**
Skype interoffice communication	**Free**
Skype Video Conferencing	Includes one US/Canada out **$9.99**
Skype phone numbers and US/Canada	(2.99+5.00) X 2 = **$15.98**

Grasshopper Incoming Phone (RAMP PLAN)	$24.00
Total per Month Cost	**$49.97**

Employee Training

I don't pretend that this book is a training manual of any depth. The book's purpose is to help you understand what technology is available and how to make good decisions in choosing and using the new virtual cloud based services. It tells you how to save money and run a more efficient office. However, reading one of the how-to-do chapters are a start.

There are YouTube videos, many put up by Microsoft, Google or Zoho. Lynda.com has a video course on Google Drive and SkyDrive. There are many other videos courses you can find with a Google search.

All services have documentation and support sites:

Google Drive

http://learn.googleapps.com/drive

Gmail

https://support.google.com/mail/?hl=en#topic=3394144

Microsoft SkyDrive

http://windows.microsoft.com/en-us/skydrive/skydrive-help#skydrive=other

Zoho Docs

https://www.zoho.com/docs/help/getting-started-guide.html

Zoho CRM

https://www.zoho.com/crm/help/

Skype

https://support.skype.com/en/

Grasshopper

https://support.grasshopper.com/home

TeamViewer

http://www.teamviewer.com/en/help/index.aspx

Transitioning to Virtual

Chapter 18: Wrapping it All Up

As we mentioned in the opening chapter, going virtual and moving into the cloud is not an all or nothing decision. Starting from a workplace, here might be a logical progression:

- Learn to use Skype for computer to computer communications. It's free, easy to use and will keep people at their desk.
- Move to one of the cloud services and upload all of your individual computer's files. Even if you cannot open them in the cloud, you could always download them later.
- Switch your phone system to Skype and Grasshopper. Sell that expensive PBX system on eBay.
- Learn how to use computer monitoring software and make sure your staff knows it is in place. Explain you are not trying to be a slave master, but if their work is done on a computer, you need a way of judging their output. This prepares them to work alone, at a remote site, should you go that way.
- Your staff are now trained and used to working in the cloud, so you can start going virtual.
- Move staff that seems to be, by nature, self-starters to their new home office. Set expectations and limits and then monitor their successes and failures.
- When that expensive office lease comes up for renewal, go for it.

If you have enjoyed this book, have found it useful and have **purchased it from Amazon**, please do me a favor. Go back to my book's Amazon page and give it a fair review.

If you liked it, please tell why in the review. Buying any book and taking time to read it, is a risky proposition and I carefully read others reviews before purchasing. It is reassuring when others, like me, think a book is valuable.

Thanks for buying and then reading How to **Move Your Expensive Office to the Free Cloud**. Contact me if you have questions or suggestions for a book you would find valuable.

Dave Armstrong

daveea@email.com

Index

Conferencing and Screen Sharing, *285–304*
Dropbox, 18, 19
    Storage, 18
Elance, 9
Evaluate Your Business as a Candidate, 2
Excel
    DATA tab, *42*
    HOME tab, *41*
    INSERT tab, *41*
    VIEW tab, *43*
Excel Survey
    EDIT QUESTION box, *55*
    Sending the link, *58*
    Testing the survey, *57*
Freelancer, 9
Gmail, 5, 19, 79, 99, 100, 103, 126, 127, 140, 141, 157, 158, 161, 162, 165, 169, *157–73***, 175, 191, 196, 349**
    Email Address, 100
    Email address and password, 5
    Email, contacts and calendar, 17
Google, 4, 8, 15, 17, 18, 19, 37, 59, 66, 101, 102, 106, 108, 111, 112, 120, 122, 123, 125, 131, 132, 134, 159, 160, 162, 168, 183, 185, 187, 188, 189, 190, 191, 192, 194, 196, 197, 227, 274, 295, 320, 349
    + Community, 113
    Account, 17
    Calendar, 99, 127, 157
    Docs, 5
    Docs, 100
    Docs, 103
    Drive, 17, 99
    Drive. *See* Google Drive
    Drive Enterprise. *See* Google Drive
    Free?, 16
    Google Play, 17
    Hangouts, 99
    Secure Server, 4
    Security, 15
    Sites. *See* Google Sites
    Storage, 19
    Storage, 100
    Storage space, 5, 16
    Task, 171
    Web applications, 15
Google Calendar, *177–82*
    Adding a New Event, *181*
Google Cloud Printing, 185–94
    Registering Your Printer, 186
Google Docs, 109
    Authorizing Script Automation, 148
    Automation Using JavaScript, 145–56
    Collaborating, 125
    Collaboration, 126
    Creating a Merge Email, 147
    Creating a survey form, *135*
    Customizing a Spreadsheet with Automation, 146
    Document, 230
    Document's Menu, *110–13*
    Form, 129
    Form Analytics, 139
    Form's File Menu, *132, 133, 134*
    Form's Toolbar, 131
    Picking an Email Template, 149
    Presentation, 113
    Present's Menu, *116, 117, 118, 119, 120*
    Print, 128
    Ready to Run Scripts From the Script Gallery, 155
    Spreadsheet, *120*
    Spreadsheet's Menus, *122, 123, 124, 125*
    The Script Editor, 154
    Walking Through a Google Doc Script, 154

Chapter 18: Wrapping it All Up

Google Drive, 1, 2, 100, 103
    Add on Apps, 106
    Convert Format, 103
    Dashboard, 103
    Desktop App, 100, 101, 102
    Email and password, 17
    Enterprise Version, 183
    HelloFax App, 107
    native App, 102
    Tamplates, 106

Google Sites, 333–48
    Creating a Company Intranet, 345–48
    Editing a Template, 339
    Managing a Google Site, 342–44
    Picking a Template, 334
    Project Planning and Collaborating, 333
    Touring the Google Sites Intranet, 345

Google+, *158*, 160

Grasshopper, *306–24*
    Configuring, *309*
    Pricing, *306*
    Recording Your Voice Greeting, *313*
    Setting up Call Forwarding, *310*
    Using Grasshopper, *316*
    Using Grasshopper on Mobile, *320*

Guru, 9

Hangouts, *17, 37, 99, 157, 173, 174, 175, 173–76, 349*

Independent Contractors, 10

Microsoft, 1, 2, 4, 15, 17, 19, 21, 39, 43, 59, 62, 66, 76, 79, 109, 123, 128, 139, 196, 278, 329, 349
    Desktop Excel, 102
    Dynamics CRM, 195
    Free?, 16
    Master Plan, 40
    Missing Apps, 103
    Monthly upgrades, 16
    Office, 17
    Office, 103
    Office 365, 5
    Office apps, 32
    Office installed, 35
    Office on Demand, 16
    Office upgrade, 16
    OneNote app, 50
    PowerPoint, 113, 115
    Ribbon, 230, 250
    Security, 15
    SkyDrive, 17, 21
    Skype, 99
    Small Business Premium, 18
    Storage, 19
    Storage space, 16
    Storage space, 5
    Upgrades, 8
    Web applications, 15
    Windows 8 blocks, 23
    Word, 17, 111
    Word, 107
    Word, 230

Microsoft Outlook. *See* Outlook Web App

Mobile Access, 19

oDesk, 9

OneNote
    HOME tab, *52*
    INSERT tab, *52*
    PICTURE TOOLS FORMAT tab, *53*
    VIEW tab, *53*

Oracle's RightNow Web Experience, *195*

Outlook Calendar
    Adding new appointments, *94*
    Main screen and month view, *88*
    Menu bar, *88*
    View/set Outlook options, *91*
    Viewing a day's events, *93*
    Viewing all upcoming with agenda, *93*
    Viewing task, *94*
    Viewing the week, *92*

Outlook Contacts

Index

Adding a new contact, *85*
Menu bar, *83*
Merging duplicates, *82*
Uploading existing list, *79*
Outlook Web App, *18, 65, 196, 224*
Adding contacts to email, *74*
App switch menu, *66*
Creating New Email, *73*
Creating rich text (HTML) emails, *76*
Inserting images, *78*
Manage your options, *71*
On behalf of issue, *70*
Sorting and filtering emails, *73*
Top menu bar, *67*
PowerPoint
ANIMATIONS tab, *48*
DESIGN tab, *46*
HOME tab, *45*
INSERT tab, *45*
TRANSITIONS tab, *47*
VIEW tab, *48*
Print over the Internet, *2*
RingCentral, *325–32*
Salesforce.com, *195*
Sites
Inserting an images and links, *341*
SkyDrive, *1, 2, 17, 19, 21, 22, 24, 25, 26, 31, 32, 45, 50, 54, 59, 60, 61, 76*
Accessing your desktop, *31*
Account, *37*
Breadcrumb links, *26*
Delete document, *24*
Documents, *24*
Downloads into desktop office, *35*
Excel, *232*
File upload, *29*
Files matching SkyDrive apps, *31*
Linking Skype, *87*
Office apps, *65*
Outlook menu bar, *65*
Paid version of SkyDrive, *70*

PC app, *22, 23*
PC folder, *24, 25*
PC folder, *36*
Profile menu, *72*
Smart phone app, *24*
SkyDrive Pro
Lync and Skype, *62*
Office 365 Home Premium, *59*
Office 365 Misdize Business, *61*
Office on Demand, *62*
Office s365 Small Business, *60*
Skype, *257–84, 306*
Calling Landlines and Mobiles, *277*
Click to Call Add-in, *283*
Group Video Conferencing, *274*
Instant Messaging, *263*
Main Screen, *261*
Making Skype Calls, *270*
Microsoft, *259*
Recording video calls with Evaer, *274*
Searching for Contacts, *262*
Sending Files, *267*
Sending SMS, *265*
Sharing Screens, *272*
Skype menus, *278–81*
Skype Pricing, *281*
Using Office with SkyDrive Pro, *59*
Using Outlook Calendar. *See* **Outlook Calendar**
Using Outlook People (Contacts), *79*
Using the Excel App, *39*
Using the Excel Survey, *54*
Using the OneNote App, *50*
Using the PowerPoint App, *43*
Virtual Office
Global Employee Pool, 8
Google tools, 100
Motivation to Use, 7
Pros and Cons, 3
Rent Cost Savings, 7
Staff sizing flexibility, 10

Technology, 1
What is the Clolud, 15
WizHTMLEditor
A free HTML editor, 77
Word
FILE
About, 39
Help, 39
Info, 38
New, 38
Open, 38
Print, 39
Save As, 38
Share, 39
FILE tab, 37
HOME tab, 33
INSERT tab, 33
OPEN IN WORD, 35
PAGE LAYOUT tab, 34
Renaming new document, 33
VIEW tab, 34

Work in the Cloud
How to, *4*
Zoho, 1, 2, 4, 18, 19, 195, 196, 197, 198, 199, 204, 228, 229, 246, 253, 255, 256, 274, 349
CRM, 18
CRM and Docs, 18
Free?, 16
Office Suite, 5
Storage, 19
Storage space, 5, 16
User ID and password, 5
Zoho CRM, *198–226*
Zoho Productivity Apps, *227–56*
Docs for Desktop, 254
Sheet's Macro and VBA, *243*
Zapier SkyDrive Integration, *256*
Zoho Sheet, *230*
Zoho Show, *249*
Zoho Writer, *229*

Made in the USA
Charleston, SC
17 February 2014